PROTESTANT *AND* IRISH

The minority's search for place in independent Ireland

Protestant *and* Irish

The minority's search for place in independent Ireland

Ian d'Alton & Ida Milne
EDITORS

CORK UNIVERSITY PRESS

First published in hardback in 2019 by
Cork University Press
Boole Library
University College Cork
Cork
T12 ND89
Ireland

This paperback edition printed in 2019

Reprinted 2020

British Library Cataloguing in Publication Data
A CIP record for this book is available from the British Library.

ISBN HB: 978-1-78205-298-2
ISBN PB: 978-1-78205-381-1

Printed by Białostockie Zakłady Graficzne S.A. in Poland.
Print origination & design by Carrigboy Typesetting Services,
www.carrigboy.com

www.corkuniversitypress.com

We dedicate this book to Deirdre McMahon—historian, mentor and friend. If she had not kept encouraging us to meet as we had things in common, we might never have found ourselves publishing it. We resolutely absolve her from any errors in what follows.

Contents

I. Belonging

II. Engagement

III. Otherness

Contributors

Frank Barry grew up beside the beautiful All Saints' Church in Raheny and was educated at the north inner city Christian Brothers school whose presence pervades James Joyce's Araby. Though he admired from afar the only two Protestant girls in his neighbourhood, he could never muster up the courage to speak to such exotic creatures. No-one of his ken seemed to know the Quaker family that occupied the big house across the road from him. He recalls his delighted father coming in mud-caked from the garden one afternoon having just dug up a gold half-sovereign that must have been dropped there in Lord Ardilaun's time. Frank Barry is Professor of International Business and Economic Development at Trinity College Dublin.

Philip Bull is an Adjunct Professor in History at La Trobe University, Melbourne, and a Visiting Professor with the Centre for the Study of Historic Houses and Estates at Maynooth University. Author of *Land, Politics and Nationalism: A Study of the Irish Land Question* (Dublin: Gill & Macmillan, 1996), he has written extensively on nineteenth- and twentieth-century Irish history. He is currently organising and cataloguing the large archive of papers at Monksgrange, County Wexford, and writing a history of that house and its occupants from the mid-eighteenth to the mid-twentieth centuries.

Ian d'Alton, as a member of the Church of Ireland, observes his tribe carefully and sometimes warily. A former civil and public servant, he was always somewhat bemused at the deference shown to his—clearly out-of-this-world—opinions. As a very young Assistant Principal in the Department of Finance, he was once summoned into the presence of an extremely senior Assistant Secretary—a.k.a. God—and asked, quite solemnly, if there was a Protestant 'take' on the recent budget. Educated sublimely and ridiculously in UCC and Cambridge, he now mixes with Trinity types as a Visiting Research Fellow in the Centre for Contemporary Irish History. A former Visiting Fellow at Sidney Sussex College, Cambridge (2014), he is a

Fellow of the Royal Historical Society. His most recent publication is 'Journeying into a wider world? The development of the histories of the Church of Ireland since 1950', in M. Empey, A. Ford and M. Moffitt (eds), *The Church of Ireland and Its Past: History, Interpretation and Identity* (Dublin: Four Courts Press, 2017).

Niamh Dillon has recently (2018) completed a PhD thesis from Goldsmiths, University of London. Her thesis, the 'British Diaspora: Race, Return Migration and Identity', explored the means by which a sense of British identity was transmitted and retained amongst southern Irish Protestants and the British community in India during the late British Empire in Ireland and India. It assessed the extent to which this sense of identity was challenged or confirmed when these two groups 're-migrated' to Britain when Ireland became the Free State in 1922 and India achieved Independence in 1947. She has been working on oral history projects for over twenty years and is currently lead interviewer for *Architects' Lives*, an oral history of British architecture based at the British Library.

Roy Foster is Emeritus Professor of Irish History at the University of Oxford and Professor of Irish History and Literature at Queen Mary University of London. He is a Fellow of the British Academy, the Royal Historical Society and the Royal Society of Literature, a Member of the Academia Europea, an Honorary Fellow of Trinity College Dublin and an Honorary Member of the Royal Irish Academy. He has received honorary degrees from the University of Aberdeen, Queen's University Belfast, Trinity College, Dublin, the National University of Ireland, Queen's University, Canada, the University of Edinburgh and University College, Dublin as well as an Honorary Fellowship at Birkbeck College, University of London. His books include *Charles Stewart Parnell: The Man and His Family* (1976), *Lord Randolph Churchill: A Political Life* (1981), *Modern Ireland 1600–1972* (1988), *The Oxford Illustrated History of Ireland* (1989), *Paddy and Mr Punch: Connections in Irish and English History* (1993), *The Irish Story: Telling Tales and Making It Up in Ireland* (2001), which won the 2003 Christian Gauss Award for Literary Criticism, *W.B. Yeats, A Life. I: The Apprentice Mage 1865–1914* (1997) which won the 1998 James Tait Black Prize for biography, and *Volume II: The Arch-Poet, 1915–1939* (2003), *Luck and the Irish: A Brief History of Change 1970–2000* (2007),

Words Alone: Yeats and His Inheritances (2011) and *Vivid Faces: The Revolutionary Generation in Ireland 1890–1922* (2014), which won a British Academy Medal and the Frokosch Prize from the American Historical Association. He is also a well-known critic and broadcaster.

BRIAN HUGHES is a lecturer in the Department of History, Mary Immaculate College, University of Limerick. His most recent publications include *Defying the IRA? Intimidation, Coercion, and Communities during the Irish Revolution* (Liverpool: Liverpool University Press, 2016) and, with Fergus Robson (eds), *Unconventional Warfare from Antiquity to the Present Day* (Basingstoke: Palgrave, 2017).

TOMÁS IRISH is lecturer in modern history at Swansea University. He completed his PhD at Trinity College Dublin in 2012 and was a postdoctoral research fellow there from 2012 to 2015. He is a historian of universities, intellectual life and internationalism in the early twentieth century and has published two monographs on these themes: *The University at War 1914–25: Britain, France and the United States of America* (London: Palgrave Macmillan, 2015), and *Trinity in War and Revolution 1912–23* (Dublin: Royal Irish Academy, 2015). He was elected a Fellow of the Royal Historical Society in 2015.

FELIX M. LARKIN is a former academic director of the Parnell Summer School, and a co-founder and former chairman of the Newspaper and Periodical History Forum of Ireland. He has written extensively on the press in Ireland in the late nineteenth and early twentieth centuries, and his publications include *Terror and Discord: The Shemus Cartoons in the* Freeman's Journal, *1920–1924* (Dublin: A. & A. Farmar, 2009). He edited *Librarians, Poets and Scholars: A Festschrift for Dónall Ó Luanaigh* (Dublin: Four Courts Press, 2007), and co-edited *Periodicals and Journalism in Twentieth-Century Ireland* (Dublin: Four Courts Press, 2014) and *Lawyers, the Law and History* (Dublin: Four Courts Press, 2013). Having studied history at University College Dublin, he was an Irish public servant for thirty-six years and served in the Department of Finance and in the National Treasury Management Agency. He is a director and former chairman of the Sick and Indigent Roomkeepers Society, Dublin's oldest charity—founded in 1790.

MARTIN MAGUIRE is senior lecturer and director of the BA (Honours) Digital Humanities Programme in the Department of Humanities, Dundalk Institute of Technology. He has published many articles on the history of Irish Protestantism with a particular emphasis on social class and identity. He has also published extensively on the history of civil service trade unions and state building in Ireland. His latest book is a co-edited collection of essays on County Louth in the revolutionary period: Donal Hall and Martin Maguire (eds), *County Louth and the Irish Revolution 1912–23* (Newbridge: Irish Academic Press, 2017).

IDA MILNE is a social historian and European history lecturer at Carlow College. She held an IRC Marie Sklowodska Curie Elevate Fellowship at Maynooth University and Queen's University Belfast, 2014–2018, where she also taught oral history and nineteenth- and twentieth-century Irish and European history. Her principal research interest lies in the social history of disease, but she also works on working lives in the newspaper industry and in medicine. She is vice-chairperson of the Oral History Network of Ireland, reflecting her strong interest in expanding the ethical practice of oral history in academia and the community. She serves on the international committee of the Oral History Association and on the historical sciences committee of the Royal Irish Academy, where she represents HSTM Network Ireland. Being intensely curious by nature, she describes herself as reversing into twenty-six-county Irish Protestant identity (informed by a family background of 400 years of Wexford Protestantism) when she notes silences in the historiography. Her monograph on the 1918–19 influenza, *Stacking the Coffins: Influenza, War and Revolution in Ireland, 1918–19*, was published by Manchester University Press in 2018.

MIRIAM MOFFITT, a graduate of National University of Ireland Maynooth, University of Nottingham and Queen's University Belfast, has written on various aspects of the history of Protestantism in Ireland. Her publications include *Soupers and Jumpers: The Protestant Missions in Connemara, 1848–1937* (Dublin: Nonsuch Publishing, 2008); *The Society for Irish Church Missions to the Roman Catholics, 1849–1950* (Manchester: MUP, 2010). She recently co-edited (with Mark Empey and Alan Ford) *The Church of Ireland and Its Past: History, Interpretation and Identity* (Dublin:

Four Courts Press, 2017). She lectures in Church History in St Patrick's College, Maynooth.

CONOR MORRISSEY is lecturer in Irish/British history at King's College London. He holds BA, MA and LLB degrees from National University of Ireland, Galway, and a PhD (2015) from Trinity College Dublin. Following a spell in the National Museum of Ireland, he returned to Trinity for an Irish Research Council Postdoctoral Fellowship, 2015–2016, and was then a lecturer at Hertford College, Oxford. His research focuses on Irish nationalism and Irish Protestantism.

DEIRDRE NUTTALL grew up on the outskirts of New Ross, County Wexford. She studied folklore and archaeology at UCD, and took a master's degree in social anthropology at the University of Durham, before returning to UCD to complete a PhD in folklore, which explored migratory legends of the supernatural in the south-east of Ireland and Newfoundland. She has carried out research in Ireland, Newfoundland and Guatemala. Deirdre currently lives and works in Dublin's historic Liberties area. Her current research project explores the folklore, traditions and narratives of the Protestant minority in the Republic of Ireland. With the support of the National Folklore Collection, she is looking at the cultural, rather than specifically faith, aspects of the group, incorporating folk history, custom and belief, identity and more.

CATHERINE O'CONNOR completed her PhD at the University of Limerick in 2007, on 'Southern Protestantism: the inter-relationship of religious, social and gender identity'. Her PhD publications include 'Mixed Marriage, "a grave injury to our church": An Account of the 1957 Fethard-on-Sea Boycott' in *The History of the Family: An International Quarterly* 13.4 (2008) and 'The Church of Ireland Diocese of Ferns, 1945–65' in M. Busteed, F. Neal and J. Tonge (eds), *Irish Protestant Identities* (Manchester: MUP, 2008). She continued to explore issues of identity and gender in postdoctoral research projects including the 'Inventing and Re-Inventing the Irish Woman, External Influences on Gender Construction, 1760–2005' project (funded by the Irish Research Council) at UL and the Changing Ireland: Migration and Cultural Heritage project (UCD, IVRLA, 2009). As well as teaching women's history and oral history in UL from certificate to postgraduate level she has worked as an oral history consultant and trainer on heritage and community projects in counties Kerry and Clare, where she lives. She has recently been engaged in projects with Dublin City Council including the Mansion House Commemorative Oral History Project (2015) and the 'Dublin a great place to start': Digital Storytelling Project (2015). She teaches the Dublin City Library and Archives Certificate in Oral History and interviews for the University of Limerick Oral History Project. Her current research interests include memoir writing and genealogy.

Caleb Wood Richardson is Assistant Professor of History at the University of New Mexico. His work has appeared in *New Hibernia Review/Iris Éireannach Nua* and *Éire-Ireland*. His manuscript, *Smyllie's Ireland*, is currently under contract with the University of Indiana Press. He is a contributor to *Reconstruction's World: Connections and Contexts*, with a chapter on the Irish-American nationalist group, the Fenians, and *Nations on the Move: Ireland, Scotland, Wales and Native America 1960–Present*. He is immediate past-president of the American Conference for Irish Studies–Western Regional.

Joseph Ruane is Emeritus Professor of Sociology at UCC and currently Adjunct Professor at the Geary Institute in UCD. His research interests include historical and comparative sociology, religious and ethnic conflict, colonialism, core–periphery relations with a focus on Ireland and Europe. He has published widely on the conflict in Northern Ireland and, more recently, on Catholic–Protestant relations in the Republic of Ireland and France.

Anthony Varley is an Adjunct Lecturer in Politics and Sociology at the National University of Ireland, Galway. His comparison of aspects of the political careers of George O'Callaghan-Westropp and Bobby Burke comes out of a long-standing interest in the way some early twentieth-century Irish farmers struggled to represent themselves independently in the sphere of party politics. He has recently reconsidered the agrarian aspect of the 1916 Rising in the west in a paper entitled 'The Eclipsing of a Radical Agrarian Nationalist: Tom Kenny and the 1916 Rising in County Galway' in M. Mannion (ed.), *Centenary Reflections on the 1916 Rising: County Galway Perspectives* (Galway: Galway County Council, 2016), pp. 92–113.

Acknowledgements

Ida Milne wishes to thank all her interviewees and also Andrew Deacon, John Nangle, Sheila Milne, Robert Milne, Tom Hunt, Eoghan Corry, William Murphy, Donal McAnallen, Paul Rouse and many others to have advised on her 'Quiet Corner Back' research over the years. Niamh Dillon would like to thank all her interviewees for their generosity and patience, without which she would not have been able to carry out this research. Ian d'Alton thanks TCD Centre for Contemporary Irish History and the American Conference of Irish Studies for opportunities to run the project through critical audiences. He offers thanks to Professor Eugenio Biagini and his deep appreciation to the Master and Fellows of Sidney Sussex College, Cambridge for the stimulation provided by a Visiting Fellowship in 2014, during which the early ideas for this book first emerged. Both editors give thanks to the essayists and the publishers, Cork University Press, for permitting them to bring this project to fruition; in particular, CUP's editor, Maria O'Donovan. They apologise humbly to all who have had to listen to their endless ramblings on this topic. For being so patient and understanding, in providing a hospitable refuge for editing, and for tea, sympathy and those restorative egg sandwiches, they also owe a serious debt of gratitude to June d'Alton.

Abbreviations

BL	British Library
BMH	Bureau of Military History
CDB	Congested Districts Board
CO	Colonial Office
CoIG	*Church of Ireland Gazette*
DED	District Electoral Division
DIB	J. Maguire and J. Quinn (eds), *Dictionary of Irish Biography* (Cambridge: Cambridge University Press, 2009), 9 vols.
DMP	Dublin Metropolitan Police
EEC	European Economic Community
GAA	Gaelic Athletic Association
GPO	General Post Office, Dublin
HL	House of Lords
ICA	Irish Citizen Army
IDL	Irish Dominion League
IFU	Irish Farmers' Union
IGC	Irish Grants Committee
IRA	Irish Republican Army
IRB	Irish Republican Brotherhood
ITUC	Irish Trades' Union Council
JP	Justice of the Peace
IWWU	Irish Women Workers' Union
MGA	Monksgrange Archive
MP	Member of Parliament
MSPC	Military Service Pension Collection
NAI	National Archives of Ireland
NLI	National Library of Ireland
NUIM	National University of Ireland, Maynooth, now Maynooth University
OTC	Officer Training Corps
RCBL	Representative Church Body Library, Dublin
RIA	Royal Irish Academy
TCD	Trinity College, Dublin

TCD[DM]	Trinity College, Dublin [Department of Manuscripts]
TD	Teachta Dála
TNA	The National Archives, Kew, UK
UCC	University College, Cork
UCD	University College, Dublin
UCD[AD]	University College, Dublin [Archives Department]
UL	University of Limerick
UUC	Ulster Unionist Council
UVF	Ulster Volunteer Force
WS	Witness Statements, Bureau of Military History

This Book: An explanation

We set out to write one book, and found ourselves assembling the material for another. The concept for this collection of essays arose out of years of debate between the authors, and anyone who cared to join in, as we tried to unravel Irish Protestant loyalties in the period immediately succeeding that crucial decade in Irish history—the 1910s—when all preconceived ideas about what might happen were overcome by events. Those 'events'—war, revolution, partition and the spinning of the new nation as an old Catholic-and-Gaelic one—have tended to blur the complex realities of just who the people of the newly-independent state were. We—each from a different community within the broader religious minority as well as historians—wanted to tell a side of history that history, which so often looks to the 'bad' stories (bad news is easier to see), had downplayed. We felt few had told the important story of the Protestant fitting in, living in harmony with their neighbours, inconspicuously 'keeping the head down', not out of a sense of unease, but because things were just fine, and it suited. And then . . . the material that came back from our wonderful contributors persuaded us of another axis for this work, to allow the same idea to be realised in a different way. In other words, we were introduced to some of our own blind spots, sometimes to our discomfort. Just as we felt others were not writing about 'our' sort of Protestant—the farming families of the south-east or the suburban middle classes of Dublin—we realised we needed to widen our definition of 'fitting in' here. So in response to, and acknowledgement of, the complexities and contradictions of our 'tribe', we have tried to show a broad spectrum of how Protestants—gruntled and disgruntled—sought to find, and often found, place in the new Ireland, either noisily or through 'keeping [that] head down'. We hope you, our readers, will feel as enlightened by their work as we do. If you chuckle in recognition at the twenty-six-county Protestant condition you know, or come to understand just a little bit better the one you do not, then we will have succeeded.

PREFACE

The Protestant Accent

ROY FOSTER

A mischievous memoir by Malachi O'Doherty is entitled *I Was A Teenage Catholic*; for those of us who were teenage Protestants in the 1960s, much in this collection strikes sharply home. Growing up in Waterford city, which was something of a time-warp in itself, I was struck by the remnants of what had once clearly been a purposeful Protestant world. Besides the stately Georgian cathedral designed by Roberts, surrounded by a Trollopean townscape of Deanery, Widows' Apartments, and Bishop Foy's School, there was a smorgasbord of non-Catholic places of worship: smaller Church of Ireland temples (St Olaf's, St Patrick's), Presbyterian churches, establishments for Baptists and Methodists, and a strong Quaker presence centred on Newtown School (founded in the resonant date of 1798). As the years passed, these minor establishments contracted, closed, or combined, though the Quakers are still there, in a meeting-house built when other halls were closing. Roberts's cathedral is beautifully restored, but is now the centre of a museum quarter.

This may be emblematic—or not. In recent decades, Irish Protestantism has received several shots in the arm, from unlikely sources, including both immigration and the input of disillusioned ex-Catholics during the era of scandalous revelations. However, this collection of essays addresses the period of reassessment and cautious restabilisation which began with the establishment of the Irish Free State and ended in the 1960s—consciously setting out to examine the social and cultural identity and existence of the Protestant *menu peuple* rather than the decaying world of 'Big House' grandees explored by novelists such as Elizabeth Bowen and Molly Keane. For example, essays such as Ian d'Alton's examine what lay beneath *causes célèbres* such as the Fethard boycott or the Tilson affair; Ida Milne draws a fascinating picture of rural Protestants passionately affiliated to GAA games; Martin Maguire looks at Protestant republicans and revolutionaries; Frank Barry explores the theme of Protestant influence in the commercial world. The picture is not that of an Irish 'establishment', or at least not in the over-simplified sense in which that concept is sometimes employed.

Nor is this book a portrait of 'former people', in the poignant phrase applied to *çi-devant* Russian aristocrats after 1917. Rather, it is a picture of an element in Irish life whose Irish identity is unequivocal and who did not share the uneasy feeling of ill-gotten historical privilege, delineated in Bowen's autobiographical writings. Even within the fortress of Trinity College, explored by Tomás Irish, the sense of an 'anti-national' identification seems an invention of nationalist zealots rather than a reflection of the place itself (which Eamon de Valera seems to have held in more affection than he did UCD). There may also be more to say about the complexities and snobberies within the Irish Protestant community: hints can be picked up through mordant asides in some of Hubert Butler's essays on the subject, such as 'Portrait of a Minority'. But 'the Protestant accent', if anyone even remembers it, is now gone (along with Protestant cuisine—an unregretted sub-culture of a sub-culture). And the notion expressed in Brian Friel's uncharacteristically maladroit play *The Home Place*—that Irish Protestants, since they are the descendants of settlers, carry within their DNA a longing for a 'home' in England—finds no purchase in the following pages. Rather, we are reminded that Irish Protestants were expert in keeping themselves warm in cold houses.

The period covered is important. One of the most suggestive arguments implied by this book is that the development of a secure Protestant identity within independent Ireland was facilitated by the gradualist schedule whereby independence was formally achieved. The fact that the Free State was a Dominion within the Commonwealth softened the impact of absorbing its nationalist rhetoric and semi-theocratic adoption of Catholic social teaching; even de Valera's 1937 Constitution could be accepted more easily, since by that date he was no longer seen as a demonic Lenin-type figure, even by the most nervous of Protestants. Moreover, the rights of non-Catholics within the pale of the state were (at least formally) recognised in the 1937 document. Had the declaration of a republic followed hard upon the new Constitution, reactions might have been rather different; but again, there was a cooling-off period of eleven years before Costello's initiative cut the links to the Commonwealth. By then, the identity of southern Protestants was more or less uncomplicatedly Irish.

The word 'southern' is important here, too, and by 1948 the contrasting experiences of both parts of Ireland in World War II had driven the wedge of differentiation far and deep between Protestants north and south—a syndrome which continues to this day. Ida Milne's essay on the GAA emphasises the marked contrast in Protestant conceptions of the Association north and south of the border. I was reminded that as Provost of Trinity in the 1970s, F.S.L. Lyons gave a splendid reception in the Provost's House for the winners of the All-Ireland football final; it would be hard to imagine such a thing happening in the Queen's of the day. Around the same time, the great Trinity botanist and all-round intellectual D.A. Webb, who came from a distinguished Irish Protestant family (his mother Ella Webb was a pioneering medic and feminist), was routinely describing himself as a 'twenty-six-county nationalist'. This was, I suspect, a pretty general response in the Irish Protestant world, and it could only be accentuated by observing the horrors developing north of the border after 1969.

The previous era had seen the slow accommodation of Irish Protestants to a new world, where they had at first feared becoming what Ian d'Alton resonantly calls 'a beached people'. This did not happen, nor did they withdraw into 'inner emigration'. (Actual emigration was another matter, especially in the early 1920s, but recent academic analysis tends to the conclusion that this has been exaggerated.) While W.B. Yeats's great philippic in the Senate about the Irish Protestant contribution to intellectual and cultural life is necessarily quoted more than once in this book, it is worth remembering his brother Jack's salty aside that the Yeats family 'had no gate-lodges or carriage-drives'. This applies to most of the people whose lives are reflected in this book; even the third Lord Glenavy, better known as the humorist Patrick Campbell, came from middle-class legal and shop-owning stock. Campbell's autobiography,

My Life and Easy Times, published in 1988 and penetratingly discussed here by Caleb Richardson, broke a cardinal rule by insouciantly quoting the slighting way his parents used to refer to Catholic mores. But the interesting thing is that, by then, Campbell felt he *could* break this rule. It is of a piece with the determination of the late Victor Griffin, legendary dean of St Patrick's (1968–1991), to 'rock the boat' as much as he could, by emphasising the unashamed position of Protestants in Irish public life, and announcing (in the campaign against the anti-abortion amendment in 1983) that Ireland 'had to choose between republicanism and confessionalism'.

This indicates that by then Irish Protestants were breathing a freer and healthier air than for much of the period surveyed in this book. The essays here rather reflect an era when Hubert Butler, another great advocate of rocking boats, used to bemoan the caution of the mid-twentieth-century Irish Protestant mind. In the 1950s he described the Church of Ireland as 'a poor old phoenix, moulting and blind and bedraggled, gazing mesmerized into the fire, but unable to summon up the courage to take the last leap'. Yet, he continued, 'I still think it has the power to lay a very fine egg'. In the following pages, we can see that a certain vibrancy and combativeness persisted within the ostensibly dusty and downbeat image of southern Irish Protestantism. The essays gathered here reflect this, and do it ample justice. They remind us that though the Protestant accent may have vanished, independent Ireland was characterised by a Protestant intonation, and was all the richer for it.

INTRODUCTION

Content and Context

IAN d'ALTON AND IDA MILNE

James Campbell, Lord Glenavy, may have been a single-minded careerist with the nerve to seek a British judicial position while at the same time acting as the first chairman of the Irish Senate.[1] But he was also a realist about the condition of, and prospects for, his tribe—southern Irish Protestants[2]—demonstrating, in Patrick Maume's words, that 'many of his adaptations reflected a desire to shape a changing situation rather than fighting in the last ditch irrespective of consequence'.[3] That embodies what this book is about. It emerged from the editors' many discussions about exactly who our 'tribe' was in the early days of the nation, and how many of our own very positive experiences and our sense of belonging, of being Irish, are not reflected in a trope of 'descendancy' where, in that worldview, the religious minority is forever MOPE (the Most Oppressed Protestants Ever), mirroring Kevin Myers's and Liam Kennedy's characterisation of the Irish generally as MOPE (the Most Oppressed People Ever).[4]

We cannot cover in one volume the totality of the Protestant experience in independent Ireland, nor do we claim to do so. What we have aimed to do is uncover a southern Irish Protestant story more nuanced and complex than a Dostoyevskian dystopia of unhappiness and alienation.[5] This book aims for a wider and more inclusive canvas: to present a colourful and intricate picture of what it meant to be part of a community that was delimited both by what it felt it was; and—often as significantly—by what it was not. Majority–minority situations are widespread and unexceptional, both in time and space, and this particular one is little different. What we hope is that the essays here, while dealing with the particularity of Irish minority–majority relationships, will have relevance to wider historical scholarship on the nature of how a formerly dominant minority coped with and adapted to changed circumstances. And it was (and is) a two-sided process, a meld of accommodation and a type of tolerance by the majority with an acquiescence by the minority that it needed to find a place in the new dispensation if it was to survive. 'Protestant' and 'Catholic' may no longer be the fundamental labels that once gave you your identity in southern Ireland (they still resonate in Northern Ireland); but they were largely self-evident and accepted for many centuries before independence, and for many decades after it. That is why they mattered and, to an extent, *still* matter. Such an historical albatross is not easy to shift.

Long before war or revolution complicated allegiances, Protestants within families and communities had to deal with complexities. For example, take the south-east. Here was an area that, in 1798, was riven, we are told, by sectarian violence; a little over a century later, relations seemed determinedly cordial, neighbourly even. Here is a tale of two Erskines: in 1914, Erskine Barton, a unionist magistrate in New Ross with connections to the Orange Order in Belfast (and brother of Robert), was reported as telling a south Dublin Orange Lodge meeting that Protestants in Wexford were afraid to declare their unionism in the lead up to Home Rule; at the same time, his cousin Erskine Childers and a party of other like-minded Protestants were planning the Howth gun-running.[6] Another Wexford Protestant, farmer Willie Thorpe, disassociated himself from Barton's claim at a meeting of New Ross Board of Guardians, saying that it was insulting for Wexford Protestants to have their nationalism denied them.[7] War throws cold water on the heat of the Home Rule issue, but this is just a sample of the intricate loyalties among the Protestant populations, even before war, rebellion, revolution and civil war. This continues after the change of regime; a vital part of the Protestant story from 1922 is precisely that allegiances and loyalties were not static, not set in stone. They could, and did, adapt where circumstances demanded and as the generations moved on.

The alternative to an independent Ireland may not have been entirely congenial for Protestants. Imperious attitudes often irritated; though, as Elizabeth Bowen put it, '. . . our politeness to England must be a form of pity . . .'.[8] Imperial governments had had a long track record of doing what they wanted, ignoring unionists as well as nationalists, creating 'the Ireland that we made' as former Tory Chief Secretary Arthur Balfour rather proprietorially asserted in 1928.[9] Conservative and Liberal governments from the 1890s to the 1910s were arguably more 'revolutionary' in Ireland than what emerged eventually from the 1919–23 period; and post-Great War socio-economic change might have been greater if Ireland had remained an integral part of the United Kingdom. The modernism displayed by Chief Secretaries Gerald Balfour, George Wyndham and Augustine Birrell might have been continued by Labour governments in 1924 and 1929, and an even more radical one in 1945. Instead, independent Ireland remained largely encased in aspic: landed, conservative and devout. Balfour was pleased. That suited many Protestant economic and denominational interests and government was relatively sensitive to its minority, more or less leaving it to its own devices. But the corollary was a subterranean exclusion. If the Protestant intelligentsia often champed impatiently at the bit in the *Irish Statesman* and the *Bell*, waiting for an invitation to run Ireland better, they would be largely disappointed.

Voices are not always heard in proportion. The elites will usually get the best lines and the most space, simply because they are rich, educated and articulate. In 1929, the *Irish Times* decried 'too frequent suggestions' that southern Protestants had 'an alien creed, an alien culture and alien aspirations'.[10] Taken at face value, the noisy parts of political Protestantism—before independence as well as occasional bursts of sour nostalgia after it—often did little to disabuse that notion. Some communities and individuals were more adept, or luckier, at putting words on paper and therefore leave an evidentiary trail of their allegiances and presence. Farming families or urban working-class families seldom wrote books, or had letters published in the newspapers. Oral history offers a path to excavating hidden stories, and several essays in this volume use it profitably.

Content

The ability of Protestants in the new Ireland to shape-shift and engage with the contemporary, using chameleon-like or parasitic traits to adapt to local conditions, is considerably underreported and underestimated. This book attempts a corrective, from various perspectives of Protestant participants in this new-old Ireland, such as former landlords, clerics, academics and students, working-class Protestants, businessmen, a journalist, revolutionaries, farm families. Roy Foster's preface picks up on the fact that by the time of the 1937 Constitution 'the identity of southern Protestants was more or less uncomplicatedly Irish'. The essays themselves are organised around three themes. In the first, 'Belonging', Ian d'Alton argues that southern Irish Protestantism's identity was an ongoing battle between contemporary experience and imagination and he analyses the construction of different types of loyalty and 'belongingness' between 1922 and 1948. Then Brian Hughes examines how 'loyalism' was portrayed to the Irish Grants Committee, focusing on a border county, which carries its own dynamics. Conor Morrissey looks at one way of redefining loyalty and to signal engagement, writing of Rev. Bolton Waller, who saw unity—national and ecclesiastical—and internationalism as the essential badges of Irish Protestantism. Miriam Moffitt discusses, through the prism of the 'State Prayers' controversy, how Protestants saw their place in the new republic after its declaration in 1948. Folklorist Deirdre Nuttall uses voices of the formerly unheard to show how Protestant 'stories' have coloured, shaped and fed back upon identity.

Experimenting with 'Engagement' was another facet of southern Protestantism's journey post-independence, and covered by the essays grouped in this second theme. Tony Varley compares the career of ex-landlords and ex-unionists George O'Callaghan-Westropp in County Clare and Robert Burke in Galway, and how class politics began to trump the religious–political divide as early as the 1920s. Tomás Irish deals with 'official' relations between Trinity College Dublin and the new state in the 1920s and 1930s, focusing on the work of Trinity's TDs, the university's public ceremonials and the way in which it used these to align itself—cautiously and carefully—with the Free State. Philip Bull's essay on the life and work of Edward Richards-Orpen, interested in progressive farming and politics, further develops this participatory theme. Protestants were significantly embedded in the commercial and professional world at independence. The nature of that business nexus is detailed and examined from 1922 to EEC accession in 1973 by Frank Barry. Lastly in this theme, Ida Milne describes the ways in which Protestants in the rural south-east normalised community relationships by participation in Gaelic games.

The Protestant story is shot through with a sense of difference, or often even mild surprise at its absence. Thus, 'Otherness' and its consequences is our third theme. 'Double-outsiders' perhaps, cut off from one community while never quite able fully to enter the experience of the other, were the Protestant revolutionaries and independence fighters recorded and discussed by Martin Maguire. Niamh Dillon's essay is a revealing comparative study of two 'outsider' communities at their respective independences: Protestants in Ireland and the British in India. Catherine O'Connor explores a rather less comfortable aspect of otherness through a nuanced examination of attitudes amongst Protestant women to social issues, including mixed marriages in 1940s and 1950s Wexford. Humour—the safety valve of a nation, to quote *Dublin Opinion*—can have two meanings. Felix Larkin, in an illustrated essay, looks at whether cartoonists humoured Protestants and their cherished institutions, or were more acerbic and critical. Also on the funnier side of the street, Caleb Wood Richardson examines the use of humour by Patrick Campbell as a form of a self-deprecatory Protestant and 'Anglo-Irish' defensive mechanism. The collection is brought together in a concluding overview by Joseph Ruane, who has contrasted perceptively the 'historical sociology' of Protestants in twentieth-century Ireland and France. He poses the question of whether some (not all) southern Protestants have developed a generic Irish identity that is independent of an ethno-religious base. If so, this just might be a model for a future Irish identity—whether twenty-six counties or island-wide—that could transcend the ethno-religious divisions of the past.

The time-scale for these studies lies largely between 1922 and the mid-1960s, which reflects this book's aim to assess a formative period in a new political environment for a formerly dominant minority. Paradoxically, the one group that had to maintain a dynamism, if only to survive, were Protestants. Daithí Ó Corráin has forged the way for a more subtle understanding of that dynamism, of how the Church of Ireland in particular and Protestants in general were more comfortable with, and in, the state from the late 1940s onward.[11] By the early 1960s, as Eugenio Biagini has written about Irish Methodism, 'there was a new sense of ease and satisfaction with conditions in the Republic'.[12] The politico-social climate was becoming—or was *perceived* to be becoming—more benign. The state may have still been a chilly place for some Protestants, but the temperature was improving. The *Zeitgeist* was undergoing a shift—not necessarily to do with the Northern Ireland disturbances, but rather reflecting the liberal *intifada* of the decade, as Ireland picked up on the modern. State and nation were becoming more open, economically secure, tolerant of plurality and the expression of sometimes uncomfortable opinions. This is particularly demonstrated in Patrick Campbell's 1967 autobiography, where he does not hide his parents' references to Catholic piety and backwardness. Such belittling and mockery took place in private all the time; by 1967, it was acceptable to mention it in public.[13] Jack White's 1975 volume *Minority Report* argues that ecumenism in religion, allied with the deletion of the article in the Irish Constitution relating to the 'special position' of the Roman Catholic church, represented clear markers between that and previous times.[14] *Ne Temere* still exerted a baleful influence, but youth on both sides was already beginning to query its premises and ignore its proscriptions. There is another volume to be written about southern Protestantism in the turbulent years shaped by the Northern Irish conflict, economic boom-and-bust and the Weberian 'protestantisation' of Irish Catholic society. This volume, however, marks the beginning of the end of a significant period of adjustment for the minority community in independent Ireland: it is a natural boundary.

Context

Who *were* these southern Protestants? The *Catholic Bulletin* represented them as tattered remnants of Ascendancy, seeing freemasons (and Free Staters) under every bed. This simplistic view painted the Protestant 'community' as socially, culturally, politically and economically homogeneous. That vision was not, of course, confined to the *Bulletin*; even today, the pastiche images of the

Irish Protestant as a foxhunting, heartless landlord or as a land-grabbing planter have a residual currency, as social media comments often reveal. Historical analyses, such as Fergus Campbell's *The Irish Establishment 1879–1914*[15] and Ciaran O'Neill's *Catholics of Consequence: Transnational Education, Social Mobility and the Irish Catholic Elite 1850–1900*[16] have focused on the elites who came to shape Ireland in the period from the mid-nineteenth century to its end. In particular, Campbell's work suggests that the 'greening' of the Irish administration, business life and policing was not so advanced as previously thought.[17] As Campbell writes, 'by the end of the nineteenth century . . . attempts to transform the composition of the Irish establishment had done little to alter the impression of Protestant domination'.[18] But whatever about the agency and influence of the elites, at independence Protestants covered a wide socio-economic spectrum, found as domestic servants, teachers, shop-owners and shop assistants, policemen, nurses, farmers, poets, revolutionaries, industrialists, trade unionists and university lecturers. They included the likes of poet and cultural nationalist W.B. Yeats; erstwhile Home Rule MP and dominion Home Ruler Stephen Gwynn; revolutionaries Sam Maguire, Harry Nicholls and Kathleen Lynn; Major James Myles, international rugby player, decorated Great War soldier and independent Protestant TD for east Donegal, 1923–43; playwright and writer Lennox Robinson; suburban journalist Brian Inglis; Anglo-Irish writers Elizabeth Bowen, Molly Keane and Hubert Butler; businessmen Richard Beamish and Andrew Jameson; politicians Jasper Wolfe and Bryan Cooper, unionist MP and then Cumann na nGaedheal TD; writer and socialist Seán O'Casey; entrepreneur and champion of co-operatives Sir Horace Plunkett. The professional classes living in suburban Rathmines and Dalkey; the Orange tinge of Cavan; the Palatines of Wexford and Limerick; the farming communities in west Cork, Carlow, Wicklow and Wexford and isolated Protestants of Kerry, Clare and Mayo—all these demonstrate Protestantism as possessed of anything but coherence and organic unity. Hubert Butler once famously suggested that southern Protestants were incapable of congealing into block opinions on religious issues; perhaps that reflects the innate diversity of their situations.[19] Gender, educational, class and cultural nuances cross-cut and complicated the picture. In imitation of animal territories, patterns and structures of plantation and migration could be invisible arbiters of identity, differing from locality to locality. Protestants in the southern state were largely Anglican, in marked contrast to the situation in Northern Ireland—one more reason why the southern and northern wings of the Church of Ireland tended towards divergence, in politics as well as theological outlook. In 1926, Anglicans accounted for nearly 75 per cent of all Protestants in the Free State. There were some 32,500 Presbyterians (of which 65 per cent were in the three border counties) and about 10,500 Methodists. By 1961, the situation was little different; Anglicans still comprised 72 per cent of the total non-Catholic population.[20] This had consequence; in the formative decades of the new state the Church of Ireland tended to make the pace when it came to asserting a distinctive Protestant ethic, demonstrated particularly in the Patrician celebrations of 1932. Political quiescence and virtual invisibility tended to be the default option for the minor Protestant denominations in the period covered by this volume, as they concentrated upon their evangelical and theological mission. As Eugenio Biagini has pointed out, Methodists in particular embarked on a new enthusiasm for evangelism and renewal following partition; colporterage—the visiting of homes to distribute and sell the scriptures and devotional books—was a particular feature. Bicycles were the chariots of this anti-Roman invasion, belief its armour and devotional literature its weaponry. This is also an illustration of how a particular Protestantism, now firmly in a minority without back-up, adjusted to the new circumstances—'an open-minded attitude to the new Ireland and a determination to identify with it'—where open-air meetings were less combative and contentious.[21]

For the purpose of placing the essays in this book in context, here we set out those essential characteristics of the southern Protestant population at independence and afterwards that, in our view, most impacted upon their social and economic lives. Historians, sociologists and demographers have seen the percentage and numerical decline of the southern Protestant population between 1911 and 1926 as a most significant determinant of the Protestant condition after independence. It shrank by about a third—from 313,000 to about 208,000 or from 10 per cent to 7 per cent of the total—in contrast to only a 2 per cent drop in Catholic numbers.[22] This generality, though, can mask the significance of the changes to the internal dynamics of the Protestant communities. As an example: when treating of the departure of the 'temporaries'—the British military, policemen, civil and public servants—the emphasis is on what proportion of the total decline it accounts for. However, for the structure of Protestantism as it faced the new dispensation, what is perhaps more significant is the *local* effect of the departures. Customers and sociality suffered, especially in the towns, where the population drop was significantly greater than in country areas.[23] In Naas and Fermoy, both with large barracks, the Protestant population declined by over 90 per cent; in Newbridge, Tipperary and Mullingar it was over 80 per cent. When the British presence finally melted away, what was exposed was the inherent demographic weaknesses of the indigenous community, such as loss of future members courtesy of conversion (mainly through the operation of the *Ne Temere* decree), low fertility (late marriage, a *soupçon* of contraceptive practices) and net 'normal' emigration.

The pace of demographic change for Protestantism also coloured the sense of where Protestantism felt it was heading. Between 1926 and 1991, the Protestant population declined by a much greater proportion (48 per cent) than between 1911 and 1926, but the later decline was a slow burn. The drip-drip of loss through conversion, *Ne Temere*, emigration and a low birth-rate seemed to be part of the natural order of things; the suddenness and trauma of 1919–23 evidently were not. Other demographic elements were perhaps more significant in the Protestant scheme of things, for example Protestant population density. A statement that in 1911, Protestants numbered about 313,000 in the area that was to emerge as the Irish Free State, representing 10 per cent of the population, is useful, but not particularly so. It masks a wide range from locality to locality, differences that had consequences for how Protestant social organisation, and a 'Protestant' economy, actually worked. Protestants in Dublin city and county, with 21 per cent of the population (and furthermore concentrated in pockets within that area) felt and acted differently compared to isolated and fragmented communities and families in Connacht (2.6 per cent) and Munster (3.6 per cent).[24] One other significant difference between the structures of the Catholic and Protestant populations might be noted here: the imbalance between the sexes. Gender difference represented some 1.7 per cent of the Catholic population, compared with 2.4 per cent for Protestants. Again, the Catholic population had more males than females in 1926—the Protestant imbalance was substantially the other way around, with some 101,000 males and 107,000 females.[25] Together with the 'clumpiness' of Protestant population distribution, this put further pressure on the relative stability of the Protestant tribe.

Drilling down further to the local raises some questions. Was the fact that those areas of west Cork that came to symbolise apparently sectarian unrest in the 1919–23 period had Protestant population proportions of between 8 and 15 per cent significant, when compared to relatively quiescent areas with either much higher, or lower, proportions of Protestant populations? Overall, Presbyterians in the twenty-six counties were a minority of a minority; but in certain border counties they were much more visible.

There were differing economies too, with pockets of poverty—rural and urban—such as 'the Protestant poor who are in distress', assisted by the Association for the Relief of Distressed Protestants in May 1916 after the Rising, and still there in 1922.[26] Small farmers struggling to subsist, single ladies beggared enough to need support from aid societies, domestic servants and an urban working class were not unknown to Protestantism by any means, but their voices were seldom heard or their concerns and lives articulated. The emphasis often placed in the narratives of elites has the effect of masking what, perhaps, is obvious—that Protestantism was not just composed of higher-order professions, managers and large farmers. For instance, the predominant stereotypes of ex-landlords and large farmers have cloaked the much larger numbers more concerned with saving hay than family histories. In 1926 there were 19,459 non-Catholic farmers in the Free State, but of these only 1,638 (or 8.4 per cent) were owners of farms greater than 200 acres (87 per cent of whom were Anglicans). The vast majority of Protestant farmers were middling owners of land. Within the Protestant communities, the 3,500 or so Protestant agricultural labourers in the state cannot have been entirely invisible, either.[27] We rely on fiction to give us a sense of what life was like for the approximately 8,800 Protestant domestic servants in the state in 1926.[28]

In its external characteristics, Protestantism in the aggregate exhibited some significant differences compared with the social and economic structure of the majority. When compared with the Catholic community, southern Irish Protestantism was not as 'agricultural' or rural; it was also more 'professionally' oriented—about 6.5 per cent of Protestant males were in the professions, compared to 2.4 per cent of Catholics. In 1926, it might have been seen as somewhat counter-intuitive to find that the proportion of Protestants in 'public administration and defence'—at around 4 per cent—still pipped Catholics, at 3.4 per cent.[29]

Protestants were undoubtedly more prosperous than the general population; in 1916 in Cork they comprised a mere 7 per cent of the population but owned 60 per cent of the motor cars.[30] This stemmed from their employment at higher income grades. They were only 2 per cent of the unskilled workforce but made up 17 per cent of the persons employed as 'employers, managers and foremen', whereas the comparable percentage for non-Protestants was 7 per cent. In a typical chicken and egg process, their prosperity was reflected in male involvement in the higher status occupations—senior bank officials (53 per cent), chartered accountants (46 per cent), barristers (39 per cent), solicitors (38 per cent), medical doctors (22 per cent), civil servants (15 per cent) and teachers (10 per cent)—all substantially in excess of the Protestant proportion of occupied males in the general population, at about 7.5 per cent. In 1926, Protestants still accounted for nearly 15 per cent of 'civil servant officials and clerks' (but only 5 per cent of local authority officers, and 2 per cent of the new Civic Guard).[31] Much of this represented an historic hangover. By 1926, the proportions in all these categories had decreased from those recorded in 1911, but that was a secular trend which predated independence. The 1926 census gives a pointer to the future, though: only 6 per cent of teachers in training were Protestant.[32]

Rural occupations show a similar grounding in relative prosperity. The landed economy demonstrated over-representation in its more prosperous parts; Protestant males, while close to the average (7.3 per cent) in the category of 'all farmers', comprised 27.5 per cent of farms over 200 acres, and a quarter of farm managers. Prosperity crossed gender lines. Of female farmers with farms over 200 acres, a quarter or so were Protestant.[33] In contrast, just less than 3 per cent of male agricultural labourers were Protestant.[34] In fourteen counties Protestants owned over one-third of the larger farms (over 200 acres) in 1926 and accounted for over half such farms in five: Carlow, Longford, Wicklow, Cavan and Monaghan.[35] Likewise in the commercial world. Of the managerial classes in 1926, over 15 per cent were Protestant, with a heavy over-representation in certain industries, such as brewing and distilling, textiles and construction.[36] What all this signalled was the vital interest that influential Protestants had in how the economy of the new state was to be organised, especially in its tariff, taxation and land-distribution policies, and in its attitudes toward education, the professions and the public service.[37]

Class was perhaps as important as religious denomination; settlement patterns reinforced the sense of ghettoisation that characterised many of the occupational categories. Thus in Dublin, while the bourgeoisie of both religions clustered together in areas of relative salubrity in such as Clontarf and the townships of Rathmines and Rathgar, Pembroke and Kingstown,[38] social intermixing between them was limited. The Anglo-Irish novelist Elizabeth Bowen's Dublin Edwardian childhood memories were of a Protestant bubble, in a small but comfortable house on the south side of the city at Herbert Place, close to the Grand Canal. Here, Catholics were in 'a world that lay alongside ours, but never touched';[39] the people that the Bowens mingled with were almost exclusively Protestant and of their own social class.[40] Even odours seemed sectarianised; the Molesworth Hall, where she learned dancing, 'had a Protestant smell'.[41]

A universe away from Bowen was a more pungent odour, and a different sort of admixture, characterised by Seán O'Casey's Bessie Burgess in his play about 1916, *The Plough and the Stars*. A loud-mouthed drunken unionist working-class Protestant harridan, she lives in the same tenement building as the Catholic Nora Clitheroe. While seemingly forever baiting her nationalist neighbours—'Has th' big guns knocked all th' harps out of your hands?'[42]—O'Casey has Bessie siding with Nora when disaster strikes and class and gender solidarity is called for. But we should not be overly seduced by his wishful invention. Looking at a typical north city working-class Dublin street in the 1911 census—in this case, North King Street—a mere 31 residents were Protestants in a total population of some 1,600, or 1.9 per cent.[43] Mirroring the rural situation, only 3 per cent of the 17,000 general labourers in the city—some 500—were Protestants,[44] suggesting that, like anxious Irish Catholic ecumenists in the 1960s wondering if there would still be enough Protestants to be ecumenical *with*, the actual opportunities to practise O'Casey's form of solidarity may have been rather thin on the ground.

Changes in the urban class structure had the effect of making Protestantism in places like Dublin more middle-class. Dublin's Protestant working-class numbered some 10,000 in 1911, but was already declining, a trend that had started in the nineteenth century. The class had largely vanished by the late 1940s,[45] picked off by manufacturing decline, emigration to Britain and further afield (and not being replaced, as Catholics were, by migration into Dublin from rural Ireland) and by increased intermarriage with Catholics (and, before 1922, by marriage with the itinerant British military). Pockets of the Protestant working class were scattered here and there, often dependent upon special factors, such as the *coterie* of domestic servants employed by the substantial Protestant middle class in the south city, county and township areas and beyond or the skilled working-class Protestants in the suburb of Inchicore, with its railway works.[46]

There is little doubt that the period between 1919 and 1923 was uncomfortable for many segments of the Protestant community. Some came through the period relatively unscathed: 'we were all uneasy enough at the time, never knowing what would happen next . . . though the Catholics were good neighbours on the whole'.[47] This, however, was not always the case and many were subjected to such a degree of intimidation and boycotting that they felt compelled to relocate outside the new state.[48]

It is clear that Protestants were not randomly or routinely attacked. Those who suffered—and some suffered greatly—were generally targeted on account of their public hostility to republican ideals or because of long-standing resentments over landownership. Indeed, the person mentioned above as having relocated out of the state had, between 1918 and 1922, kept authorities informed of the 'seditious tendency or the Bolshevik character of the various local movements'. Negative experiences often had deeper origins. Land and landownership is a potent motivator in rural Ireland and it is clear that the unsettled conditions of the revolutionary years provided an opportunity where old scores were settled.[49]

Whether one agrees or disagrees with the thesis of a species of 'ethnic cleansing' (or its variants) in Cork during the revolutionary period, the fiery tone in which the controversy is carried on has ensured that the position of southern Irish Protestants is a particular focus for debate and has provoked some research that might be described as 'brave'. New explorations of a perceived Protestant 'exodus' between 1920 and 1923 from UCC historian Andy Bielenberg suggest that there is now 'a consensus that revolutionary violence or intimidation was of far less consequence than a host of other factors'.[50] His estimate of 'involuntary emigration' is between 2,000 and 16,000,[51] significantly different from other estimates that place the number at closer to 40,000.[52]

Whatever about the numbers, intimidation and flight was as much about psychology, a matter of differing perceptions and motivations. As Charles Townshend has written: 'Protestants' own sense of persecution should not necessarily be taken at face value—insecurity is more a psychological than a physical state'.[53] Protestants may have felt that they were being targeted merely as Protestants, while at the same time militant republicans and anti-Treatyites perceived *their* actions as against those supporting the authorities, or betraying them. Everywhere, there are the handed-down stories the history books largely do not contain, the undocumented kindnesses from Catholics who put in a good word to rescue Protestants in times of trouble, or to let them know there *would* be no trouble. Sometimes, only personal perspective decides whether that glass of *uisce beatha* is half full or half empty. While there were those who viewed the IRA grave dug as a warning to leave, others noted the neighbours interceding to persuade that the chap wasn't so bad after all.

While the period from the start of the guerrilla war in 1919 to the end of civil strife in 1923 was indisputably a period of trauma and dispossession,[54] the demonstrative effect of the murders and burnings between 1919 and 1923 was what counted. While this was no Armenia or a re-run of 1641, it may have felt like it. Yet even where Protestants were driven out, or fled, David Fitzpatrick posits that 'If any campaign of "ethnic cleansing" was attempted, its demographic impact was fairly minor'.[55] Barry Keane has estimated that even taking the 3,632 total claims made to the Irish Grants Committee up to 1928 and assuming that they were all from Protestants (unlikely), the numbers would still only account for about 3 per cent of the Protestant population decline between 1911 and 1926.[56] Again, while it is estimated that about 400 Protestant homes and businesses were burnt in the period 1919–23,[57] this was a relatively modest tally for a revolutionary period in which the minority was seen as at best neutral to the majority aspiration and, at worst, often actively hostile towards it. Houses suffered more than halls; the structures of purely *religious* difference (churches, schools, parish halls, graveyards) remained largely untouched. Where such attacks did occur—for instance, the five churches in Clare, Limerick and Galway burnt between 1920 and 1922, a Protestant orphanage in Connemara and a parish hall at Bandon—it might be held that they demonstrate a very definite 'particularity' rather than a generalised animus against Protestants.[58] This was a golden opportunity to attack those individuals and families who had most provoked personal animosity from individuals on the other side, for whatever reason—imagined or real slights, agrarian jealousies, the wrong politics, over-zealous religiosity, aggressive loyalism.

The remnants of the gentry (few in numbers, but significant socially and economically—and noisy, especially from the safety of the Houses of Lords and Commons in London)—were particularly targeted in two phases. During the War of Independence, some were singled out as a result of their connections with the military; during the Civil War in 1922–3, senators such as Sir Horace Plunkett and Lord Mayo were placed in the firing-line.[59] But the destruction of upwards of 275 'Big Houses' between 1920 and 1923 represented only about 4 per cent of the total.[60] Economic inutility and local taxation policies of the Free State government and its successors were probably responsible for far more deroofing than the incendiaries ever were.

At the last, Belfast-born southern unionist historian R.B. McDowell's cool judgement was that 'hardships sustained by the southern loyalists were on the whole not excessively severe nor long-lasting'.[61] It does appear that tensions, on the surface at any rate, died down quite quickly. One commentator maintains that catharsis eventually produced deliberate amnesia on both sides.[62] Another explanation is that even if memory was buried, most quickly forgot where its tomb even lay, because it was neither necessary, nor important, to remember.[63] Those who remained were the beneficiaries of the tragedies of those who had fled. Nevertheless, there is still within some elements of the Protestant community homage to a *sensitivity* to a presumed memory of murder, persecution and flight; whether real or imagined is beside the point.[64]

Working a Passage

For Protestants in the new state, identity was always the elephant in the room. Edna Longley remarked in 1989 that if Catholics were born Irish, Protestants had 'to work their passage to Irishness'.[65] That begs the question as to what cleaving to this idea of 'Irishness' actually meant. Catholics, by and large, had to operate within a relatively constricted and historically predetermined template. By contrast, Protestants—in theory, at any rate—had the opportunity to work their passage towards a different, but equally legitimate, concept of *patria* in which *their* historic Irishness could be expressed in more contemporary terms. In this, they have been broadly successful. If they had not been, this formerly dominant group would have withered and died. In the main, southern Protestants preserved their economic, cultural and social status without much disruption or cost, and their elites continued to have a considerable influence in certain aspects of independent Ireland's life, even if their political power was close to negligible. Above all, most stayed because they did not see themselves as belonging anywhere else. As the Irish of every hue have done the world over, those who arrived as planters or in search of fortune put down roots; 400 years later, those roots had gone down deep.

One strand of southern Protestant history sees this community as almost revelling in victimhood and marginalisation. The other recognises that many Irish Protestants were content to find a place in the new dispensation, and to contribute to civic society. If southern Irish Protestants are now more or less 'uncomplicatedly Irish', the journeys to get there are anything but uncomplicated. That is what the essays that follow attempt to describe and analyse, providing an illustration of the interweaving and complexities that these conflicting visions of history have thrown up. They speak for themselves.

PART I

Belonging

CHAPTER ONE

'No Country'?: Protestant 'Belongings' in Independent Ireland, 1922–49

IAN d'ALTON

Introduction

On 12 June 1922, the forgotten imperial southern Irish loyalists, overwhelmingly Protestant, experienced the last great death of the Great War. The bureaucrats in the War Office had accomplished what kaiser, emperor and sultan had not, the disappearance of several Irish regiments. The obsequies were held at Windsor Castle as the regimental insignia were surrendered into the king's bosom. The ceremony bore all the characteristics of a funeral; in the sad, angry words of the *Irish Times*, the regimental representatives 'were entertained to luncheon on the completion of their pathetic errand' and the band 'in the quadrangle played plaintive airs'.[1] If it seemed the ineluctable end of something, it also marked the start of an intriguing triangulation of identity between Britain, Ireland and this apparently beached people, wherein it had to make some sense of living in a Free State that betimes seemed anything but free.

Even before the end of the union, southern Irish unionists were being characterised as stateless; in the words of a 1916 Cork Protestant novelist, they were little but the 'illegitimate children of an irregular union between Hibernia and John Bull'.[2] In 1898 an über-nationalist Catholic curate, Rev. Michael Kennedy, in the course of a philosophical diatribe against the minority, had claimed that 'They are not born from our race…the Irish Unionists have no country'.[3] This was echoed nearly a quarter of a century later at independence, when Major Somerset Saunderson of Cavan sighed, 'Now…I have *no* country!'[4]

This interpretative essay offers another perspective. It argues that the essential resilience of those southern Protestants—largely uncomprehending of the transcendental nature of Irish nationalism, often cleaving to Ireland as a place, not a nation, and wanting, and needing, to stay—required them to invent other 'countries' for themselves. And despite living in an Ireland which maddeningly and inexplicably demanded their adherence to and exclusion from the nation at one and the same time, they were broadly successful in squaring the circle. Most got from independence to the 1960s with relatively little dislocation to their lives, livelihoods and culture when contrasted with other stranded ethnic communities elsewhere in Europe after the Great War, such as the German minorities in Estonia, Latvia and Prussian Poland. It saw them finding an engagement with the contemporary, allowing a relatively peaceful transition to a different status while not jettisoning the characteristics of their peoplehood; and a language, a discourse and a use of symbolism that was designed not to throw out the British baby with the Irish bathwater.

Coming to Terms

Southern Irish Protestantism's identity was a constant battle between experience and imagination. As regards the experience, then, what was the approach of southern Protestants to this alien polity of which they perforce were now part? What came to their rescue was the very concept of 'loyalty', which was almost part of the southern Protestant DNA. Protestants used it to come to terms with the changed dispensation and they did it through three modes: acceptance, obedience and participation.

Acceptance was a pragmatic decision. They had little choice. In December 1921, on behalf of southern members of the Church of Ireland, Archbishop Gregg of Dublin offered 'our loyalty and our good will' to the Irish Free State,[5] although privately he felt as if he had been banished from the Garden of Eden.[6] While the Presbyterians too were prepared to support the new state, it was on the basis of 'where liberty and honesty and good-will rule'.[7] Others were more conscious of their vulnerability; when Sir Henry Wilson in late April 1922 cast the position of Trinity College as parlous under the new regime, he provoked a highly critical response from the provost, the university's MPs and the *Irish Times*.[8] In 1949, when Ireland finally left the Commonwealth, that newspaper exhorted its Protestant readership to be 'unconditionally loyal' to the new republic.[9] These were all sensible approaches.

Obedience was based on the 'rendering unto Caesar' principle. In 1913, Lord Barrymore, a leading southern unionist, had put it thus: 'if Home Rule is forced upon us we shall have to bow under it and get on as best we can'.[10] Archbishop Gregg was prepared to accept the regime change 'as a constitutionalist...if it is imposed by lawful authority'.[11] The dean of Ross said in 1933: 'the Church of Ireland has remained true to the guiding principle of obedience to constituted authority since "the powers that be are ordained of God"'.[12]

Participation was more problematic. It was sensible, on the 'head-above-the-parapet' principle, well-learnt by Protestant soldiers during the Great War, not to be too enthusiastic. The ballot-box was the safe option, and its use was encouraged.[13] A separate 'political Protestantism' was not feasible, apart from localities where there was a numerous Protestant population, such as in the border counties of Donegal, Cavan and Monaghan[14] and the townships of Pembroke, and Rathmines and Rathgar in suburban Dublin. Otherwise, Protestants, often holding their noses, voted for the guarantors of order and economic orthodoxy.[15] That is not to say that Protestants completely opted out of visible politics; in the 1923 election, apart from the Trinity seats and those in border counties, ex-unionists participated through membership of smaller special-interest and class-based parties such as Cork Progressive Association and the Businessmen's Party.[16]

In 1933 the dean of Ross suggested of the Church of Ireland that 'her sons and daughters have taken part in everything that concerns the welfare of the country, and their only wish has been that a larger share should come into their hands'.[17] The problem with the dean's wish was that of a zero-sum game; Protestant gain might be perceived as Catholic loss. Irrelevance had little value, but visibility could carry a high price. The minority well knew that the majority's benign toleration was only certain if they did nothing that would strain that toleration. As Senator Sir John Keane put it at the Church of Ireland's Patrician conference in October 1932, in an extended metaphor about the lamb lying down with the lion, 'he has no alternative but to lay low and hope he is unnoticed'.[18]

Experiencing the New Ireland

The sectarian environment could not easily be finessed. If 'white mice' was one description applied to southern Protestants, it was an apt one.[19] Cowed by the strident voices of Catholic triumphalism in the 1920s and 1930s—evidenced by legislation in favour of the Irish language and censorship and restrictions on liquor sales, divorce and contraception—southern Protestants were encouraged to keep a low, even a cringing, profile. In the context of public comments like those of J.P. Ryan, secretary of the ultra-ultramontane Catholic lay organisation *Maria Duce* that 'all non-Catholic sects…are false and evil', made as late as 1950,[20] and, more mainstream, Cardinal MacRory declaring in 1931 that the Protestant Church in Ireland was not a part of the Church of Christ at all,[21] one could perhaps see why. Sometimes they didn't even register on the radar. When a Catholic priest suggested a 'Christian' constitution to de Valera in October 1936, it was based on the Portuguese Catholic constitution of 1933. Here, 'Christian' meant 'Catholic'; for all intents and purposes, 'Protestant' Irish simply did not exist.[22]

Protestants could keep themselves warm by huddling together in their own social, economic and cultural redoubts but, even occasionally, they perforce had to venture out into a colder Catholicism. It may be possible to paint a picture of non-discrimination at official level and find evidence of integration, but the oral histories presented by Heather Crawford and Deirdre Nuttall also illuminate the underlying sense of otherness and isolation that often characterised the Protestant psyche.[23]

Engagement by individuals might be seen as relatively un-threatening. Examples are Colonel Grove White (former JP and DL), nominated rather unwillingly for Cork County Council in 1925 on a Farmers' Party ticket, but elected; and George O'Callaghan-Westropp and Robert Burke, dealt with elsewhere in this volume. Yet, if Protestantism, as an 'ism', felt that its 'loyalty and good will' entitled it to a newly legitimised push to maintain its cultural and social identity, it ran the risk of being rebuffed, or worse. But within broad limits, freed from the dead weight of history, Protestants could, and did, stand their ground, although not as firmly as those such as Hubert Butler and W.B. Stanford might have liked.[24] 'Expert at keeping themselves warm in cold houses',[25] they may have considered that a bargain had been struck. In return for an outward acceptance of the constitutional dispensation, Protestants had expiated their former sins; the responsibility for Irish history was no longer theirs to bear. They could start with a cleaner sheet.

That didn't always work. Few might disagree with Alan Ford's assertion that 'Religion has been woven into the very fabric of Irish identity and culture…inextricably bound up with political, intellectual, economic and social developments'.[26] But to interpret specifics wholly or largely as 'sectarian' can sometimes ignore other factors in play. When the appointment of Letitia Dunbar-Harrison as Mayo County Librarian in 1930 was blocked by the county council on the basis of a lack of Irish-language skills, it seemed that the real reason may have been her Trinity credentials, shorthand for her Protestantism. On the face of it, this represented simple sectarianism. Nevertheless, seen from other angles the dispute also carried overtones of the position of women in Irish public administration, and where the Catholic clergy stood in determining what their flock might be permitted to see and think. Above all, it was as much about a governmental power struggle between the centre and the periphery as about a 'religious' issue. Methodists (Dunbar-Harrison became one, later) even felt that the outcome was encouraging, since government had faced down—and seen off—local bigotry.[27]

Another example of imputing simple sectarian motives to complex situations were the arson attacks on Protestant churches, businesses and homes in July 1935 in Limerick city, Kilmallock, Galway city, Dunmanway and near Thurles. As in Cork in 1922, these appear to have been ignited by sectarian pogroms in Belfast, but—as in 1922—other, baser, motivations may have been at work. A Garda superintendent, commenting on the Thurles attack on a local landowner, ventured that 'On the surface the motive would appear to be sectarian and the attacks to be a reprisal for incidents against Catholics in the North. This I believe to be merely a cover for the outrages, as in my opinion the real reason is prompted chiefly by agrarian motives.'[28] In the same vein, the 1950 Tilson child-custody case was as much about money and Ernest Tilson's flawed character as *Ne Temere*; and the 1957 Fethard-on-Sea boycott of Protestants can be interpreted in part as a flexing of muscle by the local priest, anxious to ensure that sacerdotal domination of his community remained unchallenged.[29]

The important point, though, about these public entanglements was that there were not very many of them. That may have been due to an elaborately choreographed dance in this 'ballroom of romance'. Protestants went out of their way to avoid confrontation in the first place; and official Ireland, officially at any rate, was often prepared to wrap its minority in cotton wool, for fear it would break or, more importantly, leave, taking its talents (and its shekels) with it, fatally damaging the nascent Free State's fiscally orthodox reputation and giving priceless ammunition to diehard Northern Irish unionists, always looking for golden 'I-told-you-so' opportunities.[30]

There are other narratives: one scholar has largely demolished the myth of an alienated minority in the late 1950s and onwards;[31] while, as Ida Milne writes elsewhere in this book, Wexford Protestants engaged with, and were involved in, the wider community through sport. Protestantism's willingness to accept the prevailing wisdom of the Catholic state has been underestimated, for instance, in the areas of balanced budgets, education management and protectionism.[32] As the *Irish Times* stated in 1936, 'On many points of policy we agree, more or less cordially, with Mr de Valera'.[33] In the 1920s and 1930s Protestantism often seemed, in public at any rate, to offer a perhaps rather surprising cosying-up to the state.[34] On one level, there is evidence that Protestants *were* willing to engage; they were over-represented not only in the Senate, but also in the Dáil in the early years of the Free State and, importantly, in the judiciary and civil service.[35] Like many Catholics, Protestants were often condemnatory of socialism and suspicious of statism.[36] An innately conservative Protestantism sometimes found itself on the same side of the Catholic 'counter-revolution'.[37] This conservatism was—at least until the 1960s—not much less illiberal than Catholics on many social and economic issues. One instance was the *Church of Ireland Gazette*'s characterisation of the 1951 mother-and-child scheme as 'communist interference in the family'.[38] The advance scouts of Yeats, Stephen Gwynn, Butler and successive editors of the *Irish Times* often found themselves cut off, dangerously ahead of their imagined army.[39]

Imagining a Congenial Ireland

If sectarian fracases were relatively rare, post-1922 public Ireland was still not a particularly happy place for many Protestants. The *Irish Times* could declaim that they 'accepted the great changes of 1922; they threw themselves heartily into the working of the new Constitution; the Church's money was invested largely and promptly in the Free State's loans';[40] but how could they identify with a *patria* that carried the unacceptable whiff of a specifically Catholic nationalism? One way was to create an 'imagined Ireland', in Colin Reid's striking phrase about how Stephen Gwynn, a Protestant nationalist, came to terms with an uncongenial and inconvenient reality.[41]

The literary offered an almost irresistible path towards such an imagined Ireland but that was one of 'grand tragedy'. Primarily the construct of an elite often resourceful enough to lead a transnational existence, it possessed the luxury of wallowing in decline and decay—Robert Tobin's 'imagery and language of extinction'—and what Elizabeth Grubgeld has characterised as 'a sense of continuity and dissolution, influence and irrelevance, identity and nothingness'.[42] A large corpus of nostalgic, acerbic, Protestant autobiography and chronicle appeared from the 1920s onwards, from the likes of Tom Henn, Hubert Butler, L.A.G. Strong, Joan De Vere, Monk Gibbon and Annabel Davis-Goff, all more or less saying the same thing: we are outsiders, aren't we just! Most are preoccupied with lineage, economic hardship, a vanished utopian childhood and a degenerative view of history.[43] The 'Big House', with collapsing architecture and crumbling families, is used ruthlessly by a spectrum of writers—from Edith Somerville through Elizabeth Bowen and Molly Keane to Jennifer Johnston, John Banville and William Trevor—as a metaphor for the generality of Protestantism. 'The atmosphere which pervades

Anglo-Irish writing', as one scholar has put it, 'both fiction and non-fiction, is moribund'.[44] Largely ignoring the lively and more integrated rural and suburban,[45] the fiction of Anglo-Irish nostalgia has possessed a life outliving its subject-matter. What this type of literature represents is not just story-telling, but a particular *kind* of story-telling, with its images of decomposition, wandering, dream-like otherness.

The problem with this seductive and subversive aesthetic is that it infected the historiography, with the elegiac and regretful tending to come to the fore.[46] This need not have been. The picking-over of the Protestant condition by writers in such periodicals as the *Irish Statesman* and the *Bell* in the 1920s and 1940s was relatively brisk and contemporary. There have been some correctives, mainly from outside the history academy, in the works of the social historians Don Akenson and Heather Crawford, the cultural scholar Declan Kiberd, the political scientist John Coakley and the sociologists Kurt Bowen and Joe Ruane.[47] As Terence Brown has pointed out,[48] urban middle-class Protestantism is largely unable, or unwilling, to express itself about itself in print (it does muscular things like rugby, hockey, tennis and yachting somewhat better). By default it tended to leave the field to rural 'Big House' literature. In the main, the historiography has followed that literature and its associated memoir in positing what Robin Bury has characterised as the 'low-intensity unhappiness' of the southern Irish Protestant.[49]

It didn't help that the finishing line always seemed to be slipping tantalisingly out of reach. Devotion to Celtic mysteries and the Irish language may have been sufficient, just, in 1912 to establish a legitimate Irishness. Not so a decade later. Independence changed the terms of reference. The bar was now set higher; geography, economics and cultural adherence were no longer enough, leading a Protestant letter-writer in 1924 to complain that 'many of our people feel *less* [my emphasis] Irish than formerly'.[50]

Alternative Belongings

George Boyce has maintained that 'Irish society was too divided on sectarian lines to enable any Protestant, however talented or committed, to enter into the experience of the other side'.[51] Many might have been happy to avoid calling Lionel Fleming's head or harp at all, hoping that, by some serendipitous chance, the coin could always land on the edge.[52] That was close to impossible, of course, and they had to come to terms with that. To cope with this, other 'belongings' emerged: different loyalties, alternative conceptions of citizenship, that could jump over, bypass, or lie alongside the slightly odiferous Catholic Free State. One well-remarked-upon parallelism was a variant of what Neal Acherson has characterised as 'inner emigration',[53] the creation of an economic, social and denominational stockaded community, a comfortable temporal, spatial and cultural ghetto. At a civic level, this Lilliput existed by virtue of an already existing Protestant infrastructure. Synods and parish vestries aped parliamentary and local government. Wider public service could be undertaken in the governance of hospitals, schools and a university. Voluntary engagement was through a cat's-cradle of church and charitable bodies, choirs and freemasons, sporting and cultural organisations. Economic security was underpinned by Protestant firms and farms. This was a positive, lived-in reality for some. Yet, for poorer Protestants, especially urban ones, the ghetto hardly existed and they were picked off all the easier by mixed marriages and economic emigration. The ghetto was an abstraction in rural areas, too, where loneliness and isolation, as for Catholics, were endemic.

At a constitutional level the fancy that nothing much had changed could be indulged in. The foundational notion of this continuity, grounded indeed in the legal position to at least 1935, was one of a complex citizenship, summed up by the *Church of Ireland Gazette*'s assertion in 1921 that the categories of Irishman and loyal Briton were not mutually exclusive.[54] As Rev. Dudley Fletcher said in 1922: 'I am proud of my British blood and name. I allow the same privilege to my Gaelic neighbour. We both want to be proud of being Irishmen'.[55]

This 'Brireland' was what might be called the 'Protestant Free State', presided over, in TCD Provost Bernard's revealing description, by 'The King's Government in Ireland'.[56] An emotional attachment to the crown, representing connectivity with a residual sense of British values—relatively harmless—took the place of substance.[57] Even if dominion status was a lesser state of being than hitherto—in Bernard's words written a few days after the Treaty in December

1921: 'I confess that I don't like to think of myself as a "Colonial"! Yet that is what it has come to'[58]—Irish Protestants could represent themselves as in a game of thrones, still subjects of His Majesty in this revived 'Kingdom of Ireland'.

This was not wholly just a little Britain, nor a nostalgic never-was Ireland. It was a parallel universe that worked so long as it carefully tracked what the Free State was up to, and touched it, and be parasitic upon it, when necessary or desirable. The use of the Senate as a sort of Protestant mini-legislature is an example; Lord Glenavy's vision as chairman was that 'I was acting under the firm conviction that I was doing my best for the welfare of our beloved and native land'.[59] Minority parallelism such as this was not unique to Ireland. French Protestantism exhibits similar characteristics,[60] and a study by Rebecca Bennette on the position of German Catholics following unification in 1871 argues that they responded to the challenge in much the same way, coping with Bismarck's *Kulturkampf* by asserting their idea of a distinctive German national identity that ran side-by-side with the 'official' version.[61] The 'Protestant Free State' was out of sight of most Catholics. In this, they mirrored the Protestant way of dealing with the Other by, in effect, pretending it didn't exist. From the Protestant viewpoint operating on a different wavelength, it was exemplified by one rural Protestant's comment that 'Nothing counted for about three miles on any side of us, because there were no Protestants until then',[62] or another's 'High on the hill behind two white gates, we were a world and a law unto ourselves'.[63]

From 1922, political unionism rebranded itself as cultural royalism.[64] 'Over the Irish Free State we are still to have our King', a Dublin Anglican cleric reassured his flock on 11 December 1921.[65] Curtseying to governor-general Tim Healy was perhaps not quite the same as to Lord FitzAlan of Derwent, but it was better than to nobody. In 1935, on King George V's jubilee, Sir John Leslie, as (former) lord lieutenant of Monaghan, organised 'the best means of affording the people of the County an opportunity of expressing their loyalty to Their Majesties',[66] while Bishop Godfrey Day of Ossory ordered special church celebrations. Private expressions of loyalty, as in Armistice Day church services, allowed greater enthusiasms to flourish. Occasionally this one-way traffic was acknowledged and validated in the other direction: the former Anglican bishop of Limerick, Harry White, received congratulations from King George VI on the diamond jubilee of his wedding in 1939.[67]

The 'Protestant Free State' saw what it wanted to see and heard what it wanted to hear. Protestant architecture and loyal street-names (Dublin continued, pro-rata, to have nearly twice as many streets called after Queen Victoria as had London);[68] yacht and golf clubs and professional bodies with a 'Royal' prefix; Saorstát Éireann postboxes still with the king's cipher; and British coinage circulating even if, from 1928, the king had to slum it with the pigs and chickens on the new Free State money: all this allowed a sense that nothing much had changed.[69] Irish Ireland could simply be ignored. In private discourse, Dún Laoghaire was still Kingstown,[70] Cobh, Queenstown and Port Laoise, Maryborough; 'Queenstown' took a long time to be supplanted in the Royal Cork Yacht Club's lexicography,[71] and the letter-headings of the Royal St George Yacht Club bore the address 'Kingstown' well into the 1930s.[72] The *Irish Times* played its part, with its court and personal columns, headed by the royal coat-of-arms, only removed in March 1942 as a result of wartime censorship.[73] Despite the new Chief Justice Hugh Kennedy's apparent predilection for scrapping some of the ceremonial, the courts continued much as they did before.[74] The availability of appeals to the Privy Council, Irish representative peers in the House of Lords, and the investiture of the Prince of Wales and the royal dukes of Gloucester and York as Knights of St Patrick in 1927, 1934 and 1936 respectively had little practical significance, but they mattered to the minority.[75]

If there was any irredentist intention in this, it was relatively toothless. Even in Cavan, Monaghan and Donegal, a cross-border loyalty was not to the northern state as such, but to co-religionists, family and land, and the Orange Order. Lodge meetings doubtless were peppered with loyalist references and sentiments but publicly, the Order accepted the new dispensation, changing its own rubrics to take account of the new political realities. 'We are not going to be sulky in a corner', said Alexander Haslett, deputy grand master, in 1923. 'We are now citizens of the Free State ... we are all determined to do the best we can to support it', declared William Martin a year later.[76]

Expressions of Belongingness

If displays of Britishism were either unwise, pointless or impractical, belongingness could be expressed in other ways. One was to appropriate, somewhat cheekily, those features of national identity which did seem congenial. Thus, in 1932 briefly emerged what we might call the 'Protestant Patrician state', an enthusiasm engendered by the 1500th anniversary of St Patrick's reputed landing in Ireland. In a heady bubble of dubious ecclesiastical history and a critical examination of contemporary Ireland, the Church of Ireland asserted its pre-reformation credentials, retrofitting St Patrick into Irish history as a sort of proto-Protestant, and creating the trappings of statehood with Patrick's red saltire flag, 'for flying on church towers and in private grounds on national holidays or feast days', and bolstered by a rather ambiguous anthem, Cecil Spring-Rice's 'I vow to thee my country'—this last a reminder that there was always a heavenly citizenship awaiting if the earthly one was hell.[77] This was the painting of an Irish *patria* in which Protestants could feel they had a legitimate place, by leapfrogging backwards over the inconveniences of a contested history, and even allowing them to present their well-articulated unease with the contentious language issue in a different context. At the Patrician conference there was an entire session in Irish (printed in the official report), which was 'very well attended, especially by young people', as the official report expressed it.[78]

Moral and cultural superiority was another way of demonstrating, rather smugly perhaps, but not necessarily oppositional, loyalty to the polity. Grounded in a heritage of empire values—'our birthright and heritage of British tradition and culture which I am not ashamed to regard as the finest in the world…traditions of honour, straight-dealing, and tolerance'[79]—it was an Irishness defined more by moral than national boundaries, emphasising the generic virtues of probity, honesty, tolerance, internationalism and purity. Manifestations were the Church of Ireland's disapproval of the Irish state-supported lottery, the Irish Hospitals Sweepstake, in the 1930s, and the Methodist Gold Triangle, founded in 1944, essentially an abstinence association, with its name symbolising duty to God, good citizenship and self-reverence.[80] In particular, Methodists—strongly anti-fascist in the 1920s and 1930s—were uneasy at the de Valera government's ambivalent attitude towards the continental regimes. This was not only triggered by an interpretation of the Christian message, but also because of how the regimes in Germany, Italy, Spain and Portugal mistreated and vilified minorities.[81]

If seeking refuge from the Catholic Free State in these modes seemed somewhat desperate and faintly risible, it smoothed over loss and anxiety. In this reading Trinity College's flying of the union flag alongside the Irish tricolour until at least 1939, or use of the royal toast until about 1945, need not necessarily be seen as, in the words of one 1927 commentator, 'a gesture of bitter hostility to the Saorstát'. As Nora Robertson put it in 1960: 'In respecting new loyalties it had not seemed incumbent upon us to throw our old ones overboard'.[82]

Conclusion

Yeats captures a Protestant *Zeitgeist* that might just have achieved traction. Writing to Annie Horniman in 1907, he articulated a form of emotional engagement with Ireland that was in essence indifferent to the nature of emotion. 'Ireland' was all. Passion could swing as a pendulum: 'I shall write for my own people—whether in love or hate of them matters little—probably I shall not know which it is'.[83] But it was a dangerous road to take, never mind explaining it to closed minds. And so we are left with the idea of 'identity' espoused by the likes of Lyons, McDowell, Kurt Bowen and Bury. This thesis essentially rested on a sense of living on after demographic catastrophe and it has considerable validity. Churches were indeed closed and parishes amalgamated.[84] A population under triple threat from the *Ne Temere* decree, emigration and not producing enough babies might have seemed a hopeless case. However, it is not the whole story. The actuality was a lot fuzzier. 'Ex-unionists' were just that, with nowhere to look but in the rear mirror. But as 'Protestants', they could chart the road ahead, and develop a believable dynamic reality for themselves. This was an identity evolving and adapting, not just to external circumstances, but with positive feedback; in Joe Ruane's and David Butler's phrase about southern Protestants, 'the uncertainty and complexity of their status may itself shape that experience'.[85]

For a community with little but words as weapons, language and its uses take on an almost Foucaultian spirit. Even before independence, southern Protestants had learnt to be careful. At a meeting of the unionists of Munster in April 1912 to protest the third Home Rule Bill, Lord Barrymore put it thus: 'They did not speak there in the same loud and plain tones that their friends in Ulster did.'[86] That carefulness continued into the 1920s—thus the shock occasioned by Yeats's outburst in the Irish Senate in 1925 on the occasion of the outlawing of divorce. It jolted the Protestant community not only because of what he said, but how he said it. His language—'We, against whom you have done this thing, *are* [my italics] no petty people'—hijacked, with one provocative present tense, the sensitive Catholic ownership of 'now'. Leaving aside its possibly mischievous intent, it evidences resilience in a Protestant peoplehood for perhaps longer than some have suggested.[87] Where this can be best found demonstrated publicly is in newspapers and journals. For instance, in its jousts with officialdom during the Second World War the *Irish Times* exhibited a cheekiness which it could only have done from a sense of confident position within the modern Ireland.[88]

The declaration of the republic in 1948 was an attack on the symbolism that had sustained the royalists. It was, in retrospect, a seminal point of departure for southern Protestantism. The change was encapsulated in the Church of Ireland having to decide what to do about praying for the monarch in its services. The prayers had to go, of course. It was not an uncontested decision. But Anglicanism is rather good at muddling through, and the Church more or less slipped into praying for 'our Rulers' rather than the king. The response, though, remained a supplicant 'And mercifully hear us when we call upon thee' changing to a considerably more doubtful and secular *cri-de-cœur*—'And grant our government wisdom'—in 1984.[89]

This is where this essay has a natural end. While for nationalists it may have finally settled an issue of domestic politics that had festered since 1922, it was no less significant for southern Protestants. Departure from the Commonwealth—unnecessary in the eyes of many—was not easily borne. Some sort of umbilical cord had been snapped. But it opened the potential, for the first time since independence, of a truly common patriotism to emerge, the

Enlightenment concept of a *res publica*, facilitated by a generational change from those who had experienced the 1922 settlement;[90] and by the opposition, the Catholic world, itself entering a prolonged period of disorientation.

Faced with an unfamiliar political dispensation in 1922, the southern loyalists had had to juggle with the potentially disastrous disconnect between a genuine place-based patriotism, an uneasiness with an ascendant 'National Catholicism' and an inherent otherness. In addressing this, though, it is argued that this was mitigated by an extensive à la carte menu of other 'belongingness' to draw upon, ranging through traditional participatory citizenship, a practical desire to make the new state work, utilising their denominational and religious loyalties, seeing themselves as the repositories of moral precept and, of course, still being a willing part of the British and empire worlds. There were many setbacks, often in the sectarian sphere; the sobriquets 'West Brit' and 'Proddy-woddy' were still muttered from time to time. Yet if it took until the early 1960s for southern Protestantism to declare itself 'A confident minority',[91] that declaration had a basis in its history since 1922. We might say that southern Protestantism before then had cleaved to the *Titanic* model: a community feeling relatively good about itself, broadly happy with its current accommodation on board, sailing on, blissfully unaware of the icebergs that would lie ahead. If they had to take to the lifeboats, sans baggage, it may have been a frightening experience, but it was also liberating. They were able to claim ownership of their own identity formation, and to establish an autonomous equilibrium with the contemporary. A journey over some forty years was not spent only in a lonely wilderness. Its protective caravans were the 'Protestant Free State' and other explorations of identity and belongingness. It got them from there to somewhere safer and more congenial, in a 'gradualness of inevitability' (to invert Sidney Webb), as the Catholic state began to be 'Protestantised' and secularised, and as the European project and globalisation opened minds as well as borders.

CHAPTER TWO

Defining Loyalty: Southern Irish Protestants and the Irish Grants Committee, 1926–30

BRIAN HUGHES

Introduction

'It is very difficult to define the word "loyal"', wrote Rev. W.A. MacDougall,[1] Church of Ireland rector for the Cavan parish of Arva (or Arvagh), in September 1928. MacDougall was responding to a query about a claim for £157 compensation to the Irish Grants Committee (IGC) by parishioner John Lang. The second IGC, a Treasury-funded compensation scheme aimed specifically at southern Irish loyalists, sat first in 1926 and continued to deal with applications until its final session in February 1930.[2] Lang was seeking compensation for losses in his trade of livestock owing to boycotting from 1920 to 1921 and damage to his property in April 1922 when 'armed and masked Republicans raided my dwellinghouse'. 'It was', he insisted, 'well-known in my district what my politics were. I am District Master of the Royal Black Preceptory; Master of the local Loyal Orange Lodge No. 378; Deputy Grand Master of the County Grand Black Chapter; and hold other offices in connection with same.' To explain his loss, Lang suggested that 'I was always a loyal subject of the Crown and my persecution was due to my action in assisting to provide comforts for His Majesty's

Troops during the Great War and to my position in the Orange Institution.'[3] John Lang was one of over 4,000 self-proclaimed loyalists to submit a claim to the IGC, and among 900 to receive an award.[4] He had put himself forward as a committed and active supporter of the crown and the British administration in Ireland, but also as a victim of revolutionary persecution. It is this process of self-description, the potential cross-over between identity and experience in the way in which compensation seekers like John Lang defined themselves, that will draw most attention in this chapter.

The southern Irish Protestants who applied to the IGC were required to 'define the word "loyal"' for themselves and (perhaps more pertinently) for the committee. The testimony here—based on claims from Cavan[5]—can tell us something about what it was like to be someone who defined themselves as Protestant, loyalist or both in revolutionary Ireland. It can also give us some sense of how these applicants viewed themselves when asked to reflect on their revolutionary experiences and allegiances in the years after the foundation of the Irish Free State in 1922. The aim here is not to get to the bottom of what *actually happened* to southern Protestants in revolutionary Ireland. This chapter is not about how the IRA viewed its supposed 'enemies' among the Protestant population, but how those Protestants viewed themselves. To what extent was the loyalty of Protestant IGC applicants—and therefore the victimisation that had allegedly followed—linked specifically to their religious denomination? What forms does loyalty take, and is there a specifically Protestant loyalty to be found within the claim files? This chapter will assess the witness testimony provided to the IGC as a catalogue of depictions of loyalty; it will discuss, maybe even debate, what it meant to be a loyalist in southern Ireland as it moved towards independence and came out the other end.

Labels and Designations

Part 5 of the IGC application form asks, 'Do you claim that the loss or injury described was occasioned in respect or on account of your allegiance to the government of the United Kingdom? If so, give particulars on which you base this claim.' While the occasional applicant relied on a simple, self-evidential 'Yes', most offered a sentence or two, maybe even a paragraph. One could only be recompensed for post-Truce loss—sustained between 11 July 1921 and 12 May 1923—but was required to provide evidence of pre-Truce loyalty.[6] Bank passbooks, valuations, medical certificates and other documentation were necessary to prove financial loss. But applicants were left relatively free to decide on the particulars that would best emphasise their allegiance to the British government and its consequences. The terms of reference made no mention of religious denomination and no information on faith or religious practice was actively sought, so any reference made in that line was deliberate and used to serve the purpose of emphasising either allegiance or suffering.[7]

Even a cursory survey of the language of compensation testimony points to a range of potential labels and designations. Isabel O'Connor, an English Protestant, vaguely described herself as 'one of the lot they wished to drive out'.[8] Mary Fletcher was from the 'class which always supported British rule'.[9] When a Protestant referred to their 'lot' or their 'class' like this they were usually ambiguous and could refer to denomination, political allegiance, social standing, or a combination of all three. Ella Browne was 'an enemy on account of my class, a Protestant and a loyalist'.[10] Loyalty and religion could be variously co-dependent or mutually exclusive. Bandon Church of Ireland Protestant Joseph Northridge suggested that it was association with the crown, rather than religion, that singled people out: 'It was only persons who were known for their allegiance to the Government . . . who were driven or tried to be driven out'.[11] But for county co-religionist William Bradfield, it was 'only loyal people and Church people who were interfered with in my district'.[12] Tipperary native John Switzer claimed he 'was always known as a loyalist and Protestant which was a sin in the eyes of these gangs'.[13]

Among a sample of sixty-six non-Catholic applicants registered to County Cavan (fifty-eight Church of Ireland, six Methodist, one Episcopalian, and one Presbyterian), only nine directly mention their religion in response to part 5 of the IGC application form. For a few, the very fact that it was Protestants who were targeted was enough to prove that Protestants were loyal, and thereby confirm their own allegiance. David Henry Long, an Anglican in Cootehill, claimed for goods stolen by the IRA and asserted that 'it was only Protestants suffered though they passed R.C. on there way [*sic*]'; additionally, Long 'never hid' his politics.[14] Neighbour and co-religionist James Anderson made a similar observation about the motivation for a raid on his home in 1923: 'Suppose just owing to the fact that I'm a Protestant, as they were all Protestant houses which were raided.'[15] Anderson's response also suggests that this was not something that was made explicitly clear by raiders in Cootehill, but rather a conclusion that he had come to on his own. For another applicant, the rector in Gowna, Rev. Isaac Hill McCombe, it was enough to 'presume that being a clergyman of the Church of Ireland and therefore a loyal subject I was considered a suitable victim for such an outrage'.[16] His colleague Rev. MacDougall offered a slight variation on the same theme. He told the committee that in Arva 'every Protestant house was visited not because they were Protestant but because every Protestant had and has a liking for the Union Jack'.[17] In another letter he attested that:

> All the Protestants in this neighbourhood identified themselves with the Crown Forces during their stay in Arva and for that reason made themselves obnoxious to the rebels. They went out of their way to be friendly to the young Auxiliary police and for that reason I think they are deserving of consideration.[18]

Recent scholarship on the revolution has made increasingly clear the impossibility of assigning such singular or catch-all motivations for violence against individuals or groups; that not all attacks against Protestants, or ex-servicemen, or 'Big Houses' were motivated by the same factors or even the same combination of factors.[19] Compensation testimony further suggests the fallacy of any assumption that large collections of individuals necessarily shared the same perceptions of what was going on around them, that they all viewed their own status, loss, or victimhood on the same terms. There are some notable local and regional differences in how Protestants ascribe the motivation for violence or animosity directed against them. Some Cavan applicants assumed that Protestants were deliberate victims. In west Cork, John Bolster Barrett was much more sure: 'I was told on two occasions by Sinn Féiners that all Protestants in West Cork were going to be shot.'[20] Charles Mayne was forced from his land in Mayo in 1920 but, rather than speculate on an agrarian motive, wrote that 'all Protestants in this area were regarded as Pro-British. I being a prominent member of the Church of Ireland was singled out for exceptional treatment.'[21]

Richard Reynolds told the committee that 'A Parish Priest in a local chapel advised his congregation not to shoot Protestants but to make their existence impossible.'[22] In Cavan, though, as we have seen, only nine of fifty-eight Protestant applicants to the IGC made a direct link between their religion and the loss they had sustained. David Fitzpatrick has studied claims from west Cork Methodists and found that a higher proportion, six of thirteen, used the terms 'Protestant' and 'loyalist' in answer to Part 5 of the application form. The fifteen Protestant 'planters' who applied from Luggacurran, County Laois, 'widely agreed', according to Leigh-Ann Coffey, 'that they had been targeted because of their religion and loyalty to the British crown'.[23] In contrast, while Michael Farry found that 'a campaign of loyalist extermination' was mentioned in three claims from Sligo, religion was not often noted on claim forms from the county.[24]

The comparative strength of a Protestant community does seem to have been reflected in the ways in which individuals responded to the IGC. Sligo had a smaller non-Catholic population than Cavan in 1911 (8.75 per cent against 18.5 per cent), but in both counties clusters of applicants can be found in parts of the county with relatively strong Protestant communities.[25] Testimony suggests that in areas where the non-Catholic loyalist presence was strong, but not strong enough to protect against republican incursion, Protestant compensation applicants are less likely to associate their loss with their religion.[26] Isolated Protestants, or those forming part of a tiny minority, were most ready to describe their treatment by republicans as anti-Protestant. In Cork, William Hosford described himself as 'an isolated loyal Protestant'.[27] Sligo Presbyterian Jesse Hunter, living in a townland with only one neighbour in a largely Roman Catholic DED, wrote that 'I was a well known Protestant loyalist living in a very disaffected area and because I was alone, unprotected and a supporter of British rule in Ireland these persistent outrages were committed on me'.[28] Gemma Clark has examined Civil War violence through compensation claims from Limerick, Tipperary and Waterford and argued that in small 'Protestant enclaves' it was possible 'to easily identify and root out virtually the entire minority population'.[29] Even if no such deliberate attempt was being made, those in small communities may have perceived that this was happening, or chosen to frame it that way after the event. Claimants surrounded by a reasonable number of co-religionists, on the other hand, tended to refer to their politics rather than their religion.[30] Something similar may also apply among Protestant denominations, but in different ways in different places. Methodists were a 'tiny minority twice over' in west Cork, and Methodist applicants there were more than usually likely to refer to their religion, but none of the six Methodists who applied from Cavan does likewise.[31] This suggests that there are denominational differences in experience and attitude that need further exploration, but not necessarily that these were consistent across the country. Moreover, the broader term 'Protestant' is almost always preferred to any specific denominational nomenclature in the claim forms and this might also invite some reflection.

It is clear from claim files that religion rarely, if ever, was alone in defining an applicant's relationship with, and support for, the British government, nor their interaction with the IRA. Instead, it is one of a number of strands to their loyalist identity. Often, when denomination enters the discourse it does so as a more subtle acknowledgment of implicit communal boundaries. In the town of Arva, where 14 per cent of the population was non-Catholic in 1911,[32] an alleged IRA boycott brought Church of Ireland applicants to reflect on denominational behaviour in the town. Mary Anne Curtis was certain to point out that the boycott enforced against her specifically meant the loss of Catholic customers.[33] Shopkeeper and auctioneer Simon Henry Hewitt was similarly sure that half of his customers had been Catholic but 'since July 1921 not a single Roman Catholic has patronised me'.[34] Bernard Matthews, a tailor, claimed that serving the RIC in 1920 and 1921 had made him 'obnoxious to the Sinn Feiners and their sympathisers on whom I was largely dependent for trade support'; his wife later wrote to the committee to emphasise that 'the I.R.A. boycotted him and all his Roman Catholic customers withdrew their trade and never returned'.[35] There is an implicit suggestion here that Catholics in the town immediately and naturally aligned themselves with republicans or the IRA. But there are also acknowledgements that this was often reluctant, or simply pragmatic. Hewitt insisted that many of the Catholics who stopped coming 'informed me that they were sorry to have to leave me, but that they had been threatened with dire penalties if they transacted business with me'; his nephew Johnston Hewitt, a painter, made an identical claim.[36] Moreover, there were Roman Catholics in the same town who also considered themselves loyal; seven applied to the IGC in Arva and Catholics make up almost a quarter of a sample of eighty-six claims from County Cavan.

The significant number of Catholics who applied to loyalist compensation schemes—including, but by no means restricted to, ex-policemen and servicemen—challenges the notion that 'the overwhelming majority of loyalists were Protestants' (which is not the same as saying that most Protestants were loyalists).[37] So is there anything uniquely Protestant in definitions of loyalty expressed to the IGC? For some Protestant applicants, their attachment to the British government was continued across generations. William Irwin was 'always loyal to the British Government and my father before me', while Frederick Howell described himself as 'protestant and loyalist as my family have been for hundreds of years'.[38] 'During the old troubled times in Ireland', wrote Joseph Benison, 'his Majesty's Government could always rely on the allegiance of my family, when the Phoenix Park murders took place, the Castle authorities in Dublin consulted my father as to what steps should be taken in his district in the event of a rising.'[39] For others, their loyalty was almost obvious, self-evidential. Kate Pinkerton simply suggested that 'I could not help being Loyal to England because [the] best of our days were when under the Union Jack.'[40]

Leigh-Ann Coffey has suggested that 'most' Protestants in independent Ireland 'believed that the values they associated with their Britishness were derived in part from their reformed faith, yet within the southern Protestant population there was a surprising amount of debate regarding the exact relationship between religion and loyalism'. For some, 'Protestantism was a central element to loyalism', and allegiance to the Vatican rendered Catholics incapable of true loyalty to Britain. Yet others remained uncomfortable with the idea that loyalty was an exclusive preserve of Protestants, and 'were willing to overlook religious differences for those who had suffered during the revolution for their loyalty to Britain and who continued to support the remaining ties between the Free State and Britain'.[41] While applicants to the IGC were being asked to retrospectively articulate their pre-independence loyalty, rather than comment on their current feelings or political convictions, the potential for complexity highlighted by Coffey is also evident in their testimony.

Certainly, Protestant loyalists were aware of Catholic neighbours who shared their political views. William Henry Carleton, a Church of Ireland parishioner in Arva, wrote two letters of reference on behalf of his Catholic neighbour Maggie Masterson, certifying to 'Mrs. Masterson's loyalty to the British connection during the troubled times'.[42] But this did not mean that individuals or groups were immune to the assumption that loyalism was a specifically Protestant identity. The willingness of one influential referee, Rev. MacDougall, to suggest that all Protestants were loyal and, by implication, all loyalists were Protestant may have caused problems for Catholic applicants in his district; none of the seven who applied there received an award.[43] Several had strong cases for loyalty based on criteria often accepted by the committee: Mary Sheridan's son and husband had served in the British army; James Culley was the son of an RIC pensioner; ex-policemen and Protestant neighbours testified to Maggie Masterson's loyalty.[44] When Catholic shopkeeper Ellen Reilly submitted her claim, MacDougall insisted that 'there is no person of this name in business in Arva. I would go further and state that no person of that name in Arva in business or not was ever boycotted on account of loyalty to the British Government.' As Reilly was able to provide suitable evidence that she had, in fact, run a small business on Arva's Main Street for many years, a new informant was sought. Rev. George Ingham, who had acted as preacher while the district was without a Church of Ireland incumbent prior to February 1921, confirmed that Reilly 'cannot be charged with loyalty to the British Government as her efforts in that direction tended towards ordering goods from Belfast firms and when the northern boycott came on refusing to pay for them'. She had earlier remarked that 'A friend told me that I had no chance of getting anything from your Committee as I am a Roman Catholic, evidently my friend was correct in his opinion.'[45]

Affiliations and Behaviours

Applicants to the IGC are repeatedly referred to (by themselves and others) as a 'staunch loyalist', a 'determined Unionist',[46] a 'most loyal subject',[47] or a 'firm supporter of the British Government in Ireland'.[48] How, for Protestants, was this manifested in action? Unsurprisingly for compensation claims—where emphasising victimhood was to the applicants' benefit—the overwhelming sense from this testimony is vulnerability rather than brave resistance. Edward Goldrick's claim that he refused to 'join the Sinn Fein movement or support them in any way' is much more representative than Travers Blackley and his son inflicting casualties on a group of raiders in April 1922.[49] But is there anything notably 'Protestant' about the more subtle forms of 'loyal' behaviour articulated in the compensation testimony?

One way in which a distinctly Protestant loyalty might have been expressed was through affiliation with an Orange or Black institution. It might even be expected that organised Protestant institutions would be a particularly prominent feature of the loyalism depicted in a border county like Cavan. But, in fact, membership is only mentioned directly, or even implied, in a small number of Protestant claims from the county. John Lang directly offered his part in local Orange and Black institutions as evidence of his loyalty.[50] Arthur McClean similarly insisted that he had 'always been an Orangeman'.[51] Robert Johnstone, county grand master of the Loyal Orange Order, sought compensation, as did his wife Mary, president of the Women's Loyal Patriotic Association in her district and grand mistress of the women's Loyal Orange Order in Ireland.[52] Robert Browne described himself as a 'well-known member of the Loyal Orange Institution in the district where I live. To my membership of this Order and my consistent support of the British Government, I directly attribute the bitter and persistent hostility shown towards me'.[53] But much more often, applicants had not been affiliated with these organisations, or at least chose not to say so. Indeed, a prominent member of the Orange Order in Cavan, Travers Blackley (one time deputy grand master for Ireland), failed to mention this at all in his correspondence with the IGC.[54] Robert Graham did not describe himself as an Orangemen but—highlighting the extent to which such labels could be applied interchangeably by others—noted that during a raid on his home in January 1922 he had been told that 'you Orangemen thought you were safe but we'll show you now that you'll suffer for supporting the English government'.[55]

Active loyalty is sometimes expressed through less formal communal solidarity. David McNeill, for instance, had been placed under a republican boycott in 1920. In 1929 he told the IGC that John Ryan had 'helped me to sell and buy and did all he could to assist me and after I was chassed [*sic*] from home assisted my wife and family at great risk to himself'; another referee suggested that this was the start of Ryan's own 'trouble'.[56] Martha Jackson claimed she had been shot at and wounded as she cycled to warn a neighbour that his house would be burned down.[57] Another applicant wrote of how he 'had been loyal in helping my other brother (an ex-serviceman) to escape from republicans'.[58] For some, simply refusing to support republicans was evidence enough of their loyalty, especially in comparison to less robust (anonymous) neighbours: George Nicolls ruefully told the IGC that 'if I had to join up with the rebels to shoot down his Majesty's forces, as some of my Protestant neighbours have done, I would not be raided at all'; William Henry Carleton similarly insisted that 'I would not back the Rebels in any way against his Majesty's forces . . . If I had to join up with them against the British Government as some of my Protestant neighbours did I would not be interfered with'.[59] In Arva town, Peter McBrien's claim to loyalty consisted of 'not joining the Volunteers when asked and remaining loyal to the British government'.[60] After the revolution, loyalists continued to band together to support isolated and distressed neighbours and colleagues.[61]

More broadly, there is relatively little inherently unique about the ways in which the majority of Protestants describe loyal behaviour when compared to Catholics. Just as Peter McBrien pointed to his refusal to join in with the rebels, his Catholic neighbour Mary Sheridan believed that 'Had I let my son join the Irish Volunteers it is pro[b]able I might not be living on the Charity of friends today.'[62] And just as a relatively small number of the Protestant applicants made explicit reference to their religion, it is a minority who point to what might be seen as Protestant manifestations of loyalty: membership of a loyal organisation exclusively or predominantly populated by their co-religionists. In fact, the most common demonstration of loyal behaviour offered by applicants of all denominations was supplying the police and other loyalists with goods and services—and generally being 'friendly'—in the face of threats and persecution.[63] As R.B. McDowell has pointed out, 'Loyalists were naturally very ready to afford aid and comfort to the Crown forces. Being friendly with the army and the constabulary was, they repeatedly asserted, normal social behaviour for unionists and loyalists.'[64] But this was just as much the case for ex-policemen, ex-servicemen and their families as it was for members of Protestant congregations.

In the Front Line: Loyalism in the Border Counties

Being an IGC applicant from a 'border county' brought its own unique set of issues. The Protestants of the 'lost' counties of Ulster—Cavan, Donegal, Monaghan—were considered 'southern loyalists' for the purposes of the IGC. But in September 1912, very many Protestants in these counties had publicly declared a different type of loyalty in signing the Ulster Solemn League and Covenant and the Women's Declaration. In Cavan, 4,423 men signed the covenant and 3,722 women put their names to the declaration; 71.3 per cent and 65.4 per cent of the respective non-Catholic adult populations.[65] At least forty-one of the non-Catholic Cavan IGC sample had signed the covenant or declaration but only Arthur McClean (indirectly) mentioned this on his applicant form—'I was a loyalist organiser at the time of the signing of the Ulster Covenant'—while another, David Maguire, stated that his brother had signed while Maguire was in the USA.[66] The nature of the loyalty put forward to the scheme was, by necessity, dictated by and adapted to suit the task of declaring 'allegiance to the government of the United Kingdom'. But signing the covenant or the declaration was something different, an assertion of a specifically 'Ulster' identity and not an act of loyalty to the crown or the British government then attempting to bring in Home Rule legislation. This is not to say that these were entirely incompatible (or unchangeable) allegiances, but if such distinctions had the potential to cause concern to applicants, they were very simply avoided or ignored.

Loyalists in Cavan might also be expected to have joined the Ulster Volunteer Force (UVF). Again, some Protestant applicants point to UVF activity as evidence of their loyalty—ignoring the potential for it to be viewed as an act of *dis*loyalty to the British government—but few offer any suggestion that they were active after the Great War. Arthur McClean 'was a loyalist organiser at the time of the signing of the Ulster Covenant'; Robert Graham was 'a prominent member of the Ulster Volunteers and during the Great European War I took an active part in recruiting for the 36th Ulster division and thereby incurred the animosity of the Sinn Feiners'.[67] By May 1914, 55.8 per cent of eligible Protestant males had joined the UVF in Cavan,[68] the highest proportion in Ulster.[69] While the organisation retracted significantly after the war, it had not disappeared completely by 1921, though it might appear to have done so based on the application testimony.[70] This may be explained by the age profile of IGC applicants from the county: the median age was fifty at the time of application, with seventeen septuagenarians. Only three had joined the Ulster Special Constabulary after its foundation in 1920 but others claimed to have had sons who did and a younger, more active generation is sometimes evident in the background.[71] It may also be the case that many of those who had been active as loyalist paramilitaries had been reasonably well able to protect themselves, and thus did not need to seek compensation afterwards.

Categorising the loyalists of Cavan, Donegal and Monaghan as 'southern' at all is not entirely straightforward. Partition brought additional complexities for loyalists caught, as they saw it, on the wrong side of the border. As six-county partition became inevitable, the upper- and middle class unionist leadership in these counties saw it as a breach of the covenant and a callous betrayal by their fellow covenanters.[72] Three days after the UUC's decision, Lord Farnham wrote to Tyrone unionist Hugh de Fellenberg Montgomery lamenting that 'what we feel more than anything is that we can no longer call ourselves Ulstermen. We in Cavan were prouder of being Ulstermen than anyone in the whole province.'[73] By the time loyalists in Cavan were preparing their compensation claims, the border was at least six years old and a Boundary Commission had failed to change it.[74] In 1922, Somerset Saunderson, son of deceased unionist leader Edward, had declared that 'Now . . . I have *no* country!'[75] Three years later, his brother Edward petitioned the Boundary Commission to have the 'whole demesne of Castle Saunderson . . . transferred into Northern Ireland'.[76] By the end of the decade, with no hope of the border being redrawn, Somerset and Henry Saunderson applied to the IGC as southern loyalists.[77]

Seeking redress might well be seen as part of the process of assimilation, of coming to terms with what had gone before or finding a place in the new disposition. In doing so, southern Protestants were able to shape and define their allegiances to suit. If the loyalists of Cavan had felt the same betrayal articulated by Lord Farnham in 1920, for instance, by the end of the decade the blame was being laid firmly at the door of the British government. Rev. MacDougall was probably not alone when he argued that 'Everyone who was raided has more or less a claim on the British Government for it was their policy of surrender & weakness which made the raids possible.'[78] But this, of course, made perfect sense when claiming compensation from the British government, and may reflect canny pragmatism as much as any willingness to forgive or forget the actions of their Ulster brethren. Being an 'Ulster' Protestant was important to delegates on the UUC from the 'lost' border counties in 1920, but was of little or no relevance—the phrase is never used by Cavan applicants—less than a decade later to those seeking compensation from a scheme devised for southern Irish loyalists.

An 'Exodus'?

The Irish Grants Committee that operated from 1926 to 1930 was born out of an earlier process of aid and redress. In May 1922, a Treasury-funded Irish Distress Committee, chaired by Conservative MP Sir Samuel Hoare, was founded to provide ex-gratia loans and grants 'where refugees from Ireland were in pressing need of assistance' until they found work or decided to return home.[79] Up to May 1923, when it was reconstituted as the first Irish Grants Committee under Sir Eustace Percy and its remit greatly expanded, the Committee had received 5,600 applications for what it described as 'immediate relief' and approved 4,330 to the cost of about £24,000 (almost £1.2 million today), less than half of which was made up of loans to be repaid.[80] This influx of what were widely depicted in government and in the press as southern loyalist 'refugees'[81] is relevant to one of the most contentious issues in current modern Irish historiography: the so-called 'exodus' of southern Protestants from the twenty-six counties that became the Irish Free State in 1922, and the 32 per cent drop in the minority population between 1911 and 1926.[82] Central to this debate are attempts to establish or demolish claims of deliberately targeted sectarian violence by the Catholic/nationalist/republican majority against a Protestant/loyalist/unionist minority leading to large-scale migration, particularly during the revolutionary triennium, 1920–3.

But historians arguing (necessarily) over the timing and nature of this movement have tended to ignore something equally as important: what those on the ground *believed* was happening. Whether the numbers of migrants are found to be large or small, the rhetoric of crisis that emerges in the sources remains important. An estimate of 20,000 southern Irish loyalists (including both Protestants and Catholics) arriving on British shores by spring 1922[83] appears exaggerated, for instance, but perhaps says something of contemporary perceptions of the sudden scale of movement. For those seeking the assistance themselves, it is likely to have felt very much like a crisis too.

Travers Blackley was one of these 'refugees', having fled Cavan after shooting raiders who had come to his home in 1922. The Free State government, unable to offer any protection, had initially advised Blackley to leave.[84] But fifteen months later the government stopped paying his under sheriff's salary on the basis that it was then safe for him to return to his work. While some Protestant migrants did feel safe enough to return after the Civil War had ended, 'Mr. Blackley naturally took a different view of the situation' and remained in London. By 1926 Blackley was still there earning a 'precarious living by selling on Comm[ission]'.[85] It is perhaps an extreme case, particularly in a Cavan context, but it is one that highlights the potential discrepancy between official pronouncements and local or individual knowledge, perception and assumption.

James Heaslip was, as he put it, 'chased out' of Cavan town in July 1921 while Arthur McClean described signing away his land near Kilnaleck 'under duress' in April 1922, giving a Belfast address in 1928.[86] Many other IGC applicants also wrote of feeling compelled to flee their homes under threat or fear, either temporarily or permanently.[87] Even while treating compensation testimony with due caution, this language of expulsion should not be ignored or dismissed, nor should the voices of stubborn resistance, of indifference or apathy, of those who carried on. All can exist (or co-exist), and be equally genuinely felt. Most of the Cavan IGC sample surveyed here described no compulsion or desire to leave, though some of the younger generation—sons and daughters—did not stay after 1922.[88] There was no Cavan equivalent of the Bandon Valley killings of April 1922, and thus no propaganda pamphlets proclaiming a 'Massacre of Irish Protestants', a campaign 'To Exterminate Protestantism', and Protestants 'living in a state of most abject terror because of the shooting of members of their creed'.[89] Even if this was just atrocity propaganda, and the residents of Cavan could feel far enough away from the worst of it, its resonance in west Cork must have felt rather different. Local reports of an 'Exodus from West Cork' in the aftermath of the shootings, even if temporary, seem to suggest as much.[90]

But at the same time, Cavan certainly saw its own Protestant migration; according to the rural dean's reports for the parish of Arva (a community that accounted for a relatively large proportion of IGC applicants), the number of Church of Ireland families dropped from 119 families in 1920 to 80 in 1922. The rector, Rev. MacDougall, put the 1922 drop down to 'Migration'.[91] Similarly, a small 'census' of Protestant migration into Fermanagh alone includes 145 Protestant persons or families who left Cavan between 1920 and 1925.[92] It might be tempting to equate a short hop across the new border with revolutionary persecution, the fear of a repeat of the Bandon Valley, or pessimism about the abilities of a Dublin government to protect and serve. Few of those listed in the Fermanagh census seem to have applied for compensation for loss or damage to property, hinting that personal experiences of violence or intimidation were not primary reasons for their decisions to leave.[93] But as motivations are unrecorded in the Fermanagh census or the dean's reports, assumptions of homogeneity and all or nothing answers will remain unsatisfactory. Andy Bielenberg has pointed to regional variations in the scale of and motivations for Protestant migration.[94] This might be stretched further. Even the brief comparison made here suggests that, regardless of the figures, the experience, the atmosphere and the perception of migration in Protestant Cavan is sufficiently different from that in Cork to prompt further thought. Much more needs to be done to go beyond the numbers—as important as they are—and to understand the 'experience' of Protestant migration in this period, in all its complexity.

The Fluidity of Allegiance

The narratives submitted to the IGC—and the process of seeking redress more broadly—can serve to highlight the fluidity of allegiance, the range of 'loyalties' found among southern Protestants, and the difficulty of placing them in a neat and easily defined box. Equating behaviour with loyalty is equally tricky. Simon Henry Hewitt, for one, had trouble convincing the committee that serving crown forces was unambiguously 'loyal'. The documentary evidence of loss Hewitt submitted was (probably correctly) queried, but, more significantly, so too was his motivation for serving the crown. For Hewitt, dealing with 'Black and Tans' in spite of threats and boycotting was entirely natural; they had 'flocked' to him and he had readily served as they were English and 'Church men' like himself. But IGC secretary and contradictor, Major A. Reid Jamieson, concluded that it was 'preposterous for applicant to claim he was the victim of an extensive boycott and I submit that his loss of profit was due to economic conditions and trade depression'.[95] The crown forces were a profitable batch of customers, but had left in 1922. How exactly does one prove that one had served them as a result of an avowed allegiance to the British administration and not just because it made financial sense? Was Jamieson correct when he pointed out that, in the case of Hewitt's brother, 'The presumption arises that the Royal Irish Constabulary and Government Forces were such good customers, that other trade could be ignored; boycotting made it impossible to trade for a time, but that the departure of their customers was the chief cause of the loss'?[96]

IGC applicants consciously labelled themselves as loyalists and victims of the revolution. In that sense alone, they are a valuable cohort. But this was self-description taking place within a very specific context, the parameters of which clearly influenced the narratives produced. Even the range of applicants available offers a limited window into the scope of Protestant experience and opinion. Applicants from Cavan were mostly male (78 per cent) and generally older, with sons and daughters sometimes mentioned in passing. Almost 60 per cent worked in agriculture, the vast majority land-owning, and almost 30 per cent worked in commerce and industry, a breakdown at odds with the rest of the country.[97] What of the loyalists who did not apply at all, because they missed the deadline or never heard it existed? What of those who felt no desire to rake up the past to seek redress or right perceived wrongs, those who preferred to forget and move on, or those who never felt loss and slight in the first instance? Their voices remain unaccounted for here. Nevertheless, for all their limitations, the files of the IGC offer a valuable record of first-hand testimony and experience, accessible to historians and ripe for further mining.

CHAPTER THREE

Peace, Protestantism and the Unity of Ireland: The Career of Bolton C. Waller

CONOR MORRISSEY

Writing in 1963, Walter Starkie, Trinity College Dublin professor and travel-writer, recalled one of the outstanding personalities of his undergraduate days:

> I remember one very constant devotee of Thomas Davis—Bolton Waller, who used to gather us in his rooms late at night and cook for us a frugal meal of sausages and bacon on his Primus stove. Then as he filled for each guest from a big brown teapot . . . he spoke like one inspired of 'a nation once again' . . . a nation in which all Irishmen no matter to what religion and class they belonged would collaborate together in making a nation that would be rooted in the affections of Ireland's people, not in any exclusive principle of blood or creed or culture. . . . Many of us placed great hopes in Bolton Waller in later days, after the Anglo-Irish Treaty of 1921, when men of his calibre and tolerant humanism were desperately needed . . . but alas, he died after a short illness.[1]

For the southern Protestant minority, the Great War, the Easter Rising, partition, and the turmoil that followed, proved traumatic. Broadly speaking, the Protestant response to finding themselves part of the Irish Free State, with its strongly Catholic ethos, was, in Terence

Brown's words, 'a sense of isolation and political impotence'.[2] One figure who reacted differently to this trauma was Bolton Waller. Bolton Charles Waller (1890–1936) was a journalist, soldier, public servant, pamphleteer, ecumenist, anti-sectarian campaigner, peace activist and, latterly, Church of Ireland clergyman. Unlike many of his co-religionists, he did not retreat into convivial social networks post-independence, but rather embarked on an extraordinary career that had three main objectives: first, the peaceful unification of Ireland and the reconciliation of Irish factions; secondly, the revival of Protestant influence in public affairs; and thirdly, the promotion of a progressive internationalism, largely by means of international arbitration, protection of small states, and the League of Nations.

The Waller family was of English descent, settling in Ireland in the 1630s, becoming prominent landowners in County Limerick, with a seat at Castletown Manor, near Pallaskenry.[3] The family was notable for producing clergymen; Bolton was the fourth of his line to attend Trinity College and enter the Church. His father, also Bolton, served as rector of St Munchin, Limerick.[4] Born in County Wicklow, Bolton Charles Waller was educated at Aravon School, Bray, before entering Trinity College in 1908 with the intention of taking holy orders. Waller enjoyed a stellar college career, being elected a scholar in 1911, taking the Brooke Prize in classics in 1912 and the Carson Biblical Prize in 1915, before graduating BA.[5] He was a popular figure and a distinguished debater, being elected president of the Philosophical Society in 1914. In 1915 (presumably just before he enlisted in the army) Waller made his first contribution towards ecumenism and anti-sectarianism, when he founded the Irish Christian Fellowship. The Fellowship was 'A comradeship of Irish men and women who desire, as followers of Christ, to understand and express His spirit in relation to the whole of life'.[6]

Waller's political views first became evident during the student protest against the Campbell Amendment. In October 1912, the board of Trinity College voted a resolution exempting the college from the jurisdiction of the proposed Home Rule parliament. James Henry Campbell, a unionist member for Dublin University, moved the amendment in the Commons, which had the reluctant consent of the Irish Parliamentary Party.[7] However, a group of students and staff, of differing political persuasions, understood that the amendment would have a disastrous impact on the standing of the college in Ireland.[8] Waller was instrumental in organising student resistance to the measure; in late October a protest against the exclusion signed by 184 students appeared in the press.[9] However, the Campbell Amendment foundered, not on student opposition, but on a revolt by staff. On 11 November 1912, a meeting of fellows and professors voted by twenty-four to thirteen against the amendment, killing the measure.[10]

In November 1914, Waller gave the inaugural address as president of the University Philosophical Society. He argued that Home Rule was inevitable, at least in the south, and warned against any attempts to coerce Ulster. He urged Protestants to play a full role in the coming dispensation:

> If Protestants stood apart from the operations of Home Rule, and took no interest in local or national politics, Ireland would be deprived of the services of some of her ablest men, she would have to carry a dead weight of permanent opposition, and would be thrown more and more into the hands of extremists. It was sheer foolishness to wait and grumble till they were bayoneted in the 'last ditch' when it was to their own interest and to that of the enemy that they should become friends.

Finally, in warmly received comments, he stated that Ulster, having gained the respect of nationalist Ireland by the strength of her determination, should now negotiate entry into a united Ireland.[11] Themes that would recur throughout Waller's career are evident in this address: the need to treat Ulster honourably, the importance of Protestant influence in Irish affairs and, above all, a concern to unite the country.

Waller's perspective was not as eccentric as it might seem. The third Home Rule crisis saw the emergence of several members of the Church of Ireland to challenge Carsonism, argue against partition and work for conciliation. Prominent 'conciliators' included Rosamond Stephen (1868–1951), whose Guild of Witness organisation sought to promote unity among Christian denominations.[12] The leading figure was Sir Horace Plunkett (1854–1932), the cooperative pioneer, whose 1914 pamphlet *A Better Way* proposed implementing Home Rule for the whole island, but allowing Ulster the right to secede after a stated period.[13] Waller, Stephen and Plunkett point to the existence of a strand within Irish Anglicanism that avoided explicit endorsement of the Home Rule Bill in 1912, but which became reconciled to self-government in the years that followed, as a means of preserving the unity of the nation, the people and the church.

Waller's prediction that Home Rule would be introduced was not borne out. With the entry of Britain into the European war in August 1914, the Government of Ireland Act was suspended for the duration of the conflict; events over the next four years would ensure it would never be implemented. Waller was among the approximately 206,000 Irishmen who volunteered to fight in the war.[14] He abandoned his divinity studies, obtained a commission in the Royal Army Service Corps and served in Mesopotamia for four years. There, he achieved the rank of captain (temporary) and was mentioned in dispatches. Waller's wartime experience marked him for life. He later recalled that he regarded his service as 'a duty, though a detestable duty'.[15] His obituarist would note that 'His war experiences influenced his mind to such an extent that on his return to Ireland he determined to devote his time to the cause of peace'.[16]

The 1916 Easter Rising represented an enormous setback for those who sought a constitutional settlement to the Irish crisis. In the aftermath of the rebellion, a group of southern Irish Protestants and well-to-do Catholics, fearful of partition and separation from the empire, came together and sought to promote a peaceful all-Ireland settlement. This group, which initially called itself the Irish Constitutional Association, was soon renamed the Irish Conference Committee. Members included the artist Dermod O'Brien, Lord Monteagle, Joseph Johnston, James Creed Meredith, James Douglas, Diarmid Coffey, Walter MacMorrough Kavanagh and Wilbraham Fitzjohn Trench. They sought to bypass the Irish Parliamentary Party and reach out to southern unionists in the hope of building a broad pro-self-government coalition. In a letter to the secretary of the Irish Conference Committee, Waller lamented his inability to take part in the group's activities, although he promised to lend moral support.[17] Such support was apparent in Waller's pseudonymous pamphlet, *Ireland's Opportunity: A Plea for Settlement by Conference*, which appeared shortly after the Rising. This argued for a representative conference to be convened in Dublin that would draw up a constitution for a self-governing Ireland.[18] The Irish Conference Committee, believing that such a proposal would avert partition and save the cause of constitutional politics in Ireland, went on to make representations to the British government in favour of a delegate conference.[19] This, alongside pressure from other quarters, led to the summoning of the Irish Convention of 1917–18, chaired by Horace Plunkett. Although the Convention saw a degree of rapprochement between southern unionist representatives and the Irish Party, it broke up without securing the wide consensus needed to allow the government to legislate for Home Rule, and thus save constitutional nationalism.[20]

Following his demobilisation in 1919, Waller moved to London, where he became involved in two closely connected initiatives. In June 1919 Plunkett founded the Irish Dominion League (IDL), which agitated in favour of awarding an all-Ireland parliament a degree of independence similar to that of Canada or Australia. The IDL, which was mostly comprised of former supporters of the Irish Parliamentary Party, as well as Protestant Home Rulers, made limited impact, being squeezed between Sinn Féin, which refused to countenance anything short of an all-Ireland republic, and the Ulster unionists, who had settled on partition. Significantly, southern Irish Protestants, who might have been expected to form the IDL support base, largely scorned the movement; the emotional connection to the union remained too strong. Much of the League's publicity work was carried out by its London branch, of which Waller was an active member. More high profile was Waller's work with the Peace with Ireland Council. The Council, which was largely comprised of writers, churchmen and politicians, sought to rouse British public opinion against the war in Ireland. As secretary of the Council, Waller was involved in publicising the ill-treatment of republican prisoners and internees during the war.[21]

The IDL was outraged by the 1920 Government of Ireland Act, which created the self-governing state of Northern Ireland within the United Kingdom. Partition, and its threat to southern Protestants, was at the core of their objections; it meant the 'casting off by the Ulster Protestants of their co-religionists in the south and west'.[22] However, to Bolton Waller's horror, IDL unanimity was undermined when Stephen Gwynn, an independent-minded former Irish Party member, declared in favour of the measure, and chaired the Government of Ireland Bill Amendment Group, which sought to promote amendments to make it more acceptable to southern Irish opinion.[23]

This crisis in moderate nationalism prompted an emotional appeal from Waller. In a letter to the press he outlined five distinct groups which desired an all-Ireland peaceful settlement, which, he said, should cohere under one agreed leader. These were: the remnants of the Irish Party; the unionist Anti-Partition League; moderate elements in the Irish Labour party; the IDL; and the Government of Ireland Bill Amendment Group. 'Past controversies and minor disagreements', he said, were keeping them apart. Only by uniting together could the unity of the country be preserved. He addressed his own people directly:

> Especially to the South of Ireland Protestants would I appeal. We have been too late again and again. This is perhaps our last chance. Are not we ready to sink a great deal for the sake of Ireland?[24]

This appeal itself came too late. No union between the moderate groups was brought about. In November 1921, after several months of inactivity, the IDL, whose efforts to preserve constitutional politics in Ireland had failed, was dissolved.[25] Partition, and the collapse of the small moderate movement might have proved dispiriting to Waller. However, he turned away from possible careers in London and Geneva, and returned to Ireland. Here, he would devote the remainder of his life to working towards conciliation and the union of Ireland.

One figure to whom Waller reached out was John Frederick MacNeice (1866–1942), the rector of Carrickfergus, County Antrim, and later the bishop of Down, Connor and Dromore. In ways MacNeice resembled Waller and other southern Protestant conciliators, modified for Ulster conditions. As David Fitzpatrick has shown in his biography, MacNeice was an all-Ireland rather than an Ulster unionist, who opposed Carson and the Covenant, detested partition, and joined the Orange Order in the hope of acting as a restraining force on the rank and file. MacNeice's address to Orangemen in July 1922, written in the midst of sectarian murder in Ulster and at the outbreak of civil war in the south, was a plea for reconciliation between factions, in which he suggested that the country could eventually be reunited.[26] This address prompted a response from Waller, who suggested they collaborate on 'some sort of unofficial body working for conciliation'.[27] Although such a movement did not transpire, MacNeice and Waller would each engage in a similar pursuit of intercommunal peace in succeeding years.

From 1922 Waller sought to promote a more concrete form of unity. In that year the provisional government of the Irish Free State appointed him researcher at the North Eastern Boundary Bureau, a position he would hold until 1926.[28] The Boundary Bureau was set up to liaise with Ulster nationalists, monitor the Northern Irish government, produce propaganda and prepare data in anticipation of the Boundary Commission, which was expected to draw the border between the Free State and Northern Ireland.[29] Waller's appointment, which was made at the request of Kevin O'Shiel (1891–1970), a Tyrone-born barrister and assistant legal advisor to the provisional government, was testament to his growing reputation as an expert on minority rights and the settlement of boundary disputes. Eda Sagarra has criticised Waller's initial memorandum to the Boundary Commission.[30] This memorandum argued against the use of plebiscites, on the basis that the 'wishes of the inhabitants are already well known by the results of the elections and other indications, and where unnecessary the expense and possible danger of a plebiscite are best avoided'.[31] Plebiscites along the border region, reminiscent of those held in Upper Silesia and Schleswig after the war, may have led to the award of substantial Catholic-majority districts to the Free State. However, it is possible that Waller was working with a different intention in mind. Rather than seeking to draw an ethno-religiously-clean border, with few Catholics on the northern side and few Protestants on the southern, Waller sought to produce a settlement that would allow Ireland the chance to eventually reunite. The creation of a homogeneous Protestant state in Northern Ireland would preclude this.[32] Certainly, in 1924, Waller was among the authors of a report that recommended to the government that it should aim for the creation of an all-Ireland assembly, while allowing the Northern Ireland parliament to remain *in situ*.[33]

The story of the wrecking of the Boundary Commission—and with it the hopes of northern nationalists—is well known. On 7 November 1925 the London *Morning Post* leaked the contents of the Commission's report, which recommended only small transfers to the Free State and, to the horror of nationalist opinion, sought transfers of some southern territory to Northern Ireland.[34] Amid the furore, the British and Irish governments agreed to suppress the Commission's report, and an agreement was reached by which the Free State recognised Northern Ireland's boundaries in return for a financial settlement. This agreement, although seen by some as copper-fastening partition, did not deter Waller, who continued to apply his mind to peacefully reuniting Ireland.

With the Boundary Bureau wound up, Waller developed his parallel career in journalism. Between 1924 and 1930 he contributed at least ninety-nine articles and reviews to Plunkett and George Russell's liberal and pluralistic *Irish Statesman* journal. Equally productive was his work for the *Church of Ireland Gazette*, on whose editorial staff he served for four years. The task closest to his heart, however, was his editorship of *Concord*, the journal of the League of Nations Society of Ireland. By the mid-1920s, Waller was acknowledged as the country's leading expert on, and proponent for, the League of Nations.

In March 1923 Waller produced a memorandum for the cabinet on the question of Irish Free State membership of the League of Nations. He argued in favour of joining, stating that the chief advantages of membership included gaining recognition of the country's independent status, providing a means of publicity and protest against aggression by another state, and allowing for an opportunity to influence world affairs and work towards world peace.[35] In 1927 he became secretary of the League of Nations Society of Ireland, holding the post for three years. The Society aimed to educate public opinion and gain support for the League by means of lectures, public events and publications. Waller proved active in this regard, and by the late 1920s he was among the country's best-known commentators on international affairs. He also began to build a reputation outside Ireland: in 1924 he won the £1,000 Filene Prize for the best proposal for the restoration of peace in Europe, and in 1927 he won the Bok Prize for the best essay on the solution to world peace.[36]

It is unsurprising that the attainment of peace and security proved so important to him. Waller's war experience had been transformative and the cessation of hostilities did not fulfil his hopes: 'The Peace Settlement proved a staggering disappointment'. The creation of the League was the sole glimmer of promise; he would state that its 'establishment was the greatest advance ever made out of international anarchy and towards international order'.[37] Waller was not a pacifist, however, and in common with many Christians of his generation he believed that the use of force, for example during the Great War, was justified in certain cases.[38] His aim, rather, was for the League to develop into a potent world arbitrator, which would eventually render violence obsolete in pursuit of political aims. Waller saw that a small country such as Ireland, with its history of conquest by a larger neighbour, could be a force for good in the League.

> We have talked much of our own right to freedom; now that we have gained it, we will stultify ourselves if we do not use that position to help to establish freedom elsewhere. To some of its supporters, especially in the larger countries, the League seems to stand almost solely for the preservation of peace. But the maintenance of peace is not by itself good enough. We can remind them that a peace which permits oppression or merely perpetuates injustice is no real peace and does not deserve to be lasting.[39]

Waller's background was key to his thinking. The southern Protestant population in the twenty-six-county area had fallen from about 10 per cent in 1911 to about 7 per cent in 1926.[40] This small, scattered community, which was largely now without political influence, had reason to fear the repercussions of border tensions between Northern Ireland and the Free State. North–south conflict would leave southern Protestants and northern Catholics vulnerable.[41] Among southern Protestants, Waller was far from alone in admiring the pacific and internationalist perspective of the League. Of the thirty members of the Council and Committee of the Irish League of Nations Society in 1923, a total of sixteen were Protestant, among them the earl of Wicklow (a southern unionist senator), Sir William de Courcy Wheeler (a distinguished surgeon) and Charles

E. Jacob (a prominent businessmen and leading figure in the Society of Friends).[42] Protestants with a Home Rule pedigree were especially strongly represented; six individuals had advocated self-government for Ireland within the empire during the period before 1920.[43] For these individuals, the precepts of the League seemed to offer the best protection for endangered minorities, those who found themselves on the wrong side of a newly drawn border. Membership of the League of Nations Society may have offered southern Protestants, starved suddenly of the opportunity to contribute to public affairs, a suitable forum in which to do so.

As a well-known figure, whose views commanded some attention, Waller was tempted by public office. In 1927 he announced his candidacy for the Dublin University (Trinity College) Dáil constituency, in the June election. Waller was a high-profile alumnus and was frequently invited to take the chair in debates and other college events. The three sitting TDs, William Thrift, Ernest Alton and Sir James Craig, were generally seen as providing quiet, yet effective representation in parliament; Waller argued that they, and other southern Protestant representatives, should play a more assertive role. However, Waller found that his work with the North Eastern Boundary Bureau was a hindrance to a public career. The Trinity electorate, which comprised scholars and graduates of the college, included a substantial Ulster unionist or Ulster unionist-sympathising segment. These took a dim view of the Boundary Bureau's attempts to undermine the integrity of the northern state. In late May 1927 a meeting in the Examination Hall in support of Waller's candidacy erupted in chaos. A gleeful *Belfast News-Letter* recorded events under the heading 'Uproar at Trinity College: Egg-throwing in excelsis':

> The Examination Hall was crowded with elderly graduates and students. It was evident that many of the latter had little sympathy with Mr Waller, and that they were prepared to make their disapproval of his candidature manifest. Mr E.J. Gwynn, FTCD, who presided, had uttered only a few sentences when a rotten egg, thrown from the back of the hall, fell in his lap. . . . The egg-throwers were cheered to the echo, and for a few minutes pandemonium prevailed. Appeals for order were met by egg-throwing and laughter, and the atmosphere at the

> platform became most unpleasant ... Mr Waller was received with applause mingled with catcalls. A slight man, he stood well forward on the platform, and showed remarkable ability in dodging the eggs that were thrown at him. He could not, however, escape them all. Once he put up his hand and caught an egg, which ... broke and ran down his sleeve. ... Mr Waller was warming to his subject when there was an enormous noise outside. The doors were thrown open, and a band of students, carrying Professor [William] Thrift, whom they had 'kidnapped' marched in. They placed the professor on the platform and cheered him.[44]

Thrift, who presumably had been 'captured' while strolling through Front Square, was visibly unimpressed at events; he mounted a chair and insisted that Waller should be allowed to speak.[45] Waller received a total of 332 first preferences, placing him in line for the third seat. However, when Thrift's surplus was distributed, Alton overtook him by just eight votes.[46] A friend later suggested that the failure to take a seat was 'one of the greatest disappointments of his life'.[47]

Waller's interest in public affairs remained undimmed. In 1928 he took part in a Church of Ireland delegation to the minister for justice, James FitzGerald-Kenney, to seek amendments to the Censorship of Publications Bill. Peter Martin, in his study of censorship in Ireland, discusses a letter by Waller in which he described the interview:

> Waller ... reported that FitzGerald-Kenney was 'polite and patient but extremely obdurate'. The Minister was 'unyielding' over ... the use of the term 'public morality' in the bill. He explained that he wanted to ban anything 'attacking the institution of marriage' ... On the question of contraception 'the minister was still more stiff' and opposed anything which 'even incidentally advocated it'. When asked if this included the works of George Bernard Shaw or Dean Inge he replied that 'he was not afraid of big names ... if they were as I alleged they would have to go'. Waller [stated] that 'a large number of Protestants do, absolutely genuinely and sincerely regard this as an intolerant and unfair bill' ... 'I want to avoid sectarian controversy of the old type but this bill makes it very difficult'.[48]

During this period Waller, alongside Yeats and Russell, became that rarest of figures: an advocate for a more assertive Protestant political voice in the Free State. He argued that the older generation of Protestants, having relied 'on supports which proved untrustworthy', that is, Ulster unionists and the British government, had damaged themselves beyond repair. He looked to the younger generation to regain Protestant self-confidence, and play a forceful role in society:

> What too many Irish Protestants suffer from at present is timidity, combined with superciliousness. Having been so long denounced as a tyrannical 'Ascendancy' they seem now—to avoid odium—to have gone to the opposite extreme . . . In both the Senate and the Dáil Protestants are numerous, but, with a few exceptions, they are content to display a vague amiability rather than to make any definite contribution. Such timidity is bad both for themselves and for Ireland. Outspokenness is needed, combined with a readiness to join energetically in any effort for the benefit of Ireland.[49]

The unity of Ireland, which, peacefully effected, would allow for an enhanced Protestant voice in national affairs, remained his principal objective. Waller's pamphlet, *Hibernia, or the Future of Ireland*, published in 1928, gives insight into his thinking during this period. This work, although striking an optimistic tone about the future of the country, argued against any attempts to view members of different religions as being ethnically dissimilar. He also argued against attempts to impose a Gaelicising policy, such as by means of compulsory Irish, which he argued would further alienate Protestants. Northern Ireland, he believed, could be tempted into a united Ireland, but only on the basis of continued membership of the Commonwealth: 'the choice before us is transparently plain. Do we want complete independence for three-quarters of Ireland, or Freedom, with Unity, for the whole?'[50] Unity, he argued, could only be brought about by degrees, and with consent. He remained as convinced of the potential of settlement by conference in 1928 as he had been in 1916; he looked forward to the day when 'Representatives of North and South will . . . meet in Conference to consider the general question of the future government of the country'.[51]

Waller's inclusive vision of Irish nationalism was evident two years later, in his Trinity Monday memorial discourse on Thomas Davis. This was the first time one of Trinity's nationalist alumni was the subject of such a discourse.[52] Waller urged Trinity College to take pride in its nationalist alumni and highlighted how Davis, a Protestant, had sought to forge a conception of Irish nationalism that would incorporate all classes and creeds.[53] This appeal for the creation of a unifying, non-sectarian form of nationalism was not welcomed by the Catholic press, who denounced Waller's speech and made the rather dubious claim that Davis, were he alive in 1930, would have sought a Catholic Ireland.[54]

In that year, at the comparatively advanced age of forty, Waller renewed his divinity studies in Trinity. There is a sense, throughout the 1920s, of an ambitious, talented figure, applying himself to many things, but never quite finding his calling. The Church, his first love, would provide focus in the last six years of his life. Waller was ordained a deacon in 1931, and a priest the following year. He initially took a curacy in Rathmines, where he proved a parishioners' favourite, before being moved to the incumbency in Clondalkin in February 1936.[55] He quickly became one of the best-known Anglican clergymen in the country.

If Irish unity was his principal objective throughout the 1920s, unity of the churches became his great cause as a clergyman. Waller was the chairman and moving spirit behind the Irish branch of the 'Friends of Reunion' movement, which sought to unite all Protestant denominations into a single church.[56] He lost none of his appetite for public debate. The founding of the Irish Hospitals' Sweepstake in 1930 had seen several Protestant (although few Catholic) clergymen denounce the measure.[57] Waller was among the most prominent critics of the Irish Sweep, publishing a pamphlet that highlighted the infinitesimally small chances of winning a prize, and casting doubt on the benefit of actually doing so.[58] He also showed there were strict limits to his ecumenism during this period. Claiming that Catholics were making systematic efforts to convert Irish Protestants, his pamphlet *The Pope's Claims and Why We Reject Them*, offered an assertive refutation of the doctrines of papal supremacy and infallibility.[59] All this time Waller maintained a parallel career as an indefatigable proponent of the ideals of peace and of the League of Nations, through print, public addresses and on the airwaves.

The durability of these ideals would be challenged in the mid-1930s. In October 1935 Mussolini launched his invasion of Abyssinia. Waller, unsurprisingly, was outraged. In fact, addressing the League of Nations a month before, Éamon de Valera, the President of the Executive Council of the Free State, had delivered the sort of defence of smaller powers that Waller had always argued could be undertaken by Irish representatives.[60] Waller threw himself into anti-Italian agitation, addressing several meetings and writing numerous letters and articles, demanding that a stronger line should be taken by the international community to prevent the aggression.[61] Walter Starkie, whose recollections of Waller open this chapter, adopted an entirely different approach. Starkie came from a 'Castle Catholic' background and his family were loyal to the crown. For Starkie, his outsider status led him towards open support for fascism. He accepted Italian hospitality and ventured to Abyssinia, from where he dispatched propaganda that praised 'the great colonising work that Italy is doing in this far-off land', at a time when Mussolini was using mustard gas against civilians.[62] There could be no greater contrast with his old college friend.

The death of the rector of Clondalkin in the Adelaide Hospital on 28 July 1936, following a brief illness, came as a great shock to his friends, colleagues and parishioners. The press, which provided extensive coverage, was united in viewing him as among the most gifted figures of his generation. For the *Church of Ireland Gazette*, he was 'A man of very wide sympathies, allied to the gift of single-mindedness; it was generally thought that he would be numbered not many years hence among the Bishops of the Church of Ireland'.[63] The *Irish Times* wrote:

> To know him was to love him, for he had just those qualities that will always attract. A genuine humility, a sincerity of purpose, a strong sense of duty—these made Bolton Waller the man he was. And with them was combined a warmth of heart which won for him the love he deserved.[64]

His friends rushed to memorialise. Members of the Irish Christian Fellowship, which he had founded over twenty years before, produced a festschrift.[65] Subscribers from Ireland, Britain, France, Switzerland and the United States raised over £500 towards creating the Bolton Waller Memorial Trust, which between 1938 and 1950 held seven lectures in his honour.[66] The topic of these lectures, fittingly, was peace and international affairs.

When making sense of Waller's career it is tempting to consider him primarily as a peacemaker, one of a number of Protestant clergymen such as Robin Eames, John Morrow and Joseph Parker who contributed, in various ways, towards reconciliation in Ireland. However, we should give equal weight to his strenuous efforts to revive Protestant political influence in the Free State, at a time when his community was content to lie low and pray for good treatment. Southern Protestants, declining in numbers and labouring under a sense of dispossession, were probably never going to reorganise and assert themselves politically; this makes Waller's stand all the more impressive. During the 1920s and 1930s, his was a lonely voice indeed.

CHAPTER FOUR

This 'rotten little Republic': Protestant Identity and the 'State Prayers' Controversy, 1948–9

MIRIAM MOFFITT

Introduction

When Taoiseach John A. Costello announced in September 1948 that it was his government's intention to repeal the 1936 External Relations Act and to declare the twenty-six counties of southern Ireland a republic, he reflected the desire of the majority of the population to sever the last constitutional link with the United Kingdom.[1] There was, however, a cohort of Protestants[2] who wished to retain some form of imperial connection and whose feelings have not, until now, found expression in the mainstream public arena. The impact of this domestic political change was amplified by the withdrawal of the new Republic from the British Commonwealth of Nations, thereby ending all connection with the former empire.

The passage of the Republic of Ireland Bill in 1948 was never in question, as it commanded the support of the government and the opposition; however, the Dáil and Seanad debates help estimate the enthusiasm for these political developments across the Protestant faiths.[3] Speaking in the Seanad, William B. Stanford (Church of Ireland) insisted that three-quarters of the overall Protestant population strongly supported the concept of an Irish republic.[4] Stanford's sentiments were echoed by other parlimentarians such as James G. Douglas of Fine Gael, a Quaker, and Denis Ireland, a Presbyterian.[5] In contrast, Presbyterian J.W. Biggar, nephew of Francis Joseph Biggar, opposed the break from the Commonwealth, reminding the Seanad that his family had long supported self-government for Ireland but within a Commonwealth framework, a view shared by Dáil deputies Maurice Dockrell and W.A. Sheldon, both members of the Church of Ireland.[6]

The removal of the proposed republic from the Commonwealth had practical implications for the Church of Ireland, which spanned the two jurisdictions on the island. Roughly two-thirds of its membership lived in the six counties of Northern Ireland, which remained under British rule and within the Commonwealth, while the remainder lived in what was about to become an independent Irish republic outside the Commonwealth. Prayers for those in authority (termed the State Prayers) are an intrinsic part of Anglican liturgy since the sixteenth century, set out in the Book of Common Prayer. The leadership of the Church of Ireland appreciated that the remit of the British king would no longer obtain in the portion of Ireland outside of the Commonwealth and that it would no longer be appropriate to offer prayers for his welfare in the new Republic. The fact that the Church straddled two jurisdictions created a potentially awkward situation and some feared that the Republic's subsequent departure from the Commonwealth could bring about a lack of liturgical uniformity, which might lead eventually to a total rupture. It was believed, therefore, that a single prayer-book for use in Northern Ireland and in the Republic was essential if the unity of the Church was to be maintained.[7] As the date of commencement of the Republic of Ireland Act (18 April 1949) preceded the General Synod by three weeks, John Gregg, primate and archbishop of Armagh, and Arthur Barton, archbishop of Dublin, devised temporary prayers for use in the churches of southern Ireland in the intervening period. It was expected that these temporary prayers, from which all mention of the monarch was omitted, would be adopted for permanent inclusion in the Book of Common Prayer at the General Synod of 1949.

It is difficult to disentangle the attitudes of southern Irish Protestants regarding the declaration of the Irish Republic, their rupture from the Commonwealth and the fact that their bishops forbade prayers for their former monarch. It is clear that the three factors just mentioned were intertwined. Belonging to the Commonwealth had welded together the Church of Ireland population in northern and southern Ireland. Some southern Protestants aspired towards a republic and favoured the removal of prayers for the king;[8] others were indifferent;[9] still more, although regretting their removal, accepted that liturgical changes were necessary;[10] while a further cohort was horrified when all mention of the king was removed from the regular order of service.[11] The strong affinity with the British monarchy among the latter grouping inspired a movement for the retention of prayers for the king in the churches of southern Ireland. Chief among those who battled for the reinstatement of these prayers was Hugh Maude, who spearheaded a well-organised crusade (the 'State Prayers controversy') to publicise his objections to the bishops' temporary prayers and to prevent their permanent inclusion at the General Synod of 1949.[12] The archival sources generated by Maude's campaign provide a window onto the conceptions of identity pertaining to southern Irish Protestants at a crucial and cathartic point in the mid-century.

In 1948, Hugh Arthur Cornwallis Maude (1904–82) was forty-four years old. He had been educated at Malvern College in Worcestershire, was unmarried and lived with his mother in Belgard Castle, Clondalkin, a few miles south of Dublin. The Maudes were a Norman family and, like his father, Hugh Maude was agent for a number of landowning families. Maude had good social connections; his occupation ensured contact with many persons of note and his mother, Eva Emily Maude (died 1960), was the last surviving granddaughter of archbishop of Armagh, Marcus Gervais Beresford.[13] He was the third and only surviving son; his two elder brothers had been killed on active service with the British army, aged twenty-five and twenty-six years respectively. He had two younger sisters, both of whom were married by 1948.

Maude fully accepted that some Protestants supported the political changes and were not minded to maintain prayers for the king.[14] The Church of Ireland and her principal organs in the twenty-six counties—the *Church of Ireland Gazette* and the *Irish Times*—were at pains to point out that most southern Protestants were supportive of the new regime and willingly embraced the concept of a republic. Indeed, many who favoured retention of the State Prayers were critical of the support given to the Republic by the *Irish Times*, *The Times* and the *Gazette* and commented that letters of opposition were unlikely to be published in these papers.[15]

Hugh Maude's Campaign

Maude began his public campaign with a letter to the *Gazette* in which he outlined his 'duty and privilege' to pray for the monarch, chiefly because the latter had undertaken a coronation oath to act as 'Defender of our Faith'[16] This letter drew a torrent of responses. Although some supported Maude's stance,[17] many advised him to accept political realities and suggested that the Church of Ireland had not been well served by her close connection to Great Britain.[18] Maude's opponents claimed he was trying to turn the Church of Ireland into 'the last stronghold [of] a political party now defunct in the greater part of our country', and that many of his co-religionists were whole-heartedly in favour of the Republic, and against the partition of the island.[19]

The General Synod of 1949 approved the use of the bishops' temporary prayers in the churches of southern Ireland pending further discussion at the General Synod of 1950 but, within weeks of the synod, Maude, in conjunction with three Dublin-based clergy—Dean E.H.C. Lewis-Crosby of Christ Church Cathedral, Canon Cecil Proctor of Harold's Cross, Dublin, and Rev. J.R. Colthurst of Greystones—launched a crusade to provide an alternative form of wording. Their campaign began with a meeting on 16 June 1949, after which Maude informed the primate that laymen 'from all walks of life' were distressed by the amended liturgy.[20] Gregg's response granted no concession to Maude's concerns; the archbishop outlined his fear that Protestant churches would be vulnerable to attack had prayers for the king been continued and emphatically ruled out any deviance from the decisions of the synod.[21] Maude interpreted Gregg's response as 'an acknowledgement of weakness & of intimidation',[22] and was delighted that a number of clergy, like Rev. Bird of Delgany, simply continued to pray for the king as before.[23]

Maude persisted in his efforts; through his influence, the East Glendalough Clerical Society passed a resolution in September 1949 which proposed the retention of prayers for the monarch. This led, ultimately, to the formation of a sub-committee of the Standing Committee of the General Synod to examine the question and to a discussion at the Dublin and Glendalough Diocesan Synod in October 1949.[24] Success now hinged on the General Synod's sub-committee, established to devise a form of words that would be liturgically, politically and culturally acceptable to members of the Church of Ireland in both Northern Ireland and the Republic.[25] An unexpected vacancy on this sub-committee in January 1950 was filled by Maude, to the delight of his supporters as, prior to this, only two members were supportive of his views: Frank Fitzgibbon and Robert McNeil Boyd, bishop of Derry and Raphoe.[26] The latter came up with an ingenious wording which solved the problem of praying for the British monarch while not appearing disloyal to the Republic by suggesting that prayers be offered for the king 'in whose dominions we are not accounted strangers'. (This reflected the legislation introduced in Britain which ensured that Irish citizens were not considered 'aliens'.)

The proposed prayers were approved by the Standing Committee and introduced as Bill No. 1 at the General Synod of May 1950.[27] Great care was given to prevent the proposed prayers giving offence to members of the Church of Ireland in Northern Ireland or in the Republic. It was essential that the monarch be referred to as 'King George VI', not as 'our king' or 'our sovereign',[28] and the eventual wording was selected so that the overwhelming portion of the Prayer Book was applicable in both jurisdictions.

Conceptions of Identity Among Southern Protestants in the Late 1940s

The significance of the State Prayers episode is that it provides a snapshot of Protestant conceptions of identity some thirty years after the establishment of the Irish Free State. When it was founded in 1922, most of the Protestant population of the island favoured the retention of British rule. This was outlined in an editorial in the *Gazette* in 1920, which explained that Protestants were baptised 'not only into a religious faith, but into a political camp'.[29] Identification with the British perspective had been inculcated in

Ireland's Protestant population through its associational culture and education, as Irish history, although taught in Catholic schools, was entirely omitted from the curriculum of Protestant schools until the teaching of history was made mandatory in all national (primary-level) schools in Ireland in 1908.[30] Some Protestants recognised their lack of awareness of Ireland's past, complaining that 'It is a dreadful thing to be born into one country and educated as a citizen of another'.[31]

The curricular changes of 1908 facilitated an increased awareness of Ireland's past among her younger Protestants, which was further increased when control of education passed into the hands of the strongly nationalist and almost exclusively Catholic Free State government. This meant that, by the time of the State Prayers controversy, Irish history had been taught in the Protestant schools of southern Ireland for four decades and under a system dominated by a Catholic-nationalist ethos for over thirty years.[32] Many Protestants like Rev. Victor Griffin (1924–2017) came to 'feel uneasy' about the past, and especially about the eighteenth-century penal laws against Catholics,[33] so that, by the mid-twentieth century, there was a distinct intergenerational difference between the awareness and interpretation of the history of Ireland found among the younger and more senior cohorts of the Church of Ireland population.

An obstacle towards identification with the predominantly Catholic Irish State (both pre- and post-1949) was the paucity of interaction between its confessional communities as, owing to the evolution of denominational systems of education and healthcare in the nineteenth century, it had become possible to live one's life without significant interaction with persons outside of one's own faith.[34] Protestants were especially vigilant in discouraging intermingling of the confessions; they were concerned about the implications of the papal decree *Ne Temere* (1908), which stipulated that children of mixed marriages must be reared as Catholics, a practice which Protestants feared would ultimately lead to their extinction.[35] Protestants who fraternised with Catholics were subjected to criticism by their peers as happened to 'C.I.R', who told how his co-religionists looked at him like 'quizzed terriers' after he joined avowedly Catholic organisations in his provincial town.[36]

In 1948, most Protestants over fifty years of age had been educated to support the British connection, although a significant number had subsequently reappraised the attitudes absorbed in their schooldays. Many accepted the political changes and agreed with the views expressed in an editorial in the *Irish Times* which noted that the Protestant community had formerly been regarded as 'a kind of relic of the British garrison'.[37] Echoing the above sentiment, 'Clareman' warned that if young Protestants did not enter fully into Irish life, they would disappear as a community.[38] 'Another Protestant' told of growing support for the Republic, especially among younger Protestants. Rev. Ernest Daunt of Killiney in County Dublin stated in 1949 that the removal of prayers for the king would have been unacceptable even ten years earlier but explained that the political climate had changed in the interim to the extent that everybody, Protestants included, had 'gone green'.[39]

This was indeed a reorientation of political opinion. Arthur Gray, rector of Castlelyons in County Cork, was embarrassed to recall that, as a schoolboy, he heard the bells of Portora School in Enniskillen, County Fermanagh, ring out to celebrate the defeat of Gladstone's Home Rule Bill in 1894. Noting the shift in Protestant opinion in the intervening decades, he explained: 'To me, then, that seemed quite natural. But that is what we have to live down.'[40] Maude admitted indifference among the younger generation but claimed support from laymen of middle age and upwards,[41] and insisted to the primate that 'many of us—certainly for a generation, will be British subjects'.[42] He believed many were unwilling to articulate their real feelings, and that businessmen were especially fearful of speaking out lest they 'store up trouble for themselves'. Some of Maude's supporters believed this observation could be applied to the behaviour of the episcopate, too.[43]

Change was certainly underway and was making an impact on the younger generation. Trinity College, a bastion of unionism, was initially suspicious of the new state but moved towards an accommodation over time, which intensified after it negotiated a much-needed government grant in 1947. Some students realised as early as the 1920s that they were not bound by their parents' attitudes and that their Protestantism was not necessarily synonymous with loyalism, so the average student in the mid-1940s adopted a form of moderate nationalism: Ireland first and then the Commonwealth.[44] The Union flag was not flown officially in college after 1935, 'God Save the King' was last sung at commencements in

1939 and the king's health was toasted at a college dinner for the last time in 1945.[45] By the mid-1940s, Trinity had aligned itself with political reality; it could no longer be presumed that southern Irish Protestant students would adhere to the attitudes of their elders.[46]

Many of Maude's supporters were dismayed that sympathy for their cause was not universal, even among the older segment of the population.[47] Maude's opponents explained that a nationalist sentiment would soon prevail in the southern section of the Church, pointing out that numbers favouring an imperial connection were every day decreasing and that younger Protestants could not remember life before the First World War.[48] Not all southern Protestants were so pragmatic, however, and some remained resolutely hostile to the Irish state. For instance, W.A. King-Harmon from Boyle in County Roscommon was highly critical of the 'rotten little Republic' in which he was forced to reside and insisted that he would have moved to Britain, except for his advanced age and for the fact that Britain had allied herself with 'those filthy socialists'.[49] Doris Weir, wife of the rector of Irishtown in Dublin, expressed her dismay at the severing of the British connection in a touching letter to the king in which she explained that

> We may not use now in Church the prayers for Your Majesty and for the Royal Family. In our Parish Church, once the royal Chapel of St. Mathew, Irishtown, on Easter Sunday evening we sang, with sorrow, for it was the last time, the National Anthem. It was a prayer from all our hearts—God Save the King. Legislation does not kill love and loyalty. We will continue to pray for you and for your family, and to hold you in deep affection.[50]

Support for the monarchy within a segment of the Protestant laity and a counter-balancing disquiet within the institutional church are encapsulated in an episode which took place in St Patrick's Cathedral, Dublin, in November 1949, seven months after the Republic came into being, when the congregation sang 'God Save the King' after service, despite the organist's best efforts to drown them out.[51]

The political and cultural identity of southern Protestants, therefore, spanned a spectrum which ranged from a desire for complete political autonomy on one hand, and for retention of an imperial link on the other. Levels of support varied within the laity, within the clergy and even within the episcopate. The identity-balance tipped in favour of separation among younger Protestants, while those educated before the turn of the twentieth century were more likely to want a link with Britain. However, it is clear that identities were not uniform even within these age-groupings and while most of Maude's firm supporters were elderly—Rev. Colthurst was seventy-four years old in 1948 and Dean Lewis-Crosby was eighty-four—Canon Proctor of Harold's Cross was only forty-five years old at that time while Maude himself was a year younger still. In contrast, Rev. Arthur Gray of Castlelyons in County Cork, who criticised the celebration of the 1894 Home Rule Bill, was in his seventies. An obvious pattern emerges, however, and it is clear that identification with the empire was less evident among the younger generation of southern Protestants. In a manifestation of Sidney Webb's 'inevitability of gradualness',[52] the younger cohort of southern Protestants had loosened their identification with Britain in the years following independence. By 1948, an entire generation had been reared and educated in an independent Ireland and it could no longer be presumed that a Protestant baptism implied an affiliation with the crown. The observation made in 1915 was now redundant; a southern Protestant was no longer born in one country and educated as a citizen of another.[53]

Maude's reliance on the monarch's coronation oath as 'Defender of the Faith' drew considerable comment as many felt it unwise to defend the Protestant faith on the basis of a papal award.[54] Maude insisted—incorrectly—that the king was head of the world-wide Anglican Communion, of which the Church of Ireland was a member;[55] and although he agreed to desist from referring publicly to the monarch as 'Defender of the Faith', he remained convinced in his opinion.[56] The rationale underpinning this belief provides an insight into the manner in which war and loss of life in the service of the crown had shaped his conception of religion, politics, identity and belonging.[57] Maude insisted that British monarchs swore to uphold Protestantism as the established religion in the United Kingdom and her dominions in a coronation oath termed the 'Protestant Declaration'. This practice, which had originated in the Parliamentary Test Acts of 1677 and was extended by the Bill of Rights in 1689, obliged each monarch to repudiate the teachings and practices of the Roman religion as 'superstitious and idolatrous', although the wording of the oath was greatly softened in the course of the twentieth century.[58] Although it was pointed out that the king's undertaking regarding religion did not extend to southern Ireland, and therefore did not apply to the whole of the Church of Ireland, Maude persisted in this assertion.[59]

Maude had his own, very particular, interpretation of how and why the British monarch was indeed the 'Defender of the Faith'. He believed that British monarchs had fulfilled their coronation oaths by countering the 'forces of evil' in two world wars, and had therefore safeguarded the functioning of the British Protestant faith.[60] He seems to have created a simplified, if confused, interpretation of wartime conflict, military success and British religious identity whereby the preservation of the British way of life, the defeat of Nazism and fascism and the continuance of Anglicanism as the state religion in England (but not in Ireland) became consolidated and attributed to the king's efforts as 'Defender of the Faith'. Having recently experienced a large-scale war (admittedly as the resident of a neutral country) and having lost two brothers and numerous cousins to the conflict, it is perhaps understandable that Maude should imbue his political and cultural admiration for the monarchy with semi-religious attributes.

The Episcopate, the Clergy and the Laity

Although Maude attempted to mobilise the general Protestant population to resist changes to the State Prayers, the bishops hoped the matter would proceed quietly to a conclusion. Archbishop Gregg took an authoritative stance on the matter; his opening address to the 1949 General Synod stressed the necessity for unity in the church and explained, very firmly, that the wording of the Book of Common Prayer needed modification 'even if it wounds our sentiment'.[61] The bishops' actions drew criticism from some quarters as some felt that the State Prayers had been removed too hastily.[62] However, it is likely that the bishops' strong stance represented an attempt to protect their clergy from pronouncing on the matter at local level,[63] as a parish rector could find that he had

> On the one hand . . . the old die-hard Unionist, who often tries to rule the parish . . . On the other the Protestant Republican who would look with contempt on a Church and Service where we prayed for a non-existent person—our most gracious King and Governor.[64]

The actual locus of arbitration between the General Synods of 1949 and 1950 is unclear as the bishops entrusted the decision to the synod; but when the temporary prayers were not adopted automatically in 1949, the synod decreed that they should be retained pending further discussion the following year and passed the onus back to the episcopate. Some viewed this as an attempt to distance the episcopate from the ultimate decision.[65] Maude and Colthurst believed the primate was 'weak', and 'ignorant' of the true situation and that Archbishop Barton was trying to appease everyone. In reality, though, the archbishops recognised the complexity of the situation and appreciated the shifting nature of cultural and political affinities within southern Protestantism.[66]

Support or otherwise for the amended prayers was not uniform across the episcopate and only one bishop (Boyd McNeil) on the sub-committee supported Maude's campaign. As the episode coincided with the quatercentenary of the Book of Common Prayer (1549–1949), and as many diocesan magazines contained articles outlining its origin and development, bishops were presented with a ready opportunity to explain the rationale behind the current amendments. The *Kilmore and Elphin and Ardagh Diocesan Gazette* used the anniversary to explain the official stance regarding the alterations in the State Prayers:

> Prayers for the King and for the Royal Family will seem out of place in a Twenty-six county Republic, as indeed they have been for some years past. Converts from the Roman Catholic Church must have been embarrassed on hearing these prayers read in Church. Added to that, they must have sensed their unreality.

Kilmore Protestants were assured that 'Protestantism is still Protestantism, and quite independent of Pharaoh whether he be Seán [Taoiseach John A. Costello] or Seoirse [King George VI]'.[67] In contrast, the *Diocesan Magazine of the United Diocese of Killaloe,*

Kilfenora, Clonfert and Kilmacduagh published a letter in which Bishop Hedley Webster outlined the history of the Book of Common Prayer, but which totally ignored the contemporary debate, thereby passing up on the opportunity to explain the official position taken by the House of Bishops.[68]

Those inside and outside of the corridors of power held different perspectives on the episode and some—mostly older people who had been reared in a largely pro-British mould—felt disempowered by the attitude of the church leadership. The inability of ordinary parishioners to influence the decision regarding the removal of State Prayers mirrors their inability to influence the political events which underpinned the episode, and their sense of powerlessness and hurt is revealed in their letters to Maude.[69] These persons had few avenues through which to voice their protest and resorted to small individual and collective acts of defiance. Mrs Doris Kennedy of County Wicklow told Maude she was 'furious' at the omission of what she termed the 'old prayers', which she considered 'by far the most important part of the service' during the recent war in which her youngest son was killed in the service of the crown. This lady's hurt is palpable and her response to the alteration in the liturgy is poignant, as there were few ways in which this sixty-two-year-old widow could voice her opposition. When her rector was unable to reinstate prayers for the king, Mrs Kennedy utilised one of the few avenues through which she could voice her displeasure; she sent her manservant to her parish church to bring home her footstool.[70]

Conclusion

It is clear that a number of factors impacted on the way in which persons reacted to the changes in the State Prayers. Some were driven by an obligation to pray for the king as head of the Anglican Communion (which was not actually the case), while others wanted to pray for the British monarch as the Defender of the Faith. While doubt may be poured on the validity of either title in the context of southern Ireland, the correspondence surrounding the State Prayers controversy confirms that succour was given to Irish Protestants by their confidence in the king as holder of the above offices, especially during the recent war.

Analysis of the State Prayers controversy confirms that this was a complex and confused episode in which religious, political and cultural affinities were shown to be completely entangled. In Maude's own case, it is clear that his opinions were based on religious beliefs in which politics played a large part; it is also clear that, although these beliefs were based on rather dubious grounds, he was convinced of their validity. It is evident that although the Church authorities took a strong stance, the bishops were themselves somewhat divided on the matter but were determined to appear to give strong leadership. It can be seen that those outside the debate did not always appreciate the complexity of the issue and some considered their opinions disregarded, which amplified the sense of impotence occasioned by the unwelcome rupture of the British connection.

This essay shows that southern Protestantism was not a uniform entity and that its members' conception of identity ranged from ardent support for the Republic to determined affiliation with Britain. It reveals that the episcopate was not entirely united in its attitude, and that persons who lived at the farthest remove from the decision-making process felt their voices went unheard. Shifts in communal identities happen over time; an intergenerational change was underway by 1949 and was especially evident in the younger cohort of southern Protestants. It is not possible to identify precisely how and why their altered conception of identity evolved in the intervening decades, nor to state whether opinions and attitudes flowed from the core to the periphery or in the opposite direction. Evidence from the Maude correspondence, though, suggests a two-way flow of influence; affiliation with the Republic and dissociation from Britain was promoted publicly by the church leadership (core to periphery) but the establishment of a sub-committee to adjudicate on the matter, and the subsequent modifications of the bishops' wording, was an acknowledgement of church members' strong opinions (periphery to core).

The unexpected eruption of the State Prayers controversy presented the Church of Ireland with an awkward dilemma. It was determined to retain unity between the various segments of its membership: between its older and younger generations, its northern and southern populations, those favouring independence for Ireland

and those leaning towards a connection with Britain and various factions which had emerged as a result of differences in liturgical, doctrinal and theological opinion. The political developments of 1949 challenged the Church of Ireland's sense of unity; it weakened the north–south connection by removing the bond of Commonwealth membership and it tested the cohesion between the old and the young, and between nationalist and imperialist. The episcopate was aware that this episode had the potential to sunder the church along a number of fault lines. Although the situation demanded strong leadership, Hugh Maude's intransigence forced church leaders to concede that strongly held conceptions of identity can neither be discarded nor disregarded.

It can be argued, however, that the real importance of the State Prayers controversy lies in the archival material generated by the episode. This permits a unique insight into the diverse conceptions of belonging found in the southern Protestant community at the mid-point of the twentieth century. Analysis of this material reveals that, for some southern Protestants, their understanding of their political and cultural identity was closely connected to their religious beliefs. It confirms that, by mid-century, a distinct shift had taken place within the southern Protestant community with regard to perceptions of identity, and that individual Protestants experienced this modified sense of affiliation in different ways and to varying degrees. It proves that changes in political attitudes were embraced by a significant portion of the southern Protestant population, especially among the younger cohort. But it also shows that a minority, often persons of more mature years, clung steadfastly to an identification with the British state and empire, maintaining a sense of identity that, with the passage of time, was increasingly out of line with political reality; and that these persons found themselves sidelined as the mainstream Protestant culture in southern Ireland adjusted to a post-imperial existence.

Appendix

State Prayers as Laid Out in the *Book of Common Prayer*, 1936[71]

A Prayer for the King's Majesty	O Lord, our heavenly Father, high and mighty, King of kings, Lord of lords, the only Ruler of princes, who dost from thy throne behold all the dwellers upon earth; Most heartily we beseech thee with thy favour to behold our most gracious Sovereign Lord, King George; and so replenish him with the grace of thy Holy Spirit, that he may always incline to thy will, and walk in thy way: Endue him plenteously with heavenly gifts; grant him in health and wealth long to live; strengthen him that he may vanquish and overcome all his enemies; and finally, after this life, he may attain everlasting joy and felicity; through Jesus Christ our Lord. *Amen.*
A Prayer for the Royal Family	Almighty God, the fountain of all goodness, we humbly beseech thee to bless our gracious Queen Elizabeth, Mary the Queen Mother, the Princess Elizabeth, and all the Royal Family; Endue them with thy Holy Spirit; enrich them with thy heavenly grace; prosper them with all happiness; and bring them to thine everlasting kingdom, through Jesus Christ our Lord. *Amen.*
A Prayer for the King and Commonwealth	O Lord, God of our fathers, we humbly beseech thee to look with thy favour upon our Country and Empire, and preserve them from all perils. Save and protect our Sovereign Lord, King George, enrich him plenteously with heavenly gifts, and prosper his counsels for the welfare of his people. Bless also our gracious Queen Elizabeth, Mary the Queen Mother, the Princess Elizabeth, and all the Royal Family. Guard in thy good providence this our land, Bless and direct the Chief Governors in Ireland, and those who bear rule under them. Endue with wisdom and strength the ministers of the Crown, the Parliaments in Ireland, at this time assembled, and all who are set in authority; grant them so to use the power entrusted to them for thy honour and glory, that righteousness and peace may be established among us for all generations, through Jesus Christ our Lord. *Amen.*

State Prayers as Agreed at the General Synod of 1950[72]

[N.I.] *A Prayer for the King's Majesty*	As per the 1936 Book of Common Prayer
[N.I.] *A Prayer for the Royal Family*	As per the 1936 Book of Common Prayer
[N.I.] *A Prayer for the King and Commonwealth*	As per the 1936 Book of Common Prayer
[R.I.] *Prayer for The President and all in authority*	ALMIGHTY God, who rulest over the nations of the world; We commend to thy merciful care the people of this land, that, being guarded by thy providence, they may dwell secure in thy peace. Grant to The President of this State and to all in authority, wisdom and strength to know and to do thy will. Fill them with the love of truth and righteousness, and make them ever mindful to serve thy people faithfully to thy honour and glory; through Jesus Christ our Lord. *Amen.*
[R.I.] *A Prayer for King* George, *the Sixth.*	ALMIGHTY God, the fountain of all goodness, we humbly beseech thee to behold thy servant, King *GEORGE* the Sixth, in whose dominions we are not accounted strangers. Endue him with thy Holy Spirit; enrich him with thy heavenly grace; prosper him with all happiness; and bring him to thine everlasting kingdom; through Jesus Christ our Lord. *Amen.*

CHAPTER FIVE

Count Us in Too: Wanting to be Heard in Independent Ireland[1]

DEIRDRE NUTTALL

Introduction

In independent Ireland,[2] the stories of the Anglo-Irish gentry and of the affluent Protestant professional classes are well-preserved. While interesting and significant, theirs are not the only 'Protestant' tales. The voices of ordinary Protestants are under-represented. While congregation numbers recovered in many areas (census returns between 1991 and 2006 showed an increase of 46 per cent in Church of Ireland adherents, although the latest (2016) shows a further slight drop),[3] the distinctive cultural aspects of Irish Protestantism are in decline, as Irish Protestants are increasingly assimilated into the mainstream. It is important to listen to, record and understand the stories of this group—which have often been experienced as difficult to discuss outside the safe zone of community or family—as they will soon be gone.

Popular history and stereotyping in Ireland typically view Irish Protestants as privileged, wealthy and exclusive. Indeed, Protestants have historically been over-represented among the wealthier social classes. However, there is a substantial disconnect between the idea of Protestants as gentry or as wealthy professionals and the reality of many as ordinary folk.[4] This is described very succinctly by Eugenio Biagini, an Italian historian whose research focuses on the history of minorities, ethnic and religious, in twentieth-century Ireland:

> for most of the past century Southern Protestants did not attract much attention: they were too quiet to make headlines, and did not fit in with the dominant Irish national narrative, focusing on an 800-years struggle against English oppression, of which many Irish Protestants were (or were supposed to have been) the agents and beneficiaries . . . [relatively unknown] was the experience of the rest, those living in rural areas, the non-intellectuals, the working class, and the shopkeepers.[5]

For many years, Irish nation-building included the 'active forgetting' of history associated with British colonialism, including 'the wiping out of the positive aspects of this legacy', by removing references from curricula, or deferring to a bias.[6] The education system was designed to create a 'strong, reasonable and enthusiastic national feeling', inculcating in the national psyche mythologised versions of real events.[7] In the independent south, history promoted 'the belief in an inner spirituality of the Irish people, demonstrated by their abiding fidelity to the twin ideals of Catholicism and political freedom'.[8] Political bodies tend to promote official memory that 'claims to be collective, but is also inevitably selective, since it includes memory of only events which are convenient in a given historical moment', while inconvenient memories are omitted and 'forgotten'.[9] The collective memories of the majority were harnessed to embrace the 'official mnemonic discourse':[10] the story of a grievously oppressed Catholic people that struggled for independence against a Protestant oppressor. Shades of grey were often overlooked.

Irish Protestants integrated their own history into that of Ireland,[11] and many Protestant schoolchildren of earlier generations studied history books written specifically for them, because Protestants wanted histories that depicted them positively.[12] Many Protestants—especially those outside the cocoon of wealth and privilege—retain stories (often relating to earlier times) of feeling marginalised in a society perceived as indifferent, or even hostile, to their interests. Drawing from a selection of interviews with over fifty people from diverse Protestant backgrounds, this chapter seeks to provide some insight into the counter-narratives they provide. The interviews were carried out by the author between 2013 and 2015 as part of a larger, ongoing, research project in collaboration with the National Folklore Collection that collects and explores southern Irish Protestant identities and narratives from a folkloric perspective. Interviews were open-ended, predicated around personal and family memories and history, and lasted from approximately half an hour to three hours. The urban/rural divide is approximately 50/50. The age range of interviewees is from twenty-six to ninety-five, with a majority aged from fifty to seventy-five. At the request of the interviewees, aliases are used here, and potentially identifying factors are omitted. Use is also made of memoirs and other sociological and historical sources.

Background

By listening to Protestants from less privileged socio-economic backgrounds, and in areas where the Protestant community is small, scattered and not in a position of influence, we gain insight into the complexity and nuance of the Irish Protestant experience. While 'Irish Protestants' have never been a hermetic unit, as social anthropologist Frederick Barth writes:

> Categorical ethnic distinctions do not depend on an absence of mobility, contact and information, but do entail social processes of exclusion and incorporation whereby discrete categories are maintained despite changing participation and membership . . .[13]

Protestants and Catholics have worked and even lived together despite taboos against intermarriage and factors that tended to maintain a degree of separation. Yet each group generally holds core values. The flow of ideas and shared stories within each group can also create a sense of cultural identity, making a 'mnemonic community'.[14] While (for example) rural Protestants may share more economic and local concerns with their Catholic neighbours than with their urban counterparts, Irish Protestants nonetheless view themselves as sharing certain outlooks, stories, customs and traditions that are integral to their identity. Today, the stories told by people of Protestant origins encapsulate feelings of belonging and difference that are a feature of their group identity.

History, Memory and Folk Narrative

Popular histories of Ireland are, of course, rooted in elements of historical truth. Throughout much of the colonial period, Ireland's elite was predominately Protestant (mostly Anglican). In the early 1880s, for instance, more than 70 per cent of all justices of the peace (across the whole island)[15] were Protestants, and 250 members of the Church of Ireland's general synod cumulatively owned about a million acres of land,[16] while the Free State's 1926 census shows that 'other religions' (mostly Protestants) remained disproportionately represented in skilled work and professions.[17] The landscape still contains many of the 'Big Houses' that feature in stories about injustice and persecution. However, the homes of Protestants who are not wealthy can easily be overlooked, just like their inhabitants and their stories. Ireland's many chronicles of collective victimhood are a marker of ethnic Irishness from which Protestants can feel excluded, because they are considered perpetrators, who can never be seen as victims[18] and who are not always accepted as truly Irish.

Stories of Marginalisation

There is a common thread in the narratives of less well-off Protestants: a feeling of public invisibility and the sense that the experience of being Irish and Protestant without wealth or status is unrecognised in Ireland's dominant historical story. These feelings often coexist with intense feelings of Irishness and belonging that can be experienced as contested. Protestants have also sometimes felt excluded and marginalised in their local areas. Sometimes they report behaviours of their own (usually relegated to the past) that have contributed. Irish Protestants who did not live in a relatively populous community and who were not protected by affluence, have found it difficult to relate to stories about the landlord in his 'Big House', or to the affluent professional in a leafy suburb. Many define themselves negatively: not Catholic, not Anglo-Irish, not wealthy, not recognised. 'Shirley' said: 'They can't even see that we are here at all; sometimes even I wonder', and talks of revealing herself as a Protestant at her job as a cleaner. Her colleagues did not believe her, as she did not look like a 'Protestant' to them: 'You're not, love.'[19]

In the early years of independence, southern Ireland tended to remain 'an overwhelmingly rural, peasant economy'. State policy then was to promote Ireland as Catholic, Gaelic and predominately rural. Perhaps inadvertently, Protestants who were poor, whether urban or rural, seemed not to belong; to have 'different intellectual understandings of the world, consciousness and different ideals of truth and reality'.[20] Politicians and civil servants managed to shape national identity as culturally Catholic as well as Gaelic by filtering their ideas through the education system. When the new Constitution was drawn up in 1937, these ideas were 'incorporated . . . as the moral core of the Irish state',[21] imposing a surprising level of 'culturally manipulated homogeneity'.[22]

From the 1920s, Protestants gradually started developing a new understanding of their identity. For some, it wasn't easy. In September 1923, the *Church of Ireland Gazette* lamented that it was 'all very well to say that loyalty can be transferred . . . but [loyalty] is an affair of the heart and it is not possible to force the heart to follow the hand'.[23] Many of the working-class Protestants in Dublin left (as many Irish did) for economic reasons, but also because life had become difficult in other ways. 'Harold'[24] discussed his grandfather, who grew up in an inner-city tenement. Although many of his friends left, in part because of the marginalisation they experienced, he stayed and often described a young life marked by sectarian bullying. 'It would have been hard core' in the 1920s and it left him bitter and angry. In later life, this bitterness sometimes emerged in commentary on the past that ran counter to the officially endorsed narrative:

> I remember my granddad saying once, I suppose it was a Protestant joke . . . He and my dad were driving out to Raheny or somewhere and they were driving down the road . . . 'Sean Moore Road' or something. My dad said to my granddad, 'I wonder who this chap is. I never heard of him. Why did they name a road after him?' And my granddad said, 'He probably shot some Englishman in the back and ran!'[25]

Throughout much of the twentieth century, Protestant communities diminished in size. The process of the de-peopling of Protestant parishes, especially in more remote areas and in inner-city areas, took some time. Today, older Protestants remember seeing churches and community centres steadily closing. Their stories of culture and community often start with a litany of loss. 'Donald'[26] remembered:

> The first to go, St Mathias [demolished in the 1950s], was so strongly resented that people went around with petitions and knocked on doors. St Peter's was demolished [in 1983] . . . St Luke's [closed in 1975 and burned by an arsonist in 1986] was reduced to ruin, St Mary's [closed in 1986] is a pub. St Luke's is the ruin on Cork Street. Most of them are gone . . .

To avoid being assessed for rates, roofs were often removed from unused buildings, which rapidly deteriorated. These decaying or repurposed buildings can still prompt memories that lead to story-telling of early generations and their fate. Many Protestants comment that their decline and perceived loss of status led to anxiety that prompted 'keeping themselves to themselves'.

Where Protestants are few and not especially wealthy, some express that there has been a perception of public space as belonging to 'the other crowd'. In such areas, some describe the feeling that their right to use public spaces, like parks or streets, where they were very much in a minority, was once conditional on 'keeping the head down'. Stories are told by Protestants from small or scattered communities of finding oneself in a public space during a Catholic procession and feeling suddenly vulnerable and lost, even when nothing happened and nobody even looked at them; they were not necessarily resented, but simply irrelevant.

Although Irish history records the words and deeds of famous Irish Protestants, some notable nationalists, there is a widespread sense among those from less-wealthy backgrounds that 'my people aren't there'. 'Heather'[27] remembered from her time in secondary school:

> I started to puzzle and it really bothered me that I couldn't find one positive line about Irish Protestant people. And that

> saddened me. I thought, 'Where am *I*?' and all you could find were the Anglo-Irish and the big houses and the way they behaved in the Famine and the way they did this and the way they did that and I thought, 'Where's *my* people?'. . .

'Heather' commented that, after free secondary education was introduced in the 1960s, Catholic small farmers could afford to send their children to schools reflecting the family's faith and cultural identity. There were no local Protestant secondary schools and people like her family (also small farmers) could not afford boarding school. In the Catholic school, Protestant children often had to deal with their classmates' assumptions, sometimes accompanied by sectarian bullying, that they were rich, when the reality for many of them, growing up on small farms as the first generation to get a secondary education (like many of the Catholic students), was very different.

Protestants with a family history of poverty, such as families descended from tenement dwellers or very small farmers, often feel they are not allowed to 'own' their stories of hardship. Whereas Catholic poverty can be blamed on injustices inherited from the colonial era, poor Protestants seem to feel that they are being blamed, or suspected of 'pretending'. Poor Protestants' family memories of poverty can be rejected as lies, misunderstood or ignored. 'Heather's' teacher assured her that no Protestants died during the Famine, despite the stories 'Heather' had heard to the contrary, because the Protestants caused the Famine and could not have suffered in it. 'Harold' was beaten as a child by classmates yelling, 'Where's your butler?', believing that Protestants are English and English people are rich. 'Priscilla'[28] compared her family's experience of being poor Protestants to that of poor whites in South Africa: 'We were like the poor whites. We had nothing but they resented us anyway.'

Wealthier farmers and substantial landowners often hired a disproportionate number of Protestants to work as servants and labourers and, as many of these employers left after independence, an important source of employment for working-class Protestants dried up.[29] There are stories told about how wealthier members of congregations and communities dominated vestry and other organisations, but that they left, leaving the cost of the upkeep of local Protestant infrastructure (often too big for the community even at its peak) to those who could not afford it, leading to yet more closures. 'Penelope'[30] commented that her church was built and subsidised by 'very gentry people' who 'were able to afford to put money into it', but that 'those people are all dead and gone now' and 'it's really the ordinary people as I say, people with just ordinary jobs . . . have to come up with the money'. The difficulty of maintaining buildings has led to the need to rent churches and community halls to local (including other religious) groups. While this can cause stress, it has also helped to break down barriers between communities that were once quite separate.

'William'[31] described a mostly happy childhood in which Catholic and Protestant children played together. But he and his brother dreaded being sent 'for a few messages' because an older boy in the area would 'call us old Protestants and all that sort of stuff . . . Really nasty . . . there was kind of an undercurrent of that sort of thing . . . we were *always* conscious of the fact that we were a different religion'. He said that 'It wasn't a nice feeling. It was a bad feeling, really it was, I think it's not good for young people to feel like that.' He and his brother complained about the bullying but were advised to 'keep their heads down' for fear that an intervention would damage the family's relationship with the neighbours in a small rural community with very few Protestants.

Even today, some Protestants describe feelings of worry when they have to reveal their background. 'Henry'[32] said, 'I would discuss my own ancestry only on a one to one basis with anyone from a Catholic background who is open-minded'. 'Shirley' said that while her lifestyle and outlook are similar to her Catholic neighbours', 'I don't really tell people what I am . . . I don't want to get into an argument about it and I don't want to flaunt it. They'd still . . . "Oh God, she's one of *them*!" I still feel like that.'

Narratives of belonging can coexist with these accounts of marginalisation. 'Shirley' said that while she has 'nothing against England', she has always felt intensely Irish, saying, 'We're very proud to be Irish and my dad always loved Dublin.' As a youngster, 'Harold' asked his parents, '*Why* are you Protestants?' They didn't know what to say; 'they were open-mouthed looking at me . . . I think their angle was more "We're not Catholics" rather than "We're Protestants".' He feels that their identity largely sprang from how they were treated as young, working-class Protestants in the 1950s.

They reported being bullied and marginalised in their community: 'heavy duty'. However, he was always aware of a keen sense of Irishness: 'sympathetic towards the English but first of all Irish. If England were playing Ireland, we'd be screaming at the telly for Ireland most certainly.'

The Threat of Intermarriage

Historically, intermarriage, while disapproved of generally, was seen by Protestants as a huge existential threat. The idea that these marriages would contribute to the demise of the community evokes a population experiencing anxiety about its future, even relatively recently. 'Eleanora'[33] gave a very typical account:

> the Ne Temere rule enforced by the Catholic Church had a disastrous effect on the Protestants who had family members in mixed marriages. That member would often have been excommunicated from the family. In many cases grandparents never knew their grandchild, it caused untold heartache on both sides. Thankfully, its effect is gradually disappearing.

Heather Crawford writes of how parishes had to provide occasions for in-group socialising: 'their need to police group boundaries to enhance their likelihood of surviving as a community by avoiding assimilation'. Bishop Paul Colton remembered, as a young man in the 1970s, having to carry 'social cards' signed by Protestant clergy to gain admittance into the parish dances where young adults could meet 'one of their own'.[34]

For some older Protestants who remain unmarried, particularly in rural areas, their stories reveal sorrow over opportunities lost, especially now that they have seen how well many 'mixed marriages' turn out. They lived through a period when marrying 'out' was intensely shameful to many families, and they may have seen some 'mixed' couples being ostracised on both sides. For 'William', the fact that he never married causes grief and loss, not just because he is alone, but also because he believes that his rural parish misses the children who never came. While many rural Catholic men also remained unmarried, 'William' blames the lack of Protestant girls in the area in his youth and states that low marriage rates impacted more severely on the tiny local Protestant community. Services are now held just once a month, and he is alone in a pew that was once filled with children:

> I blame myself, really . . . If I had made more of an effort to meet someone, and had a few childer, maybe we could have kept it going. Even if she had been a Catholic, it might have worked out. I wish I'd known when there was still time . . . but I can't see much future for the parish really . . . it is hard . . . and I blame myself as much for that but when we were growing up there was a great shortage of ladies in the area. A great shortage . . . in fact quite a number of the people here would be related. There weren't that many people to marry, you see.

The notorious Fethard boycott took place in 1957 when the Protestant woman in a 'mixed marriage', Mrs Cloney, changed her mind about the vow she had taken to raise her children as Catholics and left the family home in Fethard-on-Sea, a small village on the Wexford coast, with her daughters.[35] Mrs Cloney had been visited repeatedly by local Catholic priests, who insisted that her children would be educated in the Catholic school.[36] There were widespread suspicions among the Catholic community that the local Protestants were conspiring to remove children from the Catholic Church. There were two small Protestant businesses in the area, a hardware shop and a newsagent. Both suffered devastating loss of revenue as local Catholics, following the parish priest, stopped buying anything. The local piano teacher, a Protestant, lost most of her pupils[37] and the Church of Ireland school closed because the teacher left.[38] Protestants elsewhere were concerned that the boycott would spread.

Many were thinking of another highly publicised case in 1950 in which a Protestant, Ernest Tilson, who had married a Catholic, had promised to raise their children as Catholics, only to seek custody of three of the four and place them in a Protestant orphanage when the couple experienced difficulties. Although the Tilson case was more complex than it seemed (and is not discussed in detail here, for reasons of space),[39] Tilson's actions were consistent with the legal view at the time, that the father's wishes trumped the mother's.[40] When Mrs Tilson took a legal case against the orphanage, the

High Court and the Supreme Court both ruled against him. Irish Protestants generally felt that 'the courts had abandoned a rule of law which was impartial between denominations in favour of one which benefited the Roman Catholic Church'.[41] Although the later Supreme Court ruling had rested less on religious matters, Protestants remembered that when Mr Justice Gavan Duffy made the High Court ruling, he stated that Tilson was bound by the *Ne Temere* decree he had signed and said, 'The right of the Catholic Church to guard the faith of its children, the great majority, is registered in our fundamental document [the Constitution]'.[42] This made Protestants feel that the state was intrinsically Catholic,[43] and very anxious about the likelihood of impartiality should the Fethard case eventually come before the law. The Fethard boycott was eventually resolved, partly because de Valera, the Taoiseach, denounced it on 4 July 1957,[44] describing it as 'ill conceived, ill-considered, and futile'.[45]

For many older Protestants, the Fethard boycott is an important folk narrative as well as a fact of history, providing a way to discuss old hurts and anxieties and to compare the difficulties of the past with the much more positive present, while referring indirectly to more personal incidents. For example, 'Dorcas'[46] segued from a discussion of the Fethard boycott to a story of her cousin who married the Catholic nurse he had hired to care for the children after his wife's death. There was a great 'hullaballoo'. 'When you look back', she said, 'you think, "What was it all about really?"'

Being 'Put Out'

For many, school was a time when difference was reinforced, particularly for Protestants who could not attend a Protestant school because there was none in the area, or because their family could not afford a boarding school. 'Mabel'[47] attended the local Catholic school with her siblings and cousins. It was a generally positive experience, but they felt very different during catechism when they were 'put out'. 'Albert'[48] and his sisters, the only Protestants in the school, stood outside the classroom door when religion was taught. This was the beginning of a great feeling of difference that has persisted:

> it has lived with me quite a bit too, that I am quite aware of it . . . you were almost different . . . It wasn't a very nice feeling. You didn't altogether belong . . . you knew that you just weren't quite the same.

'Ian', the only Protestant child in a small rural school, was nine at the time of an all-Ireland schools' folklore survey carried out by the Irish Folklore Commission in 1937. He was told not to participate, as the teacher believed the state body was uninterested in collecting 'Protestant' folklore. Although generally happy in the school, he often recalls this moment, and the feeling of difference it elicited. He commented also that his sisters were educated at home, as a Catholic school was seen as being less 'safe' for Protestant girls than for boys.

Rural Protestants who could afford to often sent their children to boarding school, with the result that they had few local friends. Many rural interviewees mention that this lack of local friends was problematic in terms of developing local personal and business relationships in the area as adults, typically when they returned to run the family farm. 'Ian' returned from his secondary school and struggled to develop a social network in an area with very few Protestants: 'Not going to school with them I think was the main reason . . . You were taken away when you were 12 and you were away to 17 or 18 so you were gone out of the area so you had to make friends again.' When 'Ian' had children of his own, he decided to educate them locally so that they would not have a similar experience:

> Because they haven't been so long away and they went to Catholic schools, the convent and the brothers . . . They weren't cut off entirely. They would meet people on the road who went to school with them and that. I wouldn't meet anyone from [his Protestant boarding school] going down the road!

Johnston identifies the problem of education for rural Protestants as a factor that contributed to high levels of emigration. In areas where there were few Protestants, catchment areas for schools had to be enormous to assemble enough children to run a school, and when children went to secondary schools, boarding was the norm, with the inevitable result that they had few friends in their home areas, did not have local contacts when they were growing up, and were more likely to move away.[49]

Not Joining In

Historically, observing the Sabbath by not working or playing sports on a Sunday has been important in Protestant communities. While for many this may have been primarily a matter of faith, some describe it as also having been a 'convenient excuse' to facilitate some rural Protestants' active participation in their own marginalisation. Some rural Protestants who came of age in the fifties, sixties and even seventies and eighties, describe being socially isolated because of this rule. The Sabbath rule enabled communities already very anxious about intermarriage, and other ways in which cultural and religious integrity might be compromised or diluted, to avoid 'mixed' activities, including games and dances. 'Thomas'[50] said that, when he was young in the 1940s, no Protestant would have been 'caught dead' playing Gaelic games, nor would they have been welcomed ('Thomas' also comments that things have changed greatly, and that his grandson is a keen hurler). While feelings may have been stronger in border areas, similar accounts are heard from rural areas distant from the border, sometimes with the caveat that, despite not participating in the GAA, Protestants nonetheless shared in Catholics' pride when the local team prevailed. These stories of voluntary self-exclusion generally come with the comment that things are happily no longer the same today.[51]

Conclusion

While Protestant communities in Ireland today are increasingly assimilated into the mainstream (and subject to the trend towards secularisation that is general in Ireland today), a folkloric approach to collecting their narratives offers us great insight into how being an Irish Protestant has been experienced in recent history. These narratives can run counter to those that dominate popular history and discourse. For Protestants who live in areas where their numbers are few, and/or those with family backgrounds of poverty or other forms of social marginalisation, there is a widespread sense of invisibility. Among the themes that emerge from the narratives collected in this study are those of marginalisation, a sense of Protestantism as a cultural, rather than strictly religious group and the idea that 'ordinary' Protestants are rarely heard; a sense that the story of the 'Big House' is taken as a metaphor for the Protestant community as a whole and not as just one aspect of it. These narratives often coexist with others about neighbourliness and cooperation in mixed communities.

In gaining a better understanding of the Protestant experience in Ireland, it is important to look beyond that of Protestants whose histories are rooted in affluence, privilege and areas with relatively high Protestant populations, and to include the narrative accounts of those who, for various reasons, have been less audible. Recording, listening to and understanding people's stories—as in the case of the archive of Irish Protestant narratives and experience that is currently being assembled at the National Folklore Collection—offers a way to gain insights into lived experience that complements what historical research reveals about how Irish Protestants across the social spectrum and in a variety of geographic locations have adapted to, and continue to live in, modern Ireland.

PART II

Engagement

CHAPTER SIX

Gentry Inclusion via Class Politics? Negotiating Class Transition Politically in the Irish Free State

TONY VARLEY

Introduction

As the southern Anglo-Irish landed gentry faded as a class in the twentieth century, some of them moved to acquire, or to consolidate, a new class position and identity for themselves as farmers. How this process played out in public life during the early decades of native rule, and with what consequences will be explored here with reference to the experiences of two members of the southern landowning class. Our task is to examine how the landed backgrounds of George O'Callaghan-Westropp (1864–1944) and Robert Malachy Burke (1907–1998) influenced their involvement in contrasting forms of class politics, their political advances and reverses and how they assessed whether their activism enabled them to move from one class position to another.[1]

By 1923 the demise of southern Ireland's landed gentry, a class in steady decline economically and politically for decades, was visibly accelerating. During the revolutionary years between 1920 and 1923 at least 275 'Big Houses' (about 4 per cent of the total) fell prey to arson attacks,[2] and some landed families would depart Ireland for good. Others were to follow in succeeding years.[3] Some of those who remained on—as was true of many with unionist sympathies more generally—thought to survive by keeping their heads down to the point of adopting a 'ghetto mentality' that desired to have 'nothing whatever to do with the new regime'.[4] Such a response was evidently encouraged by the manner in which 'both the British government and their northern brethren were content to leave them to sink or swim by themselves'.[5]

The 'daring few' encouraged by the Cosgrave government to become senators 'felt that the best hope for the future was loyal co-operation'.[6] Even if sixteen of the thirty government-nominated members of the first Free State Senate were 'ex-unionist' and included some prominent former landowners, F.S.L. Lyons has suggested that 'while what they had to say was important for the record, it did not have very much bearing on events'.[7]

The same cannot easily be said of either George O'Callaghan-Westropp or R.M. (Bobby) Burke, each of whom was intent on making a stir politically. Col. O'Callaghan-Westropp's political project was to see Irish farmers emerge in the interwar period, via the Irish Farmers' Union (IFU) and the Farmers' Party, as a worthy successor to a once economically and politically dominant landlord class. For a short spell he even contemplated the new farmer-owner class becoming sufficiently powerful to push for the creation of a farmers' state in southern Ireland. Bobby Burke's contrasting political project in the 1930s and 1940s was to look to the Labour Party and the trade union movement to mobilise the working classes—including self-employed working farmers and farm labourers—behind the ideal of creating a just and Christian social order in Ireland. Burke's profit-sharing farming, a major focus of his Christian radical reformism in north Galway, was partly conceived as a model that might inspire others to adopt large-scale cooperative farming as a more Christian (and more socially and economically efficient) alternative to private small-scale farming.

Even if their politics moved in very different directions, these two figures nevertheless did share much in common. Each came from a minor landowning gentry family in western Ireland,[8] was a Church of Ireland member and a staunch defender of the rule of law and of constitutional politics. Each had a troubled agrarian family history, had attended the same English public school, had served as a British army officer, and had inherited family land and other wealth. Each was determined to make (or to consolidate) a class transition to large-scale farming, albeit of a markedly different kind. And each was inclined to link his farming fortunes with those of Irish farmers more generally. Besides viewing political activism as a crucial aspect of their personal class transitions, each saw it as embedded in wider struggles to rebuild Irish society civically as well as socially, economically and politically.

To frame our discussion of the fate of the Irish gentry after they ceased to be landlords and after British rule had substantially ended, two competing imagined futures can be contemplated. A classic expression of the 'inclusionist' imagined future is found in Charles Stewart Parnell's 'long-term hope' of achieving 'a socially stable partnership between "reformed" landlords and a "satiated" class of peasants' in Ireland.[9] Members of the old landed class, once reconciled to the land settlement and moderate nationalism in Parnell's hoped-for new dispensation, would be ready to play 'their part for which they [were] fitted in the future social regeneration' of the country.[10] Assuming that the required reconciliation was achievable, a bright future lay ahead for the Irish gentry.

The 'exclusionist' imagined future, on the other hand, found a classic expression in Michael Davitt's portrayal of the Irish landlords as a parasitic garrison class, the 'bastard offspring of force and wrong' and the 'scourge of our race since it first made Ireland a land of misery and poverty'.[11] In light of the general representation of the Irish gentry in nationalist eyes as a reviled and disreputable class forever burdened with a dark and shameful history of rack-renting and mass evictions,[12] it would be well nigh impossible for the ex-landlords to shake off their stigmatised identity. The bleak imagined future here—even if stopping short of expulsion on the grounds that all 'the Landlords deserve of Ireland is a single ticket to Holyhead'[13]—is one in which members of the ex-gentry could be expected to play no worthwhile part in the new state's public life.

These optimistic and pessimistic imagined futures—lying at opposite ends of a spectrum of real world possibilities—provide us with a general framing narrative that can help us set the wider scene contextually and historically. Taking them as contending interpretive benchmarks or points of reference, we will first consider whether O'Callaghan-Westropp and Burke, as they pursued their individual class transitions at a time of consequential change, entered public life to fulfil a perceived duty to lead or to shed a perceived stigmatised identity. The sense in which their landed class backgrounds helped or hindered their efforts to build political careers will then be examined. Finally, how they subjectively saw their political activism influencing their individual class transition prospects will be explored.

Embracing Political Activism

George O'Callaghan's early politics were staunchly unionist and defensive of the old landed order.[14] The only child of an east Clare landlord notorious in nationalist Ireland and beyond for the Bodyke evictions of June 1887, the young O'Callaghan attended Cheltenham College and Sandhurst before beginning a military career that culminated in him serving as the Clare Artillery's last colonel. In 1893 he inherited his maternal uncle's, Capt. Ralph Westropp's, estate at Coolreagh, Bodyke. Two years later, in compliance with Ralph's will, he changed his surname to O'Callaghan-Westropp by royal licence.

Convinced that a medley of agrarian, nationalist and state forces were threatening them with extinction, O'Callaghan-Westropp's 'class that goes to the wall' letter to the *Irish Times* in 1897 was intended to wake up 'the latent force of the vast mass of Irish landlordism which at present is sleeping itself to death'.[15] The Colonel would pay a heavy price for his pro-landlord activism. Writing to George P. Stewart of the Irish Landowners' Convention and Irish Land Trust in 1913, he revealed how

> For six years prior to 1903 I had been boycotted, not for any local or personal quarrel but entirely because of my position and acts on the Landlords' Executive Committee, and I had been repeatedly told that the Boycott would have been withdrawn if I left that Committee, which of course I did not do.[16]

Only when faced with compulsory purchase proceedings had the Colonel accepted the Congested Districts Board's (CDB) 'final offer' for Coolreagh. The 'price was so bad', he informed Lord Castlereagh

> that I had to let go my [*c.*550-acre] Coolreagh demesne and Home Farm as I could not afford to live there on the balance of the purchase money interest except as a common farmer.[17]

Besides accusing the CDB of paying deplorably low prices, he believed that its 'settled policy' was 'to clear Protestants and Unionists as far as possible out of counties within their jurisdiction'.[18] After selling Coolreagh, and taking up residence on his recently deceased father's Maryfort estate at nearby Lismehane in the summer of 1912, further bouts of agrarian trouble awaited him. All the while the Colonel's class transition from landlord to farmer was being smoothed by his long-standing practice of immersing himself in day-to-day farm management,[19] even to the point of being ready to toil alongside his men.[20]

David Fitzpatrick has suggested that O'Callaghan-Westropp's prominence as an IFU activist during the revolutionary period helped him make an 'idiosyncratic' transition from 'extreme Unionism to non-partisan Irishism'.[21] 'It is likely', Fitzpatrick further contends, 'that many former landlords entered the movement, like O'Callaghan, to escape from their past rather than to recapture their stranglehold over the unruly lower classes'.[22] Certainly O'Callaghan-Westropp's recognition of landlordism's defeat and his disenchantment with the Irish Landowners' Convention, of whose executive committee he was still an active if deeply disillusioned member, counted for much. Of greater significance were the Colonel's strongly developed sense of duty to lead the way forward and his desire to belong to a well-organised *dominant* class. With the landed class on its last legs, completing land purchase on acceptable terms and using the IFU to turn the new farmer-owners into a dominant class appeared to offer the best prospect of securing an acceptable future in a partitioned independent Ireland.[23] Such was the vision fundamentally informing O'Callaghan-Westropp's leadership.

Did the Colonel see the farmers he and the IFU wished to represent constituting a single class or multiple classes? His overriding desire was to project Irish farmers as a single economic class and he very much saw the IFU's work, in terms of building that sense of all-farmer solidarity, as integral to class formation itself. A well-organised politically conservative but economically progressive farmer-owner class would not just improve farming but would possess the vital power to steer state policy.

A number of pressing threats reinforced the Colonel's gravitation to the IFU. Rural labour's militant challenge—influenced by the Bolshevik revolution and wartime compulsory tillage regulations introduced in 1917—was observed with alarm within IFU governing circles.[24] Another source of perceived menace was excessive and misguided state intervention in agriculture. Here the Selborne Report's proposals to make some wartime agricultural regulations permanent were viewed, with consternation, as opening the door to unbridled dirigisme and creeping land nationalisation.[25] For its potential to undermine the Irish cattle economy, the proposed lifting of the United Kingdom's ban on the importation of Canadian store cattle was experienced as acutely unsettling.[26]

Unlike O'Callaghan-Westropp, the much younger Bobby Burke had never been immersed in unionist and landlord rearguard politics. What befell his south Galway family, and the conduct of his father, did nonetheless have a politicising effect on him. After his family were burned out of their south Galway family home, Ballydugan House,[27] in June 1922, Burke's mother went to live with her brother Cecil Henry at Toghermore House on the outskirts of the north Galway town of Tuam. Much of the Toghermore estate passed to her and Bobby on Cecil's death in 1923.

After leaving Cheltenham College in the early 1920s the young Burke served briefly as a commissioned lieutenant in the Royal Artillery at Woolwich.[28] In 1928 he began studying agronomy at the Harper-Adams Agricultural College in Shropshire; that training would serve him well at profit-sharing farming at Toghermore in 1930. Burke's father's agrarian troubles had not ceased with the destruction of Ballydugan House. Writing in June 1930 to his older brother St George, who was set to inherit the Ballydugan property, Bobby Burke remarked of their father:

> MHB [Michael Henry Burke] is very difficult to deal with. I also know that his attitude towards his employees, from what he has said to me for the past 6 years is, in my opinion, unchristian and selfish.[29]

'I think it quite possible', he continued:

> that if MHB had treated his employees & neighbours as well as Uncle Cecil his, that Ballydugan might never have been burnt down, nor the stock driven off lands etc.[30]

As much as his own class background, his father's 'unchristian and selfish' conduct and the persisting agrarian trouble at Ballydugan made a deep impression on him, some have seen an encounter with Christian Socialism in the early 1920s— while a pupil at Cheltenham College—as the really critical radicalising influence on the young Burke.[31] Certainly by the late 1920s he was publicly proclaiming his great faith in Christianity as a world-changing progressive force and his determination to live his life according to Christian precepts. This path saw him turning away from his family's world of gentry privilege to live a disciplined and frugal life, actively siding with the Irish working classes and marginalised minorities (such as Travellers), and using his access to inherited family land and wealth to finance social improvements.[32]

Soon after settling in Tuam, Burke was to acquire a national profile as a social justice activist. A new anti-slum campaign in Dublin, partly inspired by a letter of his proposing a new housing fund to commemorate the 1500th anniversary of St Patrick's landing in Ireland, helped inspire the 1931 Housing Act.[33] Burke's campaigning on the slum issue even attracted some attention in England. An interview he gave at this time sheds some light on his attitude towards 'Christian socialism'. 'The article in the "*Daily Express*"', he wrote to the *Tuam Herald* in August 1931,

> also referred to me as a 'Christian Socialist'. I would like to state that I have no inclination whatever to that form of Socialism which is anti-religious and which is condemned by His Holiness the Pope. My aim is to help to bring about the *Reconstruction of the Social Order* according to the teaching of *Jesus Christ* as advocated by His Holiness Pope Pius XI himself in His recent Encyclical Letter.[34]

By this time Burke's Christian radical reformism was being felt locally in his use of family wealth to help house Tuam's poor and to relieve the poverty of struggling smallholders.[35] All the while considerable time and effort were being spent on organising his local farming activity along cooperative lines. Frank Kelly, one of Burke's main campaign workers in the 1933 election, could instance the Toghermore farm, operated on the principle of fair shares for the workers with the profits evenly divided every three months, as evidence that 'Mr. Burke had done something that required remarkable courage for he had broken away from the tradition of his class'.[36]

Besides viewing it as a source of cheap milk, meat and firewood for Tuam's poor, Burke's desire for the 250-acre Toghermore farm was that it should become a model of cooperatively and intensively run profit-sharing farming capable of inspiring others to emulate it.[37] Burke's Labour Party activism became a vital means of advancing this ambitious project. As much as £1,000 of Burke's inheritance had been invested in improving the Toghermore Farm by 1933,[38] and in 1941 he could point to an estimated increase of 'at least ten per cent' in farming efficiency since the profit-sharing venture had begun.[39]

An early elaboration of how Christian values might inform a new class politics (and provide a vision underpinning Burke's leadership) was offered at a meeting to revive the Tuam branch of the Irish Labour Party in October 1932. Centred on securing fairness and justice for 'working men', this new politics would shun law-breaking and inciting class or party strife. The appalling and intolerable gap between wealth and poverty in society Burke ascribed to 'the financial system of the world, which should be altered'.[40] At the same time, he made it clear that he was not

> suggesting Bolshevism. I am suggesting a scientific system of social credit, which will enable the real wealth of this world to be distributed in fair proportion for every man to get a job and fair play. It is absolutely artificial the present state of unemployment and poverty.[41]

Nor could Burke see any reason

> why Catholic and Protestant should not unite in a cause like this: the point is, we are all Christians, but the present social system is not as it should be according to the Christian type. I think the greatest cause of Bolshevism is the selfishness of the rich, and the best way to prevent Bolshevism is to work together in the Christian spirit.[42]

In late 1932 Burke had yet to pledge himself formally to the Labour Party, but he contested his first of five general elections in January 1933 as a Labour Party candidate. By 1934, when he played a part in saving Labour from anti-Christian communism,[43] Burke had come to see the party as the most committed to achieving the sort of radical reform needed to establish a 'just and Christian social order' in Ireland.[44] Such reform would require a major redistribution of wealth. In view of the limits of appealing to the rich to live in harmony with Christian moral precepts, he saw state-directed planning and regulation as 'absolutely necessary in order to raise the real wages of the lower paid workers, control prices and limit profits'.[45]

Political Advances

O'Callaghan-Westropp's and Burke's political advances depended considerably on resources derived from their class and family backgrounds. It was the Colonel's wealth that gave him the freedom to devote substantial time to activism in the farming interest and that greatly facilitated him in becoming a leading light in the IFU. Besides being a founding member and president (1921–27) of the IFU's county branch in Clare—the Clare Farmers' Association (CFA)—the Colonel sat on the IFU's national executive and standing committees and served three terms as one of the union's vice-presidents. Unlike Burke, however, O'Callaghan-Westropp declined to contest general or local elections in the post-1921 period. His response to pressure to stand in the June election of 1927 was that

> It was my desire that the farmers' candidates should be men in the prime of life and more 'men *of* the people', even though they could not be more men *for* the people's real interests than I am.[46]

With an IFU membership of almost 100,000 members in 1922,[47] the Colonel had reason to hope that Irish farmers were on the way to becoming a powerful popular force and a well-organised economic class. And for a time after the Farmers' Party's formation as the IFU's political wing in 1921–2—a move he initially opposed for fear of divisive politicisation—he even dared dream that southern

Irish farmers might become a political class sufficiently powerful to out-compete nationalists at the polls and so clear the way for a more rational form of class politics in which purely economic considerations took precedence over all others. The beginnings of a farmers' state might even materialise were the organised farmers to win control of the Dáil and the county councils. The Colonel hoped such a state would use its power to counter persisting post-war slump conditions by imposing sufficient austerity to greatly reduce public spending and farmers' costs.[48]

Equally relevant to Bobby Burke's efforts to build an activist career were inherited wealth and a strong sense of civic and public duty. Failing to win a Dáil seat did not stop him attaining a national as well as local profile as a public man. From late 1933 until he left Ireland in 1950 he retained his membership of the Labour Party's Administrative Council.[49] Within the Labour Party Burke's commitment to Christian radical reformist principles made him a uniquely attractive individual. His internationalism would also contribute to his standing in the labour movement. Revulsion at the 'evil effects' of the First World War had made him a passionate advocate of peace and disarmament.[50] Viewing labour's cause as very much a global struggle, he believed that the Irish labour movement had much to learn from progressive politics overseas.[51]

Burke found the policy advances of Swedish social democracy, and even more so of New Zealand's Labour government between 1935 and 1938, particularly impressive. He saw developments in New Zealand as validating the progressive taxation and dirigiste policies he and the Labour Party were advocating in Ireland.[52] His late 1930s election campaigns emphasised how New Zealand farmers had recently benefited from 'guaranteed remunerative prices' for their produce and how agricultural workers enjoyed a guaranteed minimum wage of £2 (40s.) for a forty-eight-hour working week (as against 27s. for fifty-four hours in Ireland).[53]

Another facet of Burke's politics that some found highly attractive was his keen desire to work closely with Catholics in building a broad Christian front for progressive economic, political and civic change. In the strongly clericalist town of Tuam, we find him collaborating closely with one of the local curates, Fr Michael Hennelly, in seeking to advance working-class interests. He was attracted to Muintir na Tíre, once the St Jarlath's Guild began to function in the town in 1939, because it enabled civic-minded Catholics and Protestants to work together in pursuit of the common good.[54] Burke went to considerable lengths to accommodate his politics to the Catholicism that was so pervasive in Irish society. He regularly emphasised how compatible his own Christian radical reformist principles were with Catholic social teaching, particularly as set forth in the papal encyclical *Quadragesimo Anno* of 1931.[55] The strongly communitarian character of Burke's class politics was also in harmony with the underlying tenor of social Catholicism. While constantly criticising the yawning gap between rich and poor, Burke's ultimate inclination was to think—as can be seen in his frequent references to 'the common good' and in his desire to avoid divisive class conflicts—as much in community as in class terms.

As a Protestant active in politics, Burke was mindful of Catholic sensitivities. He was apparently silent in his public life in the west on the way in which a whole series of laws—outlawing the availability of divorce, the importation of artificial contraceptives and imposing censorship—was heavily restricting liberal freedoms. While frequently and fearlessly traducing capitalism for its class-based inequities, Burke apparently avoided identifying himself publicly as a 'socialist' or even a 'Christian socialist' in north Galway.[56] Neither 'socialist' nor 'socialism' featured as terms in his local political lexicon. Of course, he was by no means unusual in this respect. Equally for Paddy Bergin, who became the Labour Party's national organiser in 1949–50, the word 'socialism' was taboo in rural Ireland during this period.[57]

Burke's best general election result came in 1943 when—after heading the poll in the Tuam district in the previous year's local elections—he polled 5,029 first preference votes (.56 of the quota) and had accumulated 5,756 votes by the final count.[58] Although failing again to win a seat in the new three-seat Galway North constituency in 1948,[59] Burke was elected in that year to the Seanad on the agricultural panel.[60]

Political Reverses

To what degree can the reverses the Colonel and Burke experienced in their public lives be attributed to their gentry class backgrounds?

By late 1927 O'Callaghan-Westropp's ambitious scenario of farmer political dominance lay in ruins. The Farmers' Party, in the June and September elections of 1927, had lost nine of its fifteen Dáil seats; in that same year the Clare Farmers' Association collapsed. The Colonel explained these calamities as due to rampant membership apathy and regular factional infighting within the IFU, its inability to control its political wing, the ineffectualness of sections of the IFU's and Farmers' Party's top leadership, the Farmers' Party's loss of independence following its coalition with Cumann na nGaedheal after the September 1927 election and the fundamentally changed political landscape the organised farmers faced with Fianna Fáil's rise as a political force.

He did not count his own landed class background, and that of some other prominent IFU members, among the organised farmers' difficulties. Others, however, took a different view. From early on, the IFU's Labour critics had criticised it for being merely 'a front for the Irish Unionist Alliance and Irish Landowners' Convention'.[61] Certainly some of the IFU's debilitating factionalism stemmed from the presence of ex-landlords in its top leadership. In a Dáil speech in 1923 the Farmer's Party first leader, Denis Gorey, said that:

> the Farmers' Union in those days [*c.*1920] was a Landlords' union led by a landlord, Colonel O'Callaghan Westropp, and backed by landlords' men in the union. They were kicked out of it and then we formed the Unpurchased Tenants' Organisation. They did not represent the unpurchased tenants and never acted for them.[62]

Before long, Gorey felt obliged to clarify and retract this statement and to acknowledge publicly that Col. O'Callaghan-Westropp 'occupies a respected position' in the IFU.[63] Again in 1927, however, we find Gorey describing leading ex-gentry IFU figures such as O'Callaghan-Westropp and Sir John Keane as members of an 'old gang' of Irish landlords and ex-landlords.[64] Nor, apparently, was Gorey acting alone here. 'The process', O'Callaghan-Westropp wrote in 1929,

> began with a steady undermining of all members of character and independence, and the masks were thrown off in the

> campaign against 'The Six Colonels' which followed the Congress of April 1927. It had gone on for five years and was simplified by the many counties which fell out.[65]

Gorey's attacks resonated with the view within Fianna Fáil of the Farmers' Party as 'a party of landlords and ranchers' that could never be depended on to represent the interests of small farmers.[66] In the highly competitive electoral sphere Fianna Fáil's 'small man' populism directly challenged the Colonel's ideal of farmers constituting a single all-embracing economic class capable of forging a new class-based politics. By the late 1920s the Colonel had to accept that the earlier prospect of farmers emerging as a dominant political class had now dissolved in the face of the increasing polarisation of Irish politics around the Treaty/Civil War split,[67] and the pressure on the organised farmers to support Cumann na nGaedheal once Fianna Fáil entered the Dáil in August 1927.

Did Bobby Burke's landed background contribute to his inability to win a Dáil seat? Just as Burke was advantaged politically to some degree by his open rejection of his gentry background, he equally found it impossible to draw a veil over his social origins. Along with having an Anglo-Irish Protestant landed background, Burke initially had to contend as well with his father's unpopularity in south Galway. Speaking on Burke's behalf in Loughrea during the 1933 election campaign, Frank Kelly declared:

> He knew well that in the town of Loughrea Bobby Burke's father was not a friend of the workers, but the sins of the father must not be put upon the shoulders of the son (hear, hear).[68]

Compared with T.J. O'Connell and Gilbert Lynch—each a union official who had won a Labour seat in Galway in the 1920s—Burke's political career was not helped by his lacking strong roots in the trade union movement. Neither was the relatively small size of the paid farm labourer class in Galway—an important strand of rural Labour's electoral support nationally[69]—to his benefit politically.

Despite his cleaner break with his gentry background,[70] Burke's detractors were quick to single out his gentry origins, his conception of 'Irish Freedom',[71] his religion and his hostility to capitalism as telling markers of negative identity. Fianna Fáil's immense political strength, based in part on the anti-colonial and anti-landlord political identity it cultivated for itself, was something Burke had always to battle against. At the point he entered politics in late 1932, Fianna Fáil had already become (with Labour Party support) a ruling party. Along with his Labour Party colleagues,[72] Burke found himself advocating many of the same policies—slum clearance, import-substituting industrialisation, welfare reform, expanded tillage agriculture and land division—that Fianna Fáil in power was determined to advance. Very likely Burke, in view of the party's formidable electoral strength in north Galway, and the siting of one of Fianna Fáil's new sugar factories in Tuam in 1934, felt Fianna Fáil's eclipsing effect on the Labour Party more than most.

Another disadvantage flowing from Fianna Fáil rule was that Burke's Dáil constituency had effectively lost a seat, so as to return unopposed the Ceann Comhairle, Frank Fahy.[73] Nor did Fianna Fáil's reduction of larger constituencies—that left it 'more difficult for minority interests to gain seats'—do Burke any favours.[74] Besides Fianna Fáil, Burke had to compete electorally with Clann na Talmhan from the early 1940s,[75] and with Clann na Poblachta from a little later on. Increasingly seeing it as hostile to his Christian radical reformist political project,[76] it was to be expected that Burke's challenge to Fianna Fáil's dominance in Galway would evoke a sharp response.[77] In 1942 Mark Killilea, TD, along with questioning Burke's truthfulness, accused him of proposing actions (relating to housing and wages) that could only pile more taxation on the embattled ratepayer.[78] Killilea also claimed to know 'more about the worker' and to be 'more in favour of the worker than Mr. Burke, because I come from the small farming class and I worked for my day's wages and he didn't have to'.[79] Nor was Killilea impressed by Burke's internationalism. 'Talking of New Zealand', he declared confidently, 'will never give bread to the worker and everybody knows we have not the same resources, mineral and otherwise, as New Zealand'.[80]

In response to another Fianna Fáil critic who castigated him for having 'the same "outlook" with regard to Britain' as his forbears, Burke pointed out how 'my outlook on this and on many other matters is very different from that of my ancestors'.[81] Burke's Protestantism—easily linked by his enemies to his class background—has also to be numbered among his political handicaps. The lengths he went to in accommodating his politics to Catholic social teaching never brought anything like full social acceptance or inclusion.[82] Indeed, from early on his efforts to improve the lot of Tuam's poor attracted the charge of proselytism. In late 1930 he felt compelled to write to the local press to deny rumours that he was paying 'money to Catholics in Tuam to induce them to send their children to the Protestant School'.[83] Two years later a proselytising intent was detected behind his local house-building activities.[84]

Some of Burke's political enemies—despite his strongly Christian and anti-Bolshevist stances—were quick to dub him a communist or even a 'Protestant communist'.[85] As soon as he resolved to contest elections, it appears that

> the whispering and vilification started in earnest, mainly by the two main political parties of the time and, of course, the more well-to-do professional and business people. It was whispered that Bobby Burke had communist tendencies and, if elected, would cause a lot of trouble organising workers etc.[86]

As well as the strong economic case to be made in its favour, one of the great advantages of co-operatively organised large-scale farming over small-scale private farming, as Burke argued in a Seanad debate in 1950, was that it was a more morally desirable form of agriculture and more 'in accordance with Christian principles that people should be encouraged to work together for the common good and to help each other'.[87] For all that, Burke's proposal to have the state test large-scale co-operative farming's potential experimentally could (despite having the backing of his own parliamentary party) muster but negligible support from inter-party Seanad colleagues.[88] Not only did his championing of large-scale agriculture, organised along profit-sharing and co-operative lines, set him at odds with deeply held commitments to the private ownership of land and family farming,[89] but it also brought him into headlong conflict with nationalist 'small man' agrarian populism and its policies of dividing and redistributing land. At a time of heightened 'red scare' hysteria in the 1930s, the anti-capitalist critique informing Burke's agricultural and labour activism exposed him to repeated bouts of red-baiting.

Subjective Responses

How did O'Callaghan-Westropp and Burke view their political reverses as impacting on their prospects for class transition? To answer this question we can ask whether they regarded their own farming efforts, and their attempts to improve Irish farming more generally, as a success. Convinced that wetter and cooler growing seasons had undermined the prospects for commercial tillage in western Ireland, the Colonel had always been content to raise store cattle on his Lismehane demesne and other rented land (about 400 acres in 1927). The high cost of wage-labour was another perceived obstacle to commercial tillage.[90]

Long before the Economic War with Britain (1932–38) the Colonel had felt obliged to conclude that the IFU, the Farmers' Party and the ruling Cosgrave party had all proved largely powerless to prevent a ruinous fall in Irish farming incomes. His bleak assessment, in the spring of 1932, was

> that farming in the Irish Free State has for ten years been conducted at a loss, that many farmers have lost their all in it and their lands are unstocked, that many have heavy overdrafts, that many also can no longer stock their lands and their neighbours have in past years suffered heavily in taking such lands for grazing, and in the present season are afraid to do so.[91]

It was understandable, given how much he tied his own farming fortunes with those of Irish farmers more generally, that the Colonel should take the CFA's and IFU's progressive degeneration very hard. Not alone was his own farming steadily sinking economically, but gone was the chance of turning Irish farmers into an economically and politically dominant class. Immediately after the CFA's collapse in 1927, he wrote to its organising secretary:

> I am dying a heart broken man: I thought to have helped save Ireland through her farmers; I have lived to see both accursed and hastening blindly to perdition.[92]

Again in 1930, he wrote gloomily to Conor Hogan:

> You were my trusted companion and lieutenant in the eight years of my life which I wasted, along with much of my private fortune, on trying to get that most hopeless class to take its own part! People who won't get together for their own mutual protection, and won't be educated in self defence, have to take what's coming to them, and remain at the mercy of every glib rogue and charlatan.[93]

The Colonel's sense of inclusion within the IFU may have long been challenged by those who saw him as a former landlord and landlords' man, but it would seem that Fianna Fáil's political triumph hurt him more than the gentry-bashing antics of Denis Gorey and his ilk. It signified that the prolonged post-war depression in agriculture was not just set to continue but to reach new depths. Under early Fianna Fáil rule, with its championing of increased tillage and its anti-cattle rhetoric, the Colonel feared that things were about to get appreciably worse for big farmers like himself. A letter he penned in October 1932 outlined how

> the position of medium and larger farmers who employ labour and in normal times buy young cattle from the small farmers, is now so serious that reticence may mean that most of us will be wiped out, possibly inadvertently, before the government realises what it is doing, in which case the sum of rural poverty in the Free State will be increased beyond repair.[94]

He went on to ask

> If the intention ... is to clear out of the Free State those of us who stuck to our country in spite of the terror and burnings of ten years ago, it would be less inhuman to put us out of pain quickly rather than the slow torment and ultimate ruin of farming under impossible conditions.[95]

The Colonel's class anxieties as a farmer were not solely the consequence of depressed markets and Fianna Fáil's early preference for tillage over cattle farming. The sporadic low-level intimidation he experienced at Lismehane in the 1920s took the form of interference with his farm carts, the knocking of walls and the deliberate trespassing of animals on his land. Lismehane House, he feared, would be highly vulnerable were he to absent himself from it for any extended length. In late December 1928 he confided to a close friend:

> My doctor wanted me to winter in the West Indies but, if I did, this place would be looted from end to end like Ballinahinch only two miles away—so much for the restoration of order! Believe me those who struck down Kevin O'Higgins knew well what they were doing, for he was the great shield against Bolshevism in all its forms.[96]

Under the cumulative pressure of the decline of his own farming and Irish agriculture more generally, the disintegration of the IFU and the Farmers' Party and the likelihood that political and economic instability were set to hit new heights under Fianna Fáil,[97] the Colonel (at least in corresponding with those he could trust) was ready to question whether self-government might even be beyond the southern Irish. We find him in August 1932 commending Senator Andrew Jameson for his struggle in the Senate

> to put a brake on Ireland's descent into Avernum, the fear of which in the past sent so many of us, with little taste or leisure for Politics, into the Unionist ranks. Today our justification is complete, for in my reading of history, no country has ever so mercilessly demonstrated its unfitness for self-government. You need not go beyond our last General Election, which returned the largest party, naked and not ashamed, for Perjury, Robbery and armed violence.[98]

'I have', he continued,

> too much experience of the fate of 'England's Friends' to desire any British intervention, and when the republic's [*sic*] next civil war breaks out on the six county frontier that will have to occur. I do not want to be legislated into a freak international bastard with Dago and Bolshevic traits.[99]

Even before the traumas of 1932, the Colonel's reluctance to make anything like a clean break from his previous class and political loyalties complicates any discussion of his personal class transition and his activism in the farming interest. His break with the old order, to judge by his private correspondence, was to be neither swift nor final. Throughout the 1920s he remained committed to preserving (or even adding to) old agrarian and political loyalties. He continued in his honorary role as aide-de-camp to the king, becoming a stalwart of the British Legion in Clare, remaining a member of the largely defunct Irish Landowners' Convention's executive committee, lamenting the decline of the landed class to gentry friends,[100] keeping up his membership of the Kildare Street Club, sending his son to an English public school,[101] recording the terror directed at the houses of the Clare gentry during what he called 'our two mad civil wars'[102] and preferring in some of his IFU work to be addressed by his military title.[103] On occasion, citing economic or health reasons, he made it known that he was thinking of leaving Ireland forever.[104]

Another indication of the Colonel's unease under the new dispensation is found in his analysis that the South's loss of membership of a powerful empire could only be enormously limiting on a poor agricultural state's capacity to provide public services. Still, none of this was to stop him from occasionally giving voice to economic nationalist sentiments that linked Ireland's agricultural difficulties to English trade policy.[105] Nor did it discourage him from developing a keen interest in his noble Gaelic ancestry that ultimately led him to assert an ill-fated claim to be officially recognised as 'The O'Callaghan'.[106]

Compared to the Colonel, Bobby Burke had cut his cables more definitively with the old order. Inclined to optimism as a rule, he tended to read his little advances (both in his farming and in his politics) as positive signs that boded well for a brighter future. Of course, the Labour Party—however small and volatile its electoral support and however fractious its parliamentary party—never suffered the decline and disappearance that was to be the lot of the IFU and the Farmers' Party. In contrast to the Colonel's growing disenchantment within the IFU, Burke appears to have continued to feel accepted into, and to have found genuine comradeship inside, the Labour Party.

Given the centrality of farming to his own class transition, how did Burke evaluate the position of Irish agriculture more generally? One of his abiding concerns was to tackle persisting agricultural crisis conditions. Shortly before the war began in 1939 he estimated that even up-to-date and hard-working farmers would really struggle to make 'an average income of thirty shillings a week' (compared to the 'very low' statutory minimum weekly wage of twenty-seven shillings then being paid to agricultural labourers). Speaking personally he revealed how his own

> remuneration (per hour worked) has been for several years actually less than I pay to agricultural labourers on our farm . . . I know, therefore, from personal experience what it is like to work very long hours and to receive a very small remuneration for my labour.[107]

In May 1950 Bobby Burke announced that with his wife Ann he was soon to depart Ireland to commence Christian development work in Nigeria. Was it, as Andrée Sheehy Skeffington suggests,[108] disillusion with party infighting and 'sectarian animosities' that caused him to leave? It is difficult to say for sure. We know that Burke was generally sanguine in public about the Labour Party's participation in the first inter-party government. He had, however, experienced defeat in five general elections and the outcome of the 1950 Seanad debate on co-operative farming is likely to have been experienced as a serious reverse. With almost twenty years devoted to Christian radical reformist activism in his native land, Burke was ready for a change. 'I feel', he told a reporter in June 1950, 'I can do better work in Africa than in Ireland'.[109]

Conclusion

How well did O'Callaghan-Westropp's and Burke's political activism facilitate their transition out of the gentry and into the farmer class? How close did their experience come to the inclusionist and exclusionist imagined futures introduced earlier? At the very least the activist careers of O'Callaghan-Westropp and Burke—one positioned broadly on the Right and the other on the Left—highlight the complexities of transition politics and the challenges of generalising more widely from our two cases. Their activism can nonetheless be viewed as necessarily being played out between the poles of objectivity, where initial political involvements, advances and reverses are concerned, and subjectivity, when their personal assessments of what actually transpired are considered.

The Colonel's pessimism about the future of Irish farming and his part in it was palpable by the early 1930s. Eventually he would see Lismehane pass to his Oxford-educated only son to be farmed (as it turned out) for one last generation as family land. Although he wouldn't live to see it, his early dream of seeing farmers become a powerfully organised economic—as against political—class actually did begin to be realised with the formation of the National Farmers' Association in the 1950s.[110]

Compared with the Colonel, Burke always found himself in transition to a more anomalous class position by virtue of his advocacy of large-scale co-operatively organised farming and his greater identification with struggling smallholders and farm labourers than with strong farmers. Burke, to go by his Seanad speech of 1950, believed that co-operative farming at Toghermore had made notable advances. The Toghermore co-operative experience, however, didn't in the end inspire followers sufficient to lay the foundation of a tradition that could be built upon. After his departure for Africa, the co-operative agricultural venture at Toghermore soon vanished to be replaced by private farming on a small scale.

In so far as O'Callaghan-Westropp's and Burke's contrasting visions of class politics (and versions of leadership) were closely integrated with their farming activity, political engagement became intrinsic to their respective class transitions. At times each one did make significant headway and did acquire some sense of belonging in Irish society on the basis of his activism, all of which accords with our inclusionist imagined future. Our two activists' initial political involvements would appear to have been inspired more by a perceived duty to lead and to get to grips with contemporary threats than to transcend what some might regard to be inherited stigmatised gentry identities. And far from a landed class background being an obstacle to our two activists' emergence as public men, their class backgrounds did become a valuable asset up to a point. At the same time, having gentry social origins could unleash exclusionary impulses, contributing to factionalism within the IFU (in the Colonel's case) and adding an extra sharpness to the competition between Fianna Fáil and the Labour Party (in Burke's case).

Some exclusionary consequences would also follow the ultimate failure of O'Callaghan-Westropp's and Burke's major projects in public life. By the early 1930s O'Callaghan-Westropp had reluctantly to accept, in light of the new farmer-owners' failure to use the IFU and the Farmers' Party to realise their potential to become a well-organised economic and political class, that his desire to belong to a new dominant farmer class was not to be fulfilled anytime soon. Here the Colonel's pessimistic subjective assessment stands very much at odds with the academic views that farmers constituted a dominant class or classes in early post-independence Ireland.[111] His perceived reality was one in which the new farmer-owners were fast joining the gentry as a chronically divided class whose capacity to exert collective control over the forces accounting for their progressive subordination was visibly waning.

For all Bobby Burke's desire to pursue an inclusive Christian radical reformist politics, joining the Labour Party had inevitably meant taking sides, defining himself politically in opposition to others and finding himself fighting (mostly) losing electoral battles against more powerful party rivals. Just being a Protestant in the context he found himself in—as the accusations of proselytism in particular highlight—was viewed by some as also taking sides and as someone to be opposed and excluded purely on that account. In spite of subjectively feeling a more secure sense of belonging in Ireland on the strength of his co-operative farming and his Labour Party and civic activism, Burke was ultimately to see his Christian radical reformist project fail emphatically. He was the one to give up co-operative farming and to leave Ireland altogether. It soon became evident that there was no popular constituency ready to keep alive his distinctive version of Christian radical reformist politics in north Galway or beyond. The county council seat he won in 1942 (and retained in 1945) was lost in 1950; it would be 1969 before the Labour Party contested his Dáil constituency again.[112]

For all their differences, both O'Callaghan-Westropp's and Burke's visions of class politics (and their attempts to negotiate their individual class transitions politically) came up against what proved to be a major insurmountable obstacle. This obstacle derived its complex character from that powerful mix of ethnic (as against civic) nationalism and 'small man' agrarian populism, which the early Fianna Fáil—both before and after becoming a ruling party—used to such electoral effect to woo small-farmer and working-class support.

Ultimately, the different class politics pursued by O'Callaghan-Westropp and Burke failed to become a comparable popular force, capable of swaying the masses emotionally as well as materially, and of building class-based conceptions of Irish identity—and notions of imagined political community—that could compete with those being projected by Fianna Fáil. On top of this Burke found himself having to function, outside and even inside the Labour Party,[113] in a decolonising, overwhelmingly Catholic country where 'Christian' was regularly equated with 'Protestant' and where moral panics born of 'red scare' hysteria proliferated as the prolonged Spanish crisis of the 1930s slowly reached its climax.

CHAPTER SEVEN

Ostriches and Tricolours: Trinity College Dublin and the Irish State, 1922–45

TOMÁS IRISH

Introduction

In December 1922 a contributor to *T.C.D.: a College Miscellany* wrote that 'the bald fact remains that Trinity College is not doing its duty to the country in the present renaissance'. Trinity, he claimed, 'still looks back to the past with longing, and like the ostrich hides its head that it may not see what is going on around it'.[1] This letter described a dilemma which faced many Protestant ex-unionists in the period after 1922: should they engage with the new state even if they agreed neither with its foundation nor its ethos, or should they remain aloof from both its practical day-to-day workings as well as its ideological underpinnings? For the students and staff of Trinity College Dublin, this tension, between acceptance of and participation in the Free State on the one hand and intellectual and emotional disconnectedness from it on the other, was a defining feature of the 1920s and 1930s.

Trinity College Dublin faced an acute crisis of identity in the decades following the establishment of the Free State. Simply stated, independence fundamentally threatened the shared identity which had developed at Trinity over the nineteenth century. By the turn of the twentieth, Trinity was synonymous with unionism, Protestantism (particularly Anglicanism) and cultural Britishness, perhaps more than any other institution in Ireland. The university was founded in 1592 as part of the English administration's attempt to enforce the Protestant reformation in Ireland and did not admit Catholics to study for the first time until 1793. In 1873, Fawcett's Act removed religious requirements for the holding of a fellowship or scholarship, meaning that Catholics could, for the first time, become full members of the college.[2] However, the population of the university remained strongly Anglican until the outbreak of the First World War, with around 80 per cent of students belonging to the Church of Ireland and ten per cent being Catholic around the turn of the century.[3]

By the early 1900s, Trinity (and Protestant) domination of higher education in Ireland led to the emergence of a Catholic-led movement to bring about the establishment of an equivalent university for Catholics in Ireland. The Royal University had catered to Catholic students since 1879 but was an examining body only and did not offer collegiate life like Trinity.[4] The Catholic movement resulted in the creation of the National University of Ireland in 1908. Part of this discourse was the desire of Irish cultural nationalists to revive the Irish language, a movement to which Trinity was frequently resistant. It did have a chair of Irish—established in 1838—but this had been founded to expand the influence of the Church of Ireland in Irish-speaking communities and the chair was attached to the Divinity School.[5] In general, Trinity was seen as hostile to the claims of Irish nationhood and returned unionist MPs to Westminster with regularity. Of these, Sir Edward Carson was the most prominent, although his increasing alignment with an Ulster unionist position began to trouble many at TCD—southern unionists and a growing number of Home Rulers—around 1912.[6] However, despite being the institution that educated Wolfe Tone and Robert Emmet, there was virtually no support for radical nationalism in the years before the outbreak of the First World War.

Trinity was perceived by wider Irish society in a variety of ways. Writing in 1904, William MacNeile Dixon argued that it was 'a loved and hated institution, as only institutions which are held to have a political complexion can be loved and hated'.[7] Trinity was often cited in publications as an example of what nationalists and Catholics railed against but aspired towards. It was a site of religious, educational, cultural and political ascendancy and held much symbolic value for this reason. Nationalist publications, such as the vituperative *Leader*, frequently emphasised its Protestant, 'bigoted' and 'parochial' attitudes.[8] The community of students, staff and alumni who passed through the college saw themselves as Irish, albeit with a strong cultural and political affinity with Britain. A great number of elements constituted the complex Trinity identity; while not applicable to all students, Protestantism and unionism were very important parts of this, as was living, studying, playing sport and socialising together. Trinity's privileged position in Irish society—and the attacks from outside that it provoked—were also important in galvanising a shared university identity.

Historians have argued that Trinity simply retreated inwards after 1922. F.S.L. Lyons claimed that the community within Trinity, much like ex-unionists elsewhere, felt intense self-consciousness and that TCD constituted a ghetto in the new state.[9] R.B. McDowell argued that from 1922 Trinity became 'an intellectual and social enclave in Dublin'.[10] While this may have been apparent from the outside, the analyses of Lyons and McDowell do not capture the often fractious debates about how Trinity might adapt itself to the new political reality. While it is difficult to generalise about collective identity, one thing is clear: the advent of Irish independence in 1922 initiated a period of deep introspection about what Trinity should be. This chapter will look at some of the initiatives undertaken by the university to align itself with the new state and the debates among students about what Trinity ought to be. It will conclude by looking at how the memory of the First World War further complicated Trinity's position in the new Ireland.

Relations between University and State

At an official level, Trinity had an ambiguous relationship with the new state. On the one hand, the board of the university passed a resolution in support of the Treaty in December 1921.[11] The university was also given four TDs in the Dáil to replace the two MPs who had formerly represented Trinity at Westminster (reduced to three in 1923). However, the university also suffered a significant financial shortfall as a result of the establishment of the Free State, as the British government had promised an annual grant of

£30,000 for the university following a Royal Commission of 1920. Following its establishment, the Free State government was in no position—financially or emotionally—to honour this commitment, seeing Trinity as the university of Protestantism and unionism and favouring, instead, the claims of University College Dublin, alma mater of many of the revolutionaries of 1916.[12] Indeed, it was not until after the Second World War that Trinity first received a grant from the Irish state. The 1920s and 1930s, then, were marked by cautious accommodation and mutual mistrust.

That said, Trinity's parliamentary representatives in the new state took their work seriously and quickly developed a reputation as diligent and trustworthy figures. The four chosen were non-political figures who each represented an important element of a Trinity education: Ernest Alton (a classicist), William Thrift (a physicist), Gerald Fitzgibbon (a barrister) and James Craig (a medical doctor). The backgrounds of these four men covered the arts and the sciences as well as two of Trinity's most important professional schools. Interestingly, both Fitzgibbon and Alton were veterans of 1916 who had helped the university's Officer Training Corps defend the university against a potential attack during the Rising. More pertinently, two of the TDs from this period, Thrift and Alton, would subsequently become provosts of Trinity, continuing co-operation born in the Dáil at a higher level.

The active participation of Trinity's TDs in the Dáil did not mean that they necessarily felt empathy with the Free State. However, Trinity's parliamentary representatives were important in quietly building good relationships between the rulers of independent Ireland and its oldest cultural institution. While Fitzgibbon would write in 1923 that 'I hate political life more and more every day', he also claimed that himself and W.T. Cosgrave—president of the Executive Council—were 'as thick as thieves'.[13] William Thrift's work was held in high esteem too. Michael McDunphy, a senior civil servant and later secretary to President Douglas Hyde, said of Thrift that 'although representing what might be regarded as the British tradition in Ireland he has since the inception of the new State in 1922 been extremely helpful in the building up of it, and has proved himself to be an Irish citizen in the truest sense'.[14] In conversations with Hyde, Thrift made the case that once the decision had been taken for Trinity to support the Treaty, 'he and his colleagues had made up their minds, once that step was taken, to throw in their lot wholly with the Irish nation' but that they could not be expected to 'sympathise with the revolutionary movement' which led to the establishment of the state.[15] In the aggregate, the work of Trinity's TDs served to establish a gradual trust between government and university, and this was important in the uncertain decades of the 1920s and 1930s.

Ceremonials

The files kept by Michael McDunphy for President Hyde at the end of the 1930s demonstrate the extent to which senior civil servants suspected that Trinity was not fully committed to the new state, either in terms of politics or sentiment. One file, entitled 'Trinity College Dublin: Anti-National Outlook', made this plain. It stated that 'the acceptance of the new order in Ireland by Trinity College was confined . . . to external action' while claiming that an 'attachment to British traditions remained'.[16] Trinity's public symbols of allegiance painted a complex picture, as the college flew the Union flag, the King was toasted at official functions, and 'God Save the King' was played at most official events until the outbreak of the Second World War in 1939.[17]

The ongoing prominence of British symbols at Trinity placed the university in a difficult position. It was an issue that was raised with Trinity's TDs by their compatriots at Leinster House. As early as 1925 Thrift raised the issue at a meeting of the board and it was resolved that for future ceremonials, three flags would be flown from the front of the university: the Union Jack, the flag of the Free State and the college flag.[18] However, the years that followed demonstrated how difficult it was for the university to plot a course between the new regime, on the one hand, and its accumulated traditions on the other. The university made a number of gestures to the Irish government. One of the ways in which it did this was through ceremonials, either by bestowing honorary degrees on 'national' figures or by inviting government representatives to the university for symbolic events. Ceremonials such as the awarding of honorary degrees played an important part in publicly expressing what the university claimed to stand for and where its allegiances lay. In this way they helped to create better relations between university and state by honouring individuals who were politically influential while disseminating a carefully constructed message to a wider audience.

Before 1914, Trinity tended to award honorary degrees to scholars of international eminence, those long associated with the university, or British political figures. This changed after 1922. While the university continued to honour scholars and eminent Trinity figures, it also began to celebrate men associated with Irish nationalism. These latter were usually figures associated with cultural nationalism or were political representatives of the new regime. Between 1922 and 1924, the poet W.B. Yeats, the Celtic philologist R.I. Best and the veteran Home Rule politician (and Governor General) Tim Healy were all honoured.[19] In 1928, Eoin MacNeill was given a D.Litt. Sir Robert Tate's oration for MacNeill lauded his scholarship, describing him as 'one of the brightest lights of our sister university in Dublin' and 'an illustrious man who has served his country so well'.[20] The theme continued in 1933 when Douglas Hyde, founder of the Gaelic League, was awarded a D.Litt; Hyde was already a Trinity graduate.[21]

While the university was beginning to recognise figures associated with Irish nationalism, it also honoured unionists and imperialists. Among those given honorary degrees in this period were Viscount Bryce, the earl of Birkenhead and the earl of Midleton.[22] However, the most symbolic of all of these—which demonstrated how ceremonials could simultaneously convey multiple messages—was the award of an honorary degree to W.T. Cosgrave in 1926. This ceremony came in the aftermath of the London Imperial Conference of 1926, where the British Commonwealth was established on the premise that Britain's dominions—including Ireland—would enjoy autonomous status within the British empire and would not be subordinate to the United Kingdom. For Trinity, the ceremony accommodated both the new and old regimes.

Cosgrave was not alone in receiving an honorary degree that day; W.S. Monroe, the Prime Minister of Newfoundland, was honoured at the same event, suggesting that the ceremony was presented as an imperial one. Tate's oration described Cosgrave as 'a man of undoubted vigour and courage' who had 'stood up to vindicate the laws and promote freedom' and 'established solid foundations for long-lasting concord'.[23] The ceremony was full of meaningful but contradictory symbolism. Cosgrave signed his name into the Proctor's Roll in Irish before he and Monroe left the theatre to the strains of the imperial anthem, 'God Save the King'.[24]

Cosgrave's speech expressed respect for the institution and the empire, as well as Irish freedom. He described Trinity's influence on the events leading to independence. He argued that Trinity had 'sent forth so many great Irishmen to work in the cause of their country' who had 'begot an honourable tradition which has no small part in inspiring the various movements which have so happily terminated in the political emancipation of our country'.[25] It was clear that Cosgrave saw the event as a celebration of Irish freedom, while Trinity saw it as a celebration of continued imperial affinity. He returned to Trinity the following year to speak to the Historical Society[26] and came back again in 1928—his third visit in three years—for the bicentenary celebrations of the birth of Edmund Burke and Oliver Goldsmith.[27]

The work of Trinity's TDs and the gestures made in ceremonials to the leaders of the Free State ensured that, while there was never great affection between the state and the university, and while the state had neither resources nor inclination to back the institution financially, a solid working relationship had developed by the late 1920s. This became apparent in instances where the state inherited responsibilities from the old regime, such as in 1927 when the question of appointing a new provost arose on the death of John Henry Bernard. Prior to 1922, the appointment of the provost had, by college statute, rested with the crown and was usually approved by the prime minister. In 1927, Attorney General John A. Costello ruled that the appointment should be made by the 'Governor General on the advice of the Executive Council'.[28] While relations were respectful, there was still a fear amongst some members of the college community that Cosgrave's government could make its own appointment from outside in order to 'Gaelicise' the institution.[29]

Ultimately, the appointment passed without issue. The board of Trinity proposed—and the Executive Council of the Free State approved—the appointment of Edward J. Gwynn.[30] Gwynn's promotion was an act of mutual accommodation. He had distinguished himself as one of the foremost Celtic scholars of the period and, in the words of R.B. McDowell and D.A. Webb, 'his academic reputation served to some extent as a lightning-conductor against attacks on the college as "un-Irish"'.[31] However, Gwynn viewed his Irish scholarship purely as an academic endeavour and remained indifferent to the use of Irish as a modern vernacular.

The establishment of good working relations did not mean that tensions over symbolism disappeared. In 1929 there was a controversy involving the annual College Races. These were to be attended by James MacNeill, then Governor General. At a similar event at Trinity in 1928, MacNeill's entrance had been heralded by the playing of 'God Save the King' and MacNeill was anxious that this not be repeated when he attended in 1929. The Cosgrave government had ruled that the national anthem for occasions such as this should be 'A Soldier's Song'.[32] The board of Trinity wrote to MacNeill to explain that custom was to play 'God Save the King' but, if he wished, no anthem would greet his arrival.[33] This caused MacNeill to cancel his visit and caused the university much embarrassment, demonstrating that the course it sought to chart between the new state and the old union was precarious.

Éamon de Valera, leader of the anti-Treaty Fianna Fáil party, also visited Trinity for the first time as a politician in 1929. Invited by the college Gaelic Society, he spoke of the legacy of Trinity alumnus Thomas Davis, expressing his wish that the university would honour him on the centenary of his birth.[34] In 1930 Davis was the subject of a Trinity Monday discourse, the first such occasion where a nationalist figure had been honoured in this way by the university. In his lecture, Bolton Waller identified Davis as the inspiration behind many contemporary national developments and described a 'long lasting and continuous' nationalist tradition at Trinity.[35] He also claimed that an Ireland where the religious minority was 'ignored or merely tolerated' would be despised by Davis.[36]

Student Attitudes

Commentary in student newspapers reflected this sense of conflicted identity in the 1920s and became more pronounced as the decade progressed. Student demographics at Trinity remained much as they had been before 1912: the student population remained overwhelmingly Protestant. In the 1920s, Catholics accounted for over twenty per cent of the student population before declining again in the 1930s.[37] The university remained the preserve of primarily Anglican students drawn from across the island of Ireland. It was not until the early 1970s that this demographic composition was transformed.[38] The principal student newspaper was *T.C.D.: A College Miscellany*, which had traditionally claimed not to deal with political issues, but had been forced to engage with them with regularity since 1912. *T.C.D.* tended to give voice to the elites of the student population, such as those associated with the debating societies, the Historical and the Philosophical, which were traditionally strongly unionist in their outlook.

The Historical Society debated the Treaty in February 1922 and the motion, 'that this house welcomes the ratification of the Irish Agreement of December 6th, 1921', was passed by twenty-one votes to two.[39] By February 1922 an editorial in *T.C.D.* argued that as the establishment of the Free State was a 'fait accompli', Trinity should 'throw in her lot' with the new state. This decision, it argued, was a good one and must be undertaken 'without reservation and without looking back'. This was, it claimed, the opinion of nine-tenths of the student population.[40] An editorial published in May 1923 at the end of the Civil War noted that 'The phrase "Irish national spirit" has an unpleasant sound for many of us, but the time has come for us to forget the past and live in the present.'[41] The dominant tone of editorials might best be described as a reluctant acquiescence. But how would this work in practice?

Speaking to the Dáil in November 1922, Ernest Alton, one of Trinity's four TDs, pledged to play Gaelic games, specifically hurling, at Trinity to demonstrate its cultural engagement with the new state.[42] This proposal proved divisive among students; some viewed it as a necessary act of self-preservation, arguing that 'in this new era we must in our collegiate life become Irish or go under'.[43] Others argued against it, claiming that there had never been any demand for Gaelic games at Trinity.[44] In this way, acts of accommodation threatened to undermine the traditional Trinity identity, which emphasised the playing of British sports such as rugby and cricket. Games were important parts of the ritual through which collective identity was formed and attempts to integrate new sports into the college's life challenged traditional understandings of the institution's ethos.[45]

T.C.D.'s mentions of Trinity's adaptation to life in the Free State became rarer in the post-Civil War period; after all, the newspaper claimed to be non-political and thus only commented on political issues in times of crisis. Issues relating to identity did still crop up in the magazine, however. In May 1927 an editorial argued that 'if Trinity is going to play her part in the life of the nation, we must not rest on our laurels and point with pride to the great politicians she has produced in years gone by'. It was more important to take 'an intelligent interest in the politics of the present day'.[46] However, there was also, it seems, a reluctance to deal with these issues outright. In 1929, a new student organ, *The College Pen*, was started in opposition to *T.C.D.* The publication sought to give a greater voice to the marginalised within the college community and to tackle the big political issues which it claimed the conservative and elitist *T.C.D.* would not do. Its very foundation underlined divided opinion within the university.

The *College Pen* came into being at an interesting juncture in Trinity's history. By 1929, a new generation of students was in the college and, unlike their recent predecessors, they had no experience of the university prior to independence. By the end of the 1920s, the student population averaged around 1,400 people, with women making up a quarter of that number, matching the proportion attained during the First World War.[47] As such, contributors to the *College Pen* were keen to discuss things that previously had not been given a prominent voice; salient among these was the place of Trinity in Ireland. The editorial of its first edition noted that 'Trinity has a large part to play in the Ireland of to-day and to-morrow' and that 'we shall not blink the fact that President Cosgrave and Viscount Craigavon are our rulers'.[48] The *College Pen* quickly became the forum for a colourful and contentious debate about Trinity's identity.

In October 1929 an undergraduate called Peter O'Flaherty wrote to the *College Pen* arguing that Trinity needed to engage more beyond its own walls. He argued that Trinity was 'segregated' from outside influence owing to the policy of a minority:

> In the first place Trinity must realise that it is an inseparable part of Ireland. If Ireland prospers, Trinity will share in the prosperity; if Ireland fails, so will Trinity. Therefore, Trinity's first allegiance should be to Ireland. If she is to make her voice felt in the country she can only do so by speaking as a part of it.

For Trinity to truly contribute to national life, it needed to encourage 'the fullest freedom of thought and discussion among her members'. Trinity needed to proactively engage with Ireland. As a starting point, O'Flaherty suggested that the university should embrace its nationalist credentials, reclaiming the names of Davis, Tone and Emmet from historical obscurity.[49] This letter sparked a contentious debate, demonstrating the fractured nature of student identity at that time.

J. Marshall Dudley, an officer in the Historical Society (and a Catholic), took issue with O'Flaherty's idea that Trinity owed its greatest allegiance to Ireland:

> Trinity is an inseparable part, not of a portion of Ireland divided in 1920, but of a worldwide Empire which her sons have laboured to build during the past two hundred years. To this she owes a greater allegiance. She was not founded nor did she ever pretend to be the university of an Irish Ireland. She was founded as an Anglo-Irish university.[50]

Owen Sheehy-Skeffington, who entered TCD in 1927 and who would represent the university in the Seanad decades later, sided with O'Flaherty, arguing that Dudley wished to subordinate 'the views of the majority to those of the minority'.[51] Dudley followed up by claiming that the 'belliferous curse of modern civilisation—the Spirit of Nationalism—would reduce Trinity from being the Third University in the British Empire to being the First University in an obscure island on the western seaboard of the continent of Europe'.[52] This series of letters animated the student community and demonstrated a deep-seated anxiety about the place of Trinity in Ireland and the world, which in turn undermined the traditional sense of community.

Remembering the First World War: Politics, Memory, Identity

This anxiety about wider collective identity emerged in other ways. Remembrance of the First World War was the point where official ceremonial and collective identity converged. Trinity College Dublin lost 471 students, staff, and alumni in the war, a loss unparalleled by any educational institution in what would become the Free State. The memory of the First World War was another forum through which institutional identity was shaped and negotiated.

The political environment in Ireland meant that remembrance of the war soon became by definition a political act. In the 1920s it became apparent that the legacies of the Easter Rising, on the one hand, and the Great War, on the other, were incompatible. The men who had fought and died in the Great War had done so for the 'wrong' cause and, at an official level, the Free State marginalised their memory. However, with over two hundred thousand Irishmen having served in the war and over thirty thousand losing their lives, personal and popular commemoration of the dead was widespread in the 1920s, for Catholics and Protestants, nationalists and unionists alike.[53]

As a community and an institution, Trinity was involved in many varieties of commemoration in the 1920s. When official Armistice Day ceremonies took place at 11 a.m. on 11 November, Trinity undergraduates frequently halted traffic in College Green to ensure the two minutes' silence was correctly observed.[54] From 1919 until 1926 crowds—often up to 50,000 people—assembled in College Green.[55] Participants were often portrayed as disloyal to the new state. Conflict often developed between Trinity and the more traditionally nationalist and Catholic University College Dublin students, who sang opposing anthems at one another and scuffled. Trinity students emphasised their group identity by singing 'God Save the King', waving Union Jacks and, on occasion, wheeling a captured German field gun to the Front Arch of the university.[56]

These outward signs of political provocation were offensive to many who had either served in the war or lost loved ones in it and the triumphalist attitude of some on Armistice Day became increasingly problematic. As early as November 1921, a correspondent to *T.C.D.* complained of the frivolous attitude of some of the younger undergraduates on Armistice Day, comparing the atmosphere to a '"Rugger" international or an inter-'varsity match'.[57] In 1926, A.A. Luce, one of three fellows of the college who fought in the war, wrote to *T.C.D.* to try to halt the growing politicisation of Armistice Day. He urged poppy-wearing civilians not to join in the march of ex-servicemen, however well intentioned their actions, as it would cause provocation and serve to politicise the ceremonial, giving

Trinity's opponents a pretext to condemn them.[58] Concerns were raised again in 1929, this time regarding the behaviour of a few, who, during the Armistice Day ceremonial, broke away from the main body of marchers and 'halted in the street bawling "God Save the King", waving their hats, and cheering'. The *T.C.D.* editorial noted ruefully that 'for the thousands of outsiders in College Green this pitiable exhibition represented the mind and policy of Trinity College!'[59] In November 1930, the *College Pen* reflected on the events of Remembrance Day 1929, arguing that the community had 'forgotten that the day was arranged primarily to serve the interests of peace rather than war'. It stated: 'in this country we are judged by appearances, and there is no doubt that by that standard we seem unduly ardent imperialists'.[60] While the memory of the First World War seemed to further divide Trinity from the new state, it ultimately provided a means of accommodation between university and government, although this was a difficult process with its share of controversies.

Trinity constructed two integrated buildings to remember its First World War dead.[61] The Hall of Honour was completed by 1928 and opened by the ex-unionist politician and chairman of the Senate, Lord Glenavy. There was no official representative of the government present at the opening ceremony; in his opening address, Glenavy spoke of the marginalisation of the memory of the conflict in the Irish Free State: 'There is a growing conspiracy of silence as to the deeds of our citizen soldiers by which they redeemed our Empire.'[62] Construction of the adjacent Reading Room began in 1935 and was opened in 1937 by Éamon de Valera, president of the Free State's Executive Council since 1932.[63] In one way de Valera might have seemed a strange choice to inaugurate a First World War memorial, given that he had set about dismantling the Treaty and undoing the remaining links with Britain and the Empire. However, de Valera's presence at Trinity in 1937 was at once an act of mutual accommodation between state and institution and also part of a scholarly connection.

Many years later A.A. Luce wrote that 'when de Valera came to power we were all frightened of him at first'.[64] In the 1930s de Valera, enrolled as a student in 1905–06, became a semi-regular visitor to Trinity.[65] He spoke to the Gaelic Society in 1929 and again in 1934.[66] Most significant, however, was de Valera's speech to the

Historical Society in November 1934. He was critical of ex-unionists who retained a strong affinity with the British crown, arguing that 'the greatest thing that this college can do for the nation would be to get its young men to turn their minds and their hearts in the direction of their own people'.[67]

In 1937, Provost Thrift, a physicist, knowing of de Valera's passion for the subject, invited him to dine in Trinity with the visiting Nobel Prize-winning physicist, Robert Millikan. While de Valera was unable to attend, he accepted Thrift's invitation to open the Reading Room in July 1937. This was a symbolic moment of accommodation but notable also for what was left unsaid. There was no mention of the First World War despite the fact that he walked past the rows of names of the dead on his way into the Reading Room. De Valera's speech stuck to the safe topic of Thomas Davis and Trinity nationalism.[68] The press gave positive reports of the event. De Valera's *Irish Press* noted that he had been well received and that the national anthem was played upon his entry to the Provost's Garden for a subsequent event.[69] The *Irish Times*, the traditional organ of southern unionism, was enthused by his appearance at the event and saw the ceremony as a moment from which Trinity and Ireland could be further reconciled: 'Our great hope is that before long the decency, the culture, the spirit of tolerance and of true nationalism inculcated by the University of Dublin will begin to play a determining part in Irish affairs.'[70]

Conclusion

On Victory in Europe day—7 May 1945—crowds gathered in College Green to celebrate the end of the Second World War. During the afternoon Ailtirí na hAiséirghe, a far-right group with fascist sympathies, burned a Union Jack.[71] Some students attempted to burn the Irish tricolour on the roof of Trinity, either acting in response to the burning of the Union Jack, or provoking it.[72] Two days of riots resulted, with the college being assailed by projectiles.[73] The events of V.E. Day suggested that Trinity still seemed more British than Irish.

The *Irish Press* described the incident as 'disgraceful'.[74] William Bedell Stanford, a college fellow, urged Provost Ernest Alton to condemn the act and apologise to the government, as otherwise Trinity would 'lose many friends and revive old enmities'.[75] One graduate wrote to Alton of his fear that the V.E. Day incident would set Trinity back to 1918 'with all our work to do again'. This turned out not to be the case. Alton apologised to de Valera in person, describing the Taoiseach as 'courteous and understanding'.[76]

In 1947, de Valera's government gave Trinity a state grant for the first time. This marked the culmination of a long and contentious process through which the university readjusted following the Treaty. The grant allowed the university to prosper. The path by which it came to this agreement was difficult; identity at the institution, built upon centuries of political, cultural and religious ascendancy, was debated and contested by the college community. It was only through the slow passage of time and a careful but ambiguous engagement with the new government that Trinity reconciled itself to the new state.

CHAPTER EIGHT

From Landlordism to Citizenship: Edward Richards-Orpen and the New State[1]

PHILIP BULL

Early Life and Background

Edward Richards-Orpen (1884–1967) embodied a concept of citizenship that was practical, useful and contributory to economic and social life in the new Irish state. It transcended, or attempted to transcend, a sterile vision of nationality as purely political. Like Sir Horace Plunkett and others before him, he tried to follow a path that in essence avoided the pitfalls of unionist versus nationalist, Catholic versus Protestant. He inherited the estate of Monksgrange, County Wexford, on the death of his mother, Adela Elizabeth Orpen, in 1927. Both his mother and his father—Goddard Henry Orpen, eminent historian of medieval Ireland—were strong defenders of the union, his mother publicly active in the unionist cause. The events of 1916 to 1921 were seen as a disaster by Edward's parents and, particularly by his mother, for whom the ultimate outcome represented the betrayal by Britain of Ireland's interests. Edward's sentiments were distinctly different and to understand why it is necessary to examine his background and the influences on his early life.

For those close to him Edward was a difficult person to deal with. Highly intelligent and talented, he was a poor communicator at a personal level. From his early adolescence away at school and again while he was at university his parents had great difficulty in getting replies to their letters, nor could they establish accountability from him on money matters. None of this arose from malice or deliberate indifference on his part but was the product of an extremely sharp and creative mind constantly preoccupied with the particular intellectual questions on which he was engaged. Particularly talented in mathematics and engineering, as a Cambridge undergraduate he pursued questions well beyond what the curriculum required, but neglected the more mundane issues on which he was to be examined. This, together with an active social and cultural life, meant that he did not achieve the honours degree that was expected of him.

In 1914 Edward married Margaret Tomalin, daughter of Lewis Tomalin the founder of the Jaeger Clothing Company. Margaret had to deal with his fecklessness, his forgetting of commitments and lack of capacity in financial matters. So ineffective was he in carrying through his intention to change his surname by deed poll from Orpen to Richards-Orpen—intended to please his mother—that Margaret had to resort to irony; was she to know what her married name would be before the marriage register was signed?[2] Her letters from the time they were engaged were riddled with underlined reminders of things he needed to do and which he had previously forgotten. Notwithstanding this their relationship was a strong one. Importantly, it was a match of a person from a wealthy and sophisticated English upper middle-class family to the scion of a landed, but largely impoverished, Irish family.

Both Edward and Margaret had lived the bulk of their lives in England and been subjected to largely English influences. Edward had grown up in London's Bedford Park—a significant intellectual and arts enclave on which later garden cities were modelled—where his parents had lived from their marriage in 1880 to their moving to Monksgrange in 1900. Edward remained at Bedford Park while completing his schooling before going to Cambridge. He did not, however, lack an Irish dimension to his life. His holidays were spent at Monksgrange while his grandfather was the owner and when his mother took over he began to develop ideas for its future. He had a sense of Irishness as distinct from his Englishness, rebutting fellow officers while in France during the First World War when they baited him over the Easter Rising; he responded with criticism of the English failure to understand the Irish point of view and denied he was fighting for England but rather against Germany.[3] Margaret, on the other hand, was the product of a highly successful English businessman and a mother drawn from a distinguished German family, spending considerable time during her childhood and youth in Germany. They were thus both products of dual societies and cultures and this was to give them a sense of distance from many of the assumptions endemic to his Irish social and political background.

This was to become particularly evident during the crisis faced by the Irish unionist cause in 1919. A section of unionists, led by Lord Midleton, president of the Irish Unionist Alliance, had come to recognise that the threat of partition and separation of southern Protestants from their northern coreligionists would be worse than Home Rule. At the conference of the Alliance in January 1919 Midleton sought to change its policy to one of support for a form of dominion Home Rule. Rejected by a majority, Midleton and his followers then formed a rival unionist Anti-Partition League. Edward's mother, Adela Orpen, was an outspoken opponent of Midleton and on the basis of the speech she made against him was then co-opted to the committee of the Alliance, now reduced in size by the defection with Midleton of many of its most distinguished southern members.[4] On the other hand Edward's wife, Margaret, with her English perceptions and not least the contempt felt by the wealthy English upper middle class for the landed elite, saw Irish affairs in a different light and urged her husband to follow Midleton rather than the 'die-hards' for whom she was 'convinced that the game is up'.[5]

There is no record of Edward's response to this, but there can be little doubt that he kept himself aloof from the more conservative unionist opinion. By the time of the Irish Civil War he emerged as a supporter of the Treaty side and committed to the success of the Free State government. This, together with his having the status of a captain in the British Army, put Monksgrange at risk of being burnt by the anti-Treaty IRA forces. In a deal brokered by one of their members, Myles Fenlon, also a trusted Monksgrange employee, Edward and his family left Ireland, his departure strengthening Fenlon's hand in saving the house now that he was known to have got Edward out of the country. For the family the threat that Monsksgrange might be burned down was a real one, as they were surrounded by other examples. Well known to them was the case of the Pack-Beresford sisters, whose Kellistown House in County Carlow was burnt down on 23 March 1923, a few days before Monksgrange was raided by the anti-Treatyites.[6] Earlier in July 1921, Ballyrankin House near Bunclody, home of the Skrine family, friends of the Orpens, had been burnt down, while near to the end of the Civil War in April 1923 Castleboro, belonging to the Carew family and closely connected with the Monksgrange people, was destroyed.[7] At least eight houses in County Wexford were burnt down between 1921 and 1923 (a disproportionate number for one county), so the local anti-Treaty IRA were clearly not inactive and the potential threat to Monksgrange was very real. Terence Dooley draws attention to the significant incidence of burnings in County Wexford during the Civil War period.[8]

An Idyllic Life in England

For the next four years Edward and his family lived in Chipping Campden in the Cotswolds, then the centre of the English arts and crafts movement. There his early roots in the intellectual and artistic environment of London's Bedford Park were reinvigorated by what proved a very creative and productive time. When Edward assumed responsibility for Monksgrange in 1927 on the death of his mother, he pursued a plan nurtured during his time in Chipping Campden. In what was to give Monksgrange a post-landlord identity he set up Grange Furniture Industry for the design, manufacture and promotion of furniture made by hand to arts and crafts principles, the actual labour and craftsmanship provided jointly by Edward himself and Myles Fenlon. While enormously successful in developing new designs and producing items of very high quality, the venture was not a financial success. This may have been partly because the whole arts and crafts phenomenon had passed its prime—the Arts and Crafts Society of Ireland was clearly on its last legs already, even though in 1928 Edward was asked to become its secretary[9]—together with declining economic conditions in the Irish Free State. But it was also affected by Edward's inefficiency in day-to-day management. He had difficulty meeting orders or requests for information, even in some cases accepting payment for items still to be made and then not meeting the deadlines. Whatever the reasons, the operation ceased in 1933, although during its short existence it had made an impact on Irish artistic and craft circles, demonstrating new standards of furniture design and production and introducing to Ireland principles and ideas derived from the lively artistic environment of the Cotswolds. Nicola Gordon Bowe has provided an evocative and richly illustrated account of the important influence of Edward's Cotswolds experience and shown the quality of what was produced from the Monksgrange enterprise.[10] It represented a significant statement by Edward of his intention to make a distinctive mark in modern Irish society and one that did not follow in the traditions of the landlord class.

Richards-Orpen also made it evident very quickly that he intended to play a role in the new polity emerging in Ireland in the 1920s. Already by early 1923 he had made approaches regarding a government position under the Free State government, this being conveyed by Michael Doyle, member of the Dáil for the Wexford constituency, to W.T. Cosgrave, together with the information that Edward had been 'compelled to go to England owing to [his] backing up the Government and that [he] was a staunch supporter of "The Treaty" all along'.[11] This appeal for a position was not successful but in the meantime he and Margaret had created an idyllic life for themselves and their children in Chipping Campden: Edward extended with his own hands the house they had bought, High Barn in Broad Campden; they had established a circle of close friends, including a number of distinguished artists and craftsmen; and they clearly greatly enjoyed the ambience of the villages 'with their grey stone walls and grey stone slate roofs', each house with 'an orchard attached'.[12] Returning to Ireland in 1926 represented a significant wrench for them; many years later one of their daughters recalled her sadness at leaving Chipping Campden.[13] But Ireland was his home and even before their marriage Margaret had made clear her commitment to Monksgrange.[14] Once back in Ireland, and especially after the demise of Grange Furniture Industry, Edward began to look for ways to contribute to a changing Ireland.

Contributing to Ireland

While Edward may not have excelled academically at Cambridge, what emerges from that period of his life is his passion and considerable expertise in the three disciplines of mathematics, science and engineering. It was in the interconnections of these disciplines, combined with his deep sense of art and aesthetics, his strong historical and archaeological interests, and his pursuit of his goal through politics and improved education, especially technical education, that his contribution to society is to be understood. His years in the Cotswolds refined the building and related engineering skills he had begun at Monksgrange from about 1912 with the commencement of a new wing to the house. In Broad Campden, he had not only built the extensions to his house, High Barn, but also assisted with building work for friends in the area.[15] It was also while in the Cotswolds that he began to learn the Irish language[16] and where he was initiated into grass roots political activism, canvassing for the British Labour Party during the 1924 general election campaign.[17]

The Chipping Campden artist Alec Miller knew Tom Jones, Lloyd George's private secretary, and through him Edward was invited to be interviewed at 10 Downing Street for a job in the recently established Rural Industries Bureau, part of a British government strategy 'to find out which of the rural crafts formerly flourishing in England might be encouraged to survive & which might with some modification be suitably altered to fit the changed requirements of post war conditions'.[18] Appointed to the position, Edward's job was then to travel throughout England and Wales finding practising craftsmen, advising them on how they might improve their work and showing how they could become more viable if brought to the notice of the appropriate firms.[19] These were experiences he began to apply on his return to Ireland, involving himself in a number of attempts to encourage the development of pottery and a clay pipe industry in Ireland, finding out about local established potteries and using his scientific knowledge to explore the conditions in which the industry might flourish and, in particular, the nature and quality of clay to be found in certain areas.[20] This also involved him in exploring the related area of lead and silver mining.[21] Although this does not appear to have resulted in any very tangible outcomes it revealed the basic modus operandi that marked his approach. Always beginning with what already existed he worked to add value by the application particularly of scientific knowledge, as well as developing political pressure for improved infrastructure at a communal or national level. His increasing involvement in politics and his cultivation of more local networks were all ultimately directed towards that end.

Political Involvement

On 15 September 1932 a new farmers' organisation was formed, the National Farmers' and Ratepayers' League, with Frank MacDermot—recently elected as an independent in the Dáil—as its president.[22] The organisation came into being following the demise of its predecessor, the Irish Farmers' Union, due to dissatisfaction with its political direction; shortly afterwards it was reconstituted as the Centre Party for political purposes.[23] Michael Doyle, the former TD—he had lost his seat in the general election of 1927—who had approached Cosgrave on Edward's behalf in 1923, invited him to a meeting of the new body, probably the convention held in the Mansion House on 6 October 1932.[24] Edward was surprised at how many familiar faces he remembered from his involvement before the First World War in the Irish Farmers' Union, where he had already begun to identify himself as a farmer rather than a landlord. His attendance at this meeting marked the beginning of what was to become a significant political role for him. Edward replaced Doyle on the national standing committee of the organisation and took up the role of honorary secretary for County Wexford.[25] He was then involved in a special meeting of the League Council to discuss a possible merger with Cumann na nGaedheal, out of which was to emerge Fine Gael. It was at this meeting that Edward first met James Dillon—like MacDermot, recently elected to the Dáil as an independent—beginning an association of great importance both in politics and in personal friendship.[26] Incidentally, his work for the League in County Wexford also started what was to prove a new and lifelong working partnership with his son John, then aged eighteen years, whose signature appears on behalf of his father on official letters.[27] Edward was incorporated by Frank MacDermot into his section of the new Fine Gael organisation, ironically—as later revealed—in face of opposition from his soon-to-be close associate and friend, James Dillon, who considered that an 'ex landlord, ex Army Captain, ex English public school & Cambridge would be about as bad as it could be!!'[28] Edward had no easy ride in dissociating himself from his origins, but he was to prove adept at it.

Richards-Orpen and Fine Gael

By 1935 Edward was at the heart of discussions within the Fine Gael party, becoming a principal operative for it in the area of economic policy. In October 1934 he was instrumental in putting together an economics committee for the party, including in its membership Cosgrave, the party leader, James Dillon, Patrick McGilligan, a former minister, and calling upon Joseph Johnston, an economist at Trinity College, to give evidence at its first meeting, with the eminent economist George O'Brien and other academic economists to be consulted subsequently.[29] By the following March he was describing this group as a 'night school', meeting in Cosgrave's house but with Edward wishing it could be held in his own flat in Fitzwilliam Square, as it would be 'more neutral ground' for those who would rather not 'face the publicity of the Dáil',[30] a reflection of his keenness for this group to be focused on its intellectual function rather than too connected to politics.

Edward's own objective in these discussions was to achieve a commitment to economic planning, especially in relation to the agricultural sector, and in this he had to bring James Dillon to his point of view:

> I see that it will be difficult to convert him to any measure of planning, he is not yet convinced that there is no other alternative. He still looks on it as interference rather than directional pushing from above. He feels that the opportunity for the efficient producer will go & the mediocre will benefit which is true to a certain extent. I hope . . . to convince Dillon that this is only a temporary measure.[31]

Important as it was, the relationship with Dillon was not always straightforward. Edward at this time remarked of a speech by Dillon on the agricultural estimates that 'he did not use much of the stuff I gave him . . . he said my dope was too logical & mostly sound economics & hence would cut no ice'.[32] This reflected what was often the mode of co-operation between them: Richards-Orpen providing sound background material that was not without influence on Dillon but the latter making his own judgements as to how to present it politically. Or, as Edward commented to his wife after he and Dillon had been appointed by the party to draw up its agricultural policy, 'This means really that I must do the job & then Dillon will take out the parts he wants at the same time keeping to the framework'.[33] It was his ability to accept this role that gave Edward the capacity to exercise a significant influence, often through Dillon, over the next three decades.

In assessing the contribution of Edward Richards-Orpen to Irish politics and society, recognition has to be given to his capacity to bridge boundaries between disciplines and areas ranging from what he was doing at Monksgrange, making furniture or farming, through local and county activity to national politics. In the latter area, for example, he did not limit his contribution to the economic policy discussions he initiated in his economic 'night schools'. In the very difficult discussions that eventuated in the formation of Fine Gael in September 1933 he did not hesitate to express his views about major issues, warning against political dangers facing the new party in a letter of 15 August 1934 to Patrick Baxter, a prominent Fine Gael politician elected to the Senate in 1934. Edward wrote of the risk of alienating farmers because of a previous political fusion that had seen a 'swamping of the Farmers Party' by Cumann na nGaedheal', with 'five years of total apparent neglect of the farmers interest'. He believed that farmers' votes would not be won by a party containing 'even a remnant of C-na-G'. Accordingly he argued that those identified with Cumann na nGaedheal, even though they included 'Several men of high mental capacity', should be sidelined until the new party structure had settled down: 'In time . . . they will regain their place . . . It is only in the initial stages they must . . . take a back seat.'[34] This was not to happen; W.T. Cosgrave, the leader of Cumann na nGaedheal, became leader again a year later. Although hostile to the role that General Eoin O'Duffy was acquiring, Edward urged caution in acting too strongly against him and his Blueshirt movement because of his popularity with young people: 'As yet we cannot assess the political value of O'Duffy and his youngsters [but] must realise that they are a force that may grow rapidly . . . The trend in Europe is towards the Youth, and we will do well to follow suit.'[35] In fact the Ard Fheis on 8 September 1933 that brought about the fusion of parties saw O'Duffy appointed its leader, although only for a disastrous first year, but Edward had been quick to write to him urging the setting up of an economics committee to report to the national executive, a committee that would take evidence from a variety of people including professional economists such as George O'Brien and John Maynard Keynes; he supported his argument with reference to how Roosevelt's devaluation of the United States dollar arose from suggestions from the university community rather than the banks.[36] Again in February 1934 he wrote to O'Duffy raising problems with the organisation of the party, especially regarding the relationship of TDs to the National Executive, being tactful in setting it in the context of 'your excellent scheme of organisation . . . not being given a fair trial'.[37] Edward was himself appointed to the National Executive in August 1934.[38]

In a letter to Patrick Baxter the day before the Ard Fheis that confirmed the fusion of parties Edward had again criticised the attitude of 'keeping [O'Duffy] in the background' and saw him as a means 'to prove to the electorate that it is not C-n-G reborn but a *New Party*', given that the former party 'failed to attract the youth': 'See that O'Duffy gets at least his fair share of prominence, not so much as head of the Nat[ional] Guard but as the head of a *Youth movement*.' He also outlined his views on a number of issues that should be dealt with in the party's forthcoming manifesto, demonstrating that his concerns were as much about political appeal as policy detail. He opposed any reference to the oath to the monarch that, controversially, was required of members of the Dáil on the grounds that it would look 'like digging up the past', while conceding that the question of the governor-general's position, currently under attack from the Fianna Fáil government, had to be addressed on account of its salary 'looming so large in minds of electorate'. On economic policy he wanted detail avoided in the manifesto, apart from the issue of ending the Fianna Fáil economic boycott of Britain that was proving so damaging to farmers. Noting that the new party was a coalition needing to find common ground for all groups, he stressed that 'too great detail in the *earlier stages* is liable to divide our supporters'.[39]

A letter to James Dillon containing a critique of the progress of the new party revealed the attention Edward gave to how it was operating in a parliamentary context. He complained that as an opposition it was weak because of a lack of combination between members, the attack on the government being 'simply a series of individual efforts, rather than a thought out scheme based on our agreed policy'. He argued that too often as an opposition they based their case

> on what C n G did in the past, this leads nowhere, if we are to retain the L[eague] of Y[outh] & inspire them with confidence we must be more *constructive*, & concentrate on the future etc. The L of Y do not care a button what C n G did in the past.

He stressed that Dillon was the one person able to manage a better approach as 'the other good speakers are handicapped by the past' and he suggested that the front bench should be made more constructive in its speeches, 'leaving more of the destructive criticism to the back-bencher'. He complained that 'most speakers avoid (possibly through ignorance) the novel & more revolutionary features'. Touching both on his concern to build on the involvement of the young associated with O'Duffy's movement and to take account of international developments, he claimed that the

> youth are much more interested in the Corporative State idea than many people realise. They feel that some complete change is necessary as otherwise we will perpetuate a sort of permanent stale-mate.[40]

When Dillon replied, some weeks later, he was much more sanguine than Edward about the relationship of Fine Gael and the League of Youth, while frank about O'Duffy's alienation.[41]

These concerns were to be continuing ones for Edward. While committing himself heavily to Fine Gael he remained critical of how it acted as an opposition. Some of this was frustration at his own marginalisation from the parliamentary scene, but there were two principal reasons why he was unlikely to get a seat in the Dáil. While there would be difficulty in securing one for someone with a family and cultural background such as his, he was essentially too much of an intellectual and visionary for the daily grind of constituency and parliamentary politics. His aspiration to move from the back rooms of politics to the public arena was strong and he was deeply frustrated that his first attempt at election to the Seanad in 1938 was unsuccessful, attributable he thought to Fine Gael's ineptitude in putting forward a failed and, in Edward's view at least, drunken former TD.[42] Another electoral attempt in 1944 was also unsuccessful.[43] He was eventually appointed to the Seanad in 1948, on Dillon's recommendation, as one of the Taoiseach's nominees for a term that lasted until 1951. By then his achievements outside the direct political arena were so significant that he came to that position with a capacity to contribute on a substantial scale, especially in agriculture and related economic areas.

Richards-Orpen as Public Commentator, Researcher and Writer

By the time he became a senator Edward had established himself as a public commentator, researcher and writer of considerable significance and his major role was to continue in the years after he ceased being a senator. Part of this influence derived from being a regular columnist with the *Irish Independent*, then the best-selling Irish daily newspaper, writing mainly on issues affecting agriculture and more general economic questions. Between 1947 and 1960 he contributed over seventy major feature articles to that newspaper[44] and even earlier in 1943 he had written the concluding article in a series on 'Post-war planning in Irish agriculture'.[45] The subjects dealt with were varied and included: electric power on the farm; international agricultural issues; the problem of farm surpluses; the European Common Market and related issues; nuclear power; solar power; land rehabilitation; the Irish sugar industry; maintenance of soil structure; agricultural research; pinpointing demand for Irish products in continental countries; and how transport costs affected agriculture. In some cases these were grouped into series of articles, such as four in response to the Department of Finance's initiatives on economic development and a significant series on 'How science helps the farmer', this a continuing subject of importance to Edward and underpinning the ideas in many of his articles. From 1945 he was also writing articles for the traditionally Irish-Ireland newspaper, the *Leader*.

The high profile Edward had established for himself in the public discourse by the 1950s was the result of intensive and varied work over the preceding two decades. His political involvement had its ups and downs, including the hiatus when he followed James Dillon in resigning from Fine Gael over Ireland's adoption of neutrality in the Second World War. This was partly out of loyalty to Dillon—although he fully agreed with his position—but as his wife pointed out, this left him in limbo in relation to what he had to offer 'of importance, even of urgent importance'. Although he still managed to get his views into the party's forums it was indirectly, especially through James Hughes, a farmer and Fine Gael politician who had been elected to the Dáil in 1938 but, in the words of his wife, 'he could not go on being known to be making suggestions . . . which he wasn't prepared to defend'. Accordingly he rejoined the party,[46] but much of what he was to achieve was done beyond the boundaries of party politics, achievements which marked him out in the opinion of one newspaper columnist as 'one of the most constructive minds in Ireland today',[47] while another writer in the same newspaper—in referring to his belief in science in agriculture—described him as 'a courageous thinker'.[48]

Rural Development Interests

In the years that followed, Richards-Orpen demonstrated his capacity, evident from his youth, to hold in balance a very wide range of interests and activities and to identify ways in which they interconnected. An early example of this was his support in the 1930s for an Irish tobacco growing industry. He began by setting his own example, devoting a large field at Monksgrange to tobacco plants and building a tobacco-drying house within the walled garden. He then encouraged other farmers to take up the new crop, setting himself up as a provider of tobacco plants. He was also significantly involved with, and may have been party to the establishment of, the

Tobacco Growers' and Curers' Association of Ireland.[49] This was still an important activity for him in 1942 when he applied for a new licence to grow tobacco.[50] Similarly, from the time of his return to Ireland he had worked to develop a manure and fertiliser industry. He was also involved in discussions about developing an industry for the preservation of vegetables, presumably what would now be freezing or sealed packaging, and the consequent possibilities for marketing. He was quick to take up new marketing, industrial or scientific opportunities, especially those that might help the Irish farmer.

An area of critical interest to Edward was the need for lime to improve Irish soils. He worked to improve access to lime supplies but he also had to counter an inherited view that lime was not necessary for such soils.[51] Typically he gained attention for his argument from his own experience of successfully growing barley at Monksgrange on very acid soil by adding ground limestone. But it was in the acquisition of Johnstown Castle in County Wexford that Edward saw advances being made in the whole area of soil science, an outcome to which he significantly contributed. Victor Lakin, who in 1942 had inherited Johnstown Castle from his grandmother, Lady Maurice Fitzgerald, wished to gift it to the state as an institute of agriculture, but Edward had conveyed his view that rather than turn it into just another school for teaching agriculture, it should become 'an Agricultural Research Station so that the existing schools would be able to teach real agriculture & not merely repeat parrotwise the findings of others'.[52] The records show that it was his intervention that brought about that outcome,[53] although Edward was to be disappointed at what he saw as an inadequate relationship between the research undertaken there and the education of farmers. In order to get the work of the new institute started before its own facilities were developed Edward offered a piece of Monksgrange land on the slope of Blackstairs Mountain 'to facilitate an immediate experiment on hill land reclamation'.[54] Michael Neenan, who worked at Johnstown Castle in soil research and was during the 1950s deputy head at Johnstown Castle Experimental Station,[55] has written that 'Few people know what an important contribution [Edward] made to Johnstown Castle' and that he 'was immensely popular with the staff'.[56] Neenan stated that Edward seemed to be the only person who had drawn attention to the failure of the existing agricultural colleges in serving their intended educational purpose. According to Neenan, 'Johnstown Castle became [James] Dillon's powerhouse' and Edward, as his 'friend and mentor', played an important role in advising him as minister.[57] Soil research remains to this day one of the principal activities of Johnstown Castle, a most fitting monument to Edward's work.

Although Edward was always focused on economics, both macro and micro, the practical focus of his work was on the interests of the farmer. The volume of research papers, correspondence and other literature in the Richards-Orpen papers, amounting to over seventy folders or the equivalent of approximately twenty archive boxes, on agriculture and related economic issues, is testimony to how much effort he devoted to this work. Much of this arose from the highly productive relationship with his son John Richards-Orpen, the two of them working closely together and contributing different but complementary skills and abilities. Michael Neenan wrote of the relationship that

> [Edward] was a genius in his own way—far ahead of John in my view, only that he was totally impractical! They 2 were a bit like John Stuart Mill & his father; the old man did the research and the son promulgated it.[58]

The practical dimension and organisation that John contributed—his abilities recognised later in the major role he played in the National Farmers' Association, of which he was vice-president and for a time acting president—played a very big part in the effectiveness of much of what Edward did. The work of them both was further enhanced from the mid-1940s by co-operation with Mrs Esther Bishop, a leading figure in the Irish Countrywomen's Association and at various times a member of its executive, and honorary secretary and later, after the death of her husband, John's wife.

Esther and John between them designed and built a village layout in models which they then travelled around the country, initially receiving national publicity in August 1947 when it was described as

> On a table, about 14 feet by 7 . . . sand was heaped in a low hill, to represent the earth. Some squares were filled with green or yellow stuffs, to represent fields in cultivation . . . Toy houses,

> a church, a mill, farm buildings, and on the hill top a ruined castle, a bridge over the mill stream of mirror-glass, and little model trees, all to scale, were disposed upon the scene exactly as in a thousand parishes.[59]

In the following years the village appeared in many locations, including as an extension lecture at University College, Cork, and often in conjunction with Muintir na Tíre, with which Edward was already closely associated. Although leaving the front-running to John and Esther—the latter proving an excellent public speaker and presenter[60]—Edward regularly accompanied the travelling show and sometimes spoke in connection with it. Given his excellent skills as a carpenter and builder, it can be assumed that he also played a significant role in the construction of the village; he had himself built a model railway at Monksgrange. By March 1949 the *Irish Times* could report that the village had been 'brought to most of the 26 counties, showing rural audiences how they may improve their own villages'.[61]

The village was in many ways a by-product and a means of public communication for ideas that arose out of Edward's extensive research, much of it focused on a project labelled the 'Economic farm unit', which led to many speeches and articles[62] and eventually a booklet published in 1944 and widely circulated.[63] While this concept had strong parallels with older co-operative ideas, it was based on Edward's more contemporary and relevant economic analyses. This research was but part of a much larger project intended to lead to a major book on agricultural economics, the drafts and virtually completed manuscripts for it now held in the Monksgrange archive, a total of four large folders. As well as demonstrating the impressive scale of his research, the annotations on these manuscripts also illustrate one of Edward's distinctive features, a recognition of the value of consultation and collaboration. As well as the work bearing the mark of John's integral involvement these annotations show the extent to which his ideas were subjected to very intelligent comments both from his wife Margaret and Esther Bishop.[64]

It may well have been that Edward's appointment to the Seanad in 1948 diverted attention away from his research and publication plans, as his openness to people now meant that he was vulnerable to extensive lobbying. As a result his achievements have perhaps not been acknowledged to the extent that they merited, although in a book published in 1951 by the economist and periodic senator, Joseph Johnston—the first academic Edward had involved in his economic committee for Fine Gael in 1933—paid tribute to Edward in the context of what he saw as the opportunities for Irish agriculture in the period of post-emergency reconstruction.[65] In a paper presented to the Statistical and Social Inquiry Society of Ireland on 27 November 1947, Johnston had drawn heavily on Edward's concept of the 'Economic farm unit'. This was a scheme

> in which the agricultural community, within a particular area, combine together into an economic group, making possible the use of modern methods of production and merchandising in whatever way best suits their geographical position, and the methods of husbandry suitable to the neighbourhood, instead of each producer selling individually in competition with his neighbour.[66]

While Edward's work may for a long time have fallen out of sight, it has now received a new impetus from Johnston's son, Roy, who has published a book, partly in defence of his father's work, but also referring to 'The Richards Orpen model for rural civilisation'.[67] The same writer on his website suggests that Edward's ideas 'offer an opportunity for development in a future, more "green", political environment'.[68]

A Wider Involvement

Edward's research and writings on economics and agriculture, as well as his practical interventions from his own experiences as a farmer, represent a notable achievement in the development of ideas and politics in the Irish Free State and the Republic, but they were by no means the limit of his contribution. The organisations he supported were legion and embodied his commitment to many facets of society and culture. From an early age he had shared the interests of his father, the historian Goddard Orpen, in the historical and archaeological artefacts of Ireland and in 1931 he was appointed to the County Wexford Local Monuments Advisory Committee, set up under the National Monuments Act of the previous year.[69] This was to lead later to an extended period from 1944 until his death as a member of the National Monuments Council. He was no cipher on this body; his copies of its circulated papers show very substantial annotations, often embodying detailed research he had carried out.[70] He was a member of the provisional committee that set up An Taisce (the National Trust for Ireland) in 1947. He was, as a member, a very strong participant in the Irish Grassland Association, the Statistical and Social Inquiry Society of Ireland and the County Wexford Beekeepers' Association and an active supporter of the Irish Red Cross, the Gate Theatre, the Royal Dublin Society and the Royal Society of Antiquaries of Ireland. Given his background and antecedents, this was one way in which those of Richards-Orpen's class and religion could reinvent themselves, involve themselves and be accepted, in the new dispensation.

CHAPTER NINE

'Old Dublin Merchant "Free of Ten and Four"': The Life and Death of Protestant Businesses in Independent Ireland

FRANK BARRY

Introduction

Non-Catholics made up only 7 per cent of the Free State population in 1926. According to the census of that year there were around 165,000 'Protestant Episcopalians', 32,000 Presbyterians, 11,000 Methodists, 4,000 Jews and a further 10,000 classified as 'other'. Quakers were particularly prominent in business, but were not enumerated separately. Adjusting for likely changes since the 1911 census, there were likely to have been around 1,000 in the Free State at the time.

The minority was strongly over-represented in the higher echelons of all business activities, including agriculture. Of farm holdings of more than 200 acres, 28 per cent were in Protestant hands. Across most industrial sectors 30 to 40 per cent of male 'employers and managers' were Protestant, with around 20 per cent in construction and related activities. Creameries, by then largely under the control of the co-operatives, were the exception; here non-Catholics made up only 4 per cent of the senior ranks.

Recruitment and promotion in the railway companies had long been a matter of controversy; the census revealed that more than 20 per cent of stationmasters and railway officials were Protestant. A similarly privileged position is apparent across the rest of the private sector. As outlined in the Introduction to this volume, non-Catholics comprised 53 per cent of senior bank officials, almost 40 per cent of barristers and solicitors and 20 per cent of department store owners and managers. If this represented evident bias, one common Protestant response was to point to differences in educational attainment. This was the explanation offered by the Society for the Protection of Protestant Interests in 1903 for the disparities in railway-company wages.[1] Another focused on entrepreneurial spirit, which was widely referenced with respect to the dynamism of the Ulster Protestant economy relative to the Catholic south.

Yet, as Tony Farmar and other observers have commented, at least until the 1960s most firms were known as either Protestant or Catholic.[2] Mary Daly quotes businessman Michael Smurfit to the effect that there were many companies where Catholics could never join the management team, 'no matter how good they were at their job or how considerable the contribution that they could make', while Catholic firms such as Smurfit found it difficult to make sales to Protestant companies.[3]

Developments external to the firms themselves ensured that this could not last indefinitely. As F.S.L. Lyons wrote of the Bank of Ireland:

> An increasingly Catholic representation on the Court of Directors and the recruitment of a predominantly Catholic staff would . . . have become inevitable with the striking decline of the Protestant population in the decades after independence. So far as there was a policy in this matter it was the natural and pragmatic policy of a business concern . . . to establish the maximum compatibility between its staff and its customers.[4]

Nor were all of the imbalances in recruitment and management ascribable to sectarianism, as Louis Cullen observes in his study of the Presbyterian firm Eason:

> Staff were recruited from the immediate circle of the principal, and since many recruits were accepted on the recommendation

> of the senior people in the firm, continued recruitment tended to be slanted in that direction . . . Recruitment tended to become more even over time, and a large Catholic base was inevitably reflected later in the promotion of Catholics as well.[5]

Terence Brown summarises Kurt Bowen's study of the Protestant community in Ireland as suggesting that 'until the 1960s at least, the Catholic and Protestant communities essentially lived apart . . . in a kind of mutually agreed apartheid'.[6] The term 'apartheid' seems particularly apt when applied to business. Among a small survey group of South Dublin Protestants Bowen reported that most who had entered the labour market prior to 1955 had found their first positions in workplaces where the majority of their co-workers were Protestant. The extent to which this was mutually agreed can be exaggerated however; the situation undoubtedly caused resentment.

Catholic blame was frequently directed towards the Masonic Order, which had seen an upsurge in membership in the 1920s, though there were suspicions of discrimination on the other side of the religious divide as well. In his oral history of Dundalk, Charles Flynn notes that 'allegations by Catholics of Protestant religious discrimination on the [Great Northern Railway] were matched by the Protestant community's assertion of Catholic discrimination in [tobacco manufacturer] Carrolls'.[7]

The Knights of Columbanus had been established as a counterweight to the freemasons. It saw its role as to rectify 'the discrepancies encountered at every level of Irish . . . life where non-Catholics were solidly entrenched in positions and occupations which depended on already accumulated capital or goodwill'.[8] In 1922 the Knights transferred their headquarters from Belfast to Dublin and their influence expanded within the new state.

Even in the 1970s, remnants of Protestant privilege remained. Though members of the Church of Ireland comprised less than 4 per cent of gainfully employed males in 1971, for example, they accounted for almost 15 per cent of business directors, managers and company secretaries. Nevertheless, the dividing lines between Protestant and Catholic businesses—and Protestant and Catholic positions in the employment hierarchy—had largely disappeared. The 1960s had witnessed the increasing adoption of modern management techniques and an expansion in the importance of educational credentials. Economic liberalisation was a major driving force. The traditional business practices—including overt and covert discrimination—that had characterised many family-run firms could not survive the opening-up of the economy.

Protestant Businesses at Independence

Since information on employees' identities and religious affiliations are not generally available, the definition of what is to be regarded as a 'Protestant business' focuses on ownership and how management and control were passed down through the generations. Protestant businesses clearly dominated 'the commanding heights of the economy' in the initial decades of independence. Writing of the Bank of Ireland, the most significant bank in the State, Oliver MacDonagh points out that 'even in the Catholic south, there were fair-sized branches where, as late as the 1890s, the entire staff belonged to the Church of Ireland'. Members of the court of directors in the immediate pre-independence era 'were unionists to a man, and the great majority of staff would have regarded themselves as "loyalists"'.[9] Though Catholic staff were employed from around 1850, and loans and donations began to be made to Catholic institutions and charities over the last quarter of the nineteenth century, Catholics in 1939 still made up only around one-third of the bank's court of directors.[10] Among the smaller banks, the Provincial was also regarded as Protestant. The Hibernian Bank, by contrast, had been established in a reaction to the anti-Catholic clauses of the Bank of Ireland's charter, while the National Bank had been founded by Daniel O'Connell, partly to serve as a financial vehicle for the repeal movement. The accountancy profession was even more strongly Protestant and 'loyalist' than banking. Both the president and the secretary of the Institute of Chartered Accountants in Ireland at independence were Protestant, as were most of the council and all of the partners of what were by far the largest firms, Craig Gardner and Stokes Brothers & Pim.[11]

Of the seven department stores in Dublin at the time, only Clery was in Catholic nationalist ownership, though Brown Thomas had recently been purchased by the London-based American entrepreneur Harry Gordon Selfridge and would come into Catholic ownership in 1933.[12] The principals of Todd Burns & Co. on Mary Street and McBirney on Aston Quay were a Presbyterian and a Christian Scientist respectively, though Catholics would on occasion occupy the most senior positions in both businesses from the early 1920s.

The other three department stores—Arnott, Switzer and Pim—would remain under Protestant ownership or management for far longer. Control of Arnott passed to the Presbyterian Nesbitt family after the death in 1898 of prominent unionist and owner of the *Irish Times*, Sir John Arnott.[13] It remained within the family until 2010. The Switzers were a Church of Ireland family of Palatine origins. Until the sale of the company in the 1970s, chairmanship of the board of directors stayed within the three Protestant families that had been represented on the board in 1890. Ownership of Pim of South Great Georges Street remained within the family of Quaker entrepreneurs until acquired by a British consortium in the mid-1950s.

Both of the leading coal-distribution companies, Heiton and Tedcastle, had been founded by Presbyterian expatriates. Control of Heiton passed into the hands of another Presbyterian family, the Hewats, after the founder's death, and members of the Hewat family would hold one or other of the key positions in the company until its acquisition by the Grafton Group in 2005. 'In a world where every firm was known to be either Catholic or Protestant', Farmar comments, '[Heiton] was clearly Protestant'.[14] Ironically, the origins of the Grafton Group lay in the hardware firm Chadwick, owned by the Church of Ireland family of that name. Tedcastle, meanwhile, had merged with a Methodist-owned firm in 1897 to become Tedcastle, McCormick. This firm was sold into Catholic ownership in 1952.

Builders' provisioning—into which Heiton ultimately transitioned—was also strongly Protestant-dominated. By the end of the nineteenth century Brooks Thomas and Dockrell were the leading firms in the sector.[15] Maurice Brooks and Sir Maurice Dockrell were both members of the Church of Ireland, though they differed in political outlook. Brooks was a Home Rule MP while Dockrell would later serve as a unionist MP for Dublin. Dockrell's descendants would in turn hold Dáil seats for Cumann na nGaedheal and Fine Gael. Other significant business dynasties operating largely in the services sector included the Bewleys and the Findlaters. The former were Quakers, the latter Presbyterian, though some would later join the Church of Ireland.[16]

Manufacturing experienced the most dramatic shifts in economic policy over the first fifty years of independence and is the subject of particular attention below. While nationalist historiography has focused on the decline of southern Irish manufacturing under the union, there was a number of large export-oriented and almost exclusively Protestant-owned manufacturing firms that had prospered under free-trade conditions. Two that had fared particularly well in the immediate pre-independence period were the Condensed Milk Company of Ireland and the bacon curing firm of Henry Denny & Son.

At a time when only around two dozen manufacturing firms employed a workforce of 400 or more, the Condensed Milk Company employed around 3,000 in its plants and creameries across Munster. The value of condensed milk exports from Ireland came to fully half of that of all brewery exports in 1920. The company was controlled from its Lansdowne base in Limerick by the staunchly loyalist family of Sir Thomas Henry Cleeve. Limerick was also the centre of the bacon trade. Of the major bacon-curing firms—Denny, Matterson, Shaw and O'Mara—only O'Mara was Catholic. One of Henry Denny's sons, Edward, had been the firm's London agent and would go on to become one of the most significant players in the international industry. A son of this English branch of the family was responsible for the First World War provisioning of bacon supplies for the British army.

The biscuit company W. & R. Jacob was one of the state's largest employers, with over 2,000 on its payroll. The Jacobs had been Quakers, though some had become members of the Church of Ireland by the time of the 1911 census. Guinness was even larger, with a workforce of over 3,000 in 1920. The principals of the Guinness family—Lords Ardilaun and Iveagh—were conservative unionists (two of Iveagh's sons represented English constituencies at Westminster) and members of the Church of Ireland.

In contrast to Guinness and Jacob, the whiskey distilling industry was in the doldrums in the 1920s. It had been outcompeted by Scotch whisky by the early 1900s and was suffering the effects of prohibition in America and a strong temperance lobby in the UK parliament. The major Dublin firms of the time were John Jameson,

John Power and Dublin Distillers, the latter a recent amalgamation of three separate distilleries, including William Jameson. The Jamesons were a Church of Ireland family, and the principal of John Jameson was Andrew Jameson, a former southern unionist leader, governor and director of the Bank of Ireland, and early Free State senator. The Powers, by contrast, were Catholic, as were the owners of Cork Distilleries.

Fertiliser company Goulding, owned by the Church of Ireland family of that name, was also export oriented. Operating at least six plants in the Free State and a further two in Northern Ireland, it was significant in scale relative even to the British market. The die-hard attitudes of the Gouldings and the Arnotts would be criticised by J.C.M. Eason, who worked to reconcile the Protestant and unionist business community to the establishment of the new state.[17]

There was also a number of large Protestant-owned textile and clothing companies, though most had passed their peak employment levels by 1922. The Limerick Clothing Company had been established by Scottish expatriate Peter Tait but was later taken over by a group of largely Protestant Limerick businessmen and remained under Protestant management. Its workforce was down to around 400 in the 1920s, from a high of 1,400 in the previous century. Another firm that had once had a worldwide reputation was the Balbriggan hosiery manufacturer Smyth & Co. It too employed around 400 and by the time of independence was under the ownership of a local Church of Ireland family, the Whytes, who had been active in unionist politics. Greenmount & Boyne was the largest linen firm outside Ulster, formed in 1925 when the Drogheda firm Boyne Weaving acquired the assets of the Pim family's business, Greenmount of Harold's Cross. Cork Spinning & Weaving was also of substantial size. It was established by the Cork Presbyterian James Ogilvie in 1889. Ogilvie also ran a confectionery business in the city and served as a director of the large Methodist-owned Cork bakery, F.H. Thompson.

The Quaker Goodbody family played a significant role across a range of sectors. Their jute works at Clara employed 700 and their Dublin tobacco operations were larger than those of Carroll in Dundalk. From 1894 the family also controlled the largest flour-milling business in Ireland, the Limerick conglomerate of Bannatyne & Sons. Other branches of the family ran successful legal and stockbroking businesses. Other flour millers of renown included the Odlums, the Shackletons and the Pollexfens. The Odlum mills were in the midlands, those of the Shackletons in Kildare and Lucan (County Dublin), while the Pollexfens—maternal ancestors of W. B. Yeats, of whom he wrote with such affection in his book *Autobiographies* and poem 'Pardon, Old Fathers'—had mills in Sligo and Mayo. The Shackletons were Quakers, the other two families members of the Church of Ireland.

Like flour milling, the confectionery sector was primarily home market-oriented. The Protestant-owned firm Williams & Woods of Parnell Street was the most substantial producer of sweets and jams at independence. Another well-known Dublin sweet-maker—immortalised in *Ulysses*—was the Methodist-owned Lemon, which operated from the Confectioners' Hall on Lower O'Connell Street. The printing and publishing sector was also oriented towards the domestic market. Two of the largest firms, Alexander Thom and Hely, were Protestant, as was the *Irish Times* newspaper, readership of which would long remain a marker of Protestant identity.

Business Developments over the Cumann na nGaedheal Era

Among the factors militating towards conservativism on the part of the Cumann na nGaedheal governments of the first decade of independence was the desire not to trigger capital flight on the part of the Protestant business community. It was careful; in the financial sector it had rapidly established relations with the Bank of Ireland, though it challenged the old Protestant and unionist accounting monopoly by directing state contracts, such as those for the Agricultural Credit Corporation and the ESB, to smaller Catholic firms. It was radical in a number of its programmes, however. Both in land distribution and power generation its policies had the potential to impact adversely on Protestant business interests.

Unabated land hunger represented a serious threat to the stability of the new state. The 30 per cent of large estates that remained at independence consisted of 'the hard knots that it had been impossible to disentangle under the system of voluntary purchase'.[18] With up to 1.5 million landless men prepared to enforce their claims 'with the gun and the torch', widespread agrarian violence, house burnings and threats of violence continued into 1923.[19] Compulsory land purchase and redistribution under the Land Acts of 1923 and 1927 led to a huge decline in the number of holdings of more than 200 acres. Numbers would fall further as a result of the Fianna Fáil Land Act of 1933, though Protestants in 1936 would still hold the same proportion of these holdings as they had twenty years earlier.[20] By then, however, most of the vast estates of more than 10,000 acres that had remained in gentry families at independence had been broken up.[21]

The Shannon electricity generation scheme was one of the most controversial of the new government's programmes. There were 160 generating plants already in existence. Though the bulk of these were under private ownership, most of the largest belonged to local authorities, with a particular concentration in the Protestant townships of south Dublin. Minister for Industry and Commerce Patrick McGilligan proposed that all be acquired by compulsory order. While private owners would be compensated according to a fixed formula, municipally owned undertakings were simply to be handed over to the new Electricity Supply Board. Business interests—supported by the *Irish Times*—deemed the proposal 'socialist' and 'confiscatory'. Sir John Keane, who was close to the major banking and financial interests in the state, had earlier been 'appalled by the government's "nationalisation" of land'. Now, speaking in the Senate, he criticised the proposal to subject electricity to this same 'poisonous virus of nationalisation'.[22] The most sustained opposition came from the recently elected TD William Hewat, whose coal distribution business would clearly be adversely impacted. Hewat would later also oppose the amalgamation of the railways as detrimental to private-sector interests.

With the 'national question' largely settled, independence afforded an opportunity for Catholic and Protestant businessmen to work together to protect their economic interests. An informal partnership had already developed between William Martin Murphy, Charles Eason and George Jacob during the 1913 lockout, and they, along with moderate ex-unionist leaders such as Andrew Jameson, helped to stabilise business sentiment in the troubled years of the early 1920s.[23] The unionist business community had feared that nationalist governments would be fiscally irresponsible, with the richer segment of the community—ex-unionists and business owners more generally—having to foot the bill. Fear of punitive or double taxation caused W. & R. Jacob to split its Dublin and Liverpool operations into separate companies at independence.

Seven representatives of business interests were put forward in Dublin and Cork in the 1923 general election. Four were elected with the benefit of strong Protestant support.[24] Catholic woollen manufacturer Andrew O'Shaughnessy and Church of Ireland brewer Richard Beamish were elected in Cork. The Dublin TDs, both Protestant, were building contractor John Good and William Hewat, principal of the coal business Heiton, for whom Catholic solicitor Arthur Cox acted as election agent.

The first governments of the Free State were pragmatists, not ideologues. When circumstances demanded, action could be taken. The collapse of the Condensed Milk Company led to a decision that one recent historian has characterised as 'the nationalisation of Irish agriculture'.[25] The company went bankrupt in 1923, largely due to the considerable stock-in-hand it was left with when prices collapsed dramatically from their peak in 1920. It had also suffered disproportionately from both the industrial unrest and the civil strife of the time, having been targeted by British forces, by the outbreak of 'soviet' agitation and by the anti-Treaty forces during the Civil War. In 1927 the government established the Dairy Disposal Company to purchase the assets of the private creameries—of which the re-formed Condensed Milk Company of Ireland (1924) was the largest—to end their long 'war of attrition' with the co-operatives. This effectively granted the co-operatives a state-backed monopoly of the industry.

The Dublin Distillers Company and Cork Spinning and Weaving also closed in the 1920s, though the social and political unrest of the period played little part in their demise. Meanwhile, with the death of Charles Denny in 1927, management and control of the Denny bacon company migrated to the Kent-based descendants of Henry Denny's son Edward. The firm would be denigrated as 'pseudo-Irish' by the President of the National Farmers' Association in 1966.[26]

Tariff Policy and Fianna Fáil Protectionism

Tariff policy was hugely controversial and divided opinion even within the Cumann na nGaedheal government. The leading exporting firms were strongly opposed to protection, as was export-oriented agriculture, as tariffs would raise not just input prices but also wage demands through their impact on the cost of living. The Fiscal Inquiry Committee of 1923 had reported in favour of free trade. The government nevertheless introduced a range of experimental tariffs on goods such as jams and confectionery. British firms responded by 'jumping' the tariff barriers. Rowntree and Mackintosh bought out Savoy Cocoa and North Kerry Manufacturing respectively—both small Protestant-owned confectionery firms—to produce their products for sale in the Free State. Crosse & Blackwell bought up the much larger company Williams & Woods.

British tobacco companies established three new factories in the Free State in 1923 to avoid customs duties; the consequent restructuring of the domestic industry saw the Goodbodys dispose of their tobacco interests to Carroll in 1929. The Goodbody family divested further by selling their Limerick-based flour-milling conglomerate to UK company Joseph Rank in 1930. Henceforth their manufacturing presence would be confined to the jute factory at Clara.

With the onset of the Great Depression and the collapse of export markets, support for protection of the home market strengthened. Greenmount & Boyne, for example—though it was reported in 1930 to export almost 90 per cent of its output—added its voice to the growing demand for higher tariff barriers. Cumann na nGaedheal was becoming increasingly protectionist as a result of the depression, while Fianna Fáil—regardless of world conditions—was ideologically committed to a policy of import-substituting industrialisation. Upon coming to power in 1932, it raised tariff barriers to such levels that Ireland became one of the most highly protected economies in Europe.

Home-market-oriented firms such as Lemon (maker of 'pure sweets') benefited, expanding later to a large new factory in Drumcondra. Some formerly highly export-oriented firms would also profit from Fianna Fáil's import-substituting strategy given the prevailing depression-era conditions. The newly established Irish

Sugar Company, for example, represented a welcome source of demand for the output of the Goodbody jute plant. Turning away from export markets, however, would store up problems for the future—Greenmount & Boyne's export output fell to 25 per cent by the end of the decade, though their later shift from linen into rayon would extend the life of the company. By the 1960s hosiery producer Smyth & Co. had forsaken export markets completely, while Goodbody's export-output ratio had declined to 30 per cent. Having lost touch with their former export markets, these firms would not survive the free trade environment of the EEC era. Britain and much of the rest of the world also turned protectionist in the early 1930s, but would liberalise again much earlier than Ireland. The threat of British tariffs finally swung the balance in favour of Guinness establishing a new factory at Park Royal in London in 1934.

Fianna Fáil initially planned to restrict the benefits of protection to Irish-owned firms and to maintain close control over 'tariff-jumping' foreign enterprises. The restrictions imposed by the Control of Manufactures Acts were easily avoided, however, and solicitors Arthur Cox developed a steady business in advising foreign firms on how to surmount the restrictions.

The plethora of new semi-state companies established by Fianna Fáil served to further address the religious imbalances in the accounting profession. As Farmar records, though the old Protestant firms Craig Gardner and Stokes Brothers & Pim audited the majority of large private-sector companies, the auditing contracts for Irish Life Assurance, Irish Sugar, Aer Lingus and Bord na Mona all went to Catholic firms, as did sixteen of the first twenty or so auditing contracts for companies sponsored by the Industrial Credit Corporation.[27]

Protestant firms adapted to the changing environment. Craig Gardner, the largest accountancy firm, appointed its first Catholic partner in 1944. The first appointment of a Catholic to the board of directors of Eason came in 1947. Economist R.C. Geary later recalled that he had been 'particularly struck by [the appointment of] a young Catholic graduate friend of mine to executive rank and later to a directorship in Eason's. That would occasion no comment now. It did then.'[28]

Fianna Fáil hoped that import-substituting industrialisation would help to create a new indigenous manufacturing class. By the early 1960s, however, as the protectionist era was drawing to a close, most of the firms with a workforce of 1,000 or more were foreign-owned. These included the likes of Cadbury, Rowntree, Dunlop, Halliday (producer of Clark's shoes), Player-Wills and Ford and—representative of a new breed—the General Electric subsidiary at Shannon. While a number of the old Protestant firms remained as large as they had been in the 1920s, there were now hundreds of firms employing 400 or more, compared to the two dozen or so firms in this size category in the earlier period. The dominance of older Protestant firms across most of manufacturing had disappeared. Many of the old names from the 1920s remained, however, on the 1966 *Irish Times* list of '50 largest Irish industrial companies'. As the list was based on companies traded on the Dublin Stock Exchange it included neither Guinness nor most of the foreign subsidiaries. Names that did appear however included Goulding, Hely, Switzer, Jacob, Arnott, Goodbody, Brooks Thomas, Heiton and Greenmount & Boyne.

Unidare, established by Cappoquin-born Charles Orr Stanley, of Church of Ireland background, was one of the few new large-scale indigenous firms to emerge. Although Stanley's main business interest was in the Cambridge scientific instrument maker Pye that he had purchased in 1929, he maintained strong links with Ireland. He set up an Irish subsidiary of Pye in 1936 to exploit the protected domestic market and served on the board of leading Cork firm Sunbeam Wolsey for four decades. Unidare was formed initially, under the name Aberdare, to supply parts to the ESB but rapidly proved successful in export markets also. It would go on to become one of the most substantial employers of the 1960s and 1970s.[29]

Outward Orientation

Post-war economic stagnation, continuing trade dependency on the UK, and the division of western Europe into two separate trading blocs—with Ireland facing the danger of being excluded from both—forced a change of economic strategy in the late 1950s. A new breed of export-oriented foreign multinational was attracted by the corporation-tax and industrial grants innovations of the time, and the jobs and confidence generated facilitated the dismantling of trade barriers over the following decades. The consequences for Irish businesses were dramatic. Scale was necessary for survival in a more open trading environment and most Irish firms of the time were tiny by international standards. The 1960s and 1970s saw a wave of mergers and acquisitions that paid no heed to the religious associations of earlier times.[30]

The main milk suppliers to the Dublin market in 1963 were Hughes Brothers and Merville Dairies, both owned by Church of Ireland families. The purchase of Hughes Brothers by the American firm W. & R. Grace in 1964 triggered the formation of Premier Dairies in 1966 through the merger of Merville and two Catholic-owned firms, Dublin Dairies and Tel-el-Kebir. Beamish & Crawford was sold to Canadian Breweries in 1962. By the mid-1960s many of the other Irish breweries, including Catholic-owned Macardle and Smithwick, had been acquired by Guinness. 1966 saw the merger of Jacob and Boland biscuits, while Irish Distillers was formed through the merger of John Jameson, John Power and Cork Distilleries. Two of the largest printing firms of the 1920s, Alexander Thom and Hely, had merged in 1962 to form Hely-Thom. The new firm was acquired by Smurfit in 1970. Goulding was acquired by Tony O'Reilly a few years later.

Similar developments were taking place in finance. 'To counter size with size', in the words of F.S.L. Lyons, and to avoid the threat of foreign takeover, Bank of Ireland merged with the Hibernian Bank in 1958. The merger 'would have astounded the Hibernian's founders, vociferous as they had been in 1825 that banking facilities were being withheld from a large section of the community, "owing to the political and religious preferences of the Bank of Ireland"'.[31] In 1966 the National Bank joined the new group. A similar fusion of traditions occurred with the formation of Allied Irish Banks later that year through the merger of the Munster & Leinster, the Provincial and the Royal.

An anecdote recounted by Tony Farmar illustrates the broader changes taking place within society over the decade. Asked to recommend a new company secretary for an old-style Protestant building firm, Craig Gardner felt obliged to point out (with some diffidence) that the candidate 'dug with the other foot'. They were informed that this was of no significance as long as the candidate was competent.[32] Craig Gardner itself became part of the large UK firm Price Waterhouse, while Stokes Brothers & Pim merged with the Catholic firm Kennedy Crowley in 1972 to form the largest accountancy group in the state. Control of Brooks Thomas and Dockrell passed to emerging conglomerates in the early 1970s.

James Quinn's assessment of developments in the building provisions sector—that the determination to keep control in Protestant hands had seriously restricted the talent pool and become an acute weakness in a rapidly changing environment—applies more generally to traditional family firms.[33] Though family capitalism remains relatively important in Ireland, as Patricia Kelleher and, more recently, Colm O'Gorman and Declan Curran have shown, the weaknesses inherent in family management structures become more apparent in more intensely competitive environments.[34] This applied to Guinness as well. Though it had long been a public company, a member of the family continued to serve as chairman of the board of directors until 1986. Family control ceased as a result of a share-buying scandal involving company management that erupted at the time of Guinness's purchase of the (Scottish) Distillers Company. Though the family was not involved, the hands-off approach to company affairs that it had come to adopt was widely criticised as inadequate in the modern era.

The outward reorientation of the Irish economy had one further powerful effect of relevance. As represented by the publication of the landmark report *Investment in Education* in 1965, it brought an increased focus on the importance of education. With the subsequent massive increase in educational attainment, educational credentials came to displace personal connections as the main route through which new staff were recruited in the private sector.

Conclusion

Ethnic and sectarian divisions are known to have a detrimental impact on a country's growth prospects. Though it is an achievement that is often overlooked, it is to Ireland's credit that there now remains little trace, either in business or the wider economy, of the divisions that were so apparent at the foundation of the state.

While Protestants still remained a privileged minority at the time of EEC entry in 1973, this was a reflection not of contemporaneous sectarianism but of the 'glass floor' that maintains through the generations the privileged position of those with inherited resources. By 1973, denominationally distinct workplaces had all but disappeared, long-established Protestant and Catholic firms had merged, the era of tightly controlled family businesses was past, educational credentials were displacing personal connections as the main means of recruitment and merit-based promotion was becoming more and more the norm.

It is perhaps ironic that the *Irish Times*—often the proponent of Protestant engagement with the new Ireland—should prove to be one of the last hold-outs. The Arnott family sold control in 1946, but the new owners were also Protestant.[35] In his memoir of a 1950s' Church of Ireland childhood, Homan Potterton, one-time director of the National Gallery, spoke of the paper's significance as a marker of Protestant identity: 'We read the *Irish Times*, they read the *Irish Independent* or the *Irish Press*: it was as simple, or as complicated, as that.'[36] Terence Brown refers to the office environment as being 'overseen by the formidable Major McDowell in which confessional distinctions did not always go unremarked'.

The paper's readership had begun, though, to broaden out under Douglas Gageby, who became editor in 1963. Gageby was determined—as noted by a journalist in the 1970s—'to bury the memory of the *Irish Times* as a voice of Protestant Unionism. He wanted us to be liberal but also to be part of mainstream Irish life.' Yet, not until 1986 was the first editor of Catholic background appointed.[37]

CHAPTER TEN

'The jersey is all that matters, not your church': Protestants and the GAA in the Rural Republic

IDA MILNE

The GAA in my Family's History

Some of my strongest childhood memories derive from the GAA: playing in family groups on the beach in the seaside town of Courtown, when a radio would be switched on and the fathers would be collectively lured away to the hypnotic sound of GAA commentator extraordinaire Michael O'Hehir's excitable descriptions; or watching my father, Ned Davitt and other neighbours hurl on the pitch on our farm in north County Wexford. Going to Ferns to welcome the team home from Croke Park with the traditional mountain of burning tractor tyres seemed an annual occasion, in the limited experiences of a child, the column of black smoke drawing people from miles around to the reception as Wexford celebrated yet another All-Ireland hurling championship win. In the 1960s golden age of Wexford hurling, the Rackard brothers were both sporting legends and society heroes.[1] When Nicky Rackard, a veterinary surgeon, came into the yard to treat our cattle, we children hung around, starstruck.

The GAA was and is part of my cultural background. The fact that our family went to a different church on a Sunday didn't seem to impinge on that. We were Church of Ireland, part of the Anglican

Communion (although we were not comfortable with that term), whereas the archetypal GAA player was Catholic. For our family, the GAA was and is part of the ordinariness of life, not the difference. My father, King (b. 1919), and grandfather, Harry (b. 1888), loved all Gaelic games—football, handball and, in particular, hurling—which they played, as did other Protestants in the parish. The fast-moving, skilful sport is gripping to watch, played in the air and on the ground, as players jump to intercept the flying *sliotar* or ball, their ash *camáns* or hurls clashing together in tackles, shoulders rippling as they belt the *sliotar* up the field in mid-jump. My father ploughed and rolled the pitch when the Ferns St Aidan's GAA club was established in Ferns. They were always going to matches and, as a child, I tagged along. My older brother preferred soccer. It was the 1960s after all, and television was bringing the new glamour of English football to our home. George Best was *his* hero.

Being interested in Gaelic games was just one of many ways we engaged with our cultural heritage. We were Irish; we stood respectfully when our national anthem was played; the tricolour was the only national flag we knew. In 1966, we schoolchildren raised the placard commemorating the 1916 Proclamation on our classroom wall with pride, and marched around with toy shotguns over our shoulders bawling the popular rebel ballad 'The Jolly Ploughboy'. Many of our national school teachers went to Coláiste Moibhí before teacher training college and consequently had had good Irish language skills; the focus on Irish was strong in our national schools. My sister and I went to the village hall in Ferns to learn Irish step dancing and took part in dancing *feiseanna*, dressed in elaborately embroidered Irish dancing costumes borrowed from the Davitts, our neighbours and friends. My mother, Sheila Milne, and grandaunts, Ida and Ettie Milne, were members of the Irish Countrywomen's Association which met in the hall in Tombrack once a month; before independence the grandaunts had been interested in the United Irishwomen, and in 1912 held a ball in Clobemon Hall to fundraise to get a midwife based in Ballycarney (equally, in February 1916 they held another ball to fundraise for the Red Cross). That nurse, Nurse Swaine, became something of a local hero birthing babies, including my father. Dad and his brother Harry were members of Macra na Tuaithe, the young farmers' association, and Dad was deeply involved in farming organisations, co-operatives and the County Show committee. Some members of the family foxhunted with the Island Hunt. That might seem like an ascendancy trait, but the Island has historically been a middle-class farmers' hunt, Catholic and Protestant, rather than a gentry one. Few of our fellow parishioners hunted; it was not part of their family culture. The idea that any of our co-religionists might be viewed as having a closer cultural or political affinity with Britain than with Ireland would have seemed preposterous through the eyes of a Wexford Protestant child of the 1960s. Like other local families in this tightly knit community, we enjoy warm friendships often of many generations' standing with our immediate neighbours. King, in later years, became an acknowledged expert on the 1798 rebellion and was so involved in the bicentenary commemorations that he used to joke: 'If as much preparation had gone into the rebellion, we might have won.'

In another clue to identity, the *Irish Times* in a newspaper-reading household was an occasional purchase; the *Irish Independent* was a daily necessity which my father mirthfully justified by saying he had to know who was dead: death notices of rural Catholic and Protestant alike were far more likely, in earlier times, to appear in the *Independent* than the *Irish Times*. Funeral-going was regarded by him as a duty to the community. Reading the *Independent*, of course, also carried political connotations; he was a member of Fine Gael. On reflection, I understand that King had good reason to value the community in which we lived, and to maintain those connections. When the farm hit a serious economic crisis in the 1920s, scores of neighbours flocked to save the crops. These acts of community support were repeated in other times of crisis also—including the 1798 rebellion and the War of Independence and Civil War—and make nonsense of all sorts of social and cultural boundaries that unknowing outsiders might impose on the community. These neighbourly supports have enabled a largely peaceful existence for various branches of our family over 400 years. It is important to acknowledge them.

In recent years, trawling through the literature about the Gaelic Athletic Association, I was surprised to find that the voice of the GAA-playing Protestant does not appear and that the story of my family's love of Gaelic games is one that is not considered the norm in Ireland. From our cultural and ethnological perspective, some historians seem to have missed this story. One work claimed that the early promise of strong Protestant involvement with the GAA quickly fell away as the GAA became more and more identified with nationalism and Catholicism. That we might not be perceived as nationalist (albeit with a very small 'n', a Fine Gael nationalism) was something of a surprise. The converse—implying unionism, allegiance to Britain, or a hankering for the old order—is simply not part of the Wexford or south-east Protestant identity.

Protestants in the Historiography

Marcus de Búrca contended that in the twentieth century only a handful of Protestants have played Gaelic games and of these he cited only Sam Maguire of Dunmanway, who reached iconic status when the All-Ireland senior football cup was named after him; and Jack Boothman, the only Protestant to date to have become GAA president. Cronin, Duncan and Rouse in *The GAA: A People's History* (2009) suggest that 'the GAA has made much of its Protestant members, but the reality is that Protestants have been greatly under-represented in the Association'.[2] They argue briefly that in Northern Ireland this happened because of the bind between religion and political allegiance, while in the south it emerged from a range of factors, including a divided educational system, as Gaelic games 'were not a significant presence in non-Catholic schools'.[3] They say that while the GAA had a number of Protestants involved in its early affairs and repeatedly stressed its non-sectarian nature, 'the reality of its politics saw it identified from the beginning with nationalism and Catholicism'.[4]

These arguments caused something of a puzzle for me as they were so far from my family experience and were also difficult, given our love of our country and our respect for our neighbours and their religion. At the same time, they are views expressed by leading historians in a work that I found riveting, drawing on the early research of the Boston College GAA oral history project, one to which, despite repeated calls for public engagement, few Protestants contributed. Gradually I came to view the arguments as a key research question and one for which I remain indebted to the above authors for drawing my attention to. Why was the public perception of the allegiances of southern Protestantism so far from what we lived in the private sphere, not just regarding the GAA but also our politics and national allegiances? It would appear that the very reluctance of twenty-six-county Protestants to draw attention to themselves and their opinions meant that broader society does not know them. Gaps tend to fill. So, in the absence of Protestants speaking up when they see themselves being misinterpreted, the natural conclusion by others is that they share the more publicly expressed allegiances and views of Northern Irish Protestant unionists: we are back to voices not always being heard in proportion, as mentioned in the introduction to this volume.

I started researching, initially through casual conversations and then through formal oral history interviews, exploring not only involvement but also attitudes and perceptions. I wanted to capture attitudes to the GAA among rural Protestants in the Republic, to identify their views separately from those of Ulster Protestants and urban twenty-six-county Protestants. Protestant opinion is not homogenous with loyalties and opinions shaped differently by a myriad of factors; as one interviewee said, 'There are as many Protestant opinions as there are Protestants.' The conversations and interviews indicate that there has always been an interest in and involvement with the association amongst rural Protestants, in particular in the farming communities of the south-east, but the involvement was treated discreetly. Neither they nor the organisation made an issue of their religious affiliation. As Croke Park director of games Pat Daly, a Waterford native, said, 'They just got on with it.'[5]

The material emerging from my interviews raises some contrasts. On the one hand, adult Protestant interest in sport in Wexford undoubtedly centred on rugby, with equine sports (mostly racing and hunting) a close second. One interviewee mentioned that the most important object in his childhood home was the photograph of Enniscorthy RFC, which won the Provincial Towns' Cup in 1963, with twelve Protestants on the team. 'Is it too fanciful to think that rural Protestants, feeling excluded from the influence-nexus of the new state (Catholic, GAA, Fianna Fáil), constructed, or retreated into, their own (Protestant, rugby, Fine Gael)?'[6] The interviews also produced strong evidence of living outside that local Protestant bubble, of engaging with the community in different ways, including through the GAA.

Northern Protestant Attitudes to the GAA

Perhaps observers have overly projected the attitudes of Protestant communities in Northern Ireland to the GAA onto southern Protestant communities. Many Northern unionist Protestants find it difficult to perceive the GAA as merely a sporting organisation, like the Football Association; instead it is seen as one of the chief expressions of the culture of the Catholic and largely nationalist communities. Gaelic games, as Sugden and Bairner have pointed out, are, like other games, symbolically reflective of whole ways of life and 'are distinctly Gaelic in nature and . . . a ritualistic celebration of that particular culture'. As such, they are 'intimately bound up with community structure, culture and ritual'.[7] The GAA, with its overt trappings of nationalism—the flag hanging over the pitch and the singing of the Irish national anthem before throw-in—is not, on the surface, welcoming for those of a different religious or political persuasion in Northern Ireland.

During the Troubles, tensions between Ulster GAA interests and loyalists frequently spilled over into violence and even death. David Hassan has argued that, from the 1960s onwards: 'There is no denying the reality that the GAA in Ulster, especially in its units based in Northern Ireland, was subject to attack from loyalist paramilitaries and elements within the British state.' Hassan points out that clubhouses were attacked, members were murdered by loyalist paramilitaries and grounds—infamously Crossmaglen GAC—were occasionally occupied by the British army.[8] Even since the Good Friday Agreement, which brought about the beginning of an end to the Troubles, some Protestant GAA players have sometimes been treated with suspicion and overt hostility by some Catholics. In one of the better-known instances, Darren Graham walked off the pitch after sustaining verbal sectarian abuse during a match between his club, Lisnaskea Emmets, and Brookeborough in 2007. He subsequently received a fulsome apology from the Fermanagh County Board and returned to play.[9]

But all was not necessarily as it looked. GAA historian Donal McAnallen considers that, in the border counties, Protestant participation in the GAA has been

> quite normalised in recent decades as they have tended to assimilate ever more into predominantly Catholic nationalist communities, though it is clear from occasional incidents that the presence of a Protestant player is often known about and can become the subject of sectarian abuse in a match context (especially as verbal abuse of all sorts seems to be so widely accepted).[10]

McAnallen suggests that north of the border, Protestant participation has been proportionately smaller than in the Republic, but that there has been a small scattering of Protestant players over the years:

> North Antrim was noted traditionally for Protestants playing hurling with relatively little fuss. Examples include Charlie Jolly, who played for the Antrim hurling team for several years in the 1930s. Denver Campbell, a DUP local council election candidate in the 2000s, played for Thomas Clarke's reserve team in Dungannon in the early 1980s. Craig Gilroy, the Irish rugby international, is one of a number of Protestants who have played for St Paul's GAA Club, Holywood, which has always been very apolitical.

The GAA: Politically Non-aligned Intent

If the GAA is seen in the North as a heavily politicised organisation, it was not founded as such. It was established on 1 November 1884 in Hayes' Hotel in Thurles, County Tipperary, as a national sporting body, open to Irishmen of all classes, creeds and political persuasions, committed to cultivating and promoting indigenous games. It was to be politically non-aligned, but pro-national. One of the three people asked to become patrons of the Association out of that meeting was politician and Protestant Charles Stewart Parnell, alongside Catholic Archbishop Croke of Cashel and Land League hero Michael Davitt. Sports historian W.F. Mandle writes that the choice of these three as patrons represented recognition of the major forces in the Irish nationalist movement of the day: agrarianism, parliamentarianism, the Catholic church and Fenianism. Parnell was there because of his politics; he was not appointed patron through any desire to show religious tolerance, Mandle says.

The guiding philosophy of non-sectarianism continues to this day. GAA Rule 1.12 states that the association is anti-sectarian and anti-racist and committed to the principles of inclusion and diversity at all levels. This rule provides that

> any conduct by deed, word or gesture of a sectarian or racist nature or which is contrary to the principles of inclusion and diversity against any player, official, spectator or anyone else, in the course of activities organised by the Association, shall be deemed to have discredited the Association.

The penalty for breaching this rule is contained in Rule 7.2 (e) 'Misconduct considered to have discredited the Association', which states that members and teams guilty of such misconduct will get a minimum eight weeks' suspension. Debarment and expulsion from the Association may also be considered.[11]

And yet, the strict adherence to the anti-sectarian rule could be construed—particularly within the context of community conflict in Northern Ireland—as being at odds with the primary aim of the Association, stated in Rule 1.2: 'The Association is a national organisation which has as its basic aim the strengthening of the national identity in a 32 county Ireland through the preservation and promotion of Gaelic games and pastimes.' The additional aims in Rule 1.4 include the support of the Irish language, of Irish dancing, music, song and other aspects of Irish culture, and the fostering of 'the national ideals in the people of Ireland'. The various rules known collectively as 'the ban', which excluded those who played 'foreign' sports and games and those who were members of the British security forces, were seen as the 'ultimate expression of the GAA's intimate association with nationalism' and were particularly contentious in the context of the Northern Ireland conflict.[12]

De Búrca points out that amongst the members of the Metropolitan Club, the backbone of the early GAA in Dublin, were several Ulster Protestants, including Rev. Samuel Holmes of Down, L.C. Slevin of Armagh, Trueman Cross of Tyrone and the brothers Frank and Robert Patterson of Newry.[13] Mandle also mentions the early support of Protestant unionists like Rev. Maxwell Close and Protestant nationalist Douglas Hyde. When control of the Association was seized by the Irish Republican Brotherhood in the late 1880s, the 'cultural euphoria' which buoyed the GAA in its very early expansionary years evaporated, according to William Murphy: 'Revolutionary politics acted as an emetic, flushing less radical nationalists from the association at an enfeebling rate.' The Association began to recover when, as Murphy points out, the Fenian-controlled leadership was replaced by a regime that prioritised sport and was 'sufficiently centrist in its expression of the organisation's cultural ideals to accommodate most nationalists and others who had no politics at all'.[14] It left the Association, however, with a taint that may have been uncomfortable for nationalist Protestants, who tended to be moderate in their political views. Wicklow Church of Ireland member Jack Boothman always maintained that, while the Association is politically aligned, it is not sectarian. GAA historian Eoghan Corry noted that at certain strategic times in the Association's history, tensions have arisen over this dichotomy, during the IRB crisis in the 1880s and again in the 1980s, during the hunger strikes crisis in Northern Ireland, when the question of the form of expression of the Association's nationalism was the subject of heated debate at its annual congress.[15]

While attitudes of Northern Irish Protestants to the GAA are well covered in the historiography and in newspaper reports, there is little commentary in the sports histories on the attitudes of southern rural Protestants. Some authorities cite issues like the requirement to fly the Irish tricolour over the pitch and the playing of games on Sundays as factors that tended to alienate Protestants from playing or supporting Gaelic games. Some also point to diverse incidents or periods as watershed marks for turning Protestants away from Gaelic games. Among these are the deposing of Michael Cusack, who had attracted many Protestants into the GAA; the seizure of control of the organisation by the IRB in the 1880s; increasing involvement with the Catholic clergy in the 1920s and 1930s; and the Northern Troubles of the 1970s and 1980s.

What the Interviews Show

The interviews demonstrate an engagement with the GAA that can be enthusiastic but is usually typified by discretion. Some Protestant families donated, leased or sold pitches to clubs and helped to maintain them, they played and continue to play at all levels, they ferried teams to matches, washed jerseys, fundraised, listened to commentators Michael O'Hehir and Mícheál Ó Muircheartaigh, cycled enormous distances to inter-county games, followed the rows at the national congress with interest and did all the things that GAA enthusiasts do. Mostly, they participated in an unassuming way, anxious not to 'stick out'. Playing or following GAA was a mode of identifying with their local community, a way of making bonds with neighbours they could not meet in church.

For many twenty-six-county Protestants, Protestantism and nationalism are far from being mutually exclusive and therefore the trappings of nationalism that accompany the GAA—the flying of the flag, the emphasis on the use of Irish, the singing of the national anthem and even the prayers and the reverence for Christianity—are also part of their identity. None of those I have interviewed about the GAA saw any reason to object to the overt nationalism of the GAA; overt Catholicism was often described as just 'a fact of life'.

While Gaelic games were rarely played in Protestant schools (or the elite Catholic schools, for that matter), only a very small percentage of Protestants were able to afford to go to Protestant private schools. As several interviewees pointed out, even after the introduction of free secondary education and the parallel grant paid to the Protestant schools' Secondary Education Committee, many Protestants still could not afford the grant-aided boarding-school fees. Typically, the Protestant GAA player is someone who has not 'gone away' to school; that is, they attended the local, usually Catholic, secondary school rather than going to a rugby- or hockey-playing boarding school with a Protestant ethos. They played in local secondary schools and with the local GAA club. This point was continually reinforced by the interviewees.

Three interviewees—Jack Boothman, Leitrim county footballer Colin Regan and Roger Boyd, who played for Annacurra—were exceptions to this rule. Boothman played rugby and hockey when he went to the Church of Ireland-ethos King's Hospital school in Dublin as a boarder, but continued to play Gaelic football at home during the summer. Regan went to a hockey-playing boarding school in Donegal run by the Donegal Protestant Board of Education, but continued to play Gaelic football during this time. Boyd's rugby-playing started when he was a boarder in the Quaker Newtown

School in Waterford; it continued later, in parallel with Gaelic football. Some people, he suggested, had an idea that all Protestants went to boarding school. This in turn, would imply that they play rugby rather than Gaelic games or soccer, as Protestant and elite Catholic boarding schools played rugby. He said this was not the case,

> not by a long shot. In fact, in my little national school, we would have been the only ones [who went to boarding school]. People have the impression that all the Protestants went off to boarding school, and it is nonsense. But the rest, the people who stayed . . . if you wanted to kick a football locally, there were no other options locally. So of course we wanted to play football.

Boyd's sentiments were echoed by Boothman; most people play the sport that is played within their community, rather than choosing to travel distances to play another code.

Protestants whose GAA playing has actually been documented include George Magan, who won an All-Ireland football medal with Kildare in 1919, and Percy Clendennen, a member of the County Offaly senior hurling team, who played in goal for Kinnitty for more than twenty-five years. Tom Mitchell, another Kinnitty Church of Ireland hurler, was on the Kinnitty team that won the Offaly championship in 1930. Mitchell told Paddy Downey of the *Irish Times* that there were Protestants on every single Kinnitty team that had won the Offaly county hurling championship. He said: 'When it comes to hurling, religion makes no difference; hurling is the religion around here.'[16] Some of my Wexford interviewees have expressed the same sentiment.

Boothman became the first Protestant to hold high office in the GAA since the 1880s and was president from 1994–7. When I asked him about the overt nationalism that some historians see as being an obstacle to Protestants, he said that 'whereas waving the tricolour and the singing of "Amhrán na bhFhiann" [the Irish national anthem] in front of an Ulster unionist are like waving a red rag at a bull, these issues do not raise any fundamental objections among Protestants in the South'.[17] He tended to downplay his religious affiliation during his term of office. 'It wasn't important.' At the same time, he sometimes used his religion as an opportunity to challenge tradition.

When the annual GAA congress was held in Wexford town during his term as Leinster president, the officials trooped in to the local Church of Ireland for the Association's traditional Sunday morning religious service, having attended mass in the Catholic church the night before. During his term of office as president, he frequently visited clubs in the North and said that while often their members' political views might be diametrically opposed to his own, he felt 'a great bond with the Northern GAA clubs, because of the difficulties they endured'.

Boothman was firmly opposed to the relaxing of the ban on allowing members of the RUC and British army to play. It was primarily a pragmatic stance; he felt that they might come to harm. He felt that attacks on GAA-playing members of the PSNI had proven his case. During his trips to the North, he made a point of attending a Protestant church service on Sundays, in order to break down cultural barriers between the Association and northern Protestants. He was often recognised as the GAA president by the congregations, and 'had a bit of chat with them'.

He placed very firm emphasis on the GAA's stance as a non-sectarian organisation and considered that it is precluded from taking a head count of the religious affiliations of its members by the anti-sectarian rule. Anyhow, he believed that many GAA people have never actually signed up for membership, so it would be impossible to check. Over the years he had served on GAA committees with other Church of Ireland or Presbyterian members; one day by chance he would discover that they were also Protestant. He said that locals in Wicklow would know of Protestants playing in clubs around, but no remarks would be passed about it: 'it was just considered a normal part of life'. Pat Daly, the GAA director of games, himself from Tallow in County Waterford, considered that this attitude would be common in the twenty-six counties: 'In the south . . . it wasn't considered anything that unusual.'

On the issue of the close identification of the GAA with the Catholic church, and in particular with priests, Boothman suggested that by contrast to the traditional close relationship between priests and people within the Catholic church, Church of Ireland clergy, in the past, tended to be rather aloof from their flock (often of a different class), and did not socialise with them. Catholic priests seemed more approachable, so they were not as alien to Protestants as some might expect. Some interviewees commented on friendships with priests. There was also the vexed question of the Sabbath observance. Sabbatarianism—the concept of keeping Sunday holy by not doing unnecessary work or indulging in pleasure—was widely practised by Protestant families, to varying degrees. Within my own family it was acceptable to watch or play sport, but not to do work that could be done the following day; as farmers, we could save a crop if the weather forecast suggested that otherwise it might be lost. Catherine O'Connor found Sabbatarianism to be an issue that prevented some Protestants from participating in or even following GAA matches on television or radio. O'Connor interviewed Protestant women in the south-eastern Church of Ireland diocese of Ferns about their lives and social practices between 1945 and 1965. An interviewee who lived near the Rackard hurling stronghold of Rathnure said that during that era, her family placed such emphasis on observing the Sabbath that not only could they not play games on a Sunday, they wouldn't be allowed to listen to the radio, or even to knit.[18] Jack Boothman said that when he was growing up in the 1940s and 1950s, 99 per cent of Protestants observed Sunday to the point where all they did was go to church:

> Our family escaped that maxim; we were dairy farmers and we had to work seven days a week, so that set us aside from other Protestant farms. We milked the cows, went to church and after that, my father brought us to some sort of a match somewhere.

Like Boothman, Roger Boyd came from a Wicklow farming Church of Ireland family near Tinahely. He, his father Cam, uncle Harry and cousin Keith all played Gaelic football with Annacurra. Boyd says that the attitude to playing on a Sunday was fairly relaxed in his family. In relation to work, one wouldn't go out of one's way to work on a Sunday, unless there was something urgent to be done. Cam used to tell a story of going to church one Sunday morning and of the clergyman basing his sermon on breach of the Sabbath. As it was well known he was going to play football in the afternoon, Cam felt the sermon was aimed directly at him. The policy was not uniform among the Protestant clergy; when Cam was in Newtown School in Waterford, another Protestant clergyman said he could see no reason to object to lads playing football on a Sunday afternoon if they had gone to church in the morning.

Eoghan Corry suggested that some players would overcome this issue by using an alias:

> That the games were generally played on Sundays caused problems for some. Priests might not like to be seen to be playing on Sunday, their busy day, and some Protestants, while willing to play on Sunday themselves, might be afraid they would give offence to some of their co-religionists. So, in the programme or the match report, they would be identified as A.N. Other or by some other alias.[19]

Corry also mentioned that until recent times players who wanted to circumvent the ban on playing the so-called 'foreign games', usually rugby or soccer, would use aliases. By the time Roger Boyd was playing, the 'ban' had been abolished. He simultaneously played rugby with Greystones, a senior team, from the 1970s to the 1990s, and Gaelic football with Annacurra.

Boyd, a thoughtful, reflective interviewee, pointed out that his sports experience challenges assumptions that people tend to make about Protestants and sport. During his GAA playing days, he could not recall coming across religious bias, except in the form of teasing or a joke. There were other Protestants also playing for the club. Interestingly, rugby in Greystones, which had a large Protestant population, was slightly different. Boyd said at one stage he was the only Protestant and the only farmer on that team:

> I played rugby with very few Protestants, even in Greystones where you would think there *would* be Protestants. Some of those guys were my best of friends, and there was plenty of ribbing about being Protestant there, but it was all good natured.

Colin Regan, a Leitrim county senior footballer, said that for his large Church of Ireland family playing Gaelic games 'was part of a community thing'.[20] His father never played Gaelic games, although he does recall football being played on one of the meadows on the family farm in the 1940s and 1950s. Regan's four elder brothers dabbled with Gaelic football while attending the Church of Ireland national school in Kinlough, but of that generation only Barbour played to adult level (he also played with Tir Conaill Gaels for many years in London during the 1980s before returning to Leitrim and his home club). When that school closed Colin went to the Church of Ireland national school in Ballyshannon, where nobody played Gaelic games. He and his closest brothers in age, Gordon and Stuart, played Gaelic and soccer with their neighbours when they came home from school; later he played with the Melvin Gaels making up the half-back line with his brothers Barbour and Gordon on numerous occasions. He won a Leitrim senior club championship medal in 1998 with his nephew Jason playing corner back. Asked if he found the overt Catholicism of the GAA difficult, he responded:

> No more than the Angelus [bell] every day. I remember heading west to Galway for *Féile na nGael*, staying with host families, and part of the trip was mass; I went along to the mass and went up for communion. The family I was staying with were trying to arrange for me to go to church but I didn't want to, I went with the others. Mass was always put in as part of the schedule but it never bothered me, it was just part of the group mentality. Just a fact that they didn't see me as different, it was not a sectarian thing or anything.[21]

His response to a question about the Irish flag flying over the GAA grounds was that 'The tricolour is my flag as well. So that is not an issue.' Sometimes other players would jibe him about being a Protestant, just the same as he might jibe them about being fans of Ipswich or whatever. 'It was just part of who you are.'

Interviewing less high-profile Protestant GAA players has proved to be a difficult process. Many had played the games discreetly, wanting to avoid drawing attention to themselves. Several people who spoke or refused to speak to me said they preferred 'to keep the head down', not through fear, but perhaps because of the reasons they wanted to take part in Gaelic games in the first place. They were trying to fit into the fabric of their community. By talking to me about being a Protestant playing GAA, they would be effectually 'othering' themselves.

My mother, Sheila Milne, said that as teenagers she and her brothers and sisters all played hurling informally in a neighbour's field at their home in the Leap, near Enniscorthy, and that they considered it normal.[22] She spoke of her own lifelong interest in

GAA games; even now she spends her Sunday afternoons watching inter-county games on television. Her brother, Eric Deacon, said that he played everything he could when he was going to the technical school.[23] He loved rugby and hurling and was good at both. He was playing on a 'good minor hurling team' for Ballinavarry Gaels, and when they looked like getting to the county final, he gave up rugby for the year:

> out of respect for the ban I thought it was not fair to my own lads, and anyhow I wanted to win a medal as well. It never cost me a thought about religion or flag or anything else like that, I just wanted to play.

As a teacher in Gorey Technical School, Deacon was approached to train the County Wexford Vocational Schools Team, which he brought to the all-Ireland final, having beaten Kilkenny—a renowned hurling county—along the way. The final was played in Croke Park, where they were beaten by a Tipperary team. After the match, he told the other organisers: 'Lads, I'll be with you next year as one of the team, but not as the coach, because next week I am putting an advertisement in the local paper to start a rugby club in Gorey.' As a result of that advertisement, a motion to have him suspended was proposed at a county convention. He was amused, as he had never formally been a member, reflecting Jack Boothman's view that 'GAA membership' was a somewhat fluid construct.

Conclusion

That concept of fluid membership and the fact that the GAA does not ask its members about their religious affiliation make it impossible to quantify the numbers of Protestants involved in the Association. Wexford historian John Nangle identified for me several Protestants who had played with various clubs in north Wexford in the twentieth century. He said that people would be well aware that they were Protestant, and that it was accepted and not an issue. Again, he said that it would be impossible to quantify numbers, as he suggested Protestants may have used aliases to 'get around the ban' on playing rugby and soccer.[24] In an interview with Senan Lillis, who is a former public relations officer of Wexford County Board

(1987–90) and former Wexford senior football selector (1986–8) as well as being an activist in Blackwater GAA Club since 1980, he said that in his experience of the GAA in County Wexford:

> GAA involvement merged the whole community and teams and individuals organised themselves for the 'love of the little village'. Parishes with a Protestant contingent would in almost very case provide players for their local GAA clubs. This was taken for granted and no 'big deal' attached to this. The large amount of Protestant players that has won county medals, in all grades in hurling and football, is testimony to this. The jersey is all that matters, not your church.[25]

It should be stated here that most of these interviews are with those who were known for their interest in the GAA; they are friends and family, or friends of friends. It would be a mistake to suggest that these views reflect anything like the majority of the local Protestant population. However, the interviews do record views that have not been included in the historiography of the GAA, or of twenty-six-county Irish Protestantism. They show that some rural Protestants within the Republic have participated in Gaelic games alongside their Catholic neighbours throughout the GAA's history. This cohort views playing Gaelic sports as a way of identifying with their local community, of blending in. As their participation has tended to be both discreet and at club rather than the more elite county level, and as the GAA's rules do not permit tracking the religious affiliation of its members, historians may not have been aware of the scale of interaction.

In many respects, southern Protestant involvement in the GAA benefited both parties. If, for Protestants, it was done quietly, it was done of love for the sport and as a way of engaging with neighbourliness and community life. For the GAA, with hindsight, a rule book that was so clear on disallowing discrimination was a vital aid in the transition to the multi-ethnic and multi-faith society that the Republic of Ireland has become.

PART III

Otherness

CHAPTER ELEVEN

Protestant Republicans in the Revolution and After

MARTIN MAGUIRE

Introduction

Traditionally the history of Ireland's revolution, 1912–23, was written as an heroic, single, national narrative featuring biographies of the key figures along with local 'fighting stories' of ambushes and battles. Recent studies show a more complex history as new sources become available, along with the development of new perspectives.[1]

Irish Protestants as a social group and their experience of the revolution and the formation of the Irish Free State has become the focus of increasing interest, often from the perspective of conflict, alienation and what has been characterised as 'ethnic cleansing'. This essay, on the other hand, explores the experience of those Protestants on the other side, those who were republican and part of the revolutionary nexus.[2]

The involvement of Protestants in the Irish revolution was the subject of León Ó Broin's study of the Stopfords. For León Ó Broin the Stopfords, and the circle of Protestant republicans that gathered around them, were eccentric oddities best understood as deviations from, rather than expressions of, the norms of Irish Protestantism.[3] More recently Valerie Jones has written an in-depth history of a selection of Protestant rebels who engaged in the 1916 Rising.[4]

Roy Foster's history of the revolutionary generation also examines Protestant nationalists, suggesting their rebellion was against their class rather than their religion.[5] Here, I identify and examine some ninety-nine Protestants involved in the revolution (sixty-six men and thirty-three women), using the BMH WS and the Military Service Pension Collection (MSPC)[6] (see Table 1). Apart from some refusing to engage, the challenges in using the BMH witness statements are well documented.[7] Eyewitness accounts may be read as privileged knowledge or, alternatively, as self-serving distortions of reality. The witness statements were collected in the 1940s and the 1950s about events thirty to forty years earlier. Consciously created as legacy records, they are inevitably shaped by knowledge of subsequent events and by the concerns of an ageing generation. Witnesses were fully aware of the later conflicts of allegiance and the disappointments that flowed from the revolution into the Civil War and shaped the independent state. The MSPC files, never intended to be an historical source and created soon after the events of the revolutionary years as applications for a state pension, act as a corrective. Collected to evaluate demands on the public purse, these were subject to rigorous scrutiny by a joint military and civil service committee. The dearth of pension files, as compared to witness statements, for these men and women may be seen as a limitation. However, the features of the witness statements that usually generate caution are, for the purposes of this article, an advantage. Taking the organisations as mentioned in the 1916 Proclamation of the Republic—Irish Volunteers, ICA and IRB—Protestants were active in all three as well as in a myriad of cultural organisations. Are their statements coloured by a *mentalité* that is specifically Protestant? Do they propose a distinctly Protestant contribution to the Irish revolution and a distinctly Protestant response to the post-revolutionary society that emerged? If so, were these Protestants disillusioned at the Ireland that grew from their revolutionary activism? In that case we would expect to find it expressed and for it to colour the witness statements given by them twenty or thirty years later.

Protestants in Revolt

Taking 'occupation' or 'father's occupation' as a proxy for class, the Protestant republicans and revolutionaries were middle class, urban and professional. Harry Nicholls was an engineer, his father a schools inspector. The brothers Archie and Sam Heron were a physician's sons. George Irvine was the son of a religious bookshop owner. Seán Lester was also the son of shopkeeper. Several rebel women were gentry, which may indicate a revolt against gender suppression as well as class. The culture of the Irish Parliamentary Party was chauvinistic and dismissive of women, in contrast to the egalitarianism of the republican organisations.[8] These women included Albina Lucy Brodrick, sister to William Brodrick, Viscount (later earl of) Midleton, leader of the Irish Unionist Alliance and the Anti-Partition League; Constance Markievicz of the Sligo Gore-Booths; Mary Ellen Spring Rice, daughter of Baron Monteagle; and Charlotte Despard, sister of John, Viscount French, who was appointed Lord Lieutenant in 1918. Another striking pattern is the number of rebels who were the children of clergy, including Kathleen Lynn, Alice Stopford Green, Robert Lynd and David Robinson Lubbock. Alexander Hamilton Irwin was a Presbyterian minister.

Male Protestant rebels were overwhelmingly young. Over 70 per cent were aged in their twenties and thirties in the years of revolution. The youngest was Frederick Norgrove of the ICA, just fifteen years of age in 1916 when he acted as a courier in the GPO. The women show a broader spread of generations than the men. Charlotte Despard was seventy-two in 1916 and had already a lifetime of activism on philanthropic and suffrage issues. She continued to be an active campaigner in support of Dáil Éireann and Sinn Féin after 1918. Alice Stopford Green was of the same age. Protestant women aged in their fifties in 1916 included Maud Gonne, Albina Brodrick, Countess Markievicz, Alice Milligan, Nellie O'Brien and Celia Harrison. The Gifford sisters dominated the younger generation of women activists. Nellie was thirty-six, Muriel was thirty-two, Grace twenty-eight and Sydney twenty-seven. Youngest of all were the Norgrove sisters Emily and Annie, eighteen and sixteen years of age in 1916. Amongst the men and the women, the younger the age the more widespread the organisational affiliation; they were all great joiners of causes and organisations. Swept up in an egalitarian and energetic associational culture, they were a generation motivated by a vision of a new modern Ireland and they were determined that they would play a central role in making it happen. They were ultimately shaped by a determination that action was preferable to inaction.[9]

The principal introduction to radical nationalism for the middle-class activists was the cultural movement, or simply 'The Movement', centred on the Gaelic League.[10] 'Irishness' became the backbone of their revolutionary movement. They elevated 'native' peasant culture, language, music, customs and dress to a high symbolic national status. Native was defined in cultural but not religious terms, in defiance of centuries of English definitions of Irishness. The revolutionaries emerged from the cultural movement; not the other way round.[11] It was as IRB men that they then moved rapidly into the Irish Volunteers. Within the IRB and the Volunteers they were welcomed and trusted and their Protestantism was not regarded with suspicion. Thus, networks of Protestant republicans developed within the IRB and, from the IRB, in the Irish Volunteers. Within the Irish Volunteers Protestants were more prominent as officers than rank and file, though this may reflect their membership of the IRB.

Within the Gaelic League the main centre for Protestants was the Craobh na gCúig gCúigí, the Five Provinces Branch, sometimes referred to as the 'Five Protestants Branch'. The branch met at George Moore's house in Ely Place with classes in Estelle Solomon's studio. Members included Nellie O'Brien, Vera French, Ernest Blythe, George Irvine and Harry Nicholls, along with many other Protestants. For many of the Protestant men the key pathway to revolution was through the personal networks and friendships built up in the Gaelic League leading into the IRB. Many Protestant men moved through the Gaelic League into the Teeling Circle of the IRB in which Bulmer Hobson was central. Hobson was a leader of Belfast republicans and later Protestant republicans in Dublin. The Teeling Circle was considered the most rigorous and intellectually challenging IRB Circle in Dublin. Seán O'Casey brought Ernest Blythe into the IRB, Blythe in turn brought Seán Lester in and Lester brought in Alfie Cotton and Archie Heron. George Nicholls introduced his brother Harry to the Gaelic League. The Gaelic League brought him to Kerry where he came under the influence of Seán Óg Kavanagh in Ballyferriter, who swore him into the IRB. It was as an IRB man that he began his activism in the Volunteers' 4th Battalion.

While for middle-class Protestant men the Gaelic League was the initial introduction leading towards revolutionary separatism, for working-class Protestants socialism and the trade union movement radicalised and brought them into the ICA. With exceptions like Seán O'Casey, working-class Protestant radicals were less interested in the cultural movement. Instead, they aimed to transform their economic struggle into a national struggle. The Belfast Protestant Rory Haskin, son of a labourer, made the journey from militant Orangeman in the UVF to militant republican in the IRB through the network of Protestant republicans gathered in the Belfast Freedom Club and without any contact with the cultural movement. Other working class Protestants included Ellett Elmes, a casual labourer, and Fermanagh-born bricklayer William Scott. Alfred Norgrove was a Dublin northside gasfitter, who with his wife Maria and his children Frederick, Annie and Emily, were all active in the revolution. These Protestant revolutionaries, all members of the trade union movement and activists in the ICA, were mobilised on issues of poverty, deprivation and oppression and more influenced by socialism and syndicalism than by culture. The working class never achieved the iconic status in which the rural peasantry was held amongst the revolutionary intellectuals.

The Irish Guild of the Church, Cumann Gaelach na hEaglaise, was formed by Protestant cultural activists to encourage Irish language services in the Church of Ireland. The Guild was a broad-based organisation with a wide spectrum of political opinion. Members included the IRB men George Ruth, James Deakin, George Irvine, Harry Nicholls, Ernest Blythe and James Duncan. Not all Protestant language activists were radicalised: Ernest Joynt, an engineering draughtsman in the Inchicore railway works, was a lifelong language activist who took no part in the events of 1916–22, maintaining a career on the teaching staff of Bolton Street college. James Deakin, IRB President in 1913–14, withdrew as it became more actively engaged in separatist conspiracy.

The Abbey Theatre provided—literally—a stage on which a revolutionary activism was enacted and shaped.[12] Arthur Shields was a Protestant member of the Abbey Company, coming from a radical labour background. His father Adolphus Shields was a Protestant labour activist in the 1890s. As secretary of the National Union of Gasworkers and General Labourers he organised the first Dublin May Day celebration in 1890. As a member of the Dublin Socialist Club he was instrumental in bringing James Connolly to Dublin in 1896.[13] Arthur Shields' own path to 1916 began with watching the plays of the Abbey Theatre, but it was the Howth gun-running and the shooting on Bachelor's Walk that nationalised his cultural radicalism.[14]

Shields' radicalisation was a complex of labour, cultural and nationalist influences. For some, radicalisation came after rough handling by the police or military. Harry Nicholls experienced the radicalising influence of a DMP baton in the course of the 1913 Lockout, as did the Norgroves. George Plant was radicalised, aged twelve, by rough questioning at the hands of the RIC in Easter 1916. Robert Barton, an officer in the British army, had been moving towards nationalism after witnessing rural poverty in the west of Ireland, but the shock of the 1916 executions awakened his republicanism. John Nelson Beaumont, a member of TCD OTC, recounts how his brother William was radicalised by his treatment at the hands of the Auxiliaries. William carried notebooks referring to his gunnery operator training; these aroused the suspicions of the Auxiliaries searching passengers on a tram. The Auxiliaries assumed that he was training the IRA and gave him a rough time until he convinced them of his war record. They then treated him as an old comrade and he became a regular drinking companion. This socialising led to him becoming a key source of intelligence for Michael Collins.

For many of the Protestant women, social radicalism in protesting for suffrage rights and action against poverty led to political radicalism. Charlotte Despard began with philanthropic campaigns in the slums of London, becoming a labour activist. She was a suffrage campaigner and anti-war activist before becoming a supporter of the Irish republican cause. Albina Brodrick, a nurse, founded a co-operative and was an anti-poverty campaigner. She joined the Gaelic League and then Cumann na mBan and Sinn Féin. Constance Markievicz moved seamlessly between her suffrage campaigning, the nationalist organisations Inghinidhe na hÉireann and Fianna Éireann, the ICA, Irish Women Workers' Union, Sinn Féin and Dáil Éireann for her all-intersecting arenas of activism.

Kathleen Lynn followed a similar trajectory from feminism through nationalism and labour organisation to revolutionary activism in the ICA. Celia Harrison (sister to Henry Harrison MP, biographer of Parnell and founder of the Irish Dominion League) was primarily a feminist who then also campaigned on nationalist and labour rights. Protestant women were founders and activists in the women's auxiliary to the Irish Volunteers, Cumann na mBan.[15] Cumann na mBan, along with the ICA, were key organisations that drew in the younger Protestant women. Albina Brodrick, Constance Markievicz, Annie Smithson, Kathleen Lynn, Elizabeth Bloxham and Rosamund Jacob all found their radicalism being militarised through engagement with these organisations. However, a social and political radicalism did not necessarily mean a nationalist radicalism. Kathleen Holmes Emerson, who married Harry Nicholls, remained an active campaigner for women's rights into the 1930s, was internationalist rather than nationalist in her perspective, being one of the Irish women who attempted to get to the 1915 Women's International Congress at The Hague, called to mobilise against the war. Suffrage and labour activist Louie Bennett, leader of the IWWU and a significant force in the ITUC, wanted to distance the labour movement from nationalism in any form.

These Protestant men and women might have been in revolt against contemporaneous constructs of imperialism, class and gender, but they were not in revolt against conventional Protestantism. A distinct and militant sub-culture of the young, most of them conformed to Foster's suggestion of a generation in revolt against their class, rather than religious, background.[16] The multiplicity of organisations in which they were active is striking. These included the Gaelic League, drama societies, suffrage campaigns, the co-operative movement, as well as political and military organisations. Protestant women show a more intellectual and wider spectrum of radicalism, combining feminism and socialism with cultural and political radicalism. Perhaps women needed to be more determined in their radicalism if they were to overcome the limitations imposed on them by gendered assumptions.

Some occasionally reflected on the relationship between Protestantism and their nationalism. Alfie Cotton was self-conscious that he was the only Protestant in the IRB circle in Sligo in 1912. Ernest Blythe reflected that, though fascinated by the Irish language, he was, as a Protestant, afraid he would not be welcomed into the Gaelic League. His fears dissolved when he discovered several fellow Protestant members and he was soon immersed in a web of Protestant IRB and Gaelic League activists that included Seán O'Casey, Bulmer Hobson, Seán Lester, Alfie Cotton and Archie Heron. Some retained a sense of Protestant superiority. Roger Casement asserted to Hobson that only Protestants could win the freedom of Ireland because they are not afraid of any bogeymen.[17] Jack White, a founder of the Irish Citizen Army, maintained what he characterised as a 'Portadown Protestant' contempt for the Catholic church.[18] One of the few sustained reflections into the relationship between nationalism and Protestantism is in the witness statement of Elizabeth Bloxham, founding member of Cumann na mBan.[19] Her own poor, west of Ireland Protestant and unionist family were apparently quite tolerant and did not disapprove of her activism, though other local Protestant families did. She thought that Irish Catholicism conferred the resources to resist the power of the British state, a hinterland of songs, symbols and history not available to Irish Protestants. Amongst those symbols she includes, without any hint of irony, the pictures of Wolfe Tone and Robert Emmet, both Protestant, that were in every house. Bloxham's view was that as a rebel she was the best Protestant of them all, for she was *protesting*. In discussion with Seán Treacy she disagreed with his optimistic assessment of the potential of converting Ulster unionists to nationalism. The unionism of her west of Ireland Protestant community was largely a habit, but the unionism of Ulster was a unionism of conviction. The most profound shock to the habitual presumptions of Irish Protestant opinion before 1916 was not the rise of Catholic nationalism but the response of the Ulster unionists to the third Home Rule crisis. Though the creation of the Ulster Unionist Council in 1905 had already effectively partitioned Irish unionism, it was assumed that Dublin would continue to lead an all-Ireland Protestant unionism. In October 1911 the *Irish Times* could assure its readers that there was no split on opposition to Home Rule and that 'Ulster will not make a mockery of Unionism by an inglorious and base attempt to shelter herself with a separate parliament'.[20] By January 1913, with Carson's amending proposal for an Ulster exclusion, it was clear that Carson and the Ulster unionists could not be relied on and that they were in fact quite prepared to throw the southern Protestant unionist lambs to the Catholic nationalist wolves.[21]

Protestants in Revolution

The arming of Irish nationalism in the Howth and Kilcoole gun-running was the key event that began the movement from revolt to revolution, from resistance to what is, to the creation of something new. The gun-running was a Protestant-led and organised operation. Roger Casement acted as the inspiration and largely the financier; Alice Stopford Green, Darrell Figgis, Mary Spring Rice the organising committee; Mollie and Erskine Childers with Conor O'Brien the crew; James Creed Meredith and Sir Thomas Myles along with Bulmer Hobson the onshore coordinators.[22] The Howth landing was a large-scale public event, designed to generate attention and excitement. In contrast, the Kilcoole landing was a secret operation, taking place under cover of an outing to the Rocky Valley and Kilmacanogue. The guns were landed in the night and moved under darkness to safe houses.

The 1916 Rising came as a bolt from the blue. Once the shooting started, recovering from the confusion arising from Eoin MacNeill's countermanding order, all the Protestant revolutionaries threw themselves into the Rising. The witness statements suggest that for most of these Protestant activists priority lay with the act of rebellion and not with concerns about the outcome of the Rising. Cesca Trench, although convinced that the Rising was apparent madness, made strenuous efforts to engage in the struggle.[23] After the surrender and trials, the interned and imprisoned included Protestants Ernest Blythe, Rory Haskin, George Irvine (who had his death sentence commuted), Alfie Cotton, Sam Heron, Ellett Elmes, James McGowan, George Norgrove, Harry Nicholls, Arthur Shields, Kathleen Lynn, Nellie Gifford and Emily and Anne Norgrove.

The 1916 Proclamation, which lacked a precise revolutionary agenda or ideology but was resolutely egalitarian, announced the Rising as a moment of fulfilling history but also of escaping from history. It asserted the historic illegitimacy of the British imperial state in Ireland as well as the provisional establishment of a secular and egalitarian Irish republican state. The spectrum of the cultural, labour, anti-English and anti-imperial impulses that had been activated was given focus by the driving force of the IRB in turning revolt into revolution. The revolution that gradually developed in the years after 1916 was unplanned, spontaneous and in constant flux, but the lack of a precise ideology beyond separatism gave it width, strength and resilience. It engaged feminists, socialists, labour activists, cultural activists as well as republicans. Simply buying republican bonds, or voting for Sinn Féin, or reading its newspaper could show support.

The binary opposition of the revolutionary movement was between Irishness and Englishness. Catholicism was an important symbolic resource, but it was not constitutive of the revolution, which was not essentially religious. It is important to note, for instance, that the revolutionaries held a considerable variety of contradictory views on responses to Ulster unionism and its sectarianism. However, for some of the Protestant rebels, there was an unsettling realisation that, in the absence of a revolutionary ideology, Catholicism provided the mass of the rebels with a social relationship, rituals and a language of resistance. It was noticed that Arthur Shields stood apart when a prayer was being said over the body of Tom Weafer, a Volunteer killed in the GPO area. Much may be made of Cecil Grange McDowell's conversion to Catholicism and his reciting to a priest what he may have reasonably assumed was his last confession, in the heat of the battle in Boland's Mills. However, McDowell's membership of the congregation of St John's Sandymount, very High Church and considered crypto-Catholic by most Dublin Protestants, cannot be discounted as a factor in this incident. Nor were the signatories of the Proclamation typical Catholics. Pearse and Plunkett displayed an intense religiosity that bordered on mysticism, MacDonagh was irreligious, Clarke was fiercely anti-clerical and Connolly a barely hidden atheist.[24] Nonetheless, on the barricades the rosary was heard more often than the 'Soldier's Song' and assurance was sought more in Catholic rituals of confession than in revolutionary propaganda. It was clear for many of the activists it was Irish Catholicism and not republicanism that gave them the ideological apparatus to assert the illegitimacy of the British state in Ireland and allowed them to be 'revolutionary'. The devout religiosity of the insurgents was then used after the executions to confer a retrospective legitimising Catholicism to their actions.[25]

In the immediate aftermath of 1916, as W.B. Yeats wrote in his poem 'Easter, 1916', all was 'changed, changed utterly'. For some Protestants, such as Robert Barton, it was the event that brought them into republicanism. The Presbyterian minister Reverend James Hamilton Irwin became an important propagandist for Irish independence after 1916. Liam Price brought his legal expertise to the service of the republic after 1916, establishing and then practising in the republican courts. David Lubbock Robinson, who had served in the British army, became a convinced separatist and joined the IRA in County Wicklow on demobilisation. Those Protestants who were already active republicans and revolutionaries experienced the further radicalising effect of fighting in the Rising, followed by gaol, resistance and the mobilisation of public support. Most of these Protestants returned to activism, though not necessarily in the reorganised Volunteers. The Norgroves went back to the ICA and trade unionism. Archie Heron was involved in reorganising the Volunteers but, as did the Norgroves, increasingly devoted his energies to trade union organisation. Harry Nicholls returned to his engineer's post in Dublin Corporation, but also turned his activism to trade union organisation amongst the local government workers, where he adopted a strongly syndicalist position. Ernest Blythe became a political activist in Sinn Féin and was elected in 1918 to Dáil Éireann as TD for North Monaghan. George Irvine was initially selected to run in North County Fermanagh as a Sinn Féin candidate in the 1918 general election. Opposed by the local Ancient Order of Hibernians—as a Protestant and as a revolutionary nationalist—he withdrew in favour of Kevin O'Sheil, and returned to his IRA activism as vice-commandant and supervisor of training in the 1st Battalion of the Dublin Brigade. George Plant became a highly committed and effective member of the 3rd Tipperary Brigade flying column.

Protestants after the Revolution

The provisional government, driven by the demands of state-building, abandoned the mass movement of the national struggle and funnelled revolutionary energies into a militarised state apparatus that developed a reliance on repressive public safety laws. The leaders of the Irish Free State, who almost all took on military staff positions, were detached from the visionary republicanism of the revolution and were content to develop Ireland's membership of the British Empire.[26] The Treaty that had been accepted as a 'stepping stone' became an end in itself.

It has been argued that the Irish state that emerged from the revolution was one in which those Protestants who fought in the revolution lost out.[27] However, as the revolution was revealed to have been a separatist movement without a developed social ideology, it was the case that progressives of all sorts lost out: socialists, feminists, republicans and secularists. For many of the 1916 rebels, as is evident in their witness statements, the Rising was the end of a revolutionary era and not the beginning. An examination of the responses to the Treaty by the Protestant men and women listed, and their subsequent careers, suggests that their attitude towards the Treaty, and their social class, was more significant than their religion in determining their future in independent Ireland. Being Protestant was no barrier to preference for supporters of the Free State government; opposition was dealt with in a non-sectarian equality. The execution of prisoners and the brutal determination of the government to win the Civil War were as divisive amongst Protestant as amongst Catholic nationalists.

Generally, twice as many of those listed were anti-Treaty than were pro-Treaty. Supporters of the Treaty included Alice Stopford Green, who was later appointed a senator.[28] Elizabeth Bloxham was compelled to withdraw from Cumann na mBan because of her support for the Treaty. She became politically quiescent, though remaining strongly nationalist and anti-partitionist.[29] Archie Heron was also a strong supporter of the Treaty but merely as the best available outcome. He, as a committed trade unionist and Labour Party supporter, urged the republicans to enter the Dáil and join in the fight against a socially reactionary Cosgrave government.[30] His politically quiescent brother Sam secured a job in the Free State civil service in the Patents Office. Alfie Cotton, who had to flee Belfast as a 'rotten Prod', supported the Treaty and also obtained employment in the Free State civil service, in the Department of Labour. Seán Lester, who had been active in the IRB, Gaelic League and Sinn Féin, got a job in the new Department of External Affairs through the influence of Ernest Blythe. That post was to begin his distinguished international diplomatic career in the League of Nations.[31] George

Annesley Ruth, who was close to Arthur Griffith, maintained his essentially cultural-revolutionary but politically moderate position. He was appointed director of Coláiste Móibhí in 1926, the Irish language preparatory college for Protestant teacher-training.[32] James Creed Meredith, who had played a crucial role in the Howth and Kilcoole gun-running and was a supporter of the Treaty, was appointed a judge of the High Court. Liam Price was appointed a district justice for the Wicklow circuit, where he continued to pursue his antiquarian interests. Edward Millington Stephens, who had acted as legal draughtsman at the Treaty negotiations, was appointed to the committee to draft the Free State Constitution and also to the Boundary Commission. Harry Nicholls may well have felt that his progress from Assistant City Engineer to City Engineer was blocked because he was Protestant; however, it was more likely he fell victim to the iron law of seniority. His 1916 action in the College of Surgeons garrison did, however, ensure he was promoted from temporary to permanent status on his release from Frongoch.[33] Frederick Allan, a Methodist who had been active in the IRB from the age of nineteen, though he had not participated in the Rising, was appointed as secretary of the Irish National Aid and Dependants' Fund, where he came under the influence of Michael Collins. He was arrested and imprisoned for his activities in the Sinn Féin movement and the republican courts. His support for the Treaty brought him into active politics. He was appointed chairman of the committee that formed the new political party Cumann na nGaedheal from the pro-Treaty Sinn Féin. Pensioned off by the demands for austerity in Dublin Corporation, where he had established the electricity generating station at the Pigeon House, he was appointed to head the power and electricity division of the new Department of Industry and Commerce and played a key role in the Shannon Scheme.[34] Sam Maguire, who had brought the young Michael Collins into the IRB and who was a key London agent for Collins in the War of Independence, was persuaded to transfer back to Dublin and a job in the Department of Posts and Telegraphs. But he then fell foul of the government in the course of the 1924 army mutiny and was dismissed without pension, ending his days in illness and poverty.[35]

For the middle-class Protestant supporters of the Treaty the transition to the Irish Free State was largely unchallenging and, for most, an opportunity. For the middle-class Protestant republicans who opposed the Treaty the transition was more difficult and for some (especially women) traumatic. Her sex, conversion to Catholicism, or the status of being a 1916 widow did not save Grace Gifford Plunkett from imprisonment in the Civil War, due to her anti-Treaty activity. Her sister Nellie Gifford Donnelly was also jailed for her anti-Treaty activism. In a letter to Frank Aiken, included in her pension application, dated 23 October 1935, she sadly reflected, 'We 1916 people, the women anyhow, will not be given any encouragement to live. Someone else generally profits from our efforts.' Charlotte Despard was also imprisoned; she moved steadily leftward, to the Irish Workers Party and the Friends of Soviet Russia. Dismayed by the rise of the Catholic reaction and pro-fascist forces in the Free State of the 1930s, she moved to County Antrim in her last years, dying in poverty. Alice Milligan remained republican and anti-partitionist. She also moved to Northern Ireland to escape poverty and ended up living with her brother and his wife in what seems to have been a politically hostile household. By way of contrast, the equally upper-class Albina Lucy Brodrick, although remaining a life-long Irish language supporter and anti-Treatyite, moved steadily to the right politically, ending up a fascist enthusiast. Rosamund Jacob was also imprisoned, with Dorothy Price, for her resistance to the Treaty, as was Annie Smithson. Other middle-class Protestants who were less radical in opposing the Treaty and were less socially revolutionary moved towards de Valera and Fianna Fáil. Countess Markievicz was a founder of the party. Robert Barton (who had fought with Cathal Brugha in the Civil War) became a Fianna Fáil government senator, as did David Lubbock Robinson (who had been captured with Erskine Childers in Annamoe and imprisoned). Annie Smithson also joined Fianna Fáil, but is best remembered for her work in founding the Irish Nurses' Union. Kathleen Lynn, who had been an officer in the ICA for the Rising and became an active IRA supporter in the War of Independence and an anti-Treatyite, went on to found, along with Dorothy Stopford Price, the children's hospital St Ultan's.

For working-class Protestants in the ICA, the Civil War was simply a continuation of struggle, but a struggle limited by the lack of clear purpose behind the organisation. For some few the ICA had always been about the militarisation of labour and the left but, in reality, for most members it was a social club. The lack of clear purpose made the ICA largely quiescent after 1916.[36] A group of Protestant members of the ICA that included Seamus McGowan, Ellett Elmes, the Norgroves, Walter Carpenter and his sons Walter Junior and Peter were involved in a faction that wanted to develop the revolutionary objective of the 'Workers' Republic', as distinct from the ideologically vague Sinn Féin republicanism. Walter Carpenter was a founder member of the Socialist Party of Ireland in 1908 and was one of the 'Red Flag' republicans of the Drogheda 1919 Labour Party conference.[37] James McGowan moved leftward, ending up in the Communist Party of Ireland. The Norgrove family continued their ICA activism through the War of Independence, to the Civil War, in which they fought with the republicans until their detention, when they suffered internment and endured hunger strikes in the Curragh camp. (The Norgroves re-entered history in 2011 when a store of arms and explosives from the Civil War period was discovered in their former home on Strandville Place off the North Strand.)

George Gilmore remained opposed to the Treaty, arguing through his later involvement in Saor Éire and in the Republican Congress that the fight for the republic must also be an anti-imperialist and anti-capitalist struggle. His ideological development brought him to Spain in 1936, to defend a different republic. Seán Beaumont made a similar journey to the left after the Civil War, as did Captain Jack White. George Plant remained an IRA activist but, beyond an almost theological adherence to the republic as proclaimed in 1916, showed no ideological development. He was executed in February 1942 by sentence of the Special Military Court, established by the de Valera government, for his role in the murder of Michael Devereux as an alleged informer, and also for membership of the IRA. He was disinterred in 1948 and, after lying overnight in Christ Church cathedral, was brought for burial with IRA military ceremony to St Mary's Church of Ireland in Johnstown, County Tipperary.[38]

The phenomenon of conversion by Protestant rebels to Catholicism, whilst useful in retrospective portrayals of the rebels as deeply devout and not at all socially revolutionary, was in fact an exotic rarity. When it did occur, it was less a conviction of the truth of the tenets of Catholicism than a gesture of rebellion or profound emotional crisis. Roger Casement's conversion on the eve of his execution was less doctrinal than a final act of defiance.

The dramatic conversion of Constance Markievicz arose from a wish for total identification with her fellow rebels in the College of Surgeons, described as her epiphany. Nellie Gifford, on the other hand, who fought in the College of Surgeons alongside Markievicz, experienced no such epiphany and remained staunchly Protestant and suspicious of the Catholic church. The most well-known conversions were those of the other Gifford sisters: Catherine, who converted on her marriage in 1909; and Muriel, who converted on 3 May 1917, five years after her marriage to Thomas MacDonagh and precisely one year to the day after his execution. Dorothy Vera French (Deora Frínseach), the founder of the Five Provinces Branch of the Gaelic League and a prolific contributor to *An Claideamh Soluis*, also converted shortly before her death in 1925. Ellett Elmes had converted to Catholicism to marry in 1909, taking Joseph as a baptismal name, but he never used the name again. Whilst interned in Frongoch after the Rising he was included amongst the Protestant prisoners. What is most striking is the continuing loyalty of most of these rebels to their Protestant identity and their acceptance (despite being rebels) within their community. Harry Nicholls was a lifelong member of the Church of Ireland parish of St Anne's in Dublin. George Irvine continued his campaign for services in the Irish language in the Church of Ireland. Dr Kathleen Lynn, Alfie Cotton and Frederick Norgrove remained and were accepted as loyal and committed members of the Church of Ireland.[39]

Harry Nicholls, in the context of the fiftieth anniversary of the Rising, reflected soberly on what he and his fellow IRB men had hoped for in the Rising and what had been achieved. In the aftermath of 1916 the principles of republicanism came into open discussion within the IRB: 'many of us felt that this was a very conservative country and that in the early years of independence this conservatism would hold sway'. He then listed the disappointed hopes: an education system that remained conservative and elitist; the continued decline in the Irish language; the degraded condition of women in the state that was an insult to republicanism; and the stupidity of censorship. He did not include the position of Protestants as a further disappointment and he remained optimistic on the development of an independent Ireland.[40]

The Civil War ended the revolution. The Ireland that emerged was not one that the revolutionaries had envisioned. It would be wrong, however, to cast the shadow of the state that emerged afterwards over the revolution that led to its foundation. Those that launched the revolution had little influence on how it developed. The Irish Free State resulted, not from the revolutionary movement, but from an intensely fought struggle for power in which the British state was an external but threatening presence that limited the options available. Protestants in the Irish Free State may have lost a marginal political privilege but Protestantism retained economic power, with high social status, cultural prestige and respectability. In fact, in the independent Ireland 'Protestant' became a synonym for 'respectable'. The independent state encouraged self-regulation of equal, separate Catholic and Protestant religious communities in education, health, welfare and social policing. The result was the development of Protestantism in independent Ireland as a socially exclusive and inward-looking middle-class 'club' and it is striking that Protestant memoir shows an acute consciousness of social class—more acute in fact than a consciousness of sectarian difference.[41]

Hubert Butler was an uncompromising commentator on the post-revolution and post-partition conservative cultures of Ireland, north and south, that had shaped understanding of both the founding revolution and Irish Protestantism:

> I do not like solid blocks of opinion but, in fact, there is nothing very reassuring about our Southern Protestant incapacity for congealing into aggressive or defensive blocks. It merely means that the Ulster Protestant, a more fanatical and bitter champion of the Reformation, assumes the leadership of Irish Protestant opinion. And that leadership really belongs by tradition to the Protestants of the South, the people of Swift and Berkeley, Lord Edward Fitzgerald and Smith O'Brien, Parnell. Men who often jeopardized their careers and even sacrificed their lives in the cause of an Ireland, free and united. So now our amiable inertia, our refusal to express grievances or cherish hopes about Ireland, are really delaying our ultimate unity.[42]

Butler's assertion that the republican and revolutionary tradition is in fact a Protestant tradition echoes the development of Patrick Pearse's own thoughts on revolution. In his essay, *The Coming Revolution*, dated November 1913, Pearse, signalling his shift from cultural to political activism, dismissed the Gaelic League as a revolutionary force.[43] However, out of the membership of the Gaelic League he predicted 'there will be in the Ireland of the next few years a multitudinous activity of Freedom Clubs, Young Republican Parties, Labour Organisations, Socialist Groups, and what not; bewildering enterprises undertaken by sane persons and insane persons, by good men and bad men, many of them seemingly contradictory, some mutually destructive, yet all tending towards a common objective, and that objective: the Irish Revolution'.[44] Amongst the 'bewildering and contradictory enterprises' of his 1913 essay there is a sense that Protestant republicans and revolutionaries were neither contradictory nor bewildering. As the planning for the Easter Rising accelerated he published a series of tracts in which he elaborated at length his characteristically messianic ideas on nationality, separatism and sovereignty, ideas that were to be restated more aphoristically in the Easter 1916 Proclamation of the Republic.[45] *Ghosts* was the first of these tracts, dated Christmas Day 1915.[46] In this, he explores the idea of Irish separatism as an apostolic succession, transmitted through the dead generations. This enduring tradition of Irish separatism is described variously as a Credo or as a Dogma of Freedom that was developed for the modern times by the four great minds of nationality: Theobald Wolfe Tone, Thomas Davis, James Fintan Lalor and John Mitchel. Pearse then adds Charles Stewart Parnell as a fifth great mind. These are the 'pale and angry ghosts' that, angered by the failure of the last generation to assert Irish nationality, must be appeased. These are the 'Fathers' of Irish separatism. Others, described by Pearse as the 'Commentators on the Fathers', include Napper Tandy, Thomas Russell, Robert Emmet and Thomas Francis Meagher. A fact that Pearse does not remark on is that, except for Lalor, all these great minds of the separatist tradition were Protestant. That they were Protestant is itself of interest and that Pearse, who gave a great deal of thought to the nature of an Irish revolution, did not consider this worth commenting on is of even greater interest. It has often been remarked that what made 1916 different was that for the first time the leadership of a revolutionary republican movement was Catholic and not Protestant. This assumes that revolutionary republican separatism was somehow normal to Catholics, despite the evidence that most Catholics identified with Crown and Empire. But in fact radical Protestants shared the same culture of revolutionary republicanism as radical Catholics. As revolutionaries they were committed to ideals of democracy, egalitarianism, feminism and socialism. What made them exceptional was not their Protestantism but their radicalism, their revolutionary republicanism.

Table 1. Protestant Activists and Revolutionaries

Men
1. Allan, Frederick James
2. Anderson, Bertie
3. Barton, Robert
4. Beaumont, John Nelson [Seán]
5. Best, Seán
6. Black, Hugh [Aodh de Blacam]
7. Blythe, Ernest
8. Boyd, Davy
9. Braithwaite, Richard [AKA Richard Brannigan]
10. Carpenter, Peter
11. Carpenter, Walter
12. Casement, Roger
13. Childers, Erskine
14. Coffey, Diarmid
15. Cotton, Alfie
16. Coulter, Geoffrey
17. Cunningham, James
18. Deakin/Deacon, James Aubrey
19. Duncan, James
20. Elmes, Ellett
21. Figgis, Darrell
22. Fullerton, George
23. Gilmore, George
24. Haskin, Rory
25. Heron, Archie

Table 1. Protestant Activists and Revolutionaries *(continued)*

26. Heron, Sam
27. Hobson, Bulmer
28. Hoffman, Frank
29. Hope, James
30. Hughes, Hector Samuel James
31. Irvine, George
32. Irwin, James A.H.
33. Johnson, Thomas
34. Joynt, Ernest
35. Lester, Seán
36. Lynd, Robert Wilson
37. Maguire, Sam
38. McDowell, Cecil Grange [Cathal MacDubhghaill]
39. McGowan, Seamus
40. Meredith, James Creed
41. Mitchell, Walter
42. Monteith, Robert
43. Moran, Herbert
44. Neill, Fred
45. Nicholls, Harry
46. Norgrove, Frederick
47. Norgrove, George
48. Norgrove, Robert
49. O'Brien, Conor
50. O'Casey, Seán
51. Plant, George
52. Price, Liam
53. Ridgeway, Charles
54. Robinson, David Lubbock
55. Ruth, George Annesley
56. Ruttle, Sam

57. Scott, William
58. Sennett, Graham
59. Shields, Arthur
60. Sloan, Sam
61. Stephens, Edward Millington
62. Snoddy, Seamus
63. Steepe, Peter
64. White, Jack
65. Wilson, Casey
66. Wilson, Frank

Women
1. Barton, Dulcibella
2. Bennett, Louise
3. Bloxham, Elizabeth
4. Brodrick, Albina
5. Despard, Charlotte
6. Dix, Rachel
7. Dobbs, Margaret
8. Duncan, Lily
9. Fitzgerald, Mabel [née McConnell]
10. French, Dora
11. Gifford, Grace
12. Gifford, Katherine Anna [Wilson]
13. Gifford, Nellie [Donnelly]
14. Gifford, Sydney [Czira]
15. Gonne, Maud
16. Green, Alice Stopford
17. Harrison, Celia
18. Jacob, Rosamond
19. Kearns, Linda
20. Lynn, Kathleen

Table 1. Protestant Activists and Revolutionaries *(continued)*

21. Markievicz, Constance
22. Milligan, Alice
23. Mitchell, Susan Langstaff
24. Norgrove, Annie
25. Norgrove, Emily
26. Norgrove, Maria
27. O'Brien, Nellie
28. Perolz, Marie [née Flanagan]
29. Price, Dorothy Stopford
30. Smithson, Annie
31. Spring Rice, Mary Ellen
32. Stopford Green, Alice [see Woodward or Woodard]
33. Trench, Cesca

CHAPTER TWELVE

'We're Irish, but not that kind of Irish': British Imperial Identity in Transition in Ireland and India in the Early Twentieth Century[1]

NIAMH DILLON

> My father was a civil servant and he had worked for the British civil service until 1920 when the change of government meant he decided he didn't want to stay any longer in Ireland. I think he was worried about the possibility of religious discrimination, he was a Protestant, and he transferred to what was then the General Post Office in England . . . I think probably there was a basis of truth in it, that when a situation had been so manifestly unjust that Protestants were favoured over Catholics, that when the change of government came the boot was going to be on the other foot and I think that was probably a fairly accurate perception on his part.[2]

One of the consequences of the formation of new states in Ireland in 1922 and India in 1947 was the marked reduction in the numbers of those who had been closely linked to British rule. Between 1911 and 1926 the number of Protestants living in the area of what became the Irish Free State declined dramatically. The population of Protestants dropped from about 313,000 in 1911 to about 208,000 in 1926.[3] After Indian independence the majority of the British community left the subcontinent. The aim of this chapter is to investigate the motivation for southern Irish Protestants and members of the British community to leave Ireland and India after independence. It will assess how these two groups understood their sense of British identity in a colonial context and how this was challenged upon independence. By considering the experience of two groups with long-established links to Britain and the empire, it will explore whether it is possible to consider a common imperial identity.

India and Ireland each had a radically different relationship with Britain in terms of geography, historical links and politics. However, each was important to the development of Britain as a composite nation and latterly as an empire, and independence in both were significant markers of its dissolution. The initial commercial relationship between the East India Company and the Mughal emperors in the seventeenth century offered enhanced trading opportunities and officially lasted until 1858, when the Crown formally took over the directly ruled territories.[4] This gave Britain a significant imperial presence in south Asia, supported by military forces which enforced British control across the region: from southern Africa, across the middle east, to south-east Asia. Ireland provided strategic as well as economic benefits, although the relationship was often contested. In addition, her inhabitants were Christian and white, which both challenged ideas of race supported by social Darwinism and created racial theories about the construction of 'whiteness' in the late Victorian period.[5] There had been resistance to British rule in both countries; political agitation in Ireland in the late nineteenth century had split the Liberal party in 1886, and opposition to Home Rule in the early years of the twentieth century created the conditions for civil war on British soil.[6] This was a direct challenge to Britain's imperial power at a time when the empire was at its most expansive.[7] The Indian National Congress agitated for independence in the years preceding 1947, culminating in the 'Quit India' movement in 1942, and independence was granted with the transfer of power in 1947. However, both countries experienced partition along ethnic and religious lines that caused political and religious animosity in the decades following independence. These two countries, then, highlight historical, geographical and political differences in the imperial context, but also presented commonalities.

While there was a wider community in each country that professed loyalty to Britain, and particular groups that had strong and demonstrated affiliations such as Anglo-Indians and Catholic loyalists in Ireland,[8] southern Irish Protestants and the British in India have been chosen because they saw themselves, and were seen by the majority Irish and Indian population, as having a close affiliation with Britain. They had long associations with imperial service and often identified themselves as part of a wider community of 'Britishness'. Perhaps most importantly, many retained a sense of Britain as 'home' in a colonial context. While the British community in India has been studied and much has been written about Irish Protestants prior to independence, there is very little comparative work across imperial boundaries. Instead, it is often rooted in a national experience. Nor is there much scholarship on their experience post-independence. By examining two different communities in contrasting geographical locations, it is possible to see how groups with imperial connections living outside the centre related to Britain and to consider their identity in a national and imperial context.

Linda Colley has argued that a sense of British identity was forged in the late eighteenth and early nineteenth century,[9] and that military victories against continental powers provided Britain with greater territorial opportunities, but also boosted a sense of national self-confidence.[10] This sense of British identity, forged in war and cemented by a sense of difference both from other Europeans and the peoples conquered during the period of global expansion particularly in the nineteenth century, is a useful way of considering the construction of British identity. Colley argues that the British 'defined themselves as Protestants struggling for survival against the world's foremost Catholic power . . . and, increasingly as the wars went on, they defined themselves in contrast to the colonial peoples they conquered, peoples who were manifestly alien in terms of culture, religion and colour'.[11] This belief in the rational superiority of Protestantism over other religions, and conviction in the racial superiority of British people over those they colonised, affected the way in which governance and policy was constructed and implemented in the nineteenth and twentieth centuries.

Benedict Anderson famously discussed the nation as 'an imagined political community—and imagined as both inherently limited and sovereign'. The power of the nation lies in its ability to create an environment whereby each of its members feel a connection with others of the same group despite never having met them.[12] The nation as an imagined entity presents as a fraternal and 'horizontal' society which encourages deep loyalty in its members.[13] This chapter considers the elements which encouraged southern Irish Protestants and the British community in India to feel aligned to Britain. By exploring understandings of home and belonging, it is possible to see how multiple imperial identities and associations developed within each imperial environment.

One of the primary sources for this research has been recorded interviews with Irish Protestants and British people living in India. Oral history has been used to supplement the historical record, which is limited on the experience of certain Irish Protestants in the period following 1922. It allows access to this poorly documented history, but more importantly, it allows individuals to express their hopes, feelings and disappointments during a traumatic and difficult period. In addition, it also provides a plurality of views and multiple, contrasting and complex perspectives on the same event. As Alessandro Portelli noted, 'oral sources tell us not just what people did, but what they wanted to do, what they believed they were doing, and what they now think they did'.[14]

Endings

One of the most contested debates about the revolutionary period in Ireland centres on inter-communal violence and whether it was 'ethnically' motivated.[15] Peter Hart is one of the key proponents of this view, arguing that Protestants in Cork, in particular, were targeted.[16] R.B. McDowell has assessed the death toll of civilians to be 190 in the period 1920–22, while acknowledging that many more were boycotted and intimidated.[17] Cork's War of Independence Fatality Register acknowledges that Cork suffered the highest number of fatalities. However, it notes that sources often provide conflicting evidence depending on the bias of protagonists and that the escalation of violence affected Crown forces, IRA and civilians.[18] The Irish Grants Committee case files provide contemporary accounts of those affected by the events of the period. Amongst those cases which link attacks to the political situation at the time was that of Lord Ashtown, whose 745 acres in County Galway were seized by the IRA 'as a result of the treatment of the Catholic population in Belfast and other Northern towns by the Orange gunmen'.[19] Another claimant was William Bateman, aged thirty-five, and a farmer from Timoleague in rural west Cork:

> I had to leave for England at the time of the West Cork murders in 1922. My expenses while away were £20 as well as the £34 which I lost through the taking of the animals. During the trouble I was a member of Clonakilty Urban Council and always refused to acknowledge the S.F. [Sinn Fein]. I was always in a minority of one in refusing allegiance to the Irish Republic.[20]

Protestant families actually affected by direct threats or violence to their person were relatively few in number, but within a small but interconnected community, particularly in rural areas, these threats would have created a climate of fear and unease and questioned their position in the new state. It also would have raised concerns about the ability of the nascent Free State to uphold the rule of law and resist more extreme republican factions.

Concerns about violence were also an issue as India prepared for independence. In a 'Top Secret and Personal Directive issued on 29 July 1947 on the Use of the British Troops after 14 August 1947', it was stated that 'although British troops can NOT be employed in communal disturbances to protect Indian subjects, they may be so employed to protect British lives'. This directive was only issued to the Commander-in-Chief in India and his three senior *British* staff officers, his counterpart in Pakistan, and the GOC in Chief in Southern and Eastern Command. They were instructed to destroy the document once troops had left India.[21] Therefore, violence against the British was at least considered at the most senior levels. Those who remember the growing demands for Indian independence recall the violence that sometimes accompanied such demonstrations. Wallace Burnet-Smith recalled riots in the Maidan in Calcutta,[22] and Lady Sylvia Corfield remembered the civil disturbances that followed independence:

> I can remember standing above The Mall in Simla and seeing all the shops being looted, and I can remember standing on the veranda of the United Services Club which had opened its doors to women, standing there with the Bishop of Lahore and hearing the rickshaw quarters in the lower Bazaar being bombed. We felt quite helpless listening to their cries and the dull thud of the explosions.[23]

While violence created a climate of fear as these new states were formed, it does not seem to have been the primary motivator in prompting migration. Interviews support existing arguments that one of the principal reasons southern Irish Protestants and the British community in India left after independence was because their role had fundamentally altered in both countries.[24] Since the nineteenth century the principle of 'trusteeship' had been advanced to justify and support the governance of British India. Many of those working in an official capacity were imbued with this ideal. Sir Olaf Caroe was a governor of the North West Province. When asked to comment on the impact of the British in India, he said it brought 'together the civilisation of the East and the West in a way that had not been done and has not been done in history at all by any other organisation than the Roman Empire', and he pointed to the advances in infrastructure, the penal code, and the widespread use of English as attributes given to India by British involvement.[25] Vere Birdwood echoed a commonly held view: 'We never felt that we were aliens in an alien land . . . We felt that this was our destiny. In many cases the destiny of our forebears. That we were there to serve India. That we were there at some sacrifice to serve India.'[26] This principle of trusteeship advocated British support of Indian advances in technology, social policy and education. The eventual goal was self-government. With the passing of the Indian Independence Act in 1947, this goal was now fulfilled and the role of the British replaced with new governments in India and Pakistan.

Many Protestants in Ireland, particularly the class that became known as the Ascendancy, formed a caste which provided members of the judiciary, senior administrators and military figures. They also supplied a significant number of unionist Members of Parliament. The formation of the Irish Free State ended the link between southern Irish MPs and parliament. While the new Constitution provided opportunities for minority group representation, speeches in the Dáil during this period illustrate some of the prevailing views. On 7 January 1922, Constance Markievicz called the southern unionists 'England's garrison, who had battened on the country while the Irish people were dying on the roadsides. They were capitalists of the worst kind. They were oppressors and traders, grinding the faces of the poor.'[27] W.B. Yeats countered this in a famous speech to the Senate on the subject of divorce when he accused the government of turning on the Anglo-Irish, who he said, were 'no petty people'.[28] As acknowledged by scholars of the period, 'members of the old British establishment in Ireland, who were largely Protestant, particularly the landlord class, experienced the most intense reversals during the nationalist revolution'.[29]

This reversal meant that positions of authority were no longer the preserve of the former imperial elite. In India, throughout the nineteenth and early twentieth century, the majority of the British community was employed by the state. In 1921 the total British population of India was just under 157,000. There were approximately 60,000 troops and just fewer than 22,000 in government service. In the 1920s the policy of 'Indianisation' introduced qualified Indian staff into British administrative positions in state departments.[30] However, the most senior positions in the Indian Civil Service were still held by Britons. The Indian Independence Act stipulated that His Majesty's Government had no further responsibility to the territories which formally comprised British India.[31] This had a direct effect on British staff as Indian post-holders took over their roles.

In Ireland, while senior government figures in the British administration were replaced by their Irish equivalents, Protestant civil servants or members of the judiciary were not removed from existing posts and therefore the transition was gradual and evolutionary rather than immediate. However, the change in regime meant that aspiring office-holders had to pass examinations in the Irish language in order to achieve teaching and civil service positions.[32] Interviews reveal a level of ambivalence towards the new cultural ethos of the Irish Free State. Peter Walton's family originated in Scotland and from the mid-nineteenth century lived on an estate in rural Carlow, where Peter spent his early years: 'There wasn't any question of going to day school because that would have meant going to the Board School in Carlow, and while that would have been good educationally, socially it would not have been acceptable at that time.' When asked to explain he said:

> The state schools were being run as providers of learning but also run as support to the new state of Ireland so everybody was obliged to learn Gaelic and to write it, and to learn Irish songs and the rest of it, none of which was socially acceptable to us at that time. It might be less unacceptable now but I don't know how the schools are run now and whether that is still a requirement.[33]

The prominent role of the Catholic Church in public life was another reason some families felt distanced from the new state. Ron Alcock grew up in a large Protestant family in Inchicore in Dublin. He recalled that

> The Church completely dominated everybody on the street where I lived. And even when the Pope was celebrating his birthday, or whatever celebration it was, they put up bunting in the street, house to house . . . The Church definitely dominated the whole street, and the whole of Ireland at the time. My parents argued against it and couldn't understand how people could be so dominated. And it made you feel isolated.[34]

Likewise, many British people in India felt a cultural distance from the Indian majority. From the early nineteenth century the British community had generally lived separate lives from the Indian majority.[35] This was reinforced after the Indian Rebellion in 1857. The lack of affinity meant that few considered staying on after independence to play a role in one of the new states. The formation of new states in Ireland and India created new political and cultural environments which were not always welcoming for these who had close associations with British rule.

Home and Identity

How did individuals understand home and identity in domestic, national and imperial contexts, and did these meanings collide for those considering their position in the postcolonial period? Interviews with those who experienced this traumatic period reveal conflicting conceptualisations of home: one rooted in a physical space and place; another existing at a 'nation' level; and a third relating to their experience as part of an imperial community. The rupture caused by independence resulted in the collision of these different conceptualisations.

Interviews and memoirs of Protestants living in Ireland in the early decades of the twentieth century convey ambiguous notions of home. Some strongly identified with Ireland as home whilst at the same time acknowledging British antecedents and political affiliations. Peter Walton's family had a long tradition of military service, and both Peter and his father served in the British army. When asked about his sense of home he explained: 'I have always regarded home as Ireland. And as I explained, three out of four of my grandparents were Irish so I don't feel that is a bad thing or a dishonest thing. Anyway I like it.'[36] In his interview, Walton was able to articulate clearly that the family's origins, Protestantism and political affiliation to Britain demonstrated through generations of military service, provided a link to Britain, yet at the same time he identified his strong attachment to Ireland. In this quote, he describes his grandparents as Irish, although they would have been born when Ireland was part of the United Kingdom. Peter is able to consider the possibilities of multi-layered identities and understandings of home. Robert Maude came from a Protestant family in north county Dublin. His father was an optician in central Dublin and many of his relatives had served in the First World War. Whilst the family felt betrayed by the Easter Rising in 1916, throughout his childhood his mother impressed on Robert his Irish identity and connection to Dublin, thus allowing an affiliation and connection to Britain whilst remaining rooted in Ireland.[37] However, not all Protestants living through the turbulent decades of the early twentieth century were able to separate home, nation and identity. For some, the long-standing link to Britain created a barrier to identifying Ireland as home. Ron Alcock was from a large family in central Dublin. His father was a painter and decorator. From his earliest years, he felt separate from the majority Catholic population of his neighbourhood: 'When I was living in Dublin I felt more British because people reminded me all the time, "You don't belong here!"

That may have been kid's stuff but you were always reminded.'[38] Although his family had lived in Ireland for many generations, and had not spent any time in Britain, their distant British ancestry and religion marked them out as separate and foreign. This caused Ron to feel alienated from the place in which he had grown up and resulted in a reorientation towards Britain as a site of home and belonging. These accounts suggest a multi-layered understanding of home amongst Irish Protestants in this period, with multiple associations of home and identity based on physical, imagined and imperial concepts. They were able to conceptualise home as physically and imaginatively located in Ireland, whilst also being part of a wider British imperial community.

The British in India had less ambiguous, but also multiple understandings of home. Alison Blunt suggests imperial sites created a place where subjects could be 'at home and not at home' simultaneously.[39] This concept of being both 'at home and not at home' has resonance with those who grew up in India in the early part of the twentieth century. Sue Sloan was born in Quetta in 1934. Her father was 'a farm boy from Kent'; her mother was born in Singapore to an Irish father and British mother. When reflecting on her childhood experiences she recalled an ambivalent feeling of both belonging in India, and yet regarding Britain as home. She attributed the feelings of belonging to the fact she was born in India, and to the degree of contact she had with Indian friends, which gave her a cultural anchor to the subcontinent. Both these factors allowed her to accept the cultural aspects that many British arrivals in India found shocking, such as death, disease and poverty. Yet, despite this acceptance of life in India, Sue never doubted that 'home' was Britain. She explained that the sense of home was fostered through British institutions in India, particularly the club, which served as a site of British life in an Indian environment. The internal space of the club represented British culture through furnishing, objects and imagery. British values were emphasised through the exclusive use of English as the language of communication and the whites-only membership policy that predominated throughout the subcontinent. The link with Britain as home was reinforced within Sue's family as the place to which the family planned to relocate on retirement.[40]

This feeling of both belonging within the physical space of India and yet being imaginatively connected to Britain was echoed in many interviews recorded for this research. John Outram was born in Malaya in 1934 but grew up in India until he was sent, aged twelve, to school in England: 'I was pretty focused on getting back to England. I never thought of India as my home, even though my father had been born there.'[41] Yet, when describing his early years, his feelings of pleasure at the landscape are evident. When reflecting on his childhood he noted that it was hard to feel rooted in England as an adult as he had not spent his formative years there. Both John Outram and Sue Sloan had close relatives who were born in England and were from families in which education and retirement was customarily spent in Britain.

However, there were other families who had much more long-standing connections to India who still felt this deep attachment to Britain. Betty Gascoyne's family counted six generations born in India. In the early nineteenth century her male relatives were employed by the East India Company; by the twentieth century most were working on the railways in different capacities. Betty explains that within her family Britain was considered home although her immediate family had never been to Britain and, until independence, had no immediate plans to relocate there. Her conceptualisation of Britain as 'home' was visually constructed from magazines imported from Britain such as the *Sketch*, *Daily Mirror* and *Pictorial*, which she read at the railway institute and which formed part of the cultural idea of Britain as home.[42] This cultural link to Britain, whilst remaining physically rooted in India, marks the British community as being part of an imperial diaspora. These interviews point to the fact that within the British community in India there existed dual meanings of home, which allowed them to feel both 'at home and not at home' in the subcontinent. This duality served to reinforce their status as members of a British diaspora who although located in India were always imaginatively positioned within an imperial British context.

Environment

When considering these different interpretations of home and belonging amongst these two communities, it is instructive to consider their relationship to land and environment. This offers some explanation as to why each group saw home differently. India was never intended as a country of permanent settlement; instead, from 1858, the British government encouraged 'a class of superior settlers; who may, by their enterprise, capital and science, set in motion the labour, and develop the resources of India'.[43] However, the increase in the need for technically skilled personnel to work on the railways, telegraphs and other infrastructure projects meant an expansion in the British population in the late nineteenth century. Many of these could not afford to return home and made India their place of permanent settlement. Ireland, by contrast, was 'settled' most controversially during the seventeenth century and there was subsequent migration from Britain in the following centuries. Unlike in India, land-ownership was encouraged.

Personal and statistical evidence reveals that a large proportion of Irish Protestants had strong links to the land established through generations of occupancy. Long habitation in a specific geographical area and home-ownership combined to create a strong sense of home for Irish Protestants. Home was less a metaphorical concept than a concrete reality. Elizabeth Bowen describes the family connection to County Cork established during the Cromwellian invasion and enduring continuously from this period to 1959. Throughout the memoir, Bowen frequently refers to the topography of this part of the rural south-west: 'The fields undulate in a smooth flowing way'; there are 'dark knolls and screens of trees'. She notes the distinctiveness of this part of the country: 'this is a part of Ireland with no lakes, but the sky's movement of clouds reflects itself everywhere'.[44] Bowen's familiarity and appreciation of this particular location in Ireland is mirrored by her description of her father's sense of place: 'His love of the country, his Ballyhoura country, was too deeply innate to be emotional—he had no contact with it through farming or sport, but all the same this was an informed love, for Henry knew about rocks and trees.'[45] Bowen's comments on the landscape link the family to the land and locate them in a specific area. The description of her father's relationship to this part of County Cork uses the personal to denote the strong attachment felt by Henry Bowen. It was 'his Ballyhoura country' and she uses the word 'love' twice to describe his feeling for it. This close and emotional link to the land is reiterated throughout a recording made with Peter Walton.[46] He described the farmed estate on the outskirts of Carlow where his family had lived for over 150 years. He expressed his deep affection for the house and its environs, recalling exploring the house with its nooks full of family mementoes and enjoying the freedom to roam around the countryside. Not only connected by time, the family was literally sustained by the estate; most of the food consumed was produced on their farm.[47]

Roy Strong in *Visions of England* has persuasively argued that the evolution of a sense of Englishness was emphasised in the nineteenth century, with the landscape being a fundamental part of this identity.[48] Paul Colley has researched the impact of place and identity on a sense of self,[49] and when we look at communities living in a colonial setting away from the metropolitan centre, it is interesting to consider the extent to which the physical environment shaped the sense of identity of these two communities. Irish Protestants reveal through memoirs and interviews their close link to the land and landscape. In many cases, the land sustained families and enabled their livelihood; it was an easy place in which to live. In contrast, the British in India feared its climate. Mark Harrison discusses the changing understandings of climate and its effects in colonial India. He argues that the earlier view of British acclimatisation had lost credence by the mid-nineteenth century and rather than being a sought-after outcome was seen as leading to racial degeneration. This encouraged the British to view the Indian climatic environment as potentially dangerous, damaging the body but also the racial make-up of British settlers.[50] This view is echoed in many of the interviews and memoirs of those living in India in the early part of the twentieth century. Colonel Rivett Carnac noted:

> The outlook out there [India] was entirely different to here, you had to take precautions against disease the whole time, in what you ate and what you drank, and where you walked, and where you pulled your curtains, there might be a small snake in it, or even on your bed, there were mosquitoes which carried diseases, and malaria, bed bugs in practically in every bed in the rest houses in the district and it was the land of sudden illness especially for children.[51]

This caution had a basis in reality. Before antibiotics, refrigeration and vaccination, India, for Europeans, was a dangerous place to live.[52] The physical representation of this was through clothing, particularly the *sola topi*, a cork hat/helmet worn to guard against the sun. Many remember purchasing their topis in Port Said in Eygpt, thus marking a symbolic transition from the European sphere to the eastern. Caution was also necessary in approaching food and possible contamination. It was common practice to only eat at home where food preparation could be supervised, or at the homes of other British families where similar precautions would be taken. Children were warned against eating food from the bazaar for fear of illness and any fresh food was washed in permanganate before being consumed.[53]

Nevertheless, there were attempts to control and tame the physical environment in India. This was often demonstrated through the relationship between British women and their gardens. It differed from the interior of the home with its legions of servants; this was a space in which British women could attempt to create and control their environment. However, the attempts to replicate an English garden replete with green lawns and flowering plants was often foiled by the atmosphere of the Indian plains. Lady Dring was married to an officer in the 45th Sikhs and therefore travelled extensively with the regiment. She recalled tending to the bungalow garden and attempting to create an oasis of green with flowering plants but being overcome by the heat and constant dust present on the plains.[54] These efforts to replicate the English garden within an Indian environment seem to indicate the British desire to tame the Indian landscape through determination and effort and forge a physical transformation of the landscape into one in which they could comfortably live. John Outram remembers the ambivalent relationship with the climate and landscape of India:

> We used to go to rocky gorges where all the stones were smoothed with flood water and we used to slide down stones and they had waterfalls. We were playing in a landscape, like you see in the Marabar Caves in Forster's *Passage to India*. They are fabulous landscapes. And the British just sported around in them. I was never taken to see a temple, never went near one, even to look at it, it was always the landscape and nature and rocks and trees.[55]

His familiarity and ease in the Indian landscape is in contrast to his experience of coming to England during the Second World War. However, John identified with the natural, rather than the built landscape of India. He described the British as 'playing in a landscape' and 'sporting' around in it, using the landscape as a place of recreation. His reference to never visiting a temple—the physical and spiritual representation of Indian life—indicated non-engagement with a fundamental aspect of Indian life. This suggests the British inhabited India, but never fully engaged with it.

'Home' for the British in India was an ambivalent concept as they were rooted physically in India, but imaginatively located in Britain. This separation between the physical space of India and psychological idea of Britain was reinforced through the lack of attachment many British people serving the Raj had with their homes, as they frequently moved. It was also reinforced through the contested space of the home, where the colonised and the coloniser inhabited the same space. It was further emphasised as the British came to view the Indian environment as a hazard to be guarded against, with potential dangers both within the home from disease and animals and in the wider environment from the climate. When comparing these understandings of home to southern Irish Protestants, there are both commonalities and contrasting experiences. Irish Protestants had different understandings of home: some closely identifying with home as rooted in Ireland, others allowing for multiple understandings of home which acknowledged both Irish and British loyalties. Some others felt the experiences of the early decades of the twentieth century created a climate in which they could never be fully accepted. In contrast to the British in India, however, there is strong evidence of close identification with the land and landscape of rural Ireland established over generations of occupancy.

The rupture caused by independence resulted in the collision of these different conceptualisations. Verna Perry's response to the news that the family would be returning to Britain from Bombay reveals some of the complicated feelings associated with return:

> I remember feeling really happy and excited about going home . . . I remember standing on the stairs and knew we were leaving Mulund [Bombay/Mumbai] and going to England and

> I can remember thinking, 'What a happy life, and I love this place', and feeling sad at leaving it and feeling apprehensive for the future, and with a lot of difficulty getting booked on the Largs Bay [ship] and it was a big adventure.[56]

Verna Perry reveals many of the elements discussed by those 'remigrating' to Britain in this period. She describes Britain as 'home', which co-existed with her love for her physical home in Bombay. Her feelings of return are ambivalent: happiness and excitement at the prospect of returning to Britain, tempered with feelings of apprehension for what this would actually mean for the family on their return.

Conclusion

The transition from British rule in Ireland and the Indian subcontinent to national governments caused a huge upheaval for those groups who had closely identified with the British empire. Formerly advantaged by their imperial connections with Britain, independence meant their position was challenged in these new states. Although violence was a feature it did not seem to be a primary motivator in the decision to relocate to Britain. Other factors, such as the cultural ethos of these new states, created an atmosphere in which many Irish Protestants and British people in India no longer felt comfortable. Both groups had several hundred years' connection to each place, but interviews reveal that Irish Protestants developed a firmer association with Ireland and in many instances considered it as a home. In contrast, the British resided in India while remaining imaginatively connected to Britain as home. Therefore, despite a common adherence to the idea of empire, there was not a uniform understanding of what it meant to be an imperial subject. The distant geographies and political challenges created an environment in which each group, although loyal, had different interpretations of what it meant to belong to the empire.

CHAPTER THIRTEEN

'My mother wouldn't have been as hurt': Women and Inter-church Marriage in Wexford, 1945–65

CATHERINE O'CONNOR

Introduction

The 1950s have been described as the 'lost decade' in Ireland, characterised by the emigration of thousands of young people, desperate to escape the economic stagnation and social oppression of Irish society.[1] This flood of emigration was particularly marked from rural areas. In February 1957, one rare immigrant, a twenty-five-year-old Australian woman, Denise T., accompanied her returning Irish husband, James, to live on a farm near Enniscorthy in County Wexford. Forty-six years later, she recalled her first impressions of Ireland as 'a drab grey country', where 'everyone seemed to wear long black or grey overcoats'. At her first church 'social' (dance), in the local Church of Ireland parish hall, dressed in her 'pretty summer dress with petticoats', she felt conspicuously out of place among the austere and severely dressed older men and women. Her first impression was that her generation appeared to have completely disappeared.[2] Drawing on an oral history study of twenty-one married Church of Ireland women, as well as local documentary sources, this chapter examines socialisation and attitudes to inter-church marriage in the rural Church of Ireland in the two decades following the Second World

War. The location of this study is County Wexford, the geographical boundaries of which corresponding almost identically to those of the Church of Ireland diocese of Ferns.[3]

Marriage, *Ne Temere* and Population Decline

The emigration of unprecedented numbers of young people from Ireland between the years 1945–65 worried state and church authorities alike. The *Report of the Commission of Emigration and Other Population Problems* set up in 1948 to address the issue considered the scarcity of marriage partners as a major contributor to rates of emigration among young people, with poor marriage prospects identified as a particular factor in high female emigration rates. Marriage and family life were considered in the *Report* to be intrinsic to material as well as emotional contentment in rural areas, and therefore central to reducing emigration figures. It was also recognised that 'the opportunity of marriage for members of the agricultural community depended very largely on the possibility of getting a farm'.[4]

Farmers, along with members of the professional class in the county towns dominated the social structure of the Church of Ireland population in Ferns diocese.[5] While a preoccupation with the continuation of the family farm contributed to the practice of patrilineal male succession, the average age of succession in the 1950s was between thirty-eight and forty years of age.[6] One interviewee, Janet C., who married in 1958 and lived on a small farm near Adamstown, described how her marriage was delayed until her husband could buy his own house, because 'I would not come in on [his] brother because he owned the place'. Her husband, thirty-seven at marriage, continued to work with his brother on the family farm, which he eventually inherited when his brother became sick and died at fifty-two years.[7]

Significant concerns with low and delayed rates of marriage were addressed in the official discourse of the Church of Ireland. The General Synod of 1949 was informed by the church's Board of Education that 'it is desirable to encourage young people of the Church of Ireland to interest themselves in rural life and to establish their homes and to make their living in country districts in Éire'.

It was noted, however, that this would only be possible if land, or alternative employment, was available to families.[8] Matrimonial advertisements were a regular feature of the *Church of Ireland Gazette*.[9] The Church of Ireland Marriage Bureau was established in 1962 to cater 'in complete confidence for people who may find it difficult to procure suitable partners for marriage'.[10] Nevertheless, in 1965, one letter to the editor of the *Gazette* again highlighted the difficulties posed to the church in rural areas by the continuing shortage of marriage partners. The writer, signing as 'hopeful', noted: 'We have a problem in the mid-west of good farms just requiring a woman or girl (Church of Ireland) to fill the post as farmer's wife for the middle aged lonely farmer. Needless to say the schools are facing hard times with few pupils on the rolls.'[11]

While all of these challenges significantly affected a predominantly rural economy such as that in County Wexford, the Church of Ireland also faced the ever-present challenge of the *Ne Temere* decree. This 1908 Catholic decree obliged the Protestant partner in a mixed marriage to consent in writing to the upbringing of any children of the union as Catholics. Faced with a consistently declining population since independence, the enforcement of *Ne Temere* posed a significant threat to rural Church of Ireland parishes. One church member described the fear occasioned by 'mixed' or inter-church marriage in this manner:

> *Ne temere* was the big bugbear. It was the reason that Protestant families went to extraordinary lengths to keep their children from mixing with Roman Catholics. There were terrible cases where young people had been disowned by their families for marrying a Catholic.[12]

The report of the 1948 Anglican Lambeth Conference and in particular its warning against 'mixed marriages' was reproduced in the February 1949 *Church of Ireland Monthly* inset in the *Diocesan Magazine of Ossory Ferns and Leighlin*. The report insisted that the signing of a declaration that children 'be brought up in another religious system in which he or she does not believe' was sinful and 'an abrogation of a primary duty of parents to their children'. It continued that 'in no circumstances should an Anglican give any undertaking as a condition of marriage that the children should be brought up in the practice of another communion . . . you cannot morally pawn, pledge or mortgage the faith of a little child'.[13] The Church of Ireland Primate, Archbishop Gregg, described the enforcement of *Ne Temere* as 'a grave injury to our church'. In 1951 in the light of the Tilson case, when the Supreme Court upheld the contractual validity of the pre-marriage promise given by both parties in inter-church marriage as a result of *Ne Temere*, Gregg addressed the seriousness of mixed marriage. Explaining the decision taken by the General Synod to issue cards outlining church opposition to inter-church marriage to all parishes, he advised that:

> We must create so far as we can such a deep-rooted prejudice, and such a community sense against such marriages on Roman Catholic terms, that even the thoughtless will know that they constitute a grave injury to our Church and should not be entered upon.[14]

The suggestion of 'creating a deep-rooted prejudice' is indicative of the sense of threat caused by *Ne Temere*. In a predominantly rural diocese such as Ferns, it threatened the church significantly, not only through population decline, but also in the area of land-ownership. For many decades after independence the succession of the family farm and especially the continuation of 'the name on the place' was fiercely protected. Conversion to Catholicism was common in the event of an inter-church marriage, leading to a perceived loss to the community through the transfer of land-ownership, as well as the loss of subsequent children. Interviewees—for example Susan M., who lived near Wexford town—recognised that 'the person that was getting married into the Roman Catholic church nearly always had to become a member and all the children'.[15] Joanne R., a farmer's wife from Bunclody, also described an example of a relative converting to Catholicism on marriage. She confirmed that she 'went to his church and the children were all Roman Catholics'.[16] Lesley J., on the other hand, who grew up in Wexford but later went to live in Waterford, was very clear that 'these marriages even led to a son not being passed on the farm by his father leading to family break down also'.[17]

Further personal testimony of the harm occasioned by inter-church marriage was expressed by Mary A., again a farmer's wife, married in 1946, from north Wexford. Mary was fully aware of the distress caused by inter-church marriage and spoke from the heart about its consequences. One topic that engaged her was the funeral of a neighbour's mother:

> There was a lady and her mother died around here, now she married a Roman Catholic but anyway, she was an extremist but . . . anyway, the mother died and when she came to the church that night, the daughter came to the door and then she turned around and went back. You know things like that, they were cruel now weren't they? Your mother's your mother . . . and sure what difference would it make?[18]

The oral histories reveal that many women contested the 'cruelty' of family division that sometimes resulted from inter-church marriages in rural communities. Jean A. described how her mother maintained secret contact with her sister, who had married a Roman Catholic and had been forced to leave for England.

> My mother wouldn't have been as hurt. She would have done anything for her family. She was friends with all. Actually I was amazed that she once flew over to England. She never flew in her life or went anywhere. All she did was work but she flew over to see Nellie. She would have kept up contact all the time which was marvellous for Nellie.[19]

Meeting Partners

With the exception of one candidate, all the women interviewed in the oral history study employed were married within the Church of Ireland community between the years 1940 and 1965. The majority met future husbands through family contacts, school or their local church community. Sarah W. first met her husband when he came to thresh corn at the family farm. When he returned to collect his payment for this work, they arranged to meet on the following Sunday. They went to Courtown, a nearby seaside resort, and 'sat on the wall and chatted'.[20]

The only participant in an inter-church marriage in the study, Heather B., married in the 1940s having met her husband at a dance in Dublin, where she had moved in her twenties to work, following the death of her mother and her father's remarriage. Significantly, Heather did not initially disclose this fact and was surprisingly unwilling to discuss her marriage at all. It was not until a second interview that it became apparent her husband was not Church of Ireland. In answer to the direct question: 'Was your husband Church of Ireland as well, Heather?' she replied: 'No, he wasn't. Ah sure we didn't care if they were Church of Ireland or what they were.' Later, after persistent prompting, she explained that she and her husband were married by a Catholic priest: 'we just went . . . to a Catholic place and they just go though the formula. There were no problems.' Her children were brought up as Catholics although she continued to attend her own church. When asked if religion was important to her still, she replied: 'Well it keeps you in touch, doesn't it.'[21] None of Heather's family attended her wedding and she very seldom went back to Wexford afterwards to visit. The following exchange indicates her reluctance to discuss this:

I.: Did you go home much after you got married?
H.: Well, not as much because you couldn't. You wouldn't have the same freedom or time or anything you know.
I.: Were you married in Dublin or in Wexford?
H.: In Dublin.
I.: Did the family come up to the wedding?
H.: No, it was just a matter of signing a couple of yokes. It wasn't like nowadays, a big deal.[22]

The evident reticence in this extract signifies in its exclusion of detail some of the consequences and meaning of inter-church marriage for members of the Church of Ireland in the 1940s and 1950s. All of the interviewees in the study confirmed an awareness of the desirability of marriage within the church. Within the family, the mother appears to have been the most influential in the promotion of this ideal. Hazel L. remembered her mother telling herself and her sister that 'marriage is difficult enough as it is, why make it more difficult by marrying someone of a different religion?'[23] The hurt occasioned in families through marriages and the conversion to Catholicism that was often chosen by the Church of Ireland partner was described by one interviewee, Jean A., in the context of her parents' antipathy to her sister's mixed marriage: 'It was terribly difficult; you see it was awfully hard on my parents in that our baptism wasn't recognised. They had to become Catholic and they had to be baptised, confirmed all over again, which made very little of us.'[24]

Yet in spite of this understanding, all interviewees knew neighbours, friends and sometimes relations involved in inter-church marriage. Some emphasised the subsequent marginalisation of family members. Discussion of the topic in the oral histories was characterised by a reticence otherwise absent in the interviews, indicative of a legacy of hurt and resentment.[25]

Socialisation in the Church of Ireland

Such hurt and resentment remained significant constituents not only of personal and family history but also of the history of Church of Ireland communities. They led to strenuous efforts at parish level to encourage the socialisation and, by consequence, marriage among its (remaining) young people. In Wexford, the local *Diocesan Magazine* recorded much of this activity in its parish notes.[26] All marriages and especially baptisms were announced with particular relish by the parish incumbent. The rector often looked forward to the future participation of the child in parish life.[27] The arrival of children benefited the entire parish community, for example in helping to keep small schools open. In October 1961 the rector of Kilnamanagh Union enthusiastically congratulated two parishioners on the birth of twin boys, exclaiming that 'the future of Kilnamanagh school looks rosy!'[28] Integrating children into the church community included Sunday school activities, picnics, sporting tournaments like table tennis and tennis, summer fêtes and endless fundraising gatherings. This promotion of social and community cohesion was very much dependent on women in their organisational capacity and subscription. Indeed it is evident from the *Diocesan Magazine* and these oral histories that in the local church, religious and social activity were very much synonymous.[29] Women were also vital to the promotion of segregated social activity. Church of Ireland dances—'socials' as they were popularly known—sponsored by the clergy or local parish organisations, were ostensibly part of continuous fundraising efforts for various church needs. However, all remembered their primary function as that of providing social opportunities for young people to meet prospective marriage partners. Lesley J. explained the purpose of church socials in this way: 'the division between some social activities was deliberate. Protestant socials were usually held in church halls so boys and girls could meet and prevent mixed marriages.'[30]

These events were strictly denominational. Susan M. explained that her Catholic neighbours 'understood they didn't come to our socials and they didn't hold it against us or anything'.[31] Similarly, the promotion of denominational education by the Church of Ireland in this period played a crucial role in the struggle to preserve Protestant identity. Many of the women interviewed were aware of the importance of denominational education for their children and worked very hard to support Protestant primary schools. Stringent efforts, including constant fundraising, were made in Wexford as elsewhere to maintain small national schools and to support the school transport schemes necessary to ferry pupils to and from them. Meanwhile, the selection of secondary school depended primarily on financial circumstances. The co-educational Tate School (1867–1949), established as a 'charity school' by the bequest of William Tate in 1792, had provided Protestant secondary education to boarders and day students in Wexford town until its closure in 1949 due to financial reasons.[32] There was no Protestant secondary school in County Wexford following the closure of the Tate, so young people had to attend boarding schools outside the county if their family wanted or could afford to have them receive a denominational education. Yvonne C., who lived near New Ross, admitted that: 'Protestants sent their children to boarding school so they would mix with their own kind as well as keeping them from being indoctrinated by Catholic ideas and theories.'[33] In neighbouring counties, schools such as Kilkenny College (with a Church of Ireland ethos) and Newtown School in Waterford (Quaker) absorbed these students.

It was suggested by Lynne P. from south Wexford, who came from a wealthy background and was educated in England, that in some cases: 'poor Protestants who had not been lucky or affluent enough to receive much education . . . suffered dreadfully by being the odd men out in the [Catholic] national schools'.[34] While this notion of 'suffered' is contradicted by other testimonies, it highlights an often hidden issue of social class cutting across religious boundaries in rural Wexford.

It is also apparent from the oral evidence that considerations of social class are relevant to any discussion of attitudes to inter-church marriage. The testimony of Mary A. is informative. She described how there were certain neighbouring families (Protestant as well as Catholic) whom she was forbidden to speak to as a child in the 1930s:

> Even when we were growing up, you know now we couldn't mix and we couldn't do this, and there was families you couldn't mix with or talk to, even on our road when we were coming from school now and all . . . You'd be skinned alive you know, you really would.[35]

Mary later revealed that a fear of tuberculosis, widespread in Ireland until the 1960s, lay behind this admonishment. Tuberculosis was associated wrongly in popular perception with poverty and unhygienic living conditions, and was considered by many families as a form of social taboo. At the same time, Jean A. was aware that her parents' opposition to her brother's marriage to a local Catholic girl may have also been influenced by social snobbery.

> My oldest brother married a girl nearby and my father was dead against it. She was a Roman Catholic girl and I am not convinced that that was all, I think it was because she lived in a cottage and we were farmers. If I speak from my heart. She never came into our house.[36]

A certain ambiguity emerges in the oral histories highlighting social organisation within the rural Protestant community. Very significant social distinctions existed which introduced variables of class and social position as much as religious affiliation to social interaction between Protestants and their Catholic neighbours. Lynne P., whose family wealth was atypical of this group, provided a clear example in her reflection on social difference:

> I would say the differences were cultural. We knew a great many Church of Ireland people whom I would not call friends.

> We were lucky in that we received a good education and the people whom we would not have counted as friends would not have had that privilege. But we were friends all the same with our staff (two domestic plus governess, two on the farm, a few casual workers and lots of people in the neighbourhood). We just didn't invite them to share a meal with us—the acid test.[37]

Nevertheless, the oral histories provide evidence of many examples of cross-community congeniality. All of the women interviewed admitted to having childhood Catholic friends and testified to excellent relations with their neighbours in rural communities. One respondent, Janet C., described how her childhood friend Kitty went everywhere with her:

> My friend, Kitty, she was a Roman Catholic and I was a Protestant and that time the Roman Catholic people wasn't allowed to go into the Protestant church, but Kitty didn't mind, we went everywhere, into the chapel, into the churches and we never minded whatsoever.[38]

The labour-intensive nature of agricultural work in this period necessitated a high level of interdependence among farming communities, prompting ample opportunity for socialisation. Heather B., who was born near Gorey in 1919, framed her description of good relations between Protestant and Catholic neighbours within this context. She described:

> The neighbours got on alright together you know. You would go visit them . . . they didn't make any distinction as far as we were concerned, no, we just mixed in and helped one another on the farm, you know, certain times of the year. The harvest time and that. They didn't have much distinction.[39]

Among younger respondents to the study, there is a significant shift in perception of such social interaction as the decades advanced. Susan M., born in 1938, almost twenty years after Heather, in her reflection on the discouragement of inter-church marriage, pointed to a difference between the 'old beliefs' and her own upbringing in the 1940s. She described:

> And there were old beliefs that we were led to believe, you know, that Rome felt that if you weren't that if you weren't, anyone who wasn't a member of the Roman Catholic Church, you know, would not go to heaven, it was called that time you know. But now whether, I'd say the way I grew up there was never a trace of bitterness, and I suppose it was sort of more a code of behaviour that you lived by, that you . . . felt that that was, you know . . . And I mean, some of my dearest and closest friends are members of the Roman Catholic church certainly these days and even then, very close friends.[40]

This extract exemplifies how although conscious of the difficulties involved in mixed marriage, for Susan this was almost contrary to her personal experience of inter-church relationships in the parish where she grew up. Her interview is replete with examples of convivial social relations with her neighbours. Her father was one of the first in their locality to own a radio and her house was full of neighbours on Sunday afternoons to listen to hurling matches in the period when the Wexford team won three All-Ireland hurling finals in 1955, 1956 and 1960.[41]

There is significant evidence that while women supported church activity and indeed promoted this activity within the local church, they also enjoyed increasing levels of social activity and opportunity in the 1950s. Many were active and indeed leading members of the Irish Countrywomen's Association in Wexford, such as Susan M., Denise T. and Mary A. above, together with other organisations which facilitated greater social interaction with their Catholic neighbours. As well as the ubiquitous church socials, many frequented county show dances, hunt balls and many other examples of social entertainment. Susan, who married in 1958, described going to show dances as fun: 'We would go to the show dance in Enniscorthy . . . they were fun, you know, cycling home at dawn and quite happy to, you know, and it was quite safe and nobody had anything to worry about, you know.'[42] Protestant farmers and business people were consistently well represented on local agricultural show committees, while Protestant farm women contributed enthusiastically to the produce and craft exhibitions and demonstration classes, which were an integral feature of such events.

Rose F., who married in 1963 at the age of twenty-four, enjoyed a varied social life, attending 'race' dances and the cinema regularly. The popularity of the cinema was evidenced by a number of interviewees who remembered cinema visits by bicycle during their youth. These bicycle journeys often provided opportunities for social intermingling among the sexes. The 1950s witnessed the introduction of mobile cinemas in Wexford, with film shows in many local halls. Taghmon Mobile Cinemas, among others, travelled around the county with a varied repertoire.[43] For Rose, and some of the younger interviewees, increasing social mobility in the 1950s meant greater social interaction with the local Catholic community and, perhaps inevitably, less silent acceptance of the significance and consequences of inter-church marriages. This social advancement would appear to support the possibility of what Glenfield has identified as 'the emergence of a new generation of Anglicans without many of the old prejudices of previous generations'.[44]

The 1957 Fethard-on-Sea Boycott

As the oral histories provide a more nuanced account of attitudes to inter-church marriage, they also inform on attitudes to the 1957 Fethard-on-Sea controversy in the county.[45] The boycott of Protestant businesses in this small south Wexford village was called in response to the flight of Sheila Cloney with her two daughters from their home in April 1957. Sheila Cloney, née Kelly, a member of a well-known Church of Ireland farming family in the area, married her husband Seán Cloney, a local Catholic farmer, in London in November 1949. After a short stay in England the couple returned to Fethard to farm at Dungulph Castle and subsequently had two daughters, both baptised as Catholics. In April 1957, the eldest daughter Eileen was due to start school in the local Catholic national school. This was opposed by Mrs Cloney, who wanted her children to attend the local Church of Ireland school instead. She left the family home with her children on the morning of Saturday 27 April. Rumours spread that she had been assisted by members of the Church of Ireland community and, on 12 May 1957, the local Catholic curate in Poulfur, adjacent to Fethard, Fr Stafford, called for a boycott of Protestant business until the Cloney children were returned.[46]

The boycott lasted for a number of months, inciting passionate commentary from all sides. On a visit to Wexford in July 1957, the Catholic bishop of Galway, Dr Browne, condemned the 'kidnapping' of Catholic children and the efforts of Protestants to 'make political capital' from 'a peaceful and moderate protest'.[47] Meanwhile, the Church of Ireland bishop of Ferns, Dr Phair, adopted a restrained and cautious approach to the controversy. He appealed for calm and reconciliation while acknowledging nationwide expressions of support.[48] In the September issue of the *Diocesan Magazine*, he expressed gratitude that the 'cruel' boycott showed signs of coming to an end. However, it was November before he could proclaim with any confidence that conditions in the parish were improving, although admitting that it would probably be 'some time before normal relations are fully restored'.[49] The issue of control of the children's religious formation was central to the debate. While not openly supported by the Catholic bishop of Ferns, Dr Staunton, the boycott awakened old wounds around inter-church marriage and a deep sense of resentment towards the obligation imposed by *Ne Temere*. On 4 July, the boycott was discussed in Dáil Éireann. In response to a question raised by Dr Noël Browne, former Minister for Health, Taoiseach Éamon de Valera described the boycott as 'ill-conceived, ill-considered and futile for the achievement of the purpose for which it seems to have been intended'.[50]

Hazel L., who lived in New Ross, not far from Fethard-on-Sea, remembered the boycott and its effects on the Protestant community as well as her own family. She was twelve years old at the time and recalled much adult discussion of the 'shocking' event. In her opinion, the boycott had repercussions all over the county. She remembers discussion of people coming from other counties to shop at Gardiner's shop in Fethard to show solidarity as well as to provide financial support. Hazel's family holidayed regularly in Fethard-on-Sea, and empathised strongly during the course of the boycott with the community there.[51]

The boycott did not represent a simple polarity between Catholic and Protestant interests, as is often portrayed, and was in fact contested by both communities. The recollections of Canon Edward Grant, rector of the Fethard union of parishes from March 1946 to November 1956, unveil some of these nuances. In his 'Recollections' Canon Grant described a complex system of social relations at work between the Catholic and Protestant communities in the area. He includes accounts received from many Church of Ireland clergy of increased friendliness and support from Catholic neighbours and records witnessing one instance of assistance provided by a Catholic farmer 'with a reputation for Sinn Féin activity in the "trouble times"' to Sheila Kelly's brother on the failure of his tractor. Citing some examples of previous excellent relations between both communities in the area, in the conclusion to his memoir he asserts that 'This whole affair of the "Fethard Boycott" was one awful sequel to an attempt to enforce the *Ne Temere* decree, that children of a mixed marriage should be reared as Catholics.'[52]

Meanwhile, another contemporary, Sarah Poyntz, recorded in her memoir *Memory Emancipated* her father's account of how he strongly resisted attempts by an unnamed Catholic priest to force him to discontinue business with his Protestant clients at the time of the boycott.

> He said he had been visited by a Roman Catholic Curate who said to him, 'You will of course, Mr. Poyntz, join the boycott of Protestants by refusing to be their solicitor . . . I told him I'd do nothing of the sort and he replied that if I was a convinced Catholic I'd join the boycott. I looked at him and said, 'In my more than thirty years as a solicitor I've never had to tell anyone to leave my office. Now I'm telling you to leave it this minute and it gives me great pleasure to see you to the door and to tell you never again to darken it. Go home to your church and look after it and leave me to look after my own affairs.' So I saw him to the door and out he went, his tail between his legs.[53]

Correspondingly, Elizabeth K. described how local Catholics in Clonroche continued to support the annual Protestant fête in neighbouring Killegney parish despite the boycott. There was a long-standing tradition of reciprocal support for each other's events, elaborated on in her description of the Church of Ireland fête in 1957:

> Well Castleboro fête was a big day in Cloughbawn parish, the 29th of June. A great big fête with races and bicycle races and athletics of all kinds, and stepdancing and all kinds of sideshows

> and everything, and our parishioners all rowed in and helped them with that . . . and we all used the same 'Aunt Sallys'. I don't know whether they owned them or we owned them, but the same staff ran both of them. And I can remember when the Fethard boycott was on, and it was told that no one was to go to a Church of Ireland fête. I don't know whether it was the priest or what, I suppose it was the priest in Cloughbawn, and before the gates were open Mr. A. and Mr. B. [two local Catholics] were queueing up to get in and they were sort of a prominent family in Clonroche. But they showed up at the gate to get in and then the whole village of Clonroche followed suit . . . our rectory was just a few hundred yards from Clonroche village, and everything went on as usual.[54]

Finally, Yvonne C. was anxious to assert that the Fethard-on-Sea boycott 'was given a lot of publicity, maybe more than should have been given to it, you know' and contended that 'Fethard is now the greatest example of ecumenism that you could find'.[55] Such oral and written personal accounts subvert any simplistic sectarian analysis of the boycott and contribute to a fuller historical understanding of its effects in the diocese.

Conclusion

There is no doubt that the enforcement of the *Ne Temere* decree—together with demographic trends of low and delayed rates of marriage—led to a steadily diminishing rural Church of Ireland community in the years 1945–65. Problematic in a rural community where land inheritance and possession was fiercely protected, *Ne Temere* and its effects were most vividly epitomised in the Fethard-on-Sea boycott of 1957. Inter-church marriage was perceived to present the greatest threat to the survival of the Church of Ireland population in rural Irish parishes. In the family setting, warnings against such marriages were delivered inter-generationally by women and internalised by all the candidates interviewed in the oral history study on which this chapter is based. However, the oral evidence contributes to a deeper, more nuanced understanding of this perceived threat and of attitudes to inter-church marriage.

While, in the light of *Ne Temere,* marriage to a Roman Catholic was seen as reprehensible by church authorities, many interviewees actively contested the family division which occurred in the wake of such unions.

In the oral history study women framed their narratives within the paradigm of family; indeed even their accounts are recounted primarily in relational terms. What occurred in Fethard-on-Sea represented the exploitation of a family dispute, but there is evidence that the boycott was challenged locally, as well as colluded in. Women in the oral histories were actors and exhibited vital agency in their local church communities, contributing essentially to family as well as social cohesion within their communities. But it is important to acknowledge that this activity was not exclusive in the sense that the subscription of women to the maintenance and promotion of church identity did not in any way necessitate or create social isolation. In fact, the opposite is true. Women combined this church activity with significant social interaction and close relationships with Catholic neighbours and friends.

An important feature of the oral histories is evidence of the modernisation of rural society in 1950s Wexford. For example, the widespread expansion in the 1950s of rural organisations such as the Irish Countrywomen's Association and, to a lesser extent, Macra na Feirme encouraged greater social interaction and provided important educational opportunities for women. Many women benefited from adult education classes in local vocational schools while changing social attitudes were reflected in the return to paid employment by almost all of the interviewees in this study throughout the 1960s.

It is possible to suggest that these decades witnessed a changing rather than a stagnant rural society and challenged the dismissal of the 1950s as a decade distinguished only by economic gloom and social stagnation. Local newspapers of the period after the Second World War reveal that in County Wexford many new opportunities emerged for socialisation. People came together at local level in amateur dramatic productions, dancing, music, cinema and sporting activities. There is evidence that members of the Church of Ireland community in the county participated in all the above activities. This period, therefore, witnessed the widening of social opportunities in County Wexford. The successful and enduring Wexford (Opera) Festival was founded in 1951, while the same year saw the opening of Wexford racecourse at Bettyville, outside Wexford town. When Denise T. settled in Wexford in 1957, she quickly involved herself in local non-denominational activity, joining and subsequently chairing her local Irish Countrywomen's Association in Marshalstown, as well as running art and craft classes from her home, subscribed to by many of her Catholic neighbours. It seems plausible to suggest that a more tolerant attitude to inter-church marriage discerned in the oral histories of younger respondents to the study may have coincided with this emerging modernisation.

CHAPTER FOURTEEN

Carson's Abandoned Children: Southern Irish Protestants as Depicted in Irish Cartoons, 1920–60[1]

FELIX M. LARKIN

INTRODUCTION

On the principle—as endorsed in song—that 'a picture paints a thousand words',[2] the cartoon published in the *Freeman's Journal* on 29 June 1923 (Fig. 1) captures most succinctly both the predicament and the unenviable fate of southern Irish Protestants in the period of the Irish revolution, 1912–23. A group of southern Irish unionists, apparently landed gentry now living in exile, is shown confronting Sir Edward Carson, by then Lord Carson of Duncairn, with the failure of his strategy of using Ulster—in other words, playing 'the Orange card'—to preserve the union between Great Britain and the entire island of Ireland. The cartoon is titled 'Ulster Will Fight, Etc.', but this is wholly ironic, and that gives the cartoon its force.[3] Ulster unionists had not fought to their last for their counterparts now abandoned as an insignificant minority in the new Irish Free State. Instead, in the words of Eugenio Biagini, they had been 'altogether ruthless in their determination to cut their losses and cast off not only the Southern loyalists, but also those of

1. 'Ulster will fight', Shemus, *Freeman's Journal*, 29 June 1923

the Ulster border counties' in order to secure the exclusion of the other six Ulster counties from an independent Ireland.[4]

The disillusionment of southern Irish unionists with Ulster for abandoning them is reflected in the cartoon's caption, but the caption also reflects the disillusionment that Carson felt with England for its abandonment of the southern unionists:

> Carson to Southern Unionist Exiles—'I'm sorry I ever told you to trust England!'
> Southern Unionist Chorus—'We're sorry you ever told us to trust Ulster!'

Carson was himself a southern Irish unionist, and his personal sense of betrayal which the caption encapsulates was evident in the speech—described by R.B. McDowell as 'partly philippic, partly apologia'[5]—that he gave to the House of Lords in December 1921 on the Anglo-Irish Treaty. He famously declared on that occasion: 'What a fool I was. I was only a puppet, and so was Ulster, and so was Ireland, in the political game that was to get the Conservative Party into power. And of all the men in my experience that I think are the most loathsome, it is those who will sell their friends for the purpose of conciliating their enemies.'[6] Carson, however, was being somewhat disingenuous; he had been complicit in the abandonment of the southern Irish unionists for which he so bitterly condemned others. While never wavering in his desire to maintain the union of Britain and Ireland, he had been pragmatic enough to realise early on in the crisis following the introduction of the third Home Rule Bill in 1912 that some form of Irish independence was inevitable. He had thus willingly embraced the idea of the partition of Ireland as a corollary of any independence settlement, on the basis that it would safeguard to the maximum geographic extent practicable the position of Irish unionists within the United Kingdom. To again quote McDowell, '*faute de mieux* he accepted the exclusion of the north' from the emerging independent Ireland.[7] If, as his statue at the parliament buildings in Belfast suggests, he should be regarded as the father of Northern Ireland, then the southern Irish unionists such as those depicted in the 'Ulster Will Fight, Etc.' cartoon are his abandoned children.

Carson's one concession to his abandoned children was to suggest a Council of Ireland linking the two Irish administrations post-partition as a means of mitigating the isolation of southern Irish unionists. Provision was made for that in the Government of Ireland Act 1920 and in the 1921 Treaty. Nothing, however, was done to establish it. The idea was resurrected in the Sunningdale agreement of December 1973—this time, as a means of safeguarding the Catholic, nationalist minority in Northern Ireland—but again nothing came of it.[8]

Cartoons in the *Freeman's Journal*

'Ulster Will Fight, Etc.' was the work of Ernest Forbes, who, using the pseudonym 'Shemus', was the resident cartoonist in the *Freeman's Journal* from 1920 until it ceased publication in 1924. The *Freeman* was a moderate nationalist daily newspaper—formerly

2. 'The Lion and the unicorn', Shemus, *Freeman's Journal*, 17 August 1920

the organ of the Irish Parliamentary Party—and its cartoons complemented its editorial policy. Carson, because of his leadership of the unionist cause, was accordingly the great *bête noire* of the cartoons. He was included in more of them than anyone else, and his elongated figure and doleful countenance made him an ideal subject for a cartoonist. McDowell wrote of him: 'Thin, tall, angular, with a straight nose, curving, mobile mouth, long jaw and jutting chin, he provided for his opponents a cartoonist's conception of the upholder of autocratic and alien law.'[9] The *Freeman* and its cartoonist were among his fiercest opponents.

Another—visually more vicious—example of Shemus's treatment of Carson is his cartoon entitled 'The Lion and the Unicorn' (Fig. 2), which draws its inspiration from the popular rhyme beginning 'The lion and the unicorn were fighting for the crown'. It is rewritten here as:

> The Lion and the Unicorn / Were fighting for the Crown;
> The Lion let the Unicorn / Rule from Belfast town.

Published by the *Freeman* on 17 August 1920, it recalls Carson's flirtation with armed rebellion against the British government on the Home Rule issue through his association with the Ulster Volunteers and their importation of guns from Germany in 1914; note that Carson is depicted with a sword marked 'made in Germany' in place of the unicorn's horn. The background to the cartoon is that the Government of Ireland Bill 1920, which, *inter alia*, provided for the new entity of Northern Ireland, was about to become law. The cartoon acknowledges the victory of the Carsonian unicorn in its fight with the British lion; the lion has capitulated and is being led on a leash by Carson. Later, just after the first elections to the new parliament of Northern Ireland, the *Freeman* ran a cartoon by Shemus crediting Carson with the creation of the new dispensation (Fig. 3).[10] In that cartoon, the six counties of Northern Ireland are symbolised by bubbles blown from Carson's toy pipe. Sir James Craig, the prime-minister-in-waiting of Northern Ireland, is borne aloft on top of the bubbles, while the British prime minister, Lloyd George, and Sir Hamar Greenwood, chief secretary for Ireland, observe the charade from a distance. It is one of Shemus's best cartoons, because it is so simple in conception, and it required no caption.

What, then, are we to make of the way in which the southern Irish unionists are represented in the first cartoon that we considered, 'Ulster Will Fight, Etc.'? They appear to be, as already mentioned, of Anglo-Irish gentry stock and each of them is the epitome of the gloomy loyalist ridiculed by D.P. Moran as a 'sourface' in his weekly paper, the *Leader*.[11] Their clothes, however, are threadbare, almost in rags. They have lost everything, but not just as a result of being beached on the wrong side of the recent revolution. That was merely the final indignity. Their church had been disestablished in 1869; the widening of the franchise in stages throughout the nineteenth century and the reorganisation of Irish local government in 1898

3. 'The six counties', Shemus, *Freeman's Journal*, 28 May 1921

had deprived them of local political clout; and the land agitation of the 1880s and 1890s and the subsequent ameliorating land acts had decimated their estates, many of which were in any event in a parlous state commercially. The landed gentry had become stranded gentry.[12] Ian d'Alton has characterised them as 'largely a busted flush by 1911', and he reminds us that they were only a small part of the Protestant population[13] and yet, in 1923, it was by reference to the gentry that southern Irish unionists were portrayed in the *Freeman*'s cartoon. This was because, as d'Alton remarks, the gentry 'contributed a large part of the noise'.[14] Most of that noise was generated at Westminster, where southern Irish gentry—both in the House of Lords and sitting in the House of Commons as MPs for English constituencies—wielded enormous political influence. As late as July 1916, the southern Irish unionists within the British cabinet—notably Lord Lansdowne and Walter Long—had been able to sabotage Lloyd George's attempt to introduce an emergency Home Rule measure for Ireland in the aftermath of the Easter Rising.[15] That, however, was their last hurrah; in the Irish Convention of 1917–18 they accepted that the game was up and that their co-religionists had finally cast them adrift.

Ireland's Comic Tradition

The perception of southern Irish Protestants as a powerful elite—a unionist ascendancy—acting against the interests of the majority of the Irish people made them an obvious target for satire. Satire, whether in literary form or in cartoons, is regarded as something that mainly 'punches up'; in other words, a weapon of the powerless against dominant groups and people.[16] Even in ancient times, Aristotle defined wit as 'educated insolence [*pepaidumenē hubris*]'.[17] The depiction of the southern Irish Protestant in Irish cartoons is best understood in that context. Ireland has a fine tradition of comedy, with southern Irish Protestants such as Swift, Wilde and Shaw pre-eminent among the past masters. Vivian Mercier has argued that this tradition is the central one of Irish and Anglo-Irish literature and can be traced back to oral Gaelic roots in the ninth century. He identifies the elements of the tradition as 'a bent for wild humour [and] a delight in witty word play', and he regards 'satire as one of the indispensable functions of the [Irish] literary man'.[18] Cartoons fit comfortably into this tradition and there is a very rich history of cartooning in Ireland. From the late 1870s onwards, vivid and colourful cartoons were published as supplements by the *Weekly Freeman*—a weekly digest of news issued by the *Freeman's Journal*—and by *United Ireland*, another nationalist weekly newspaper. These cartoons were a uniquely Irish phenomenon; they had no exact equivalent in Britain. According to L.P. Curtis Jr, the three artists mostly responsible for them—John D. Reigh, Thomas Fitzpatrick and John Fergus O'Hea—were 'Ireland's most accomplished graphic artists' of their generation.[19]

Their work was less humorous and more propagandistic than that of later cartoonists. When southern Irish Protestants featured in these cartoons, it was almost invariably in the guise of rapacious landlords guilty of abusing vulnerable tenants—and they were demonised. A typical example is O'Hea's 'Two Christmas Hearths'

4. 'Two Christmas hearths', John Fergus O'Hea, *Weekly Freeman*, 18 December 1886

(Fig. 4), which appeared in the *Weekly Freeman* on 18 December 1886, at the outset of the so-called Plan of Campaign. It contrasts in very stark terms the plight of an evicted family at Christmastime with the good fortune of their former landlord and his family enjoying the festive season snug inside the 'Big House' in the distance.[20] Cartoons such as this, together with the reportage and editorial comment in the newspapers that carried them, were part of a conscious strategy adopted by the leaders of nationalist Ireland at that time to court public opinion in pursuit of their twin aims of land reform and Home Rule. The manifesto of the Plan of Campaign in 1886 had stated that 'the fullest publicity should be given to evictions'[21] and accounts and visual representations—including cartoons—of evictions and related horrors were used quite explicitly for propaganda purposes both at home and abroad.[22] As a result, eviction scenes became some of the most enduring and evocative images of later nineteenth-century Ireland. These images inevitably informed how southern Irish Protestants—those who had opted not to go into exile, and they were the vast majority[23]—were presented in cartoons in Irish newspapers and periodicals after 1922 as they

5. (*above*) 'The old firm', Coll, provenance unknown

6. 'Sir John Keane', Shemus, *Freeman's Journal*, 20 April 1923

sought to adjust to the new regime in post-independence Ireland and were exploring how to be good citizens in a polity wary and still suspicious of their place and motivation. As in the 'Ulster Will Fight, Etc.' cartoon, they are almost always gentry—an elite—and thus fair game for satire. Suspicion of them is clearly discernible in a cartoon dated 1922 and entitled 'The Old Firm (but a new name)' (Fig. 5). Its provenance, unfortunately, is not known, nor has it been possible to identify the artist who signed the cartoon with the pseudonym 'Coll'. The cartoon asserts that the Irish Farmers' Union is a reincarnation of 'die-hard' southern unionism; in particular, the slogan 'acts of union our specialty' calls to mind the Act of Union of 1800.[24] By this not-so-subtle word play was 'outsider status' implied at the very moment when the Irish Free State was being born. If that cartoon tallied with Irish nationalist/Catholic opinion, then it did not augur well for integrating the once-dominant Protestant minority.

The new government of the Free State, however, made an early gesture of conciliation to that minority by nominating a number of 'the class formerly known as Southern Unionists' to the first Senate established under the 1922 Constitution.[25] Sixteen of the thirty nominated members—total membership was sixty—belonged to that class. As a gesture, it was perhaps perfunctory but, in the opinion of the clerk to the Senate, Donal O'Sullivan, it was as much as public opinion would allow.[26] No less than nine of the sixteen 'unionist' senators would later feature in a series of caricature portraits of notable persons published by the *Freeman's Journal* between late February and early July 1923. This series, drawn by the *Freeman*'s regular cartoonist, was entitled 'Snapped by Shemus'.[27] The caricatures are benign in tone, quite unlike the bitter depictions of Carson in the *Freeman*, indicating that that newspaper at least was now open to the possibility of positive unionist/Protestant engagement in independent Ireland. The *Freeman*'s proprietor, Martin Fitzgerald, had also been nominated to the Senate—as a representative of the remnant of the Irish Parliamentary Party, another minority in the Irish Free State—and so the *Freeman* was bound to support the idea of the Senate as a 'safeguard for minorities'.[28] One of the best of the caricatures is that of Sir John Keane (Fig. 6), the County Waterford landowner who served in the Free State Senate from 1922 to 1934 and again in Seanad Éireann—under the 1937 Constitution—from 1938 to 1948.

The *Freeman* in its final years—it ceased publication on 19 December 1924—was closely identified with the Free State government; the 'Snapped by Shemus' caricatures are evidence of that. It became an unofficial organ of the government, a role similar to that which it had had with the Irish Parliamentary Party until 1918.[29] Its reportage, editorial comment and cartoons were respectful of the political establishment in Dublin, its criticism being reserved for unionists in Northern Ireland and for republicans who were challenging the very existence of the Free State. This disharmony in approach was highlighted in Dáil Éireann in 1923 by Cathal O'Shannon of the Labour Party, when he commented, *à propos* of a specific Shemus cartoon, that 'you can fire artistic bombs at the Parliament of the Six Counties, but do not touch the Parliament of the Saorstát [Free State]'.[30]

Dublin Opinion

By contrast, *Dublin Opinion*—arguably Ireland's most celebrated satirical magazine—did not hesitate to fire 'artistic bombs' at the government and other institutions of the independent Irish state. It was not exactly *dis*respectful; rather it aimed, in its own words, to 'poke a little fun or make a weak jest at the expense of men of various political views'.[31] Its general policy, as explained by its principal cartoonist and joint-editor, C.E. Kelly, was to offer 'kindly criticism, as against "growing teeth" and using them on the victims' and 'that, where we did criticise, we should do so without inflicting pain, and that the successful critical cartoon or article was one which made the victim (if there was one) laugh'.[32] Launched by Kelly and Arthur Booth, both Dubliners, in March 1922 during the hiatus between the signing of the Anglo-Irish Treaty in the previous December and the start of the civil war with the bombardment of the Four Courts at the end of June, it began with an aspiration to peace and unity.[33] Its first cover featured a cartoon of Arthur Griffith and Éamon de Valera smoking pipes of peace with 'unity blend' tobacco, and its first editorial ('Pull together') expressed the hope that all will 'unite in a spirit of friendliness and goodwill'. That hope was not realised in the short term. However, after *Dublin Opinion* ceased publication in 1968, Kelly felt justified in claiming that it had done 'a little to heal the national wound of the civil war';[34] indeed Seán T. O'Kelly, de Valera's long-time deputy and later president of Ireland, speaking to the Institute of Journalists in 1940, praised it for 'pouring, month after month, the balm of laughter on our wounds'.[35]

One of the best known and most accomplished of *Dublin Opinion*'s cartoons is 'Ceilidhe in the Kildare Street Club' by Kelly, published in 1934 (Fig. 7).[36] Its humour lies in the incongruity of what was still at that time a bastion of the Anglo-Irish gentry and the Protestant professional classes hosting such an event so redolent of the Irish-Ireland cultural revival. The cartoon includes some clever word play with names and titles: the third 'f' in 'fffoulkes', Duke of Blump (but did Kelly intend to write 'Blimp'?) and Col. Mac Burst (who, flushed with indignation, looks like he might burst out of his picture-frame). The use of the Gaelic language adds greatly to the incongruity. The formality of dress—white tie and tails for the men, gowns and sparkling gems for the ladies, and liveried waiters—is complemented by the mien of the club members and their dancing partners, which conforms to the 'sourface' stereotype that Shemus also invoked in his 'Ulster Will Fight, Etc.' cartoon. This is gentle, even kindly, mockery—possibly slightly patronising—and tempered by a hint of social envy. The victims probably did laugh at this cartoon themselves. Nevertheless, it brings their 'outsider status' into sharp focus. It demonstrates how even moderate nationalists perceived southern Protestants: there existed a chasm, a separateness, that marked them as different from mainstream Irish society post-independence. Likewise, a cartoon of the newsroom of the *Irish Times*—a Protestant institution with a higher profile than the Kildare Street Club—also by Kelly and published by *Dublin Opinion* in 1930, emphasises the 'outsider status' which that newspaper retained until 'rescued by the "Protestantization" of southern Irish society beginning in the 1970s' (Fig. 8).[37] Much of the humour of the cartoon derives from the anachronistic atmosphere of the newsroom as portrayed by Kelly: most people wearing a top hat or mortarboard, a porter with medals from ancient wars, *Burke's Peerage* and *Debrett's* prominently displayed on the bookshelves, conversation about Lady Dudley's ball at Dublin Castle[38] and references to Sackville Street and Kingstown. The cartoon's *pièce de résistance* is the corral for the 'Irishman's Diary', occupied by

7. 'Ceilidhe in the Kildare Street Club, C.E. Kelly, *Dublin Opinion*, February 1934

8. 'The *Irish Times* newsroom', C.E. Kelly, *Dublin Opinion*, September 1930

9. 'The ship of state', C.E. Kelly, *Dublin Opinion*, January 1936

a peasant and his pig. That is a subtle and perceptive inversion of marginality; whereas the Protestant minority may be 'outsiders' in Irish society, the majority population is marginal within the closed world of the Irish Protestant.[39]

In fairness, *Dublin Opinion* did not concern itself very much with the Irish Protestant. It ran relatively few cartoons targeting

Irish Protestant society or institutions in over forty-six years of continuous publication. Ernest Blythe, of Ulster Church of Ireland stock, was regularly lampooned for the harsh budgetary measures he introduced as Minister for Finance, but he—a Free State government minister and former revolutionary—was an outlier among Irish Protestants.[40] No mainstream Protestants were singled out for attack by *Dublin Opinion*—as Carson had been in the Shemus cartoons in the *Freeman*. The reason was, of course, that the Protestant minority in independent Ireland was tiny and, while they may have 'punched far above their numerical weight', they no longer threatened the interests of the majority population and could therefore be ignored by cartoonists as well as by others as '"a vestigial population" in the new nation-state'.[41] However, the derision which *Dublin Opinion* heaped on the Free State Senate from its inception until de Valera abolished it in 1936 can be seen as, at least indirectly, hostile to the Irish Protestant community. The Senate is invariably depicted in the magazine as aping the senate of ancient Rome, with members dressed in togas and the inscription 'Hiberniae Senatus' above the door of their chamber. For *Dublin Opinion*, the Senate was an expensive irrelevancy; and, when it was being abolished, a brilliant cover cartoon by Kelly showed de Valera as the captain of a pirate ship, *The Ship of State*, forcing senators resplendent in their Roman togas to walk the plank, with a shark awaiting them in the water below (Fig. 9).[42] The Senate's putative role as a 'safeguard for minorities'[43] did not save it from such sustained abuse and may even have encouraged abuse, since the safeguard was for a privileged minority.

Other Cartoons and Cartoonists

Dublin Opinion virtually monopolised cartooning in Ireland during its years of publication. When the *Freeman's Journal* went out of business in 1924, Ernest Forbes ('Shemus') returned to his native England and, apart from the work of Gordon Brewster in the *Evening Herald* and *Sunday Independent*, and that of Victor Brown in the early days of the *Irish Press*, the editorial cartoon was thereafter largely absent from Irish newspapers until the late 1960s, a period outside the scope of this volume.[44] Brewster's cartoons were different from those of his contemporaries in that they mostly eschewed

10. 'A hard hit', Gordon Brewster, *Evening Herald*, 19 August 1925

strictly party politics—the old Civil War divisions—but focused instead on lifestyle and socio-economic matters; they were also more international in outlook.[45] Southern Irish Protestants did not feature in them explicitly, though Brewster often made the professions in which Protestants were disproportionately represented—banking, the law and medicine—the butt of his humour. Like *Dublin Opinion*'s assaults on the Free State Senate, such cartoons are indirectly hostile to Protestants insofar as they get some of their punch from identifying these professions with the former unionist ascendancy. One such cartoon is 'A Hard Hit', published in the *Evening Herald* on 19 August 1925, which refers to the objections of Irish doctors to the establishment of a separate medical register for the Irish Free State (Fig. 10). Breaking the link with their UK colleagues is the 'hard hit' which the Free State government is inflicting on the medical profession in Ireland. Cosgrave, as head of the Free State government, is thus shown firing a salvo at a 'Big House' suitably situated in a large demesne. The label 'Irish medical profession' attaching to the 'Big House' makes what Brewster clearly regards as an unflattering association. In another cartoon, entitled 'Jonah' and published in the *Herald* on 22 July 1926, Brewster draws a parallel between the story of Jonah swallowed by a whale and the sale of the National Land Bank—established by the First Dáil in 1920—to Bank of Ireland. It bemoans the fact that Bank of Ireland—closely identified with the *ancien régime* in Ireland and many of whose senior officials were Protestant—had absorbed a rival institution with an unblemished revolutionary pedigree.[46]

Damning his targets by associating them with the old Anglo-Irish gentry was also part of the stock-in-trade of Victor Brown. Like Ernest Forbes, he was an Englishman. His cartoons appeared in the *Irish Press* under the pseudonym 'Bee' during the first years after Éamon de Valera founded the paper in 1931 as the organ of the Fianna Fáil party.[47] They are unashamedly partisan, and the thrust of many of them was to discredit the Cumann na nGaedheal government by claiming that it was backed financially by southern Irish Protestant ex-unionists. The cartoon at Figure 11 is typical. It shows a cheque for 'Mr Cosgrave's election fund', signed by four senators of 'the class formerly known as Southern Unionists',[48] and its title, 'A check on nationalism', explains the purported motivation of the donors by means of clever word play.[49] Another cartoon—anticipating a Fianna Fáil victory in the 1932 general election—elaborates on this theme (Fig. 12).[50] An 'ex-unionist'—with the clichéd features of a 'sourface'—addresses a gathering of self-satisfied likeminded men, and he states: 'Mr Cosgrave has not been returned, but our money has been well spent. As you will see, it has been employed by Cumann na nGaedheal to defame the natives far better than we used to do it.' The use of the term 'the natives' is calculated to paint Irish Protestants in a bad light and readers of the *Irish Press* in particular could be relied upon to take offence at the presumption of racial superiority that it betrays. Even if the purpose of the cartoon was solely to damage Cumann na nGaedheal, it displays a profoundly anti-Protestant/anti-unionist *mentalité*.

Bee's most provocative cartoon from an Irish Protestant perspective was his very first one, published in the inaugural issue of the *Irish Press* on 5 September 1931. Untitled, it shows a line of men and a woman in chains en route to the guillotine; the first two

11. 'A check on nationalism', Bee, *Irish Press*, 12 December 1931

12. 'Financed by Unionists', Bee, *Irish Press*, 15 February 1932

13. 'We've got them on the list...', Bee, *Irish Press*, 5 September 1931

have been dubbed 'old order' and 'social pretension' respectively (Fig. 13). Their fate as foreshadowed here is absurd fantasy and therein lies the humour—the dark humour—of the cartoon. Beneath the fun, however, there is a serious message: Protestants, and others who do not subscribe to Fianna Fáil's version of Irishness, will find themselves beached anew on the wrong side of another revolution—albeit a peaceful one—when Fianna Fáil comes to power. That there will be no place for them in de Valera's Ireland is signalled by the caption on the cartoon which, slightly misquoting the Lord High Executioner's song in Gilbert and Sullivan's *The Mikado*, reads: 'We've got them on the list, and they'll none of them be missed.'

Conclusion

Dame Mary Beard has observed that 'laughter acts both to incorporate and to isolate'.[51] So, although the representation of Protestants in Irish cartoons tended to emphasise their 'outsider status' in independent Ireland, did the laughter inspired by the cartoons nevertheless bridge the gap between Irish Protestants and the majority population and help heal the wound of injustices perpetrated by each side on the other? Did the 'balm of laughter'—repeating Seán T. O'Kelly's phrase—weave its magic? One would like to think so, but it is notoriously difficult to assess the impact of magazines and newspapers. Walter Lippmann argued that their real importance derives from the fact that they 'signalize' an event or issue; in other words, they tell their readers what to think about.[52] The paucity of cartoons depicting Irish Protestants after 1921 may therefore be the most significant thing about them. It indicates that, despite the many advantages Protestants continued to enjoy, they were largely invisible in Irish society post-independence. That was probably by their own choice and perhaps all to the good; they wished to be ignored and invisibility was part of their strategy for survival. When, however, they found themselves in the cross-hairs of a cartoon from the 1920s onward, to be treated as anachronisms and 'relics of oul' decency' was infinitely preferable to being portrayed as a people to be feared and hated, as the landlords were in the 1880s. In that respect, the cartoons mirror a movement towards the acceptance of southern Irish Protestants as no longer a threat to Irish independence or to the economic and social aspirations of the majority population of the new state.

CHAPTER FIFTEEN

Patrick Campbell's Easy Times: Humour and Southern Irish Protestants

CALEB RICHARDSON

Introduction

Probably no piece of rhetoric is as associated with southern Irish Protestants as is W.B. Yeats's address to the Irish Senate during the debate on divorce legislation in June 1925. His summation of the group as 'no petty people' has served generations of undergraduates in search of epigrams. It is an angry address, but despite its energy it presents an essentially dark view. Yeats makes a case for the group being one of the 'great stocks of Europe', yet struggles to come up with a single member of this 'great stock' that was still alive and kicking in 1925. His mode is elegiac. However much he wants to make the case that Protestants still matter, he finds it difficult to speak about them in anything but the past tense.

Fortunately another southern Protestant was there to point this out. This was James Henry Mussen Campbell, first Lord Glenavy and the Chairman (Cathaoirleach) of the Free State Senate. After an especially long passage, Glenavy interrupted the poet in mid-flow to ask a question: 'Do you not think we might leave the dead alone?'[1] Yeats's quintessentially Yeatsian response to this interruption—'I am passing on. I would hate to leave the dead alone'—is more often remembered than the interruption itself. But for the historian of southern Irish Protestantism, the words that prompted the riposte are just as important. Glenavy's remark captures an underappreciated quality of southern Irish Protestants: their humour.

The Nature of Humour and the Southern Irish Protestant

Southern Irish Protestants came up with different ways of adapting to independent Ireland, but probably the least examined of these is humour. In part, this scholarly blind spot is because so much of the work on the group has focused on alienation and decline; historians and sociologists are as susceptible as anyone else to the demands of genre and humour seems inappropriate when telling the story of a once-great minority's decline and fall.[2] This tendency is even more marked in literary scholarship; based on much of this work, one would think that the 'great stock' that produced Swift, Sheridan, Wilde and Somerville and Ross lost the ability to laugh on or about December 1921 with the signing of the Anglo-Irish Treaty.[3] The fact that some of the greatest fictional chronicles of Protestant decline—by Elizabeth Bowen, Jennifer Johnston and Molly Keane, among others—are also quite funny seems to have been overlooked in the unrelenting search for what Ian d'Alton has characterised as 'the grand tragedy' interpretation of southern Protestant history.[4]

In fact humour played an important role in the group's adaptation to life in independent Ireland, although not quite in the ways that one might think. At first glance, the three 'classical' interpretations of humour and laughter—often described as 'Superiority Theory' 'Incongruity Theory' and 'Relief Theory'—would all seem to suit the southern Protestant situation perfectly. 'Superiority Theory' suggests that we laugh at those we believe to be inferior and in so doing reinforce our own position in the social hierarchy.[5] According to nationalist rhetoric, this would be exactly what one would expect of Irish Protestants, who had, after all, been laughing 'with foreign jaws' at the native Irish for centuries.[6] 'Incongruity Theory', which posits that humour arises out of 'incorporating into one situation what belongs to another', also seems appropriate for a group that could appear simultaneously anachronistic and anatopistic.[7] Finally, 'Relief Theory', often associated with Freud, interprets humour as a release of tension.[8] This function would also suit a group who often felt as oppressed by what was not being said as by what was. There is ample evidence for humour playing each of these roles in the history and literature of southern Irish Protestants; the character of Lady Naylor, in Bowen's *Last September*, could serve as a case study in all three.

But these explanations are not sufficient. One problem with these traditional analyses is that they oversimplify; philosophers, linguists, sociologists and literary scholars, not to mention stand-up comedians, have identified a much more complex set of functions. The other is that they are each based on a view of humour that, until quite recently, saw it as an essentially harmful force in society. 'Throughout history the vast majority of moral evaluations of humour have been negative', observes the philosopher John Morreall. The problem is that humour can promote disengagement from society.[9] In the case of southern Irish Protestants, a humour rooted in the traditional categories of superiority, incongruity and relief could have increased, rather than decreased, their alienation from mainstream Irish life. Highlighting the group's superiority and incongruity would reinforce a sense that southern Irish Protestants were fundamentally different from the Catholic majority, while using humour as a release could serve as an excuse for not bothering to integrate oneself into Irish life. Comedy could reinforce tragedy.

Patrick Campbell's Humour

Morreall highlights several important 'virtues' that humour can promote, including critical thinking, empathy, patience, open-mindedness and tolerance.[10] Much of the work of Patrick Campbell, the grandson of Yeats's genial antagonist in the Senate debate, reveals this more positive approach. In a genre full of under-appreciated writers, Patrick Campbell stands out.[11] Part of the reason may be that humour—as distinct from satire, wit, fantasy, parody and burlesque—plays a relatively small role in the scholarship of Irish literature. The pre-eminent survey of comedy in Ireland, Vivian Mercier's seminal *The Irish Comic Tradition*, has little to say about humour.[12] Perhaps this is a matter of nationality. Frank Muir, Campbell's close friend and the editor of the *Oxford Book of Humorous Prose*, argues that humour, 'the recording of "small but significant human traits"', is quintessentially English. 'It is a contribution to culture which England has given the world', he writes; 'not Britain, not Scotland, Ireland, or Wales—but England . . . no other nation [has] the word humour in its language'.[13] It is striking, however, that Muir includes Swift, Goldsmith, Edgeworth, Griffin, Shaw, Somerville and Ross, Dunsany, O'Nolan, P.J. Kavanagh, Frank O'Connor and Joyce in his collection, and introduces Campbell by writing that 'of all the humorists of his era he probably wrote the purest "humour" in this book's definition of the word'.[14]

On the other hand, perhaps Campbell's diminished reputation is a function of his professionalism. His career spanned the last three decades in which it was possible to make a living as a humorist, and even then he had to work quite hard to do so. His byline appeared in dozens of different publications. His uncredited work in the *Irish Times* and other newspapers ran to at least several hundred thousand words. He wrote screenplays, worked as a dialogue consultant for films and appeared on radio and TV. As a result of all of this activity, much of his work bears the unmistakable stamp of a looming deadline. Other pieces feel very much of their time. In some of his writing about women from the 1950s and 1960s, for instance, a miasma of aftershave, pipe smoke and slightly moist rayon practically rises from the page. Finally, there is the simple fact that, in Campbell's time as well as our own, it is difficult for an Irish humorist to make a living writing about Ireland. Much of Campbell's work concerns much more universal issues, such as death, or the etiquette of when one should play through on the fifteenth hole.

The Background to Campbell's Use of Humour

Campbell at his best illuminates the ways in which humour could be used by southern Protestants to contribute to, rather than to distance themselves from, Irish society. By exploring the ways in which Campbell's work upended the three 'classical' interpretations of humour, one can see that humour could serve to integrate, rather than to detach, southern Protestants from Irish history. First, this essay will examine how Campbell's 'Irishman's Diary' for the *Irish Times*—which, in some respects, could be seen as the pre-eminent example of 'superiority theory'—in fact represents an inversion of that theory. Secondly, it will explore how, in his later essays, Campbell turned 'Incongruity Theory' inside out: he inverted the idea of southern Protestants as victims. Finally, it will show that 'Relief Theory' does not fully account for the ways in which humour can reveal, as well as release, tension: Campbell's autobiography is a kind of model for how humour can highlight uncomfortable truths, as well as easy answers.

In some ways, the Campbell family's history serves as a species of précis of the southern Protestant Irish experience in the late nineteenth and early twentieth century. There is hardly a stereotype about the group that the family does not embody. They had deep roots in the legal profession. Before acting as Yeats's interlocutor in the Senate, the first baron had been Solicitor General, Attorney General, Lord Chief Justice and Lord Chancellor of Ireland. They had connections to the worlds of business and finance. The second baron, Charles Henry Gordon Campbell, served as secretary (administrative head) of the Department of Industry and Commerce and as a director of the Bank of Ireland; his wife was Beatrice Elvery, whose family owned the eponymous sporting goods store. They were artistic and literary. Beatrice was an artist and painter and the family was close friends to Shaw, D.H. Lawrence, Yeats and William Orpen, to name only some of the most prominent members of their circle. Finally, the Campbells managed to experience every possible variety of alienation and persecution that could possibly be suffered by southern Protestants during and after independence. The family was burned out of its house in 1922 and for weeks afterwards the second baron had to change his residence every night for fear of reprisals.[15] Members of the family that stayed in Ireland felt discriminated against; Patrick remembers his father being constantly worried about being stripped of his considerable number of directorships because 'they don't like Protestants, you see, and they can't wait to get me out'.[16] Patrick, his brother and his sister all left the country. Presumably, the Campbells also didn't wash their fruit, sing in church and eat plain digestive biscuits, but this is difficult to establish from the historical record.[17]

Patrick Campbell attended Crawley's Preparatory School in St Stephen's Green, Dublin, where he was intimidated by students; Castle Park School in salubrious Dalkey, where he was intimidated by the headmaster; and Rossall School in Lancashire, which he cared so little about that he could not even bother to be intimidated. Oxford followed, although he was sent down soon after driving his car into the Martyrs' Memorial after a long night at the pub. Although his education was, as he put it, 'of the most formal kind', he remembered that it 'failed almost entirely to make a mark on me, or me on it'.[18] In part this was because what he had received from his parents and their circle was so much more vital than anything he could have learnt at school: 'No schoolmaster could have competed with my parents, and especially my mother, in forming what I've come to regard defensively as my mind', he wrote later.[19] His mother's memoir, *Today We Will Only Gossip*, bears this out; it depicts the kind of home where, on any given day, Katherine Mansfield might be pottering about in the garden, or Paul Robeson rehearsing 'Ol' Man River' on the family piano.[20]

After being sent down, Campbell had a brief career in business. His father, who had played a key role in encouraging Siemens' investment in Ireland, managed to convince the company to employ his son at its home office in Munich. Patrick's inability to speak German and his subsequent inability to understand what he was supposed to be doing or where he should be doing it, meant that in a short time he had returned to Dublin, where he was hired by R.M. Smyllie at the *Irish Times*. He found his métier in journalism. As he put it, it was 'the only job that required no degrees, no diplomas, no training and no specialized knowledge of any kind'.[21] He contributed stories to the 'Irishman's Diary' column, reported on the local district courts, served as a literary editor and a film critic, and wrote a 'Dáil Sketch' that became one of the paper's most popular and—because of its caricatures of deputies—controversial features.

He left Ireland when offered a job with the Beaverbrook press, but returned to Ireland just after the outbreak of war in 1939. Although troubled by his decision to leave—'It's an uncomfortable feeling, to say the least, to have missed a fearful experience that millions of other people endured'—he threw himself back into Irish life, and joined the Irish Marine service.[22] He also returned to his 'Irishman's Diary' post towards the end of the war, helping to transform that feature from a kind of grab-bag of commentary, anecdote and local colour into the more individualised column that it remains today.

Despite his family background, Campbell was not really a part of 'literary Dublin', preferring the Buttery at the Royal Hibernian

Hotel to the Palace Bar, the Shelbourne Bar to the Pearl, and the golf course or racetrack to all of them. According to Ulick O'Connor, these were places where 'he felt a sense of protection amongst his own class', where he 'could play whatever role he wished without being pushed into a protective pose'.[23] As a result, his version of the 'Irishman's Diary' existed in a sphere of Irish life that, for lack of a better term, could be called 'Anglo-Ireland'. Campbell, who adopted the pseudonym 'Quidnunc' for the column, was an aristocratic outsider, coolly observing Irish life.

'An Irishman's Diary'

All of the above should have been a recipe for the 'Superiority Theory' of humour and this does occasionally show through, such as when he attends a Gaelic football match:

> I have not seen Gaelic football before. It appears to be a sequence of three inevitable events. Somebody, with exceptional length and accuracy, punts the ball high in the air. Five other players leap for it. Then the St. John Ambulance and two men with small Gladstone bags trot smartly on to the field and look after the man that the other players landed on. At one time four of the players, in small crumpled heaps, were being attended to at the same time.[24]

More often, however, Campbell undercuts his status, highlighting the aspects of Irish life that are ridiculous but also ridiculing outsiders for their ignorance of Irish life. When a foreign visitor tells him that 'What I love about your Dublin . . . is the heavenly smell of peat', 'Quidnunc' responds:

> 'Pete who?' I said, twisting another newspaper into strips and poking it into the fire lying flat on my face, with my eyes running.
>
> 'Peat,' said the visitor; 'the stuff you're lighting.'
>
> I blew madly into the fire, until the room began to swirl round. 'It's not called peat,' I said, 'it's called turf.'
>
> The foreign visitor thought for a moment, and then he said: 'But how do you light it?'

> I gave one final blast, and threw the bellows into the fire.
>
> 'You take four bundles of sticks,' I said, 'and dry them in the gas-oven until crisp. While the sticks are drying you dry a quarter of a ton of turf, piece by piece, over an electric stove. Set the fire and touch a match to it, and then start rushing up and down the back stairs, carrying up more and more turf, and flinging it on the fire, until it's time to go to bed.'
>
> The foreign visitor looked uncomfortable, and then he said: 'I mean—are you—joking?'[25]

If anything, Quidnunc reserved his most severe displays of superiority for those non-Irish outsiders—especially English ones—who don't understand Irish life, as in this list of common questions asked by postwar English visitors to Dublin:

> 'What, if I am in search of pleasure, shall I do with myself and my party after the public-houses close at half-past ten?'
>
> 'If I really do buy this castle in your Dingle Peninsula, how shall I pass the long winter evenings—apart from rushing around the house catching the drips from the roof in an enamel bucket—while a cloudburst vents itself upon the laurel bushes bordering the avenue?'
>
> 'Am I to take it, seeing that all my new Irish friends speak of their friends as chancers, cute hawks and cods, that as soon as I leave their company I, too, shall be pilloried by this indiscriminate malice?'
>
> 'What makes you think that you can hold an audience of comparative strangers by the recital of an anecdote which presents you in a favourable light, while it is perfectly obvious to any thinking listener that you have played the part, in this action, of what we spoke of at Harrow as a cad?'
>
> 'Do you pronounce it as—Devaleera, or—Devallera?'
>
> 'Will you be kind enough to take your hand off my throat?'[26]

Campbell's 'Quidnunc' may be an Anglo-Irishman, but the emphasis is on the second half of his hyphenated identity.

The most common way that Campbell upended the 'Superiority' theory of humour in his 'Irishman's Diary' column was through exaggeration. Much of his writing critiques the idea of Anglo-Irish superiority by exploding the whole concept to the point that it becomes absurd. Take this description of what many would consider to be Campbell's natural element, preparing for racing at Punchestown:

> The chaps in the tight check trousers were off to Punchestown horse-sports. What we are wearing for Punchestown this year turns out to be tight check trousers, jacket to match with a large flap at the back, woollen tie, no expression on the face and a hat the hounds have been sleeping on.
>
> If we have ladies around we have ladies with diamond horse-brooches pinned to the front of small, felt pots pulled low over the ears.
>
> Some of us, more fortunate than others, are accompanied by ladies whose diamond horse-brooches are being ridden by tiny jockeys wearing rubies, sapphires and other precious stones in the colours of the owner.
>
> In the midst of this clamour are some terrified natives carrying sardine sandwiches in raffia baskets. They, too, are going to the races, but by bicycle.[27]

The column frequently recounts Campbell's adventures in 'Anglo-Ireland', but in his hands it becomes a parody of itself. 'Laughing, standing on the stools eating wine-glasses and throwing Napoleon brandy at the barman, I am diverting myself in this fashionable sozzling spot', one column begins.[28] 'I should like it to be known that I have cancelled all my hunting engagements during the present season', another ends, after a long account of Quidnunc's complete inability to manage a horse.[29] And in another piece, he uses a long set-up to overturn assumptions. Under the subtitle 'Hunting Notes', he writes:

> If you have not yet purchased your bowler for the hunting season, do for pity's sake get a hat without that odious piece of string. String, from collar to brim, is worn only by ex-cricketers on boaters at the less fashionable watering-places.
>
> String is not worn on the hunting field for a very good reason. When you perceive Reynard, it is your duty to raise the hat directly above the head in a vertical line, holding it there

> at the full stretch of the arm, pointing, at the same time, to the direction in which the quarry has made away with the other. This maneouvre cannot be performed if the hat is made fast to the collar, unless it be your desire to pull the coat completely over the head.
>
> And now—for the younger miss. If you ride astride, never wear a veil. Veils may be worn only by ladies riding side-saddle.
>
> If you ride side-saddle, and wear a veil, never tie it beneath the nose or chin. The veil should be crossed beneath the jawbone and knotted tightly at the back of the neck.
>
> I don't know what I'm talking about.[30]

'Irishman's Diary', far from finding its humour in highlighting differences in social status, in fact holds those differences up to ridicule.

The Campbells and Irish Revolution

Shortly after the end of the war, Campbell again returned to a more profitable job in England, working for the *Sunday Dispatch*, the humour magazine *Lilliput* and the *Sunday Times*, as well as contributing to *Punch*, *Spectator* and other magazines. Much of his work did not address Ireland specifically at all, instead dealing mainly in what one ungenerous reviewer termed 'the rather well-worn groove of British humour which finds small details of domestic life to be excruciatingly funny'.[31] But in some of his best pieces, he highlighted some of the more uncomfortable situations in which the Anglo-Irish found themselves in the early twentieth century. In 'A Boy's Best Bodyguard', he recounted his family's experiences with the IRA during the war of independence and the Civil War.[32] It is a subject ripe with the potential for the humour of incongruity, but he turns that incongruity into something unexpected.

'A Boy's Best Bodyguard' takes the stereotypical image of the besieged 'Big House' and turns it on its head, twice. It is not just that, contrary to expectations, the IRA attackers in Campbell's story turn out to be polite and accommodating—Elizabeth Bowen had gotten there first, in *Bowen's Court*, by admitting of the invaders of Bowen's Court that 'even prejudice allows it that they behaved like lambs'[33]—it is that, far from being passive victims of the assault, the Campbell family, and particularly Campbell's mother, practically direct the proceedings. Beatrice's first response to one of the raiders, appearing on the stairs disguised with a cap and handkerchief and carrying a revolver, is 'If there's going to be any murder . . . you can get back out of that and go home.'[34] She immediately moves on to making sure that her books and pictures are safe.

The raiders appeal to Lord Glenavy, as a voice of reason; he suggests that the family gather a few valuables and retreat. But Lady Glenavy is having none of it: 'And leave', my mother cried passionately, 'all the children's Christmas toys behind? Certainly not!'[35] While one group of men is busy pouring petrol in the hallway, she is commandeering another group to help her:

> By the time the first whoose [*sic*] of petrol flame poured out of the windows she had five of the men working for her, running out with armfuls of books and pictures, ornaments, and our Christmas toys. They'd become so deeply concerned on her behalf that they frequently paused to ask what should be salvaged next. 'Is the bit of a picture in the passage anny good, mum?' 'Is there ere a chance of gettin' the legs offa the pianna, the way we could dhrag it out . . .?'

By the time this archetypal moment of Anglo-Irish alienation has come to an end, Beatrice is 'bathed in the light of the flames, standing guard over a great heap of treasures in the middle of the lawn, with Orpen's picture under one arm and the little drawings by John under the other—a clear winner on points'.[36]

This does not seem to be a misrepresentation of the events of the night. Beatrice's own memoirs do not always corroborate Patrick's; she, for instance, remembers that his supervisors at Siemens had written 'expressing their approval of Paddy's work and saying they would like to send him to South America on some project', and that the real problem was that he 'did not want to be a businessman'. But in this case, if anything, he seems to be underplaying her heroism. Her own memory of the event leaves her in the position of a Wagnerian heroine:

> I went round to the garden at the back of the house and stood in the wind and the rain in an ecstasy of relief—no one had been

> shot or burnt. As I watched the flames in the bedroom windows I had a most wonderful moment feeling that everything that I owned was being destroyed. No more possessions—I experienced an extraordinary sense of freedom.[37]

Far from being victimised by this event, which is the culmination of most accounts of Anglo-Irish tragedy, the Campbells are reinvigorated. Much of this, undoubtedly, is due to the remarkable character of Campbell's mother. (He remembers, later in life, being in a pub when it was robbed, and it occurs to him that if 'my mother had been there she would have cut the proceedings short by telling the gunman to do the washing up, or get us another round of drinks'.)[38] But the humorous incongruity in the story comes from a reversal of expectations: here, the persecuted minorities have become the heroes.

My Life and Easy Times

In the last two decades of his life, Patrick Campbell was best known for his appearances on television and radio rather than for his writing. He appeared regularly on *Not so Much a Programme, More a Way of Life*; *Call My Bluff*; and *That Was the Week That Was*. Although he continued to write, his most significant literary work was his autobiography, published in 1967.

If one were to translate the Irish phrase 'An Béal Bocht' into English ('The Poor Mouth' is a common, although not quite adequate, interpretation) and find its antonym, you might come close to capturing the remarkable character of Campbell's autobiography. This is a book that starts with a long description of the death of Campbell's father, and then goes on to describe Patrick contracting scarlet fever, getting in a horrific drink-driving accident, being sent down from Oxford early, almost being strangled to death by Brownshirts in 1930s' Berlin, abandoning his journalism career in Dublin to take up a position with the Beaverbrook press in London only to be fired by Beaverbrook, losing his sister in a flying bomb attack, getting divorced, being fired first from his dream job at a magazine and then from his fall-back job, and only finding success as a TV personality better known for his stutter than his literary style. The book is entitled *My Life and Easy Times*.

It is Campbell's darkest book. In part this is because it is even more relentlessly self-deprecating than his other writing. But that, in itself, is not enough. Self-deprecation, after all, is perhaps the most quintessentially Anglo-Irish comic mode; Elizabeth Grubgeld observes that 'ever since the late seventeenth century political cartoons that constitute Anglo-Ireland's first attempts at self-representation, ridiculing one's own values and traditions has been itself a valued tradition'.[39] But if one theory of humour is that it provides for the relief of tension, the book is almost pathological in its denial of that relief. In part that is because the death of the second baron looms so large over the book; it is, in a way, Campbell's attempt to come to terms with the man that he realised, too late, that he respected more than any other.

The book often feels as though it is humour writing with the humour drained out of it. Superiority theory is at work, but it is much more direct than it had been in 'An Irishman's Diary'. Campbell is unflinching in his portrayal of his parents' sense of difference from the Catholic majority. 'I came from a Protestant home wherein Catholicism, and all its words and works, was the subject of constant derision', he remembers:

> Bad Irish art was dismissed by my mother with the inevitable, 'But what else would you expect from the tenement Catholic mind?' My father, only half in jest, used to deliver great rolling denunciations based upon, 'The bottomless squalor of Roman Catholic superstition—' and conclude with a string of Hail Mary's in the genteel accents of a Dublin Civil Servant.[40]

He remembers his father 'frequently rail[ing] against the cretinous slobs who pass for people of intelligence in Ireland'.[41] And, Campbell suggests, this is not entirely inexplicable. He remembers asking his father why he had left a successful career in England to return to Ireland after independence:

> Once, when I asked him, 'why did you come back here, then?' he shook his head—an instinctive gesture that said the question was out of order.
>
> The truth was, of course, that he'd come back to Ireland because he loved Ireland, and loved the idea of taking part in the formation of what he thought of, romantically, as being a

> new and ideal Free State. One of the first tastes he got of the new and ideal Free State was when the I.R.A. burnt down our house on Christmas Eve, 1922, and it seemed for a long half hour that they were going to execute him on his own front lawn.[42]

Looked at from this perspective, Campbell suggests, his father's resentment is understandable.

Incongruity plays a role as well, but again it is less playful than it had been in Campbell's earlier writings. Campbell admits his mixed feelings upon returning home to Dublin, where his father is on his deathbed. 'I was going to have to face the fact of his death,' he writes, 'but all that I had at this moment was the feeling of excitement, of much to be done, of taking over the leadership of the family . . . It was not unpleasant to be the Hon. Patrick Campbell, receiving V.I.P treatment on the way to the bedside of his dying father'.[43] He notices that his mother's response is incongruous in a different way; she seemed to be experiencing her grief 'as an emotional phenomenon, a fascinating quirk in human nature to be discussed objectively, to be respected for itself'.[44] He wonders if this is, in part, a matter of religion:

> I remembered, when my sister had been killed, that an elderly cook we had at the time had complained to me, 'Her Ladyship doesn't suffer right.' The cook had been looking forward, with Catholic fervour, to my sister's portrait being draped in black, the blinds in the house drawn, the whole family convulsed in solitary grief. Yet everyone was sitting out in summer clothes in the patio at the back of the house, and there was even laughter, at small things.[45]

Whereas in his earlier writings Campbell was quick to use humour to undercut stereotypes and to make people think about the position of the Anglo-Irish in a new way, here he is much more straightforward.

But there is another side to this too. In her resoundingly negative contemporary review of *My Life and Easy Times*, Mary Holland condemned the book for missing the opportunity to explore the contradictions of Anglo-Irish life. Quoting the passage about Catholic 'superstition' and the 'tenement mind', she explains:

> These were sentiments that [the Campbells] would have been ashamed to express to D.H. Lawrence or Shaw when they entertained them in London. It took Dublin to bring them out. Yet there was another side to the relationship with Ireland which made Lord Glenavy the trusted friend and adviser of businessmen, farmers, trades union officials, cattle dealers [and] politicians, and drew this tribute from a workingman: 'Sure, the Lord could mind mice at a crossroads.' It was a complex affair between Lord Glenavy and his like and Ireland, for it was the result of history.

The problem is that in his book, Holland argues, Campbell 'makes no attempt to get beneath the skin to the love and hate'.[46]

In fact this is exactly what the book does so well. A more generous reading of *My Life and Easy Times* would suggest that it perfectly captures the experience of living with contradictions. And living with contradictions was the existential condition of southern Irish Protestants after independence. Campbell's refusal to reconcile or explain those contradictions—and his insistence that these contradictions were part of what made Ireland Ireland—is not so much an evasion of responsibility as an act of courage.

But this is too serious a way to end; better to finish with a passage from *My Life and Easy Times* that is much more representative of Campbell's work as a whole. In the 1930s, his parents moved to Rockbrook in south Dublin. His father used to drive to the bus stop in Terenure and on the way he experienced persecution and alienation of an entirely different kind, as Patrick remembered:

> He told me once, with great pleasure, 'Two little boys outside Doyle's cottage on the corner have it in for me. Every time they see the car coming they yell, 'Dere's Dord Dendavy—t'row de mud.' And they do.'[47]
>
> His normally gloomy face shone for a moment with pure delight.[48]

This is a species of delight that any Dubliner, of whatever confession, will appreciate. There was more to the southern Irish Protestant experience than grand tragedy and Patrick Campbell reminds us of this in a way that few other writers can.

AFTERWORD

Ireland's Mysterious Minority—A French–Irish Comparison

JOSEPH RUANE

INTRODUCTION

How Irish Protestants see themselves and their place in the wider society is one of the remaining mysteries of Irish life. In a society where virtually every social category and institution has been brought into focus, meditated on and moralised about, this one remains elusive. It might be attributed to their very small numbers. But they loom larger in the public imagination than the numbers alone might warrant. They are central to the history of the island: their imprint is on the landscape and on its cultural institutions; their churches, schools and hospitals occupy central places in its cities and towns; they inhabit leading positions in key sectors of society; they are formally represented at public events; their historic university—Trinity College—remains at the centre of Irish cultural life; their cathedrals and once great houses are must-see places for foreign tourists. There is more than enough to talk about. Instead, though, there is a wariness and a silence that points to a reluctance on both sides to engage with the issue. Protestants prefer to deal with matters of concern privately and discreetly, and Catholics are happy to oblige. This is consistent with the general pattern of majority–minority relations. Majorities tend not to think of minorities unless they are powerful, influential, or troublesome. Minorities feel vulnerable and dislike drawing attention to themselves. But there are also issues specific to the Irish case: the long history of Catholic–Protestant conflict on the island; the circumstances in which independence was secured; the question of how southern Protestants were treated by the new state. One consequence has been a reluctance on the part of Protestants to be too explicit about how they see themselves, the wider society and their place within it.

The situation of Protestants in the new state has been discussed since its foundation, though it has rarely been central to public debate. In the 1920s the *Irish Statesman* journal, and in the 1940s the *Bell* magazine, dealt with it from time to time. The 1960s saw the publication of Brian Inglis's *West Briton* and Michael Viney's series of articles, 'The Five Per Cent'. The 1970s saw Jack White's *Minority Report*. The 1980s brought Kurt Bowen's *Protestants in a Catholic State*. The 2000s saw Colin Murphy and Lynne Adair's compendium *Untold Stories* and Heather Crawford's *Outside the Glow*. So far the 2010s have seen Brian Walker's *A History of the Two Irelands*, Robin Bury's *Buried Lives*, and now the current volume.[1] Recurring themes for the immediate post-independence decades include the materially privileged position of Protestants, the fall in their numbers, their attitude to the new state, their continuing attachment to the Crown, the effects of the *Ne Temere* decree, sectarianism, the difficulty of being a tiny minority in a society that was fervently Catholic, and the (Catholic) tendency to define Irishness in terms of nationalism and Catholicity. More recently a key topic is the violence experienced by Protestants during the War of Independence and Civil War. These books were widely read within the Protestant community.[2] It is not clear how much they were read outside of it.

The reluctance on both sides to make the position of Protestants a subject of public debate has limited its capacity to deal with a range of problems, including the unresolved politics of the island. The northern Protestant response to suggestions of closer contact with the south is mediated by their perception of how southern Protestants have been treated – in their view very badly.[3] They focus in particular on the fall in their numbers, which they take to be a symptom of their marginality and lack of acceptance. Some southern Protestants contest that view; others share it. But there has been no serious debate about it. Whatever the reality, the perception is important. The Good Friday Agreement of 1998 has not stabilised the politics of the island. The prospect of Brexit has brought further uncertainty; demographic change in the North continues. The question of reunification has not gone away. Despite their small numbers, southern Protestants are a distinct and important part of the political geometry of the island. Greater clarity about how they see themselves, how they view their past, how they define their relationship to the Irish state and to Irishness, might permit a more effective response to the challenges and difficulties that reunification would pose.

The focus of this Afterword, and of the book as whole, is on the Republic's historic or core Protestant community, now centuries-old and thoroughly indigenous. This is not the total Protestant population recorded in the census. The numbers in the census have grown significantly since the 1990s, from 3.2 per cent of the total population in 1991 to 4.2 per cent in 2016.[4] Some of this is attributable to immigration, evident in the figures on ethnic and religious diversity.[5] The numbers also include the children of mixed marriages who were baptised Protestant but are not necessarily being reared as such, as well as disillusioned Catholics who have converted religiously, but remain culturally Catholic. It is difficult to give a precise figure for the core community, but, if one takes 1991 as a benchmark—before large-scale immigration and the scandals in the Catholic Church—and allows for some increase, a working estimate would be 3.5 per cent.

I begin with two opposing views of how Protestants have fared since independence. I then point to the new direction opened up by this volume: how Protestants forged their path within the new state and reconstructed their politics, identity and sense of belonging. After this, I concentrate on a specific issue and look at it historically and comparatively: the adaptive strategy that Irish and (later) southern Irish Protestants have used to meet the challenge of being a minority in a Catholic-majority society. The comparison is with the similarly sized (3.1 per cent) Protestant minority in France.[6] Finally, I contrast the responses of Irish Protestants and Catholics to recent social and cultural challenges. On both comparisons, Irish Protestants stand out as distinctive.

Current Views of Southern Irish Protestants

There are two sharply contrasting narratives of the experience of southern Protestants since independence. One speaks of 'privilege', the other of 'victimhood'. The 'privilege' view is the traditional Catholic one, though it is shared by some Protestants and also informs Kurt Bowen's sociological work *Protestants in a Catholic State: Ireland's Privileged Minority*. As the title suggests, it sees post-independence Protestants still in possession of most of the privileges they had accumulated during the period of British rule: the larger farms and better land, leading positions in banking, stockbroking, industry and the higher professions; well-appointed churches and possession of Dublin's two cathedrals; control of Ireland's oldest and highest-status university; residence in the better parts of Dublin and Cork; possession of a network of exclusive schools, sports and social clubs. If Protestants were outside the mainstream of the new society, this is assumed to be by choice based on resentment that the British link had been broken, disdain for the new state and its institutions, a sense of religious and social superiority, a way of safeguarding privileges. Those who hold the privilege view apply it mainly to the post-independence decades and either see it as no longer relevant today or are not sure. However, it lingers as a set of stereotypes and presuppositions and still has currency in rural areas. These themes are well covered in the introductory chapter of this volume and particularly in the essays by Ian d'Alton, Tomás Irish and Frank Barry.

The 'victim' view of southern Protestants is traditionally the Protestant one, though it is now shared by many Catholics. It was an important strand in Protestant writings between the 1920s and 1940s. It came back in a more nuanced way in the 1970s, became more pronounced in the 1980s and has become sharper in tone since then.[7] Robin Bury's recent *Buried Lives* is in that tradition. He describes a community subject to a terrifying onslaught of hostility, intimidation and violence during the War of Independence, followed by the forced exodus of large numbers, leaving it with a weakened and ever-weakening demographic base. There was job discrimination in the state sector, achieved in part by the Irish language requirement. Their numbers were further eroded by the *Ne Temere* decree, and the exacting of a promise by the Protestant party to a mixed marriage that the children would be reared as Catholic, a promise given legal status by the Supreme Court Tilson judgement of 1950. Added to this was the general undercurrent of Catholic resentment and hostility to Protestants that surfaced in the Fethard-on-Sea boycott of 1957.[8] Most who hold the victim view accept that the situation has changed since then, but believe that there are still issues, particularly on matters of identity and belonging.[9]

The victim view has gained strength in the recent period for two reasons. One is the much greater attention being paid by historians to the experience of Protestants during the War of Independence and Civil War. This began in the 1990s with the writings of the late Peter Hart on the IRA in west Cork during the War of Independence and Civil War, and his vivid description of the killing of thirteen Protestants in the Bandon Valley in late April 1922.[10] Though reference had been made to these killings before, this was the first time they were dealt with in detail and the claim that they were sectarian bluntly stated.[11] The timing was important. Hart's research coincided with the Northern Ireland peace process and intensified debates about the extent to which the campaign of the Provisional IRA had been sectarian. Not everyone who saw the recent campaign as sectarian extended this back to the earlier one, but some did.[12] Hart's claims appeared to find support in later accounts of killings in Cork city and at Coolacrease in County Offaly in 1921.[13] However, critics have questioned Hart's use of sources and the interpretation advanced in his and later studies.[14] The debate has been rancorous, with accusations of political bias and bad faith on both sides.

The second reason the victim view resonates more today is because of the attention given to victims everywhere in the contemporary period. Its currency in Ireland is such that it has led to victim status being conferred on a substantial portion of those who lived through the first five decades of the new state. The list is long: married women confined to the home, women pregnant outside of marriage, women who lost their children to enforced adoption, anyone seeking contraceptives or knowledge about them, girls taught by censorious nuns, boys taught by abusive Christian Brothers, boys pressured into playing Gaelic football when they wanted to play soccer, anyone who was ever in care, everyone who was forced to learn a nationalist version of Irish history and the Irish language, anyone wishing to read the banned works of modern literature, the poor, the unemployed, Travellers, emigrants. Those held responsible for all this are the Catholic Church, nationalist ideologues and the state. If Catholics were victims in the state they had built for themselves, how much worse must it have been for Protestants?

While the question of Protestant privilege or victimhood is usually treated in either/or terms, it is possible to hold both views simultaneously. One option would be to see some Protestants as privileged and others as victims. The historian John A. Murphy responded to claims of 'ethnic cleansing' in west Cork with the comment that 'there was no ethnic cleansing of the South Mall';[15] the journalist Eoghan Harris frequently contrasts the experience of isolated Protestant small farmers in west Cork with that of comfortable middle-class Protestants in suburban Dublin. A second option would be to see post-independence Protestants as materially privileged, but suffering culturally. Deirdre Nuttall's chapter in this volume brings further illumination to this issue.

Much more research is needed on this question and there are insights to be gained from both perspectives. The research benefits of doing so are obvious. But there is another reason. At issue is not simply a narrative of history, but the construction of an identity. Identities have a 'path dependent' quality, in the sense that once an identity is embraced, it tends to embed itself in ways that make it enduring. This is more likely in the case of the victim view than the privilege one. The time of Protestant privilege is over, but the consequences of demographic decline are permanent. If decline is attributed to victimisation, and a victim identity is embraced, it promises to be of long duration.[16]

This volume addresses a further issue: the tendency of the literature on southern Protestants to treat their experience in particularist terms. Irish religious divisions were far from *sui generis*. Confessional division was the norm in most of Europe from the seventeenth to the twentieth centuries, sometimes with ethnic overtones, and was often a source of conflict during periods of state and nation building. The idea of a 'Protestant Free state' might seem exotic, but there are likely to be analogous cases in other parts of Europe.[17] This highlights the need for comparison, both within and beyond Europe. In this volume, Niamh Dillon brings an India–Ireland comparison to bear on questions of Britishness. This chapter compares the Irish Protestant minority with that of France to see how two small and vulnerable minorities have dealt with the challenge of living in an overwhelmingly Catholic society. French Protestants have given much more attention to questions of history and identity than Irish Protestants. What accounts for the difference?

French Protestants

France and Ireland are polar opposites on most indicators. France has long been one of Europe's largest, richest, most populous and most continuous states, and historically an empire as well as a state. For most of its history Ireland was an English/British periphery, colonised, underpopulated, materially poor. The present-day Republic of Ireland has been independent for less than a century. The French reformation was home grown, the difference between French Catholics and Protestants was wholly religious and foreign involvement was minimal. The Irish reformation came as part of the English conquest, the difference was ethnic as well as religious, and the British state was the dominant actor throughout. In France, Catholics won the wars of religion and the French penal laws targeted a tiny Protestant minority. In Ireland, the Protestant minority won and the target of the Irish penal laws was the Catholic majority. In France political and religious emancipation came with the Revolution of 1789, and opened the way to full integration into the state and nation. In Ireland the undoing of the penal laws was dragged out, the last stage of political emancipation required mass Catholic mobilisation and, rather than integration into the (British) state and nation, the outcome was the secession of most of the island. France today is one of Europe's most secular states with a strict separation between church and state. The Republic of Ireland remains one of its most religious and church and state are still entwined.[18]

Differences of that magnitude raise the question of whether the two cases can usefully be compared. One reason they can is that the twists and turns of Irish history have produced an unexpected convergence: partition left a Protestant minority in the Republic of Ireland that today is of the same proportions as the one in France. In both countries the total Protestant population is growing as a result of immigration and conversion, but the historic Protestant community appears to be stable. This allows us to compare how two minorities of equivalent size have managed their situation.

How French Protestants have done it—and still do so today—can only be understood in the light of their history. The French religious wars of the sixteenth century were exceptionally violent, with massacres and extreme cruelty during and between wars.[19] By far the worst was the St Bartholomew's Day massacre in Paris in 1572, originally aimed at the Protestant leadership but going beyond that, and extending from the capital to the provinces. Thousands died, and many more converted to save their lives. Protestants were 11 per cent of the population of France in 1562; by 1600 they were 5.5 per cent.[20] Despite their small numbers they were sufficiently powerful militarily to secure substantial rights in the Edict of Nantes of 1598. However, as the seventeenth century progressed, their rights were cut back. From the 1660s its terms were more strictly and harshly applied, then systematically breached. In 1685 the edict was revoked in its entirety, making Protestantism illegal.

The Revocation was a disaster for an already very small Protestant community and it remains the great wound in the collective memory. Some fled the country, others converted. By 1702 their numbers had dropped to 2 per cent.[21] Those who remained faced harsh measures. Troops were quartered in Protestant homes until the family converted; churches and meeting houses were destroyed; pastors were tortured and executed; men arrested at clandestine assemblies were sent to the galleys and women to prison; children were taken from Protestant homes and placed in Catholic convents.[22] The severity with which these measures were enforced varied by time and place, depending on the attitude of local intendants, priests and bishops. The worst was over by the second half of the century, but the execution of Jean Calas was in 1762 and the last of the female prisoners in the Tour de Constance was not released until 1768.[23] Despite the persecutions, most Protestants refused to yield. When obliged to, they observed the external forms of Catholicism but dissented internally. They read their bibles in private, had their children secretly baptised by itinerant pastors, buried their dead in their gardens rather than in the Catholic cemetery and attended clandestine religious assemblies.

A measure of legal toleration was introduced in 1787. Two years later the Revolution transformed the situation and by 1793

Protestants had full religious and political rights. A succession of constitutional regimes followed, including a restored constitutional monarchy and an empire, but the principle of confessional equality had been established. The Revolution also put in place a new, citizenship-based, understanding of the French nation, undoing the *ancien régime*'s equivalence of Catholicity and Frenchness.[24]

The eighteenth century penal laws had ruled out direct participation in law and government, but did not restrict Protestants' economic opportunities. Many prospered in banking, business and trade and built up sizeable fortunes. This, together with their traditional emphasis on literacy and education, left them well positioned to take advantage of the economic opportunities opening up in the nineteenth century as France's economic modernisation got underway. One consequence was that in the religiously mixed areas Protestants were on balance wealthier than Catholics, with a stronger socio-economic profile, very often the employers of a Catholic workforce. Protestants played a key role in politics during the early decades of the Third Republic, particularly in the establishment of a second-level school system and in drafting the law of separation of church and state of 1905.[25] By this time, they had rebuilt their churches, schools, hospitals and organisations of social relief and had established colleges to educate new generations of pastors.

They also devoted much effort to reconstructing their history and to creating institutions—journals, museums—to preserve and disseminate it. They did this partly for themselves, partly to respond to continued Catholic mistrust and criticism. Religion was central to the answer of who they were; it had set them apart and continued to do so. But history came a close second. Calvinist theology pointed to an identity based solely on the faith and commitment of the present-day community of believers. But they existed as a community only because their ancestors had resisted and had survived the years of persecution. History was not incidental to who they were; it was at the heart of it, and an essential part of the explanation for why they existed at all. It was a history that was at once dolorous and glorious, and it made them more than simply a religious denomination. It made them in some sense a people, one with a tragic past and heroic ancestors to whom they owed a duty of memory.[26]

Equally important was the question of how and where they fitted into French history and society. Their exclusion from the mainstream of French life and the view that as Protestant they could not be truly French had cut deep. They argued that not alone were they wholly French and had always been loyal to France, they had brought something of great value to it: a tradition of individual judgement, freedom of conscience, religious freedom, respect for difference, rejection of arbitrary authority, a stress on literacy and education. In particular, they had contributed to the Enlightenment and through that to the Revolution. They would now help France keep pace with the technological and economic advances happening in competitor countries, in particular Protestant Britain and Germany. Underlying these claims was a view of France as historically held back by its Catholicism, a religion of superstition and clericalism, hostile to progress, education, science and modernity.

Liberal and anti-clerical Catholics were inclined to be sympathetic to these views, but the Catholic Church and those in the monarchical tradition remained hostile, holding Protestants substantially responsible for the Revolution and the Terror and the attacks on the Church that accompanied it. They challenged their theological views and version of history, monitored and denounced their influence on government and over-representation in the civil service and in finance, insisted that France was a Catholic nation, questioned their Frenchness and loyalty to France and, after the French defeat by Protestant Prussia in 1870, accused them of having collaborated with them.[27] Relations at local level depended on the demographic balance. In most parts of France there were so few Protestants that Catholics hardly came across them. In the mixed areas, particularly those in the south of the country with a history of division, Protestant claims to special virtues added to existing tensions.

The twentieth century brought a softening of attitudes, though the old attitudes survived in some places and among some families until the 1960s. The situation today—two generations later—is very different. The opposition of Protestant and Catholic no longer has the same depth or meaning. Ecumenism had a major impact, the cultural revolution of 1968 a greater one and the shift to a hyper-individualistic, advanced consumer society a still bigger one. Confessional identities are more lightly held, if held at all, and more easily bracketed. Church attendance is very low. The dynamic sectors in French Protestantism today are evangelical. Many of today's evangelicals are not descendants of the historic Protestant community and those who are, are more interested in their faith than in what happened in the past. Some of the historic Protestant community are still believers; most are not, or what they believe is only loosely based on the Bible. Intermarriage with Catholics (usually non-practising ones) is frequent, the children of mixed unions are often not baptised or, if they are, receive little religious formation. The presumption of cultural superiority to Catholics has gone; with greater education and less obedience to their Church, Catholics are thought to have now 'caught up'.[28]

These changes, in particular the decline in belief and practice, have led to concerns among French Protestants about the survival of their distinctive identity, and they work to preserve it.[29] This is done partly by practical initiatives at local level, but also by renewing the positive version of that historic identity. Its purpose is to allow younger generations of Protestants to be proud of their past, whether or not they have religious beliefs.[30] The claim is that (unlike Catholicism) theirs was a religion based on freedom of conscience, reason and the Bible; their history was one of courage and survival; their culture was progressive and enlightened; their values—rooted in their experience of persecution—include concern for the suffering of others, particularly those subjected to deprivation or arbitrary authority. At a time when other identities have become fractured or devalued, this makes an attractive package, a heritage to embrace, even if one is not personally religious. Given their small numbers and history of marginality, recognition is important. In September 2017, in a speech at the Hôtel de Ville in Paris to mark the 500th anniversary of the Reformation, President Macron stressed the profound contribution that Protestants and Protestant values had made to France, declaring that 'Protestant blood flows in the veins of France', and that 'France needs its Protestants to remain watchtowers of the Republic'.[31] The comments were appreciated, but the matter did not stop there. Some months after, twenty prominent Protestants sent him open letters detailing the things they wanted him to attend to.[32]

Irish Protestants in the Light of the French Example

The major social and political differences between the French and Irish cases were listed above. A further one will now be added: the amount of attention each Protestant minority has given to clarifying its history, identity and relationship to the wider society. French Protestants have done this for a long time, and it continues to be the subject of books, articles and conference papers, as well as a recurring theme in their weekly newspaper, *Réforme*. Irish Protestants also write books, articles and hold conferences. There are church-based history societies with libraries and archives and the Church of Ireland also has a now-monthly newspaper, the *Church of Ireland Gazette*. There are works that draw attention to some of the ways in which they feel ill-treated. There are also ones that touch on general identity issues.[33] Despite this, a clear picture of contemporary Irish Protestant identity (or identities) does not emerge. The clarity with which President Macron was able to convey French Protestant self-understanding would not be possible in Ireland.

Irish Protestants also differ in this respect from Irish Catholics, who since the 1980s have incessantly analysed their identity in an unending stream of academic and popular works, opinion columns, novels, plays, poetry, or on television and radio programmes.[34] Most of these speak of 'Irish' rather than 'Catholic Irish', but the two are almost always interchangeable. If an Irish government wanted to make a statement about how the Catholic Irish view themselves and the nation, it would have no difficulty knowing what to say. If it had to do the same for the Protestant Irish, it would struggle.

How are these differences—between French and Irish Protestants, and between Catholics and Protestants in Ireland—to be explained? There are differences between the two national cultures—the French tend to intellectualise more than the Irish—but this would not explain the Irish Catholic–Protestant difference. I begin with the French–Irish Protestant difference, explaining it in terms of the historical challenge each faced as a minority and the strategy it adopted to deal with it. I then look at the Catholic–Protestant difference.

French Protestants were the product of an indigenous reformation movement and their fate would depend on developments within France. From time to time they could get help from outside—in particular from Holland or from England—but reliance on outside help risked accusations of disloyalty that could make their situation worse. Their only real option was to rely on their own resources and talents: their economic enterprise, their political adaptability, their support for one another, their culture of resistance, their ability to spot dangers and opportunities and to respond appropriately. To do this effectively they needed a clear understanding of who they were, what their options were, and where they might fit into wider French society. This is the historical basis of the exceptional reflexivity of French Protestants; it was the adaptive response of a minority to a sustained existential challenge.

Irish Protestants faced an existential challenge of equivalent magnitude, but its origins were different, and so was their response. They came as strangers and conquerors to a land that already had its own identity and traditions. They were also assigned the task of transforming it, including converting it religiously and assimilating it culturally. From the beginning they had had to address pressing questions of legitimacy. Their claim to property and to rule rested mainly on rights of conquest, but also on their political, religious and cultural mission: to bring order, progress, religious enlightenment and political liberty to a chaotic, backward, superstitious and priest-ridden island. It was a claim that remained at the heart of their identity for generations.[35] It also contributed to the alienation of the native population, the failure of the hoped-for religious conversion and the limited nature of the cultural assimilation. It was a historic failure and it left Protestants outside Ulster as a permanently small and vulnerable minority.

Their strategy of defence was very different to that of their French counterparts. It rested on two basic principles: secure a monopoly of economic resources and political power, and retain the support of the British state. This worked for a long time, but from the second part of the eighteenth century, a Catholic recovery was underway, and the British government was becoming receptive to Catholic demands. By the end of the nineteenth the Protestant position had been substantially eroded in the Catholic-majority parts of the island.[36] By this time also any hope of holding the line by reconciling Catholic–Protestant differences or by reconfiguring identities was long gone; Catholic nationalists questioned their Irishness and their historic civilising claims, and were demanding Home Rule. The only hope now was to put their trust in the British government and the politics of unionism. In the end both let them down.

The nationalist struggle for independence reconfigured and renewed the sense of existential threat that Irish Protestants had always lived with. Some saw no future for themselves and left. Most stayed and the situation turned out to be less fearsome than many expected. The period of open war did not last long, the violence was concentrated in parts of the country, and those at risk were mainly those who served—or were suspected of serving—the British state. Once the new government had established its control, the situation became more promising. They already had a strong economic base, a well-developed ecclesiastical infrastructure, a major university, a network of schools, hospitals, sports and social clubs. The new government left all of that in place. Its own sympathies lay with the political and religious views of the majority, but it was anxious to show its neutrality and fairness. It was not the state Protestants would have chosen, but it was one they could work with. Independence led to some reflection on questions of history and identity, but not much. It was not necessary and—as the essays in this volume by Conor Morrissey, Ian d'Alton and Miriam Moffitt show—there were reasons not to dwell too much on it.

The post-independence period was a challenging time, but the challenges were manageable. The religious one is better understood from the perspective of confessionalism than of sectarianism. Confessionalism may be defined as the generally accepted activities that churches and their members engage in to mark and maintain their difference. Sectarianism is action that breaches those norms. The boundary between the confessional and the sectarian changes over time and what is seen as confessional at one point in time may be viewed as sectarian at another. Like much of Europe, Ireland had been confessionalised for centuries and the division was taken for granted. The British state had worked with it, initially to control the island, later because they had no choice. The new state did the same. In its time, the British state had tilted towards Protestantism. The new one tilted towards Catholicism, but Protestant religious rights were fully respected. The Tilson judgement is widely viewed as evidence of the sectarianism of the state, yet it was more neutral in law than in the manner in which it was presented, and Protestant opinion on it was divided.[37] The Fethard-on-Sea boycott is often taken to be clear evidence of Catholic sectarianism—and it certainly showed how a family confessional dispute on the education of the children could escalate into a communal sectarian one—but Catherine O'Connor's essay in this volume shows that it cannot be reduced to a simple Catholic–Protestant bipolarity. Equally telling, such examples were rare. The difficulty Protestants faced was less sectarianism than confessionalism in a context of severe demographic imbalance: the extraordinary public Catholicity of the country and the impossibility of getting away from it.[38] Even then, there was an upside: it provided robust and reassuring confirmation of their own religious identity.

Much has also been made of the cultural oppressiveness of the post-independence period: the identification of the state with the nationalist narrative of Irish history, the foregrounding of the Irish language and requirement that all schoolchildren learn it, the hostility shown to expressions of a British identity or loyalty. This was a burden, but it has to be seen in context. In practice, the British legacy remained all-pervasive: the English language, Georgian buildings, British street names, British coinage, statues of British heroes, country estates and mansions, TCD, the interiors of Dublin's two cathedrals, the Royal Irish Academy, the Royal Dublin Society, Dublin Castle, the Viceregal Lodge. Some steps were taken to undo this, but they were on a limited scale. New public bodies were given Irish names, there was much token use of Irish, some Georgian houses were allowed to fall down, some streets were re-named, the more prominent statues were removed, Dublin Castle and the Viceregal Lodge were taken over (though used for a similar purpose), expressions of political and cultural nationalism were at times intense. But much remained as it was. As Ian d'Alton points out in this volume, post-independence Dublin still had, pro-rata, twice as many streets named after Queen Victoria as London. Elsewhere he has shown that, if one chose carefully, one could continue to live as if not much had changed.[39]

The post-independence period was one of continuity as well as rupture and this was also evident in the adaptive strategy of the Protestant minority. Allegiance had to be transferred from one state to another, but the basic approach was the same: support and secure the support of the existing state and defend their strong economic, social and institutional base. Addressing identity issues in the manner of French Protestants was not part of it. It might have brought some additional benefit, but perhaps not much. Defending the difference was more important than analysing what exactly it was.

I turn now to Irish Protestant–Catholic differences on identity matters, focusing on their contrasting responses to recent challenges. Post-independence Ireland did not cut itself off from the outside world. The preoccupation with events and developments elsewhere continued, as did the fascination with the modern. Local and national newspapers and magazines reported on world events, there was a steady inflow of books, newspapers, magazines, films and popular music. People travelled. Emigrants wrote home and some returned.[40] But the extent of openness increased exponentially after the 1960s, making the country today one of the most open in the world. The internal changes that accompanied this opening out were also far-reaching. Post-independence Ireland was rural, agricultural, small-town, materially struggling, familistic, localistic, poorly educated, deeply religious, deferential to and fearful of state and religious authority. Very little of this remains. The population is now predominantly urban; its economy is industrial and service-based; there is wealth and affluence; education levels are high; the values are individualist and consumerist; religious belief and church attendance remain high by international standards, but secularism has taken a deep hold; there is scepticism towards all forms of authority, particularly clerical.[41] There were other developments. The Second Vatican Council opened the way to Catholic ecumenism and brought liturgical reforms that undid much of the visible difference between Catholicism and the variety of Protestantisms. The collapse of the Northern state between 1969 and 1972 was followed by more than two decades of prolonged paramilitary violence. Southerners tried to keep their distance from it, but it impinged at every level, and the condition of a settlement was an end to the politics of reunification in place since the foundation of the state. The 1990s brought further dramatic changes: an economic take-off that produced an unprecedented level of wealth, the first significant immigration for centuries and the birth of a multicultural society.

These changes can be viewed as the more or less inevitable convergence of Ireland with other western societies, later in respect to post-war modernisation, earlier as far as globalisation is concerned. But they did not just happen; they were undertaken as solutions to pressing problems and actively pursued by those in positions of leadership or by those who campaigned for them. Decisions had to be made, laws changed, policies implemented, established practices questioned, changed or abandoned. Not everyone wanted the changes and some were deeply opposed to them, but change of some kind could not be avoided. Some groups benefited, others lost. Each stage was marked by public and private debate. Ideological as well as practical choices had to be made and the ideological battles were often sharper and more wounding than the practical ones. How much the debates influenced the direction the society took is questionable; wider economic, political and cultural forces were more important. However, the debates shaped the meaning of what was happening, legitimised the decisions made and ensured continuity between past and present.

Catholics and Protestants were equally affected by the changes, but the challenges were different and their responses also differed. For Catholics there was the shock of realisation that more was at issue than simply working out new policies. The cultural certainties of the post-independence decades were dissolving. Their understanding of their state and nation was coming into question, as was the nationalism and Catholicism on which it was based. At a cultural level it was a challenge of existential proportions, and they responded to it in the way they responded to such challenges in the past: by re-opening and re-engaging with questions of history and identity. This was the context for the outpouring of reflection and analysis and the identity debates of the 1980s and 1990s. Protestants contributed to the historical research that informed these debates, but were generallly slow to participate in them, and the work of cultural and ideological reconstruction was undertaken almost wholly by those within the Catholic-nationalist tradition.

Protestants' reluctance to involve themselves closely in these debates owes much to the fact that they raised politically sensitive questions of nationalism and Catholicism.[42] But they also did not feel the need to: the new directions being taken were mostly ones they approved of and had wanted for a long time. They were also aware that Catholics were finding the work of demolition painful enough without Protestants interjecting a 'We told you so', even if it could sometimes be heard in the pauses, or read between the lines. Like their French counterparts, Irish Catholics were finally 'catching up' and they could be let get on with it.

Meanwhile, Protestants faced challenges of a different kind. From the 1970s they were opening up the sectors they had once controlled to Catholic entry: Protestant businesses, Trinity College, second-level schools, sports and social clubs.[43] There were political reasons for doing this: ecumenism made separation by religion seem backward and intolerant, and the conflict in Northern Ireland provided evidence of the dangers. But practical considerations were more important. The times were more dynamic and more competitive and it was a question of adapt or go under.[44] Their biggest problem was one of scale; their numbers and their world were too small. To grow they had to open up and allow Catholics in. This brought benefits, but at a cost. Their control of these sectors had served the community well, helping it to maintain its ethos, numbers, coherence and internal social order. They had provided spaces where patronage was exercised, contacts made, deals done, favours exchanged, networks built, matches made and the sense of an Irish Protestant world sustained. They had offered reassurance that the community was taking care of its own. The entry of Catholics complicated that.

The opening up was by no means total. There were still wholly Protestant spaces: church activities (even if participation has been falling) and the Protestant primary school sector, which brought together the children of Protestant families and—just as important—their parents. Many of the firms that had been Protestant retained the imprint of their past and even today some of these have a disproportionate Protestant presence at higher executive and board level. Trinity College retains much of its past ethos, particularly at staff level. Second-level schools use selection criteria that give priority to Protestant applicants, and their boards of management remain majority Protestant. One-time Protestant sports clubs remain disproportionately Protestant. But the extent of control has diminished, making it difficult to carry out the previous functions. There are still strong Protestant networks which do this, but they are less visible and it is less evident to the wider community that they are doing so. This coincides with increasing intermarriage and cultural convergence. These changes can be—and usually are—viewed in positive terms, but they also have implications for Protestant numbers, social cohesion and cultural distinctiveness. This raises the question of whether the traditional adaptive strategy is still fit for purpose. The state remains supportive, but the once protected

Protestant economic and social sector has been substantially eroded. This is a new situation, and it may demand a fresh approach.

Protestant leaders and members of the community are responding to the challenge in practical ways. They include special efforts to sustain the sense of community at the level of parish and school, intensive lobbying to secure state support for Protestant schools and the extraordinary efforts of some parents to secure places for their children in Protestant schools, even if the Protestantism of some of these is in question. As in the past they have not responded in the manner of their French counterparts: publicly defining and projecting a clear and positive image of who they are, what their history has been, what it means to be Protestant, and what Protestantism has contributed to their country.[45] They also differ from Irish Catholics, whose response to recent challenges is much closer to that of the French Protestants.[46]

What explains the Irish Protestant reluctance to engage with questions of history and identity in the same way? The most likely explanation is that they do not see an immediate need or benefit to doing so. There are challenges, but it is not a crisis. Protestant numbers fell continuously until 1991, but they have been stable since then, and may have grown slightly. Moreover, what works for French Protestants and Irish Catholics would not necessarily work for them, and there could be risks in trying it. Their history does not support the kind of heroic narrative available to their French counterparts and Catholic sensitivities to the past have not entirely gone away.[47] A second possible explanation is that, even if there were benefits to doing so, they do not wish to expose themselves to increased public scrutiny or to further advertise their difference. It is not as if they are completely invisible; their historical imprint is everywhere and they continue to have a strong institutional presence. Beyond that, they simply want to be accepted, to feel they belong, to have their difference respected and to be let get on with their lives. A third possibility is that since they have not done this kind of identity-work in the past, it would be difficult to begin it now.

Conclusion

A final question might be asked: is there anything that might lead southern Protestants to engage with questions of history and identity in as focused and public a manner as French Protestants or Irish Catholics? There is a possible circumstance, referred to at the outset: Irish reunification. Irish unity may never happen, it could happen a long time from now, or it could come quicker than anyone imagines. In general, southern Protestants have kept their distance from the politics of the island, but they are an important part of its political geometry. If ever there is movement towards reunification, they could play an important role. They might choose not to or the Irish government and Northern unionists could ignore them and concentrate on working out a deal with one another, but they have an interest in the outcome, and it would offer a historic opportunity to once again play a role in the politics of the island. Doing so would mean breaking with their low-key approach and asserting themselves forcefully in public debate. They could meet resistance, not least from southern Catholics long accustomed to Protestant reticence and discretion. If they choose to play such a role, they will need a clear view of who they were, who they are today and what they would like an island-wide settlement to be. It might be better to reflect on such matters now than wait until then.

Endnotes

Introduction: Content and Context

1 Glenavy's job-seeking was so notorious that he was known in popular parlance as 'Lord Glengravy'.

2 For the purposes of this book, 'southern Ireland' is defined as the area of the Irish Free State and the later Republic, i.e., the twenty-six counties. Unless otherwise indicated, Irish 'Protestants' are defined from the 1926 census as Protestant Episcopalians, Presbyterians, Methodists and Baptists: Saorstát Éireann, *Census of Population, 1926, Religions and Birthplaces* (Dublin: Stationery Office, 1929), vol. 3, table 9, pp. 13–17. See also note 22.

3 P. Maume, 'Campbell, James Henry Mussen', *DIB*, vol. 2, p. 291.

4 K. Myers, *Irish Times*, 18 August 1999; L. Kennedy, *Unhappy the Land: The Most Oppressed People Ever, the Irish?* (Newbridge: Irish Academic Press, 2016).

5 For a recent work in this genre, see R. Bury, *Buried Lives: The Protestants of Southern Ireland* (Dublin: History Press, 2017).

6 *Irish Independent*, 11 July 1914.

7 Willie Thorpe to New Ross Board of Guardians, cited in *People*, 1 August 1914.

8 E. Bowen, *Bowen's Court & Seven Winters: Memories of a Dublin Childhood* (London: Virago, 1984), *Seven Winters*, p. 14.

9 B. Dugdale, *Arthur James Balfour, First Earl of Balfour, K.G., O.M., F.R.S., etc 1848–1905* (London: Hutchinson, 1939), p. 138.

10 *Irish Times*, 22 June 1929, quoted in S. Hood, 'The Church of Ireland Commemoration of St Patrick in 1932', online presentation and digital archive, at http://ireland.anglican.org/about/165 (accessed 22 July 2013).

11 D. Ó Corráin, *Rendering to God and Caesar: The Irish Churches and the Two States in Ireland, 1949–73* (Manchester: Manchester University Press, 2006), pp. 70–114, 182–199.

12 E. Biagini, 'A Challenge to Partition: Methodist Open-air Work in Independent Ireland, 1922–1962', *Bulletin of the Methodist Historical Society of Ireland*, vol. 19, 2014, p. 41.

13 See chapter fifteen below.

14 J. White, *Minority Report: The Anatomy of the Southern Irish Protestant* (Dublin: Gill & Macmillan, 1975), pp. 2–3.

15 Oxford: Oxford University Press, 2009.

16 Oxford: Oxford University Press, 2014.

17 See particularly L. McBride, *The Greening of Dublin Castle: The Transformation of Bureaucratic and Judicial Personnel in Ireland, 1892–1922* (Washington, DC: Catholic University of America Press, 1991).

18 Campbell, *Irish Establishment*, p. 312.

19 Hubert Butler, 'Portrait of a Minority', *Escape from the Anthill* (Mullingar: Lilliput Press, 1985).

20 *Census of Population, 1926*, vol. 3, table 1A, p. 1; table 4A, p. 5; also Ireland, *Census of Population, 1961* (Dublin: Stationery Office, 1965), vol. 7, table 1A, p. 1.
21 Biagini, 'A Challenge to Partition', pp. 5–44. The quote is on p. 13.
22 *Census of Population, 1926*, vol. 3, table 1A, p. 1.
23 *Census of Population, 1926, General Report* (Dublin: Stationery Office, 1934), vol. 10, pp. 46–48; A. Bielenberg, 'Exodus: The Emigration of Southern Irish Protestants during the Irish War of Independence and the Civil War', *Past and Present*, no. 218, February 2013, table 6, p. 223.
24 R.B. McDowell, *Crisis and Decline: The Fate of the Southern Unionists* (Dublin: Lilliput Press, 1997), p. 4; *Census of Population, 1926*, vol. 10, p. 48.
25 *Census of Population, 1926*, vol. 3, table 1A, p. 3.
26 *Irish Times*, 5 May 1916.
27 *Census of Population, 1926*, vol. 3, table 18A, p. 130.
28 *Census of Population, 1926*, vol. 3, table 17, pp. 126–7. Protestant females accounted for about 5 per cent of total female domestic servants, slightly below the population average.
29 *Census of Population, 1926*, vol. 3, table 17, pp. 114–5, 124–7.
30 *Guy's Cork Almanac and Directory, 1916*, pp. 158–64.
31 *Census of Population, 1926*, vol. 3, table 17, p. 124.
32 *Census of Population, 1926*, vol. 10, pp. 54–5.
33 *Census of Population, 1926*, vol. 3, table 17, pp. 114–15.
34 McDowell, *Crisis and Decline*, p. 5; *Census of Population, 1926*, vol. 10, pp. 49–57.
35 *Census of Population, 1926*, vol. 10, pp. 51–2.
36 *Census of Population, 1926*, vol. 10, p. 52; R.B. McDowell, *The Church of Ireland, 1869–1969* (London: Routledge & Kegan Paul, 1975), pp. 121–2. See also C. O'Neill (ed.), *Irish Elites in the Nineteenth Century* (Dublin: Four Courts, 2013), p. 26; also idem, *Catholics of Consequence: Transnational Education, Social Mobility, and the Irish Catholic Elite 1850–1900* (Oxford: Oxford University Press, 2014), pp. 206–7.
37 Lord Midleton sought direct representation in 1922 for commerce as well as property in the new Irish Senate—P. Martin, 'Unionism: The Irish Nobility and Revolution, 1919–23', in J. Augusteijn (ed.), *The Irish Revolution, 1913–1923* (Basingstoke and New York: Palgrave, 2002), p. 162.
38 For the townships, see S. Ó Maitiú, *Rathmines Township 1847–1930* (Dublin: CDVEC, 1997), passim; idem, *Dublin's Suburban Towns 1834–1930* (Dublin: Four Courts, 2003), pp. 196–7.
39 Bowen, *Seven Winters*, p. 48.
40 Bowen, *Seven Winters*, p. 33.
41 Bowen, *Seven Winters*, pp. 36, 41.
42 Seán O'Casey, *The Plough and the Stars*, in S. Tucker, *Twenty-five Modern Plays* (New York: Harper Brothers, 1953), p. 753.
43 According to the 1911 Census: https://tinyurl.com/yby8csg3 (accessed 12 June 2016); also M. Maguire, 'A Socio-economic Analysis of the Dublin Protestant Working Class, 1870–1926', *Irish Economic and Social History*, vol. xx, 1993, pp. 35–61.
44 *Census of Ireland 1911, Province of Leinster, City of Dublin, Area, houses and population . . .* (Dublin: HMSO, 1912), Cd. 6049-II, pp. 16–28.

45 M. Maguire, 'The Dublin Protestant Working Class, 1870–1932: Economy, Society, Politics' (unpub. MA thesis, UCD, 1990); idem, 'The Organisation and Activism of Dublin's Protestant Working Class, 1883–1935', *Irish Historical Studies,* vol. 29, no. 113, May 1994, pp. 65–87.

46 M. Maguire, 'The Church of Ireland and the Problem of the Protestant Working-class of Dublin, 1870s–1930s', in A. Ford, J. McGuire and K. Milne (eds), *As by Law Established: The Church of Ireland since the Reformation* (Dublin: Lilliput, 1995), p. 202.

47 TNA, MS CO 762/48/14.

48 TNA, MS CO 762/42/13.

49 E. Rumpf and A.C. Hepburn, *Nationalism and Socialism in Twentieth-century Ireland* (New York: Barnes and Noble Books, 1977), p. 62. For a case study of the persistence of land-war sectarian tensions into the revolutionary era, see Miriam Moffitt, 'Protestant Tenant Farmers and the Land League in North Connaught', in C. King and C. McNamara, *The West of Ireland: New Perspectives on the Nineteenth Century* (Dublin: History Press Ireland, 2011), pp. 93–116.

50 See letters from John Regan, Martin Maguire and Tom Cooper in *Irish Times*, 17, 22 September 2014; David Fitzpatrick, Niall Meehan and others in *History Ireland* and elsewhere, 2013–14 summarised at https://www.academia.edu/5027882/David_Fitzpatrick_Niall_Meehan_debate_ethnic_cleansing_during_Irish_War_of_Independence_and_a_spoof_sectarian_ballad (accessed 19 September 2017); also A. Bielenberg and J.S. Donnelly Jr, 'Cork's War of Independence Fatality Register', at http://theirishrevolution.ie/cork-fatality-register/#.WcQTGnjqCSo (accessed 21 September 2017); and Barry Keane, *Cork's Revolutionary Dead, 1918–1923* (Cork: Mercier Press, 2017).

51 A. Bielenberg, 'Southern Irish Experiences of the Irish Revolution', in J. Crowley, D. Ó Drisceoil and M. Murphy (eds), *Atlas of the Irish Revolution* (Cork: Cork University Press, 2017), p. 780; G. Clark, 'Breaking the Silence on Civil War Casualties', *Irish Times*, 18 September 2017; Bielenberg, 'Exodus', p. 233.

52 D. Wood, 'Protestant Decline in Ireland 1911–26', unpub. paper read to a conference 'Southern Irish Loyalism in Context', Maynooth University, 21–2 July 2017, p. 25.

53 *Irish Times*, 6 Sep. 2014, review of G. Clark, *Everyday Violence in the Irish Civil War* (Cambridge: Cambridge University Press, 2014).

54 Bielenberg, 'Exodus', p. 232; J. Coakley, 'Independence Movements and National Minorities: Some Parallels in the European Experience', *European Journal of Political Research*, vol. viii, no. 2, 1980, pp. 215–47; T. Wilson, 'Ghost Provinces, Mislaid Minorities: The Experience of Southern Ireland and Prussian Poland Compared, 1918–23', *Irish Studies in International Affairs,* vol. xiii, 2002, pp. 61–86; idem, *Frontiers of Violence: Conflict and Identity in Ulster and Upper Silesia, 1918–1922* (Oxford: Oxford University Press, 2010); McDowell, *Crisis and Decline*, p. 119.

55 D. Fitzpatrick, 'Protestant Depopulation and the Irish Revolution', in *Descendancy: Irish Protestant Histories since 1795* (Cambridge: Cambridge University Press, 2014), p. 180.

56 See B. Keane, 'The Irish Protestant Refugee Crisis in London 1922 Debunked? Figures from the Irish Distress Committee', at https://www.academia.

edu/36074588/The_Irish_Protestant_refugee_crisis_in_London_1922_debunked_Figures_from_the_Irish_Distress_Committee (accessed 5 March 2018).

57 P. Hart, *The I.R.A. at War, 1916–1923* (Oxford: Oxford University Press, 2003), p. 243.

58 Bielenberg, 'Southern Irish Experiences of the Irish Revolution', p. 773; idem, 'Exodus', pp. 204, 209–18. See also P. Deignan, *The Protestant Community in Sligo* (Dublin: Original Writing, 2010).

59 T. Dooley, *The Decline of the Big House in Ireland: A Study of Irish Landed Families* (Dublin: Wolfhound Press, 2001), pp. 187–92, 287; J.S. Donnelly Jr, 'Big House Burnings in County Cork during the Irish Revolution, 1920–21', *Eire-Ireland*, vol. 47, nos 3–4, Fall/Winter 2012, pp. 141–97. It must be noted that Catholic senators—such as Count Moore—were also burned out.

60 Dooley, *The Decline of the Big House*, pp. 171–97.

61 McDowell, *Crisis and Decline*, p. 159; P. Buckland, *Irish Unionism 1: The Anglo-Irish and the New Ireland 1885–1922* (Dublin: Gill & Macmillan, 1972), pp. 190–1, 296.

62 J. O'Neill, *Blood-dark Track: A Family History* (London: HarperCollins, 2000), pp. 295–6, 327–33.

63 Church of Ireland United Dioceses of Cork, Cloyne and Ross, *Diocesan Magazine* vol. 33, no. 11, December 2008, p. 1.

64 The Bishop of Cork, Cloyne and Ross, Dr Paul Colton, admitted that many in the Church of Ireland community in Cork 'anticipate the coming centenary commemorations of the War of Independence and the Civil War fearfully and with a certain dread. Many fear that the ceremonies will re-open old sectarian wounds—particularly given that the descendants of many of those involved in the events of 1919–22 are still living in the same general area' (*Belfast Telegraph*, 11 September 2017); also *Irish Times*, 16 September 2017.

65 *Irish Times*, 9 August 1989.

1. 'No Country'?: Protestant 'Belongings' in Independent Ireland, 1922–49

1 *Irish Times*, 11 April, 13 June 1922.

2 S. Day, *The Amazing Philanthropists* (London: Sidgwick & Jackson, 1916), p. 16.

3 *Cork Examiner*, 3 April 1898.

4 H. Saunderson, *The Saundersons of Castle Saunderson* (London: pr. printed, 1936), p. 73; also see D. MacDonald, *The Sons of Levi* (Manorhamilton: Drumlin Publications, 1998), p. 214.

5 G. Seaver, *John Allen Fitzgerald Gregg Archbishop* (Dublin: Faith Press, 1963), pp. 119, 126.

6 Seaver, *Gregg*, p. 126; R.B. McDowell, *Crisis and Decline: The Fate of the Southern Unionists* (Dublin: Lilliput Press, 1997), p. 113.

7 *Irish Times*, 17 January 1922.

8 *Irish Times*, 28 April 1922.

9 *Irish Times*, 20 April 1949; T. Brown, *The Irish Times: 150 Years of Influence* (London: Bloomsbury, 2015), pp. 208–10; M. O'Brien, *The Irish Times: A History* (Dublin: Four Courts, 2008), pp. 132–3.

10 *HL Debates*, 30 January 1913, vol. 13, col. 770–3.
11 Seaver, *Gregg*, p. 116; F.S.L. Lyons, 'The Minority Problem in the 26 Counties', in F. McManus (ed.), *The Years of the Great Test, 1926–1939* (Cork: Mercier, 1967), p. 96.
12 C.A. Webster, 'The Church Since Disestablishment', in W.A. Philips (ed.), *History of the Church of Ireland from the Earliest Times to the Present Day* (Oxford: Oxford University Press, 1933), vol. 3, p. 422.
13 *CoIG*, 5 February 1932.
14 David Fitzpatrick, 'The Orange Order and the Border', in D. Fitzpatrick, *Descendancy: Irish Protestant Histories since 1795* (Cambridge: Cambridge University Press, 2014), pp. 55–7.
15 Report by Major M. Grove-White, 22 July 1925, TNA, WO 32/5315 (my thanks to Professor Eunan O'Halpin).
16 *Irish Times*, 29 August 1923.
17 Webster, 'The Church Since Disestablishment', p. 422.
18 W. Bell and N. Emerson (eds), *The Church of Ireland A.D. 432–1932: The Report of the Church of Ireland Conference held in Dublin, 11th–14th October, 1932 ...* (Dublin: Church of Ireland Printing & Publishing Co., 1932), p. 178.
19 *CoIG*, 27 April 2007, letter from Rev. A. Carter.
20 O'Brien, *Irish Times*, p. 135.
21 T. Hoppen, *Ireland Since 1800: Conflict and Conformity* (London, New York: Longman, 1989), p. 249.
22 Rev. E. Cahill to E. de Valera, 21 October 1936, de Valera papers, UCDA, P150/2393.
23 D. Ó Corráin, *Rendering to God and Caesar: The Irish Churches and the Two States in Ireland, 1949–73* (Manchester: Manchester University Press, 2006); H. Crawford, *Outside the Glow: Protestants and Irishness in Independent Ireland* (Dublin: UCD Press, 2010).
24 R. Tobin, *The Minority Voice: Hubert Butler and Southern Irish Protestantism, 1900–1991* (Oxford: Oxford University Press, 2012), p. 114.
25 R. Foster, 'Feeling the Squeeze', *Dublin Review of Books*, no. 66, April 2015.
26 Cit. in A. Scholes, *The Church of Ireland and the Third Home Rule Bill* (Dublin: Irish Academic Press, 2010), p. 1.
27 Biagini, 'A Challenge to Partition', pp. 18–19.
28 T. Fanning, 'Vicious Attempts by Catholics to Drive Out Protestants', *Irish Independent*, 22 February 2009.
29 I. d'Alton, 'Navigating the Minefield: How *The Irish Times* and the *Church of Ireland Gazette* Approached the Tilson Case and the Dogma of the Assumption in 1950', unpub. paper read at the Church of Ireland Historical Society, 7 November 2015, p. 4.
30 Eugenio Biagini makes the point that in European societies, discrimination against minorities was more often a local than an official or national phenomenon, *Irish Times*, 7 February 2015.
31 Ó Corráin, *Rendering to God and Caesar*, p. 242.
32 J. Hone, *Ireland Since 1922* (London: Faber & Faber, 1932), p. 16; I. d'Alton, 'Southern Irish Unionism: A Study of Cork Unionists', *Transactions of the Royal Historical Society*, 5th ser., vol. 23, 1973, pp. 71–88; E. Biagini, 'The

Protestant Minority in Southern Ireland', *The Historical Journal,* vol. 55, no. 4, December 2012, pp. 1161–84.

33 Brown, *Irish Times*, p. 138.

34 C. O'Halloran, *Partition and the Limits of Irish Nationalism: An Ideology Under Stress* (Dublin: Gill & Macmillan, 1987), pp. 79–85; K. Milne, 'The Church of Ireland Since Partition', in B. Bradshaw and D. Keogh (eds), *Christianity in Ireland: Revisiting the Story* (Dublin: Columba Press, 2002), p. 222.

35 E. Blain, 'The Protestant Vote in the Republic of Ireland, 1922–1969' (unpub. MA thesis, UCD School of Politics and International Relations, 2009), passim.

36 The *CoIG* frequently inveighed against the interference of the state in health and social welfare matters: C. Holohan, 'Rediscovering Poverty and Class? Ireland in the 1960s', unpub. paper read at a conference 'Class and Culture in Twentieth-century Ireland', St John's College, Cambridge, 18 April 2015.

37 P. Deighan, 'The Protestant Community in Sligo, 1914–1949' (unpub. PhD thesis, NUIM, 2008), pp. 422–8, esp. p. 425; R. Roddie, 'Editor's Note', *Bulletin of the Methodist Historical Society of Ireland*, vol. 19, 2014, p. 4: 'a Church that was largely comfortable with the moral stance of the new Irish State'.

38 P. Semple, 'Previous generations would be astounded at attitudes to churches in Ireland today', *Irish Times*, 18 November 2014.

39 L. Pilkington, 'Religion and the Celtic Tiger: The Cultural Legacies of Anti-Catholicism in Ireland', in P. Kirby, L. Gibbons and M. Cronin (eds), *Reinventing Ireland: Culture, Society and the Global Economy* (London: Pluto Press, 2002), pp. 125–33; Ó Corráin, *Rendering to God and Caesar*, pp. 97–9; R. Foster, *The Irish Story* (London: Allen Lane, 2001), p. 190.

40 *Irish Times*, 10 May 1932.

41 C. Reid, *The Lost Ireland of Stephen Gwynn: Irish Constitutional Nationalism and Cultural Politics, 1864–1950* (Manchester: Manchester University Press, 2011), p. 245.

42 R. Tobin, '"Tracing Again the Tiny Snail Track": Southern Protestant Memoir since 1950', *The Yearbook of English Studies*, vol. 35, no. 1, January 2005, p. 172; E. Grubgeld, *Anglo-Irish Autobiography: Class, Gender and the Forms of Narrative* (Syracuse, NY: Syracuse University Press, 2004), p. xi; E.M. Wolff, *'An anarchy in the mind and in the heart': Narrating Anglo-Ireland* (Lewisburg: Bucknell University Press, 2006), passim. See also A. Wessels, 'Elizabeth Bowen's "A World of Love": A "Cultural Analysis" of the Anglo-Irish Ascendancy in the Twentieth Century', *The Canadian Journal of Irish Studies*, vol. 21, no. 1, July 1995, pp. 88–95.

43 Grubgeld, *Anglo-Irish Autobiography*, pp. xi, xx, 4, 14.

44 D. O'Byrne, 'Last of Their Line: The Disappearing Anglo-Irish in Twentieth Century Fictions and Autobiographies', in M. Busteed, F. Neal and J. Tonge (eds), *Irish Protestant Identities* (Manchester: Manchester University Press, 2008), p. 46.

45 T. Brown, 'Religious Minorities in the Irish Free State and the Republic of Ireland 1922–1995', in *Building Trust in Ireland: Studies Commissioned by the Forum for Peace and Reconciliation* (Belfast: Forum for Peace and Reconciliation, 1996), p. 237.

46 F.S.L. Lyons, 'Yeats and the Anglo-Irish Twilight', and G.C. Bolton, 'The Anglo-Irish and the Historians', both in O. MacDonagh, W. Mandle and P. Travers (eds), *Irish Culture and Nationalism 1750–1950* (London: Macmillan, 1983); M. Bence-Jones, *Twilight of the Ascendancy* (London: Constable, 1987). But see I. d'Alton, 'A Perspective upon Historical Process: The Case of Southern Irish Protestantism', in F.B. Smith (ed.), *Ireland, England and Australia: Essays in Honour of Oliver MacDonagh* (Canberra, Cork: Australian National University/Cork University Press, 1990), pp. 82–6.
47 K. Bowen, *Protestants in a Catholic State: Ireland's Privileged Minority* (Kingston, Ont.: McGill-Queen's University Press, 1983); D. Akenson, *Small Differences: Irish Catholics and Irish Protestants, 1815–1921, an International Perspective* (Montreal: McGill-Queen's University Press, 1988); D. Kiberd, *Reinventing Ireland: The Literature of the Modern Nation* (London: Vintage, 1996), esp. pp. 413–67; J. Coakley, 'Religion, Ethnic Identity and the Protestant Minority in the Republic', in W. Crotty and D. Schmitt (eds), *Ireland and the Politics of Change* (London: Routledge, 1998), pp. 86–106; Crawford, *Outside the Glow*; J. Ruane, 'Ethnicity, Religion and Peoplehood: Protestants in France and in Ireland', *Ethnopolitics*, vol. 9, no. 1, 2010, pp. 121–35.
48 Brown, 'Religious Minorities', p. 237.
49 R. Bury, *Buried Lives: The Protestants of Southern Ireland* (Dublin: History Press, 2017), pp. 100 et seq.
50 *CoIG*, 15 February 1924, letter from 'Anglo-Irish'.
51 D. Boyce, '"One last burial": Culture, Counter-revolution and Revolution in Ireland, 1886–1916', in D. Boyce (ed.), *The Revolution in Ireland, 1879–1923* (Dublin: Gill & Macmillan, 1988), p. 135; F. Moffett, *I Also Am of Ireland* (London: BBC Publications, 1985), p. 72: 'there were "them" and "us"'.
52 L. Fleming, *Head or Harp* (London: Barrie & Rockcliff, 1965).
53 N. Ascherson, 'Communist Dropouts', in *New York Review of Books*, 13 August 1970, at http://www.nybooks.com/articles/1970/08/13/communist-dropouts/ (accessed 1 October 2016).
54 *CoIG*, 9 December 1921.
55 *Irish Times*, 13 May 1922.
56 J.H. Bernard to Col. Mitchell, Carnegie Trust, 28 September 1923, TCDDM, MS 2388-93/440; also Hone, *Ireland Since 1922*, p. 6, and N. Robertson, *Crowned Harp* (Dublin: Figgis, 1960), pp. 7, 9.
57 As instances, spontaneous renderings of *God Save the King* at the Armistice Day remembrance in the Phoenix Park in 1931 and 1950 were rare public manifestations of loyalty usually kept close to the chest: McDowell, *Crisis and Decline*, p. 170; *Irish Times*, 15 November 1950. See also H. Jones, 'Cultures of Commemoration: Remembering the First World War in Ireland', in John Crowley, Mike Murphy and Donal Ó Drisceoil (eds), *Atlas of the Irish Revolution* (Cork: Cork University Press, 2017), pp. 844–7. The Church of Ireland's *Church Hymnal* still contained the hymn 'God Save the King'; it did not acquire a rubric—'For use in Northern Ireland'— until the year 2000.
58 J.H. Bernard to Cecil Harmsworth, MP, 11 December 1921, Bernard Papers, NLI, MS 46,624/1.

59 Seanad Éireann, *Debates*, vol. 10, no. 34, col. 1412, 28 November 1928.
60 J. Ruane, 'After Conflict: Protestant Identity in the Gard today', in P. Bénédict, H. Daussy and P.-O. Léchot (eds), *L'identité huguenote: Faire mémoire et écrire l'histoire XVIe-XXXIe siècle* (Geneva: Droz, 2014).
61 R.A. Bennette, *Fighting for the Soul of Germany: The Catholic Struggle for Inclusion After Unification* (Cambridge, MA: Harvard, 2012).
62 Fleming, *Head or Harp*, p. 36.
63 J. Hone, *Duck Soup in the Black Sea* (London: Hamish Hamilton, 1988), p. 238.
64 J. Biggs-Davison and G. Chowdharay-Best, *The Cross of St Patrick: The Catholic Unionist Tradition in Ireland* (Oxford: Kensal Press, 1984), show a Catholic split loyalty, too.
65 *CoIG*, 16 December 1921, Rev. T.W.E. Drury; 11 December 1921.
66 R. Hartford, *Godfrey Day, Missionary, Pastor and Primate* (Dublin, Cork: Talbot Press, 1940), pp. 116–17: message of sympathy from Sir John Leslie to Queen Mary [signed as 'His Majesty's Lieutenant, Monaghan'], 25 January 1936, Leslie papers, NLI, MS 49,495/2/39; also various papers relating to George V's silver jubilee.
67 *Irish Times*, 4 September 1939.
68 Derived, by the author, from gazetteers of London and Dublin in 1925.
69 T. Mohr, 'The Political Significance of the Coinage of the Irish Free State', *Numismatic Society of Ireland Occasional Papers*, no. 55, 2014, pp. 27–52.
70 Though it may be noted that, as late as 1932, the port was described as 'Dun Laoghaire (Kingstown)' in an advertisement in Saorstát Éireann, *Official Handbook*, advertisements, p. 130.
71 A. St Leger, *A History of the Royal Cork Yacht Club* (Cork: RCYC, 2005), p. 201.
72 S. Archer and P. Pearson, *The Royal St George Yacht Club: A History* (n.p: n.d. [1987]), p. 117.
73 O'Brien, *The Irish Times*, pp. 108–11.
74 H. Geoghegan, 'The Three Judges of the Supreme Court of the Irish Free State, 1925–36: Their Backgrounds, Personalities and Mindsets', in F.M. Larkin and N. Dawson (eds), *Lawyers, the Law and History* (Dublin: Four Courts, 2013), pp. 33–4.
75 P. Galloway, *The Most Illustrious Order: The Order of St Patrick and Its Knights* (London: Unicorn, 1999), p. 100.
76 Fitzpatrick, *Descendancy*, p. 53.
77 I. d'Alton, 'Religion as Identity: The Church of Ireland's 1932 Patrician Celebrations', in J. Hill and M. Lyons (eds), *Representing Irish Religious Histories: Historiography, Ideology and Practice* (Cham [Switz]: Palgrave Macmillan, 2017), pp. 197–210.
78 Emerson and Bell (eds), *The Church of Ireland A.D. 432–1932*, pp. 147–66.
79 Emerson and Bell (eds), *The Church of Ireland A.D. 432–1932*, p. 223: the Warden of St Columba's College, Rev. C.B. Armstrong.
80 R. Roddie, 'The Ups and Downs of Irish Methodism's Temperance Crusade', *Bulletin of the Methodist Historical Society of Ireland*, vol. 22, no. 1, 2017, p. 127.
81 Biagini, 'A Challenge to Partition', pp. 22–25.
82 Robertson, *Crowned Harp*, p. 9.

83 R. Foster, *W.B. Yeats A Life. I—the Apprentice Mage* (Oxford: Oxford University Press, 1997), p. 370.
84 R.B. McDowell, *The Church of Ireland 1869–1969* (London, Boston: Routledge & Kegan Paul, 1975), pp. 126–7.
85 J. Ruane and D. Butler, 'Southern Irish Protestants: An Example of De-ethnicisation?', *Nations and Nationalism*, vol. 13, 2007, p. 619.
86 *Cork Constitution*, 22 April 1912.
87 Ruane, 'Ethnicity, Religion and Peoplehood', pp. 121–35; Coakley, 'Religion, Ethnic Identity and the Protestant Minority in the Republic', p. 102.
88 O'Brien, *The Irish Times*, pp. 101–21.
89 Ó Corráin, *Rendering to God and Caesar*, pp. 12–19. This was changed to 'Save the President' in the *Alternative Prayer Book According to the Use of the Church of Ireland* (Dublin: Collins Liturgical Publications, 1984), p. 35. Intriguingly, some clerics use a monarchical form: 'Michael, our President'.
90 Hugh Maude to Dean Lewis-Cosby, RCBL, MS 262/1/1/2/25; copy letter, Maude to Reggie [Ross Williamson], 29 December 1948, MS 262/1/1/2/7.
91 Ó Corráin, *Rendering to God and Caesar*, p. 70, quoting the title of Bishop Arthur Butler's sermon on the eve of the General Synod of the Church of Ireland, 13 May 1965.

2. Defining Loyalty: Southern Irish Protestants and the Irish Grants Committee, 1926–30

1 MacDougall to I.H.J. White, 8 September 1928, IGC papers, TNA, CO 762/186/2.
2 IGC report, 1930, TNA, CO 762/212; *Belfast Newsletter*, 6 February 1930. For more on the work and nature of the IGC, see Niamh Brennan, 'A Political Minefield: Southern Irish Loyalists, the Irish Grants Committee and the British Government, 1922–31', *Irish Historical Studies*, vol. 30, 1997, pp. 406–19; R.B. McDowell, *Crisis and Decline: The Fate of the Southern Unionists* (Dublin: Lilliput Press, 1997), pp. 130–62; Gemma Clark, *Everyday Violence in the Irish Civil War* (Cambridge: Cambridge University Press, 2014), pp. 18–53; Brian Hughes, 'Loyalists and Loyalism in a Southern Irish Community, 1920–1922', *The Historical Journal*, vol. 59, no. 4, 2016, pp. 1075–1105.
3 John Lang claim, TNA, CO 762/186/2.
4 IGC report, 1930, TNA, CO 762/212. Lang received £80.
5 The survey on which this chapter is based relates to claim files catalogued for County Cavan, excluding applicants who may have been incorrectly catalogued or moved from Cavan and were listed under their county of current residence. Several of the ninety-five claimants catalogued for Cavan have also been excluded. Three applicants requested a form but subsequently failed to submit, while six were catalogued as Cavan applicants but claimed for losses suffered in other counties. A box containing one Cavan applicant is missing and that applicant has been excluded. Two single files for losses suffered by two individuals (a married couple and two neighbours) have been enumerated as four individuals.
6 Brennan, 'A Political Minefield', p. 417.

7 IGC, Report of committee, 1930, TNA, CO 762/212.
8 Isabel O'Connor claim, TNA, CO 762/170/22.
9 Mary Fletcher claim, TNA, CO 762/134/11.
10 Ella Browne claim, TNA, CO 762/60/18.
11 Joseph Northridge claim, TNA, CO 762/37/2; Anne Applebe and son claim, TNA, CO 762/37/4.
12 William B. Bradfield claim, TNA, CO 762/186/14.
13 John Alexander Switzer claim, TNA, CO 762/186/15.
14 David Henry Long claim, TNA, CO 762/124/12.
15 James Anderson claim, TNA, CO 762/126/5.
16 Isaac Hill McCombe claim, TNA, CO 762/161/8.
17 MacDougall to IGC, 9 July 1928, in William Irwin claim, TNA, CO 762/174/4.
18 MacDougall to IGC, 6 September 1928, in Johnston Hewitt claim, TNA, CO 762/168/11. The police in Arva at this time were special constables in the RIC ('Black and Tans') rather than Auxiliaries.
19 See, for example, David Fitzpatrick, *Descendancy: Irish Protestant Histories since 1795* (Cambridge: Cambridge University Press, 2014), pp. 157–240; Clark, *Everyday Violence*; Paul Taylor, *Heroes or Traitors? Experiences of Southern Irish Soldiers Returning from the Great War 1919–1939* (Liverpool: Liverpool University Press, 2015); Brian Hughes, *Defying the IRA? Intimidation, Coercion, and Communities during the Irish Revolution* (Liverpool: Liverpool University Press, 2016).
20 John Bolster Barrett claim, PRONI, D989/B/3/8.
21 Charles E. Mayne claim, TNA, CO 762/14/6.
22 Richard B. Reynolds claim, TNA, CO 762/36/5.
23 Leigh-Ann Coffey, *The Planters of Luggacurran, County Laois: A Protestant Community, 1879–1927* (Dublin: Irish Academic Press, 2006), p. 63.
24 Michael Farry, *The Aftermath of Revolution: Sligo, 1921–1923* (Dublin: UCD Press, 2000), p. 193. Farry does not tabulate this but writes that religion was only 'sometimes given': p. 247, n. 60.
25 Hughes, 'Loyalists and Loyalism'; Farry, *Sligo*, p. 193; W.E. Vaughan and A.J. Fitzpatrick (eds), *Irish Historical Statistics: Population, 1821–1971* (Dublin: Royal Irish Academy, 1978), pp. 66–8.
26 See Hughes, 'Loyalists and Loyalism', pp. 1087–9.
27 William B. Hosford claim, TNA, CO 762/4/10.
28 Jessie Hunter claim, TNA, CO 762/51/13; Jessie Hunter, digitised 1911 census returns, http://census.nationalarchives.ie/ (accessed February 2015).
29 Clark, *Everyday Violence*, p. 48.
30 See Hughes, 'Loyalists and Loyalism', p. 1089.
31 Fitzpatrick, *Descendancy*, pp. 181, 212.
32 1911 census returns, Arvagh DED, http://census.nationalarchives.ie/ (accessed February 2015). Thirty-two per cent of the population of the DED were non-Catholic in 1911.
33 Mary Anne Curtis claim, TNA, CO 762/170/4.
34 Simon Henry Hewitt claim, TNA, CO 762/196/3.
35 Bernard Matthews claim, TNA, CO 762/23/1.
36 Simon Henry Hewitt claim, TNA, CO 762/196/3; Johnston Hewitt claim, TNA, CO 762/168/11.

37 Leigh-Ann Coffey, 'Loyalism in Transition: Southern Loyalists and the Irish Free State, 1921–37', in James W. McAuley and Graham Spencer (eds), *Ulster Loyalism after the Good Friday Agreement: History, Identity and Change* (Basingstoke: Palgrave Macmillan, 2011), p. 24. By November 1922, 598 Protestants and 1,063 Catholics had been assisted by the Irish Distress Committee (later the first Irish Grants Committee): Brennan, 'A Political Minefield', p. 407.
38 William Irwin claim, TNA, CO 762/174/4; Frederick Howell claim, TNA, CO 762/66/7.
39 Joseph Arthur Benison claim, TNA, CO 762/14/3.
40 Kate Pinkerton claim, TNA, CO 762/27/16.
41 Coffey, 'Southern Irish Loyalists', pp. 28–30.
42 Reference by William Henry Carleton, 9 January 1930, in Maggie Masterson claim, TNA, CO 762/175/16.
43 Unsuccessful applicants Patrick Drumm and Mary Sheridan had even named MacDougall as one of their referees.
44 Mary Sheridan claim, TNA, CO 762/51/9; Michael J. Culley claim, TNA, CO 762/171/12; Maggie Masterson claim, TNA, CO 762/175/16.
45 Ellen Reilly claim, TNA, CO 762/54/2.
46 Joseph Gordan claim, TNA, CO 762/78/9.
47 John Ryan claim, TNA, CO 762/113/1.
48 Robert Alexander Browne claim, TNA, CO 762/95/20.
49 Edward Goldrick claim, TNA, CO 762/36/14; Travers R. Blackley claim, TNA, CO 762/37/6. See also *Anglo-Celt*, 15 April 1922, 16 February 1924.
50 John Lang claim, TNA, CO 762/186/2.
51 Arthur McClean claim, TNA, CO 762/183/2.
52 Mary Elizabeth Johnstone claim, TNA, CO 762/66/3; Robert H. Johnstone claim, TNA, CO 762/8/6.
53 Robert Alexander Browne claim, TNA, CO 762/95/20.
54 Travers Robert Blackley claim, TNA, CO 762/37/6.
55 Robert Graham claim, TNA, CO 762/164/11.
56 John Ryan claim, TNA, CO 762/113/1.
57 Martha Jackson claim, TNA, CO 762/175/11.
58 John J. Cartwright claim, TNA, CO 762/116/15.
59 George William Nicolls claim, TNA, CO 762/175/18; William Henry Carleton claim, TNA, CO 762/78/6.
60 Peter McBrien claim, TNA, CO 762/58/13.
61 Coffey, 'Southern Irish Loyalists', p. 26.
62 Mary Sheridan claim, TNA, CO 762/51/9. See also Peter McBrien claim, TNA, CO 762/58/13.
63 See Hughes, 'Loyalists and Loyalism'.
64 McDowell, *Crisis and Decline*, p. 87.
65 Fitzpatrick, *Descendancy*, p. 243.
66 Arthur McClean claim, TNA, CO 762/183/2; David Samuel Maguire claim, TNA, CO 762/57/6. Figures for covenanters are derived from a search of the digitised Ulster Covenant signatures for Cavan, https://www.nidirect.gov.uk/services/search-ulster-covenant (accessed April 2015). One of the non-covenanters, Wilson Johnston, was under the prescribed minimum age of sixteen.

67 Arthur McClean, TNA, CO 762/183/2; Robert Graham claim, TNA, CO 762/164/11.
68 Deliberately named the Cavan Volunteer Force by its leader Oliver Nugent.
69 Fitzpatrick, *Descendancy*, p. 244.
70 See, for example, report of UVF patrol in Cootehill: *Meath Chronicle*, 9 April 1921; commandeering of goods by '"A" Company. 1st Battalion, U.V.F.': *Anglo-Celt*, 28 January 1922.
71 The applicants who joined are Robert Smith, TNA, CO 762/103/20; John Markey, TNA, CO 762/9/1; Charles Woods, TNA, CO 762/74/9.
72 Fitzpatrick, *Descendancy*, p. 43; Diane Urquhart, 'Unionism, Orangeism and war', *Women's History Review*, 2016, p. 16, n. 68.
73 Farnham to Montgomery, 13 March 1920, PRONI, D627/435/10.
74 For a recent study of the impact of the border as seen through the testimony provided to the Boundary Commission, see Peter Leary, *Unapproved Routes: Histories of the Irish Border, 1922–1972* (Oxford: Oxford University Press, 2016), pp. 31–59.
75 Henry Saunderson, *The Saundersons of Castle Saunderson* (London: pr. printed, 1936), p. 73.
76 Edward Saunderson to Secretary, Boundary Commission, TNA, CAB/61/131.
77 Henry and Somerset Saunderson claim, TNA, CO 762/91/9.
78 MacDougall to IGC, 6 September 1928, in Johnston Hewitt claim, TNA, IGC, CO 762/168/11.
79 *Irish Free State Compensation: Report of a Committee Presided over by Lord Dunedin* [Cmd. 2746], H.C. 1922; Brennan, 'A Political Minefield', p. 406.
80 *Irish Grants Committee Second Interim Report* [Cmd. 2032], H.C. 1924.
81 See, for example, Lionel Curtis to secretary, provisional government of Ireland, 13 May 1922 in *Liability for the Relief of Irish Refugees* [Cmd 1684], H.C. 1922, xvii, 532; 'IRELAND: Relief of refugees from Irish Free State', TNA, HO 45/11992. A 'Refugee Committee' was also founded by the Ulster Unionist Council for 'refugees' arriving in Northern Ireland: PRONI, D1327/15/6. The phrase is used throughout 1922 and 1923 in the unionist and conservative press, including the *Irish Times*, *Belfast Newsletter*, *Morning Post* and *Daily Mail*.
82 For some of the most recent work on this topic, see R. Bury, *Buried Lives: the Protestants of Southern Ireland* (Dublin: The History Press, 2017); Fitzpatrick, *Descendancy*, pp. 159–80; Bielenberg, 'Exodus', pp. 199–233. Non-Catholic decline in this period was earlier examined by Robert E. Kennedy, *The Irish: Emigration, Marriage, and Fertility* (Berkeley and Los Angeles: University of California Press, 1973), and Kurt Bowen, *Protestants in a Catholic State: Ireland's Privileged Minority* (Montreal: McGill-Queen's University Press, 1983), and was taken up again by Peter Hart, *The I.R.A. at War, 1916–1923* (Oxford: Oxford University Press, 2003), and Enda Delaney, *Demography, State and Society: Irish Migration to Britain, 1921–1971* (Liverpool: Liverpool University Press, 2000).
83 Brennan, 'A Political Minefield', p. 406.
84 Travers Robert Blackley claim, NAI, FIN/COMP/2/2/112.
85 Travers Robert Blackley claim, TNA, CO 762/37/6.

86 James Heaslip claim, TNA, IGC, CO 762/139/1; Arthur McClean claim, TNA, CO 762/183/2.
87 See, for example, Thomas Nagle (Church of Ireland, Cork), TNA, CO 762/3/6; Joseph Hosford (Methodist, Cork), TNA, CO 762/7/12; Richard George Hetherington (Church of Ireland, Limerick), TNA, CO 762/34/11; Pim Goodbody (Church of Ireland, Kildare), TNA, CO 762/85/1; Lewis Richard Lipsett (Church of Ireland, Donegal), TNA, CO 762/175/24.
88 Mary Sheridan claim, TNA, CO 762/51/9; Lizzie Anderson claim, TNA, CO 762/174/30; George Cartwright claim, TNA, CO 762/98/1.
89 'Massacre of Irish Protestants', *c.* May 1922, PRONI, D989/C/1/40.
90 *Irish Examiner*, 1 May 1922. See also *CoIG*, 5 May 1922.
91 Rural dean's reports, Arva, 1919–1922, Representative Church Body Library, D3/1/27, 28A, 28, 29.
92 Terence Dooley, 'Protestant Migration from the Free State to Northern Ireland, 1920–25: A Private Census for Co. Fermanagh', *Clogher Record*, 15/3, 1996, pp. 88–132.
93 See Hughes, *Defying the IRA?*, pp. 201–2.
94 Bielenberg, 'Exodus', pp. 205, 219–21.
95 Simon Henry Hewitt claim, TNA, CO 762/196/13.
96 Richard Hewitt claim, TNA, CO 762/168/12.
97 See Hughes, *Defying the IRA?*, pp. 102–3.

3. Peace, Protestantism and the Unity of Ireland: The Career of Bolton C. Waller

1 Walter Starkie, *Scholars and Gypsies: An Autobiography* (London: John Murray, 1963), pp. 109–10.
2 Terence Brown, *Ireland: A Social and Cultural History, 1922–1985* (London: Fontana, 1985), p. 109.
3 Sir Bernard Burke, *A Genealogical and Heraldic History of the Landed Gentry of Ireland* (revised by A.C. Fox-Davies) (London: Harrison & Sons, 1912), pp. 734–5; Edward MacLysaght, *The Surnames of Ireland* (Dublin: Irish Academic Press, 1980), pp. 295–6.
4 Canon J.B. Leslie, *Clergy of Limerick, Clergy of Ardfert and Aghadoe: Biographical Succession Lists* (revised by Canon D.W.T. Crooks) (Belfast: Ulster Historical Foundation, 2015), pp. 512–15.
5 *A Catalogue of Graduates of the University of Dublin*, IV (Dublin: Longmans, Green, 1917), p. 103; *The Dublin University Calendar, being a Special Supplemental Volume for the Year 1912–1913* (Dublin: Longmans, Green, 1913), pp. 75, 260; *The Dublin University Calendar for the Year 1915–1916* (Dublin: Longmans, Green, 1916), p. 56.
6 Margaret Cunningham (ed.), *Looking at Ireland* (London: Student Christian Movement Press, 1937), p. 10.
7 *Irish Times*, 28 October 1912. See also Dermot Meleady, *John Redmond: The National Leader* (Sallins, Co. Kildare: Merrion, 2013), p. 223.
8 See Tomás Irish, *Trinity in War and Revolution, 1912–1923* (Dublin: Royal Irish Academy, 2015), p. 56.
9 *Freeman's Journal*, 28 October 1912.
10 Undated clipping from unknown newspaper [November 1912], NLI, Redmond Papers, MS 15,254.

11 *Irish Times,* 6 November 1914.
12 See Oonagh Walsh (ed.), *An Englishwoman in Belfast: Rosamond Stephen's Record of the Great War* (Cork: Cork University Press, 2000), esp. introduction, pp. 1–15.
13 Horace Plunkett, *A Better Way: An Appeal to Ulster not to Desert Ireland* (Dublin: Hodges, Figgis, and London: Simpkin, Marshall, 1914), pp. 23–4.
14 For figures, see David Fitzpatrick, 'The Logic of Collective Sacrifice: Ireland and the British Army, 1914–1918', *The Historical Journal,* vol. 38, no. 4, December 1995, pp. 1017–30, at 1017–18.
15 Bolton C. Waller, *Paths to World-peace* (London: G. Allen & Unwin, 1926), p. 7.
16 *Irish Times,* 29 July 1936.
17 Waller to H.O. White, 19 September 1916, Dermod O'Brien papers, TCDDM, MS 4294/142-187.
18 'Unificus' [Bolton Waller], *Ireland's Opportunity: A Plea for Settlement by Conference* (London: King, 1916). For Waller's authorship of this pamphlet, see Wilbraham Fitzjohn Trench, *The Way to Fellowship in Irish Life* (London: Student Christian Fellowship, 1919), p. 24.
19 *Irish Times,* 13 April 1917; *The Times* 13 April 1917.
20 See R.B. McDowell, *The Irish Convention, 1917–18* (London: Routledge & Kegan Paul, and Toronto: University of Toronto Press, 1970), p. 181.
21 See, for example, Waller to Art Ó Bríain, 5 October 1921, Art Ó Bríain papers, NLI, MS 8427/28.
22 *Irish Statesman,* 13 March 1920. See also Henry Harrison, *The Irish Case Considered: A Remonstrance Addressed to the British Public* (London: Irish Dominion League, 1920).
23 For this group, see Colin Reid, *The Lost Ireland of Stephen Gwynn: Irish Constitutional Nationalism and Cultural Politics, 1864–1950* (Manchester: Manchester University Press, 2011), pp. 183–4.
24 *Freeman's Journal,* 6 August 1920. The letter also appeared in the *Irish Times,* 4 August 1920.
25 *Irish Times,* 4 November 1921.
26 David Fitzpatrick, *'Solitary and Wild': Frederick MacNeice and the Salvation of Ireland* (Dublin: Lilliput, 2012), pp. 166–8.
27 Waller to MacNeice, 22 August 1922, in Fitzpatrick, *'Solitary and Wild',* p. 168.
28 Ronan Fanning, Michael Kennedy, Dermot Keogh and Eunan O'Halpin (eds), *Documents on Irish Foreign Policy,* II, *1923–1926* (Dublin: Royal Irish Academy, 2000), p. xxv.
29 K.J. Rankin, 'The Provenance and Dissolution of the Irish Boundary Commission', *Working Papers in British-Irish Studies,* no. 79, 2006, p. 12.
30 Eda Sagarra, *Kevin O'Shiel: Tyrone Nationalist and Irish State-builder* (Sallins: Irish Academic Press, 2013), p. 204.
31 'Memorandum on European precedents for the North Eastern Boundary Bureau', by B.C. Waller, NAI NEBB 1/3/3, p. 4.
32 Paul Murray, *The Irish Boundary Commission and Its Origins, 1886–1925* (Dublin: University College Dublin Press, 2011), p. 252.
33 Proposed settlement with Northern Ireland: report of the Cabinet committee, appointed 1 October 1924, NAI, Department of the Taoiseach, S4084.

34 Jonathan Bardon, *A History of Ulster* (Belfast: The Blackstaff Press, 2001), p. 508.
35 Extract from a memorandum by Bolton Waller on admission to the League of Nations, 24 March 1923, in Fanning, Kennedy, Keogh and O'Halpin (eds), *Documents on Irish Foreign Policy,* II, pp. 74–7.
36 *CoIG,* 7 May 1926; *Irish Times,* 22 January 1927.
37 Waller, *Paths to World-peace,* pp. 8, 9.
38 *CoIG,* 7 May 1926.
39 Bolton C. Waller, *Ireland and the League of Nations* (Dublin: Talbot Press, 1925), p. 73.
40 Saorstát Éireann, *Census of Population, 1926, Religions and Birthplaces* (Dublin: Stationery Office, 1929), vol. 3, p. l.
41 For references to the League's work on peaceful arbitration and minority rights, see *Concord,* September 1927, January, February 1928, January, April 1929.
42 Nominal data derived from *Irish League of Nations Society,* leaflet no. 6, 7 December 1923.
43 Bryan Cooper, Senator James G. Douglas, Stephen Gwynn, Sir John Lumsden, George Russell (Æ); Bolton C. Waller.
44 *Belfast News-Letter,* 1 June 1927.
45 *Irish Times,* 1 June 1927.
46 Final tally: William Thrift, 614; Sir James Craig, 415; Ernest Alton, 400; and Bolton C. Waller, 393.
47 *Irish Times,* 3 August 1936.
48 Peter Martin, *Censorship in the Two Irelands: 1922–39* (Dublin: Irish Academic Press, 2006), p. 82. Waller's correspondent was Michael Tierney.
49 Bolton C. Waller, *Hibernia, or the Future of Ireland* (London: K. Paul, Trench, Trubner and New York: Dutton, 1928), p. 68. See, similarly, enthusiastically received comments to the Church of Ireland Young Men's Christian Association, in Dawson Street, Dublin: *Irish Times,* 17 October 1929.
50 Waller, *Hibernia,* p. 82.
51 Waller, *Hibernia,* p. 92.
52 Irish, *Trinity in War and Revolution,* p. 255.
53 Bolton C. Waller, *Thomas Davis (1814–1845): a Commemorative Address, Delivered in the Chapel of Trinity College, Dublin, on Trinity Monday, 1930* (Dublin: Printed at the Dublin University Press by Ponsonby and Gibbs, 1930), pp. 7, 12.
54 *The Standard,* quoted in *Kerry Champion,* 28 June 1930.
55 Canon J.B. Leslie, *Clergy of Dublin and Glendalough: Biographical Succession Lists* (rev., ed. and updated by W.J.R. Wallace) (Belfast: Irish Historical Foundation, 2001), p. 1145. See also *CoIG,* 6 February 1931; 28 February, 29 May 1936.
56 *Irish Times,* 11 May 1933, 23 April 1934, 23 September 1936. For the Friends of Reunion in Ireland, see Alan Megahey, *The Irish Protestant Churches in the Twentieth Century* (Basingstoke: Macmillan, 2000), pp. 127–8.
57 Marie Coleman, *The Irish Sweep: A History of the Irish Hospitals' Sweepstake 1930–87* (Dublin: University College Dublin Press, 2009), p. 14.

58 Rev. Bolton C. Waller, *Sweepstakes: Some Hard Facts* (Dublin: Church of Ireland Printing & Publishing Co., 1932); also Rev. B.C. Waller, 'Gambling', in Rev. W. Bell and Rev. N.D. Emerson (eds), *The Church of Ireland A.D. 432–1932: the Report of the Church of Ireland Conference held in Dublin, 11th–14th October 1932* . . . (Dublin: Church of Ireland Printing and Publishing Co., 1932), pp. 191–5.
59 Rev. Bolton C. Waller, *The Pope's Claims and Why We Reject Them* (Dublin: Association for Promotion of Christian Knowledge, 1932).
60 See Martha Kavanagh, 'The Irish Free State and Collective Security, 1930–36', *Irish Studies in International Affairs,* vol. 15, 2004, pp. 103–22, esp. 115–17.
61 See, for example, *Irish Times,* 19 September 1935, 24, 27 April, 4 May 1936.
62 Jacqueline Hurtley, *Walter Starkie, 1894–1976: An Odyssey* (Dublin: Four Courts Press, 2013), p. 233.
63 *CoIG,* 31 July 1936.
64 *Irish Times,* 29 July 1936.
65 Cunningham (ed.), *Looking at Ireland.*
66 Papers relating to the Bolton Waller Memorial Trust, NAI, M3578.

4. This 'rotten little Republic': Protestant Identity and the 'State Prayers' Controversy, 1948–9

1 In this chapter, the term 'southern Ireland' refers to the twenty-six counties which currently comprise the Republic of Ireland. For a contextual political overview of the State Prayers controversy, see D. Ó Corráin, *Rendering to God and Caesar: The Irish Churches and the Two States in Ireland, 1949–73* (Manchester: Manchester University Press, 2006), pp. 12–19.
2 Unless otherwise specified, or clear from the context, throughout the chapter the term 'Protestant' refers to members of the Church of Ireland.
3 *Irish Times*, 17, 24 November, 3 December 1948.
4 *Irish Times*, 11 December 1948.
5 *Irish Times*, 10, 11 December 1948.
6 *Irish Press*, 25 November 1948; *Irish Independent*, 25 November 1948; *Irish Times*, 10 December 1948.
7 *CoIG*, 28 January 1949. See also *CoIG*, 28 January 1949 (letter from J. Riversdale Colthurst); ibid., 11 February 1949 (letters from James B. Leslie and Edward J. Moore); *Irish Times*, 2 May 1949 (letter from Douglas I.C. Dunlop); Cecil Proctor to Hugh Maude, 28 April 1949, RCBL, MS 262/1/1/2/37.
8 *CoIG*, 17 February 1950 (letter from A.W. Cotton); *Irish Times*, 13 June 1949 (letter from 'Another Protestant').
9 Hugh Maude to Dean [Wilson] of St Patrick's, 19 January 1949, RCBL, MS 262/1/1/2/17; Rina [Ingram] to Hugh Maude, 31 October 1949, MS 262/1/1/4/147; [Mrs] D.N. Weir to Hugh Maude, 3 November 1949, MS 262/1/1/5/154.
10 Cecil S. King-Harmon to Hugh Maude, 7 May 1949, RCBL, MS 262/1/1/3/56.
11 Bob [Ashtown] to Hugh Maude, 5 May 1949, RCBL, MS 262/1/1/3/53.

12 The State Prayers controversy impacted only on the Church of Ireland, as prayers for secular leaders are not included in the liturgy of the Catholic Church; and, although they form part of the Presbyterian and Methodist services, this takes place in an extempore fashion and therefore does not require a formalised wording.
13 *Irish Times*, 8 June 1935, 19 February 1960, 20 March 1982.
14 Hugh Maude to Ynyr [Bruges], 19 April 1949, RCBL, MS 262/1/1/2/30.
15 Hugh Maude to Reggie [Ross Williamson], 25 December 1948, RCBL, MS 262/1/1/2/3; Hugh Maude to St John Ervine, 25 December 1948, MS 262/1/1/2/4; [Lord] Templemore to Hugh Maude, 2 January 1949, MS 262/1/1/2/12.
16 *CoIG*, 14 January 1949 (letter from H.A.C. Maude).
17 *CoIG*, 28 January 1949 (letter from A.A. Luce).
18 *CoIG*, 11 February 1949 (letters from A.W. Cotton, 'Celtic Christian', A.E. Gray); ibid., 18 February 1949 (letter from Martin Townsend); ibid., 28 January 1949 (letters from Ernest M. Bateman, D.A. Webb and F.H. Garrett).
19 *CoIG*, 4 February 1949 (letter from 'Celtic Christian'); *Irish Times*, 13 June 1949 (letter from 'Another Protestant').
20 Hugh Maude to Primate, 16 June 1949, RCBL, MS 262/1/1/3/93.
21 John [Gregg], to Hugh Maude, 22 June 1949, RCBL, MS 262/1/1/3/98.
22 Hugh Maude to Rina [Ingram], 29 June 1949, 1 July 1949, RCBL, MSS 262/1/1/4/101, 262/1/1/4/108.
23 J. Riversdale Colthurst to Hugh Maude, 'Confidential', 30 July 1949, RCBL, MS 262/1/1/4/120; [Lord] Templemore to Hugh Maude, 11 July 1949, MS 262/1/1/4/110; Hugh Maude to [J.R.] Colthurst, 10 August 1949, MS 262/1/1/4/122.
24 E.H. Lewis-Cosby to Hugh Maude, 17 September 1949, RCBL, MS 262/1/1/4/123; J.R. Colthurst to Hugh Maude, 24 September 1949, MS 262/1/1/4/124.
25 Hugh Maude to Lord Templemore, 1 November 1949, RCBL, MS 262/1/1/5/151.
26 J.R. Colthurst to Hugh Maude, 22 February 1950, RCBL, MS 262/1/1/5/186; Hugh Maude to Mr Barton, n.d., MS 262/1/1/5/197A; same to F. Fitzgibbon, 10 November 1949, MS 262/1/1/5/156.
27 The wordings in use before this episode, and the amended wording approved in 1950, are appended to this chapter
28 Hugh Maude to Rina [Ingram], 24 November 1949, RCBL, MS 262/1/1/5/168.
29 *CoIG*, 13 August 1920 (editorial). See also comments by T.S. Berry, bishop of Killaloe, in *CoIG*, 16 February 1917 (editorial notices).
30 Karin Fischer, 'Another Irish Nation: Some Historiographical Variations as Found in Late Nineteenth and Early Twentieth Century Schools', *Canadian Journal of Irish Studies*, vol. 30, no. 1, Spring, 2004, pp. 41–47.
31 *CoIG*, 19 November 1915 (letter from 'Member of Irish Guild of the Church'). See also ibid., 2 March 1917 (letter from Leslie Handy).
32 Robbie Roulston, 'Reassessing the Church of Ireland's Relationship with the Irish State in Education: An Archival Approach', *Irish Archives*, 2014, pp. 51–62.

33 Victor Griffin, *Mark of Protest* (Dublin: Gill & Macmillan, 1993), p. 29.
34 Ian d'Alton, '"A Vestigial Population"?: Perspectives on Southern Irish Protestants in the Twentieth Century', *Éire-Ireland*, vol. 44, nos 3 & 4, Fall/Winter 2009, pp. 9–42.
35 Homan Potterton, *Rathcormick: A Childhood Recalled* (Dublin: New Island, 2001), p. 177; Griffin, *Mark of Protest*, pp. 22–3.
36 C.I.R., 'Gigmanity uprooted', *The Bell*, vol. 11, no. 2, November 1945, pp. 694–5. C.I.R. had joined the GAA and Fianna Fáil.
37 *Irish Times*, 14 May 1949.
38 *Irish Times*, 14 May (editorial), 20 May 1949 (letter from 'Clareman').
39 *Irish Times*, 13 June 1949 (letter from 'Another Protestant'); *Our Church Review*, May 1949 (letter from Rev. E.G. Daunt).
40 *CoIG*, 4 February 1949 (letter from A.E. Gray).
41 Hugh Maude to Dean Lewis-Cosby, undated, RCBL, MS 262/1/1/2/25; same to Mrs Kennedy, undated, MS 262/1/1/4/138A; same to Rector [of Clondalkin], 11 May 1949, MS 262/1/1/3/65. See also same to J.R. Colthurst, 29 October 1949, MS 262/1/1/4/144.
42 Hugh Maude to Primate, 16 June 1949, RCBL, MS 262/1/1/3/93.
43 Rina [Ingram] to Hugh Maude, 7 November 1949, RCBL, MS 262/1/1/5/155.
44 Lionel Fleming, *Head or Harp* (London: Barrie & Rockliff, 1965), pp. 99–105; Jack White, 'Inside Trinity College', *The Bell*, vol. 10, no. 1, April 1945, p. 71.
45 R.B. McDowell, *Crisis and Decline: The Fate of the Southern Unionists* (Dublin: Lilliput Press, 1997), pp. 170–1.
46 White, 'Inside Trinity College', p. 71.
47 Hugh Maude to Reggie [Ross Williamson], 29 December 1948, RCBL, MS 262/1/1/2/7; Ynyr [Bruges] to Hugh Maude, 5 February 1949, MS 262/1/1/2/22.
48 *Irish Times*, 20 May 1949 (letter from 'Clareman'); ibid., 13 June 1949 (letter from 'Emilius'); *CoIG*, 25 February 1949 (letter from Rev. R.F. Hipwell, Castleventry, County Cork); *Irish Times*, 20 November 1948 (letter from J.S. Judge, Castlebar, County Mayo).
49 W.A. King-Harmon to Hugh Maude, 12 May 1949, RCBL, MS 262/1/1/3/66.
50 Quoted in Mary Kenny, *Crown and Shamrock: Love and Hate between Ireland and the British Monarchy* (Dublin: New Island, 2009), p. 265.
51 J. Riversdale Colthurst to Hugh Maude, 10 November 1949, RCBL, MS 262/1/1/5/159.
52 Quoted in Ian Shaw et al. (eds), *Sage Handbook of Social Work Research* (London: Sage Publications, 2010), p. 116.
53 *CoIG*, 19 November 1915 (letter from 'Member of Irish Guild of the Church').
54 *CoIG*, 14 January 1949; Hugh Maude to D.A. Webb, undated, RCBL, MS 262/1/1/3/60; Hugh Maude to Mr [Charles] Carson, 26 November 1949, MS 262/1/1/5/169A. See also Hugh Maude to the editor, *The Times*, 25 December 1948, MS 262/1/1/2/5; [Lord] Templemore to Hugh Maude, 20 January 1949, MS 262/1/1/2/17A.
55 Hugh Maude to Dean [Lewis-Cosby], 16 May 1949, RCBL, MS 262/1/1/3/69.

56 J.R. Colthurst to Hugh Maude, 2 December 1949, RCBL, MS 262/1/1/5/174; Hugh Maude to J.R. Colthurst, 3 December 1949, MS 262/1/1/5/174A. See also T.F. Campbell to Hugh Maude, 4 June 1949, MS 262/1/1/3/82; Charles Carson to Hugh Maude, 21 November 1949, MS 262/1/1/5/169; [Lord] Templemore to Primate Gregg, 6 February 1949, MS 262/1/1/2/21c; *CoIG*, 28 January 1949 (letters from A.A Luce, W.C.G. Proctor and Ernest M. Bateman).

57 Maude to Rector [of Clondalkin], 11 May 1949, RCBL, MS 262/1/1/3/65.

58 R.M. Morris, *Church and State in 21st Century Britain: The Future of Church Establishment* (Basingstoke: Palgrave Macmillan, 2009), p. 37.

59 Charles Carson to Hugh Maude, St Andrew's Day [30 November] 1949, RCBL, MS 262/1/1/5/170A.

60 Hugh Maude to Mr [Charles] Carson, 26 November 1949, RCBL, MS 262/1/1/5/169A.

61 *Journal of the Twenty-sixth General Synod of the Church of Ireland, 1949* (Dublin: APCK, 1949), pp. lxxxiii–iv.

62 W.E. White to Hugh Maude, 23 April 1949, RCBL, MS 262/1/1/2/32; same to same, 27 April 1949, MS 262/1/1/2/34; Edward F. Grant to Hugh Maude, undated, MS 262/1/1/2/39.

63 See, for instance, Arthur [Barton] to Hugh Maude, 16 May 1949, RCBL, MS 262/1/1/3/68; John [Gregg] to Hugh Maude, 22 June 1949, MS 262/1/1/3/98.

64 *CoIG*, 4 March 1949 (letter from A.E. Gray, Castlelyons).

65 J.R. Colthurst to Hugh Maude, 24 September 1949, RCBL, MS 262/1/1/4/123; Hugh Maude to Colthurst, 26 September 1949, MS 262/1/1/126; W.A. King-Harmon to Hugh Maude, 12 May 1949, MS 262/1/1/3/62.

66 Hugh Maude to Rina [Ingram], 1 July 1949, RCBL, MS 262/1/1/4/102; Hugh Maude to [J.R.] Colthurst, 10 August 1949, MS 262/1/1/4/122; J. Riversdale Colthurst to Hugh Maude, 19 July 1949, MS 262/1/1/4/11; J. Riversdale Colthurst to Hugh Maude, 'confidential', 30 July 1949, MS 262/1/1/4/120.

67 *Kilmore and Elphin and Ardagh Diocesan Gazette*, April 1949.

68 *Diocesan Magazine of the United Diocese of Killaloe, Kilfenora, Clonfert and Kilmacduagh*, January 1949; see also March, April, May 1949.

69 Hugh Maude to St John Ervine, 25 December 1948, RCBL, MS 262/1/1/2/4; Hugh Maude to Dean [Lewis-Cosby], 31 May 1949 MS 262/1/1/3/78.

70 Doris Kennedy to Hugh Maude, 5 January 1950, RCBL, MS 262/1/1/5/184; same to same, 27 October [1949], MS 262/1/1/4/138C.

71 *The Book of Common Prayer and Administration of the Sacraments and Other Rites and Ceremonies of the Church According to the Use of the Church of Ireland* (Dublin: APCK, 1936), pp. 16–70, 30–3.

72 *Journal of the Second Session of the Twenty-seventh General Synod of the Church of Ireland, 1950* (Dublin: APCK, 1950), appendix B, pp. cxxiv–cxxxi.

5. Count on Us Too: Wanting to be Heard in Independent Ireland

1 I thank the Reconciliation Fund (Department of Foreign Affairs and Trade) for supporting this research, which is carried out in collaboration with the National Folklore Collection at University College Dublin.

2 For the sake of brevity, the area now known as the Republic of Ireland is referred to as 'Ireland'.

3 M. Macourt, *Counting the People of God? The Census of Population and the Church of Ireland* (Dublin: Church of Ireland Publishing, 2008), p. 111.
4 D. Fitzpatrick, *Descendancy: Irish Protestant Histories since 1795* (Cambridge: Cambridge University Press, 2014), p. 3.
5 E. Biagini, 'The Protestant Minority in Southern Ireland', *The Historical Journal*, vol. 55, no. 4, 2012, pp. 1163–4.
6 K. Lysaght, 'Living in a Nation, a State or a Place? The Protestant Gentry of County Cork', *National Identities*, 2009, vol. 11, no. 1, p. 64.
7 G. Doherty, 'National Identity and the Study of Irish History', *The English Historical Review,* 1996, vol. 111, no. 441, p. 326.
8 Ibid., p. 342.
9 T. Banjeglav, 'Conflicting Memories, Competing Narratives and Contested Histories in Croatia's Post-war Commemorative Practices', *Croatian Political Science Review*, vol. 49, no. 5, 2012, p. 8.
10 Ibid.
11 J. Ruane, 'Ethnicity, Religion and Peoplehood: Protestants in France and in Ireland', *Ethnopolitics*, vol. 9, no. 1, 2010, pp. 121–35.
12 M. Elliott, *When God Took Sides: Religion and Identity in Ireland—Unfinished History* (Oxford: Oxford University Press, 2009), p. 10.
13 F. Barth, *Ethnic Groups and Boundaries: The Social Organisation of Culture Difference* (Long Grove: Waveland Press, 1998), p. 9.
14 B. Misztal, *Theories of Social Remembering* (Maidenhead: Open University Press, 2003), p. 15.
15 Justices of the Peace sat with resident magistrates to try minor offences and with county judges and juries for more serious offences. The role was permanently abolished by the Courts of Justice Act in 1924: http://www.irishstatutebook.ie/eli/1923/act/6/section/4/enacted/en/html#sec4 (accessed 9 March 2017).
16 T. Guinnane, *The Vanishing Irish: Households, Migration, and the Rural Economy in Ireland, 1850–1914* (Princeton: Princeton University Press, 1997), p. 75.
17 http://www.cso.ie/en/media/csoie/census/census1926results/volume3/C,19,1926,V3,T16.pdf (accessed 20 January 2017).
18 M. Elliott, 'Religion and Identity in Modern Irish History', *Faculty of History Alumni Newsletter no. 3*, Oxford University, May 2005.
19 'Shirley' is a Dublin woman in her forties from a working-class, inner-city background, interviewed in December 2013.
20 J. Dingley, 'Religion, Protestants and National Identity: A Response to the March 2009 Issue', *National Identities*, vol. 15, no. 2, 2013, p. 109.
21 B. Graham, 'The Imagining of Place: Representation and Identity in Contemporary Ireland', in B. Graham (ed.), *In Search of Ireland: A Cultural Geography* (London: Routledge, 1997), p. 193.
22 B. Graham, 'Ireland and Irishness: Place, Culture and Identity', in B. Graham (ed.), *In Search of Ireland*, p. 8.
23 A. Megahey, *The Irish Protestant Churches in the Twentieth Century* (London: Palgrave Macmillan, 2000), p. 109.
24 'Harold', in his forties, is a Dubliner from a working-class, inner-city background, having grown up in social housing, interviewed in December 2013.
25 This quote, even if jokingly said, points up uninformed stereotypical attitudes, and also sometimes the unreliability of memory and oral testimony. Sean Moore,

born 1913, was of working-class stock, a Fianna Fáil TD for 17 years, sometime Lord Mayor of Dublin, and a parliamentarian who had nothing to do with the IRA.

26 'Donald', in his mid-fifties, is a Dublin man who describes himself as coming from a 'lower middle-class' city background, interviewed in November 2013.

27 'Heather', a woman in her late forties, is from a small-farm rural background and grew up in a border area, interviewed in January 2014.

28 'Priscilla', in her seventies, grew up on a small farm in the midlands, interviewed in May 2014.

29 Macourt, *Counting the People of God?*, p. 61.

30 'Penelope', in her seventies, grew up on a small farm in the west, interviewed in November 2014.

31 'William' is from a small-farm/labouring background in the west, interviewed in March 2015.

32 'Henry', in his fifties, is from a middle-class Dublin background, 'with some Loyalist sympathies', interviewed in November 2014.

33 'Eleanora', in her seventies, is from a farming background in the west, interviewed in May 2014.

34 C. Murphy and L. Adair, *Untold Stories: Protestants in the Republic of Ireland, 1922–2002* (Dublin: The Liffey Press, 2002), p. 57.

35 E. Broderick, *The Boycott at Fethard-on-Sea, 1957: A Study in Catholic–Protestant Relations in Modern Ireland* (Newcastle: Cambridge Scholars Publishing, 2011).

36 T. Fanning, *The Fethard-on-Sea Boycott* (Cork: The Collins Press, 2010), p. 72.

37 Broderick, *Boycott,* p. 12.

38 Ibid., p. 17.

39 G. Hogan, 'A Fresh Look at Tilson's Case', *Irish Jurist*, vol. xxxiii, 1998, p. 311.

40 F. Kennedy, *Family, Economy and Government in Ireland* (Dublin: The Economic and Social Research Institute, 1989).

41 Megahey, *The Irish Protestant Churches*, p. 118.

42 D. Jameson, 'The Religious Upbringing of Children in "Mixed Marriages": The Evolution of Irish Law', *New Hibernia Review*, vol. 18, 2014, p. 79.

43 Jameson, 'Religious Upbringing', p. 72.

44 Megahey, *The Irish Protestant Churches*, p. 119.

45 Broderick, *Boycott,* p. 37.

46 'Dorcas', in her eighties, comes from a rural background in the west, interviewed together with her husband 'Ian', of a similar age and background, in April 2014.

47 'Mabel', in her seventies, is from a farming background in the midlands, interviewed in October 2014.

48 'Albert', in his seventies, is from a farming background in the west, interviewed in November 2014.

49 R. Johnston, *Century of Endeavour: A Biographical and Autobiographical View of the Twentieth Century in Ireland* (Dublin: Tyndall Publications in Association with the Lilliput Press, 2003). On the other hand, in some cases the financial pressure caused by sending children away to boarding school may have been an agent of women's empowerment, as many women returned to work, or started running guest houses or other rural businesses so as to fund school fees: C. O'Connor, 'The Church of Ireland Diocese of

Ferns, 1945–65: A Female Perspective', in M. Busteed, F. Neal and J. Tonge, *Irish Protestant Identities* (Manchester: Manchester University Press, 2008), p. 121.

50 'Thomas', in his nineties, is from a rural border area, interviewed in May 2014.

51 For a more detailed discussion of Protestants and the GAA, see Ida Milne's essay in this volume.

6. Gentry Inclusion via Class Politics? Negotiating Class Transition Politically in the Irish Free State

1 For discussion of their public lives, see T. Varley, '"The Class that Goes to the Wall": Colonel George O'Callaghan-Westropp, Class Politics and Identity in Cumann na nGaedheal Ireland', in J. Cunningham and N. Ó Ciosáin (eds), *Culture and Society in Ireland Since 1750: Essays in Honour of Gearóid Ó Tuathaigh* (Dublin: Lilliput Press, 2015), pp. 219–45; and T. Varley, 'Bobby Burke', in E. O'Connor and J. Cunningham (eds), *Studies in Irish Radical Leadership: Lives on the Left* (Manchester: Manchester University Press, 2016), pp. 163–74. In this collection, the essay by Philip Bull on Edward Richards-Orpen is complementary to many of the arguments made here.

2 A. Bielenberg, 'Exodus: The Emigration of Southern Protestants during the Irish War of Independence and the Civil War', *Past & Present*, no. 218, February 2013, p. 204; T. Dooley, *The Decline of the Big House in Ireland: A Study of Irish Landed Families 1860–1960* (Dublin: Wolfhound Press, 2001), pp. 286–7; J.S. Donnelly Jr., 'Big House Burnings in County Cork During the Irish Revolution, 1920–21', *Éire-Ireland*, vol. 47, nos. 3 & 4, 2012, pp. 141–2; R. Bury, *Buried Lives: The Protestants of Southern Ireland* (Dublin: History Press, 2017), chap. 3.

3 F.S.L. Lyons, 'The Minority Problem in the 26 Counties', in F. MacManus (ed.), *The Years of the Great Test 1926–39* (Cork: Mercier Press, 1967), p. 93; J. Rudd, '"Cast a Cold Eye": A Sociological Approach', in J. Genet (ed.), *The Big House in Ireland: Reality and Representation* (Dingle: Brandon, 1991), pp. 38–41; I. d'Alton, '"A Vestigial Population"? Perspectives on Southern Irish Protestants in the Twentieth Century', *Éire-Ireland*, vol. 44, nos 3 & 4, 2009, pp. 227–9; G. Ó Tuathaigh, 'Irish Land Questions in the State of the Union', in F. Campbell and T. Varley (eds), *Land Questions in Modern Ireland* (Manchester: Manchester University Press, 2013), pp. 14–15.

4 Lyons 'Minority Problem', pp. 99–100; see J. Coakley, 'Religion, Ethnic Identity and the Protestant Minority in the Republic', in W. Crotty and D.E. Schmitt (eds), *Ireland and the Politics of Change* (London: Longman, 1998), p. 88.

5 Lyons, 'Minority Problem', pp. 101–2. For some recent discussions of the 'integration', 'assimilation', 'de-nationalisation', 'de-ethnicisation', 'exclusion' and 'marginalisation' of southern Irish Protestants since independence, see Coakley, 'Religion, Ethnic Identity and the Protestant Minority in the Republic'; J. Ruane and D. Butler, 'Southern Irish Protestants: An Example of De-ethnicisation?', *Nations and Nationalism*, vol. 13, no. 4, 2010, pp. 619–35; B.C. Hayes and T. Fahey, 'Protestant Politics in the Republic of Ireland: Is Integration Complete?', in M. Busteed, F. Neal and J.

Tonge (eds), *Irish Protestant Identities* (Manchester: Manchester University Press, 2008); d'Alton, '"A Vestigial Population"?'; and H. Crawford, *Outside the Glow: Protestants and Irishness in Independent Ireland* (Dublin: UCD Press, 2010), pp. 197–205.

6 Lyons, 'Minority Problem', p. 93; Dooley, *Decline of the Big House,* pp. 232–40; J.H. Whyte, 'Political Life in the South', in M. Hurley (ed.), *Irish Anglicanism 1869–1969* (Dublin: Allen Figgis, 1970), p. 145.

7 Lyons, 'Minority Problem', p. 101; see also D. Cannadine, *The Decline and Fall of the British Aristocracy* (London: Picador, 1992), pp. 178–9; Coakley, 'Religion, Ethnic Identity and the Protestant Minority in the Republic', pp. 96–9.

8 For a discussion of the differences between Ireland's minor and major gentry, see F. Campbell, *The Irish Establishment 1879–1914* (Oxford: Oxford University Press, 2009), pp. 17–18. In the mid-1870s the O'Callaghans of Maryfort owned 4,842 acres (poor law valuation (plv) £1,919 10s.), the Burkes of Ballydugan 1,574 acres (plv £905 5s.): *Land Owners in Ireland: Returns of Owners of Land of One Acre and Upwards in the Several Counties, Counties of Cities, and Counties of Towns in Ireland* (Dublin, 1876 [Baltimore, Md.: Genealogical Publishing Co., 1988], pp. 112, 294.

9 P. Bew, *Enigma: A New Life of Charles Stewart Parnell* (Dublin: Gill & Macmillan, 2012), p. 61.

10 Bew, *Enigma,* pp. 61, 21–2, 74–5, 80, 194–5; Cannadine, *Decline,* pp. 167–8, 475–80; R.B. McDowell, *Crisis and Decline: The Fate of the Southern Unionists* (Dublin: Lilliput Press, 1997), pp. 168–9. For Horace Plunkett's strain of 'inclusionism', see his *Noblesse Oblige: An Irish Rendering* (Dublin: Maunsel & Co., 1908).

11 M. Davitt, *The Fall of Feudalism in Ireland or the Story of the Land League Revolution* (London and New York: Harper & Brothers, 1904), p. 155. Davitt uttered these words at the Westport rally of 8 June 1879 that became a milestone in the Land League's formation. Just before they occur in his text, it is notable that Davitt praises Parnell (another speaker in Westport and an Irish landlord) not just for his courage in appearing on the platform but for his memorable speech (ibid., pp. 151–4; see also T.W. Moody, *Davitt and Irish Revolution 1846–82* (Oxford: Clarendon Press, 1982), pp. 296–306).

12 L.P. Curtis Jr., 'Demonising the Irish Landlords Since the Famine', in B. Casey (ed.), *Defying the Law of the Land: Agrarian Radicals in Irish History* (Dublin: The History Press, 2013), pp. 20–43; D.S. Jones, *Graziers, Land Reform, and Political Conflict in Ireland* (Washington: The Catholic University of America Press, 1995), pp. 238–9.

13 P. Bew, *Conflict and Conciliation in Ireland 1890–1910: Parnellites and Radical Agrarians* (Oxford: Oxford University Press, 1978), p. 32; R.V. Comerford, *Ireland* (London: Hodder Arnold, 2003), p. 9.

14 Cannadine, *Decline,* pp. 174, 480–1.

15 *Irish Times,* 27 April 1897.

16 O'Callaghan-Westropp (O'C-W) to G.P. Stewart, 3 April 1913, University College Dublin Archives Department (UCDAD), P38/3, p. 344.

17 O'C-W to Lord Castlereagh, 28 January 1913, UCDAD, P38/3, pp. 313–15. The 'final offer' price appears to have been actually £41,000 and the Colonel disclosed to a close friend his intention of 'spreading my purchase

money all over the world in sound investments, to yield an average of 4¼%, to get peace and safety for a change as I grow old. I wish you were out of land': O'C-W to H.V. McNamara, 13 August 1912, UCDAD, P38/3, p. 244; O'C-W to Messrs Maunsell, Darley and Orpen, 7 June 1912, UCDAD, P38/3, p. 231.

18 O'C-W to Lord Castlereagh, 28 January 1913, UCDAD, P38/3, pp. 313–15.

19 The trend for post-Famine landlords to become large-scale graziers or farmers themselves is discussed by David Jones, *Graziers*, pp. 99, 103, 112–29, and T.A.M. Dooley, 'Landlords and the Land Question, 1879–1909', in C. King (ed.), *Famine, Land and Culture in Ireland* (Dublin: UCD Press, 2000), pp. 117–18.

20 It has been suggested that the occasional forced withdrawal of his paid farm workers left him with little choice but to work as '"a common labourer"': D. Fitzpatrick, *Politics and Irish Life 1913–21: Provincial Experience of War and Revolution* (Cork: Cork University Press, 1998), p. 53.

21 Fitzpatrick, *Politics and Irish Life*, p. 43.

22 Ibid., p. 222.

23 The Northern Ireland landed class was to do considerably better than its southern counterpart in the interwar period in retaining substantial economic and political power (see Olwen Purdue, *The Big House in the North of Ireland: Land, Power and Social Elites 1878–1960* (Dublin: UCD Press, 2009), chaps 4, 5 and 7.

24 See E. O'Connor, *Syndicalism in Ireland, 1917–1923* (Cork: Cork University Press, 1988), pp. 40–1, 74–6. At Lismehane the Colonel's strict policy was to employ only non-union labour.

25 T. Varley, 'On the Road to Extinction: Agrarian Parties in Twentieth-Century Ireland', *Irish Political Studies*, vol. 25, no. 4, 2010, p. 587.

26 For the background to this contentious issue, see J. O'Donovan, *The Economic History of Livestock in Ireland* (Cork: Cork University Press, 1940), pp. 227–9.

27 See A. O'Riordan, *East Galway Agrarian Agitation and the Burning of Ballydugan House, 1922* (Dublin: Four Courts, 2015).

28 C. Callan and B. Desmond, *Irish Labour Lives: A Biographical Dictionary of Irish Labour Party Deputies, Senators, MPs and MEPs* (Dublin: Watchword, 2010), p. 27.

29 Bobby Burke (RMB) to WStGB, 12 June 1930, Galway County Council Archives, Burkes of Ballydugan papers, GP6/120.

30 Ibid.

31 J. Cunningham, 'Bobby Burke: Christian Socialist', in J.A. Claffey (ed.), *Glimpses of Tuam since the Famine* (Tuam: Old Tuam Society, 1997), pp. 253, 241; B. Desmond, *No Workers' Republic! Reflections on Labour and Ireland, 1913–1967* (Dublin: Watchword, 2009), pp. 300–4; Michael D. Higgins, *Renewing the Republic* (Dublin: Liberties Press, 2011), pp. 211–15.

32 *Tuam Herald*, 1 and 29 November 1930, 7 November 1931, 25 November 1933.

33 See *Tuam Herald*, 13, 20, 27 June 1931, 18, 25 July 1931, 1 August 1931, 12 September 1931, 19 June 1933.

34 Burke went on to praise *Quadragesimo Anno*'s condemnation of the excessive inequality between capital and labour, its assertion of the

'Principle of Just Distribution' that he saw legitimating profit-sharing forms of economic organisation and the Pope's approval of 'young men devoting themselves to social reform' (*Tuam Herald,* 22 August 1931).

35 He had apparently offered 'over 450 statute acres' to the Land Commission in 1931 and, in 1949, on his mother's death, another 515 acres (*Tuam Herald,* 4 April 1936, 12 November 1949).

36 *Connacht Sentinel,* 17 January 1933. Burke's conduct did not sit well with members of his family, provoking tension in his relations with his mother and a serious rift with his brother who objected to his wanton dispersal of family wealth.

37 Desmond, *No Workers' Republic!,* pp. 122–3.

38 *Tuam Herald,* 25 November 1933.

39 *Irish Times,* 27 September 1941.

40 *Connacht Sentinel,* 1 November 1932.

41 Ibid.

42 Ibid.

43 N. Puirséil, *The Irish Labour Party 1922–73* (Dublin: UCD Press, 2007), pp. 54, 321.

44 *Tuam Herald,* 10 November 1934.

45 Ibid.

46 O'C-W to M. Molohan, 7 May 1927, UCDAD, P38/14, p. 24.

47 After an organisational drive commencing in 1917 the IFU had attracted 60,000 members in twenty-five counties by 1920 (O'Connor, *Syndicalism,* p. 74).

48 O'C-W to R.A. McCabe, Secretary, Co. Kerry Farmers' Association, 24 November 1924, UCDAD, P38/9, pp. 27–28.

49 Callan and Desmond, *Irish Labour Lives*, p. 27.

50 *Tuam Herald,* 18 November 1933.

51 *Tuam Herald,* 5 August 1933.

52 *Tuam Herald,* 21 November 1936, 4 December 1937, 18 June 1938.

53 Ibid.

54 *Seanad Debates*, 8 March 1950, vol. 37, col. 803; D. Ó Cearbhaill, 'Bobby Burke and the Tuam Parish Council of Muintir na Tíre', *Journal of the Galway Archaeological and Historical Society*, vol. 62, 2010, pp. 202–12.

55 See *Tuam Herald,* 22 August 1931, 30 January 1937, 8 April 1939, 6 April 1940.

56 *Tuam Herald,* 22 August 1931.

57 F. Devine, 'Pádraig Mac Gamhna, Paddy Bergin and Labour in Carlow', in T. McGrath (ed.), *Carlow: History and Society* (Dublin: Geography Publications, 2008), p. 935; see also Puirséil, *The Irish Labour Party 1922–73*, pp. 144–8; S. L'Estrange, '"A Community of Communities"—Catholic Communitarianism and Societal Crises in Ireland, 1890s–1950s', *Journal of Historical Sociology,* vol. 20, no. 4, 2007, pp. 564–9.

58 M. Gallagher, *Irish Elections 1922–44: Results and Analysis, Vol. 1* (Limerick: PSAI Press, 1993), p. 254.

59 M. Gallagher, *Irish Elections 1948–77: Results and Analysis, Vol. 2* (London: Routledge, 2009), p. 17.

60 Burke has the distinction of being the only person with an immediate gentry family background to have become a member of the Labour Party's parliamentary party (see Callan and Desmond, *Irish Labour Lives*, pp. 7–256).

61 Fitzpatrick, *Politics and Irish Life*, p. 222.
62 *Dáil Debates*, 5 July 1923, vol. 4, col. 289.
63 *Irish Times*, 12 July 1923.
64 O'C-W to R. A. Butler, 19 April 1927, UCDAD, P38/4, p. 865.
65 O'C-W to C. Hogan, 8 June 1929, UCDAD, P38/16, p. 319.
66 T. Varley, 'On the Road to Extinction', p. 593.
67 The Colonel's estimation in 1928 was that 'the average 100 [IFU] members would be made up of 30 for the Treaty, 20 against, 20 nationalists opposed to both wings of Sinn Fein and jealous of the government and 30 who loathed and distrusted all politicians' (O'C-W to P. Ford MP, 4 March 1928, UCDAD, P38/16, p. 43).
68 *Connacht Sentinel*, 17 January 1933.
69 M. Gallagher, *Political Parties in the Republic of Ireland* (Dublin: Gill & Macmillan, 1985), p. 134.
70 While George O'Callaghan had stayed within the gentry in marrying Rose Godbold in 1893, Bobby Burke had married outside his class of origin. Ann Grattan, a Belfast-born 'committed Young Christian' when she married Burke in 1936, had met her future husband at the All Ireland Youth Conference of the Church of Ireland (Cunningham, 'Bobby Burke', p. 246).
71 *Tuam Herald*, 19 August 1933, 9 September 1933, 4 December 1937.
72 N. Mansergh, *The Irish Free State: Its Government and Politics* (London: George Allen & Unwin, 1934), p. 290.
73 With the exception of 1948, all of Burke's general elections were subject to this constraint.
74 Lyons, 'Minority Problem', p. 102; Coakley, 'Religion, Ethnic Identity and the Protestant Minority in the Republic', p. 100.
75 After the 1942 local elections Burke declared: 'I am friendly to Clann na Talmhan because their policy is near to that of Labour' (*Connacht Tribune*, 5 September 1942; see also R.M. Burke, 'Labour and Clann na Talmhan', *Torch*, 27 February 1943; *Irish Farmers' Paper*, July 1942).
76 See, for instance, *Tuam Herald*, 30 January 1937; 19 February 1938; 4 June 1938; 19 September 1942.
77 The *Connacht Tribune*, in a leader titled 'Party Politics at their Lowest', felt compelled in 1942 to condemn Fianna Fáil's 'scurvy treatment' of Burke who found himself after his local election success excluded from all the new county council's committees (*Connacht Tribune*, 5 September 1942).
78 *Tuam Herald*, 21 November 1942.
79 Ibid.
80 Ibid.
81 *Tuam Herald*, 6 November 1942.
82 Cunningham, 'Bobby Burke', p. 248; D. Ó Cearbhaill, 'Bobby Burke', p. 210; F. Harte, 'They Weren't all Bad You Know—A Landlord with a Difference', *Journal of the Old Tuam Society* vol. 4, 2007, pp. 37–8.
83 *Tuam Herald*, 29 November 1930.
84 *Connacht Sentinel*, 1 November 1932.
85 *Tuam Herald*, 3 June 1933; Cunningham, 'Bobby Burke', p. 248.
86 Harte, 'They Weren't all Bad', p. 38. Some of the Labour Party's western enemies were advising small farmers against voting Labour in 1943 for

the reasons that city unionised workers were on average better paid and worked fewer hours than working farmers, and that maintaining Irish agriculture as a cheap food source for urban workers was Labour Party policy. In the eyes of Labour's enemies, these two reasons implied that urban trade unionists and western working farmers could never make common cause (*Torch*, 28 August 1943, 14 August 1943, 31 July 1943).

87 *Seanad Debates*, 1 March 1950, vol. 37, col. 620.

88 The minister for agriculture, James Dillon, went as far as to dismiss Burke's proposal 'as about as bad as an idea could be' (*Seanad Debates*, 1 March 1950, vol. 37, col. 647; 8 March 1950, vol. 37. col. 811). Some years earlier in 1937 the Land Commission had dissolved 'a thriving land co-op in Mountemple [Mount Temple], Westmeath, where, for two years, fifty-two families had been illustrating the superiority of co-operative farming over small-scale individualism' (C. McGuire, *Roddy Connolly and the Struggle for Socialism in Ireland* [Cork: Cork University Press, 2008], p. 168).

89 Very likely an arson attack on the Dovea co-operative farm's hay crop in the late 1940s was the work of individuals who wanted to see the 200-acre holding in Tipperary divided (Joseph Johnston, *Irish Agriculture in Transition* [Dublin: Hodges, Figgis and Co., 1951], pp. 139–40).

90 See here Niek Koning's general thesis that large labour-employing capitalist farms were finding themselves, by the late nineteenth century, at a major competitive disadvantage vis-à-vis smaller farms relying mainly on family labour: N. Koning, *The Failure of Agrarian Capitalism: Agrarian Politics in the United Kingdom, Germany, the Netherlands and the USA 1846–1919* (London: Routledge, 1994).

91 O'C-W to Secretary, IFU, 30 March 1932, UCDAD, P38/16, p. 915.

92 O'C-W to P. J. Healy, 14 July 1927, UCDAD, P38/15, p. 6.

93 O'C-W to C. Hogan, 17 August 1930, UCDAD, P38/16, p. 590.

94 O'C-W to 'The Editor', 27 October 1932, UCDAD, P38/16, p. 993. See Crawford, *Outside the Glow*, pp. 143–4.

95 O'C-W to 'The Editor', 27 October 1932, UCDAD, P38/16, p. 993. See also T. Dooley *'The Land for the People': The Land Question in Independent Ireland* (Dublin: UCD Press, 2004), pp. 103–4; Crawford, *Outside the Glow,* pp. 142–5; and M.H. Warner, *W. Lloyd Warner: Social Anthropologist* (New York: Publishing Center for Cultural Resources, 1988), p. 73.

96 O'C-W to C. Hogan, 25 December 1928, UCDAD, P38/16, p. 229.

97 Greatly adding to the Colonel's personal anxieties was his wife's death in November 1929.

98 O'C-W to A. Jameson, 20 August 1932, UCDAD, P38/16, p. 973.

99 Ibid.

100 In 1926 he compared the ex-landlords' position to 'the toad beneath the harrow' and to 'an abandoned rear-guard' (O'C-W to G. de L. Willis, 11 June 1926, UCDAD, P38/4, p. 704).

101 See McDowell, *Crisis and Decline,* p. 180.

102 O'C-W to C. Hogan, 27 October 1931, UCDAD, P38/16, p. 847; Warner, *W. Lloyd Warner,* p. 72.

103 As someone contesting elections in the early days of native rule, Burke had good reason to want to keep his brief stint in the British army a secret.

104 See, for instance, Fitzpatrick, *Politics and Irish Life*, p. 50; *Irish Times,* 18 January 1926; Dooley, *Decline of the Big House,* pp. 257–8.
105 O'C-W to Secretary, IFU, 26 May 1931, UCDAD, P38/16, p. 762.
106 See P.B. Ellis, *Erin's Blood Royal: The Gaelic Noble Dynasties of Ireland* (London: Constable, 1999), pp. 134–5.
107 *Tuam Herald,* 8 April 1939.
108 A. Sheehy Skeffington, *Skeff: A Life of Owen Sheehy Skeffington 1909–1970* (Dublin: Lilliput Press, 1991), p. 252.
109 *Times Pictorial,* 10 June 1950.
110 Varley, 'On the Road', p. 597.
111 See P. Bew, *Ireland: The Politics of Enmity 1789–2006* (Oxford: Oxford University Press, 2007), p. 568; F. Campbell, *Land and Revolution: Nationalist Politics in the West of Ireland, 1891–1921* (Oxford: Oxford University Press, 2005), pp. 303–4; T. Garvin, *Preventing the Future: Why Was Ireland so Poor for so Long?* (Dublin: Gill & Macmillan, 2004), pp. 34–5.
112 None of this is to say that Burke didn't profoundly impress some of those whose lives he touched. After a conference in Tuam in 2007 to commemorate the centenary of Burke's birth, Deirdre Manifold (a Galway-based Catholic activist and writer), who had known Burke in her young years, wrote to the local newspaper to say that when 'asked by a friend if I had ever met a saint, I said I had, and that he was both a landlord and a Protestant. That man was Bobby Burke'. Manifold went on to relate how Burke 'figured very big in my life as a child. At Christmas he gave a party for the children and in summer he brought us on a day's outing' (*Tuam Herald,* 1 November, 2007).
113 Michael Gallagher characterises the Labour Party of this period as in 'some ways . . . the most clericalist of the main parties' (*Political Parties*, p. 89).

7. Ostriches and Tricolours: Trinity College Dublin and the Irish State, 1922–45

1 'Correspondence', *T.C.D.: A College Miscellany* (hereafter *T.C.D*), 7 December 1922, p. 55.
2 R.B. McDowell and D.A. Webb, *Trinity College Dublin 1592–1952: An Academic History* (Dublin: Trinity College Dublin Press, 2004), pp. 255–8, 387.
3 Tomás Irish, *Trinity in War and Revolution 1912–1923* (Dublin: Royal Irish Academy Press, 2015), p. 28.
4 Senia Pašeta, 'Trinity College Dublin and the Education of Irish Catholics, 1873–1908', *Studia Hibernica,* vol. 30, 1998/1999, pp. 8–9.
5 Máirtín Ó Murchú, 'Irish Language Studies in Trinity College Dublin', *Hermathena: A Trinity College Dublin Review, Quatercentenary Papers,* 1992, pp. 60–1.
6 Irish, *Trinity in War and Revolution*, pp. 56–7.
7 William MacNeile Dixon, 'Trinity College, Dublin', *Times Literary Supplement*, 29 January 1904, p. 29.
8 Irish, *Trinity in War and Revolution*, p. 4.
9 F.S.L. Lyons, 'The Minority Problem in the 26 Counties', in Francis MacManus (ed.), *The Years of the Great Test* (Cork: Mercier, 1967), pp. 92–9.

10 R.B. McDowell, 'Trinity College Dublin and Politics', in McDowell (ed.), *Historical Essays 1938–2001* (Dublin: Lilliput, 2003), p. 92.
11 TCDDM, MUN/V/5/22, 10 December 1921, p. 200.
12 James Lydon, 'The Silent Sister: Trinity College and Catholic Ireland', in C.H. Holland (ed.), *Trinity College Dublin and the Idea of a University* (Dublin: Trinity College Dublin Press, 1991), p. 42.
13 Fitzgibbon to Blake, 2 June 1923, TCDDM, MS11107/41.
14 W.E. Thrift file, NAI, PRES/1/P/1780.
15 NAI, PRES/1/P3002.
16 NAI, PRES/1/P3002.
17 McDowell and Webb, *Trinity College Dublin*, pp. 433–4.
18 Board meeting of 24 October 1925, p. 202, TCDDM, MUN/V/5/23.
19 'Conferring of Degrees', *Irish Times*, 21 December 1922.
20 Robert Tate, *Orationes et Epistolae Dublinenses (1914–40)* (Dublin: Hodges Figgis, 1941), p. 86.
21 'University of Dublin: Honorary Degrees', *Irish Times*, 25 February 1933.
22 Tate, *Orationes*, pp. 20–91.
23 Tate, *Orationes*, pp. 73–4.
24 'Two premiers honoured', *Irish Times*, 3 December 1926.
25 NAI, TAOIS S 5983/4.
26 'College Historical Society', *T.C.D.*, 3 November 1927.
27 'Bicentenary of Edmund Burke', *Irish Times*, 12 December 1928.
28 NAI, AGO/2009/74/406.
29 Denis Gwynn, *The Irish Free State 1922–1927* (London: Macmillan, 1928), p. 232.
30 NAI, TAOIS/ S 5510.
31 McDowell and Webb, *Trinity College Dublin*, p. 441.
32 Cosgrave to MacNeill, 20 September 1928, NAI, TAOIS/S/6535.
33 Undated letter of the board to MacNeill, *c.*1929, NAI, TAOIS/S/6535.
34 'Cumann Gaolach an Choláiste', *College Pen*, 12 November 1929, p. 43.
35 See the essay by Conor Morrissey in this volume.
36 Bolton C. Waller, *Thomas Davis (1814–1845): A Commemorative Address, Delivered in the Chapel of Trinity College, Dublin, on Trinity Monday, 1930* (Dublin: Printed at the Dublin University press by Ponsonby & Gibbs, 1930), pp. 3–16.
37 McDowell and Webb, *Trinity College Dublin, 1592–1952*, p. 504.
38 Irish, *Trinity in War and Revolution*, p. 272.
39 'College Historical Society', *T.C.D.*, 16 February 1922, p. 98.
40 'Editorial', *T.C.D.*, 23 February 1922, p. 103.
41 'Editorial', *T.C.D.*, 17 May 1923, p. 145.
42 *Dáil Debates*, vol. 1, no. 29, cols 2126, 2144, 'Estimates, Arts and Sciences', Thursday, 16 November 1922.
43 'Correspondence', *T.C.D.*, 23 November 1922, p. 30.
44 'Correspondence', T.C.D., 30 November 1922, p. 46.
45 James A. Mangan, *Athleticism in the Victorian and Edwardian Public School* (Cambridge: Cambridge University Press, 1981), p. 206.
46 'Editorial', *T.C.D.*, 19 May 1927, p. 225.
47 *Dublin University Calendar, pt. II*, 1928–32.
48 *College Pen*, 7 May 1929, p. 1.

49 *College Pen*, 29 October 1929, pp. 4–5.
50 *College Pen*, 5 November 1929, p. 20.
51 *College Pen*, 12 November 1929, p. 37.
52 *College Pen*, 19 November 1929, p. 52.
53 Keith Jeffery, 'Irish Varieties of Great War Commemoration', in John Horne and Edward Madigan (eds), *Towards Commemoration: Ireland in War and Revolution 1912–1923* (Dublin: Royal Irish Academy Press, 2013), pp. 117–19.
54 Jane Leonard, 'The Twinge of Memory: Armistice Day and Remembrance Sunday in Dublin since 1919', in Graham Walker and Richard English (eds), *Unionism in Modern Ireland: New Perspectives on Politics and Culture* (Basingstoke: Macmillan, 1996), p. 101.
55 See, for instance, a front page article: 'Armistice Day in Dublin: Temporary Cenotaph in College Green', *Irish Times*, 15 November 1924; Leonard, 'The Twinge of Memory', p. 102.
56 Leonard, 'The Twinge of Memory', p. 102.
57 *T.C.D.*, 17 November 1921, p. 22.
58 *T.C.D.*, 18 November 1926, p. 84.
59 'Editorial', *T.C.D.*, 14 November 1929, p. 37.
60 'Editorial', *College Pen*, 11 November 1930, p. 1.
61 Irish, *Trinity in War and Revolution*, p. 259.
62 'An Imperishable Inspiration: Lord Glenavy's Tribute', *Irish Times*, 12 November 1928.
63 K.C. Bailey, *A History of Trinity College Dublin, 1892–1945* (Dublin: Hodges Figgis, 1947), pp. 65–6.
64 TCDDM MS 7939, 21 November 1971, p. 21.
65 David Fitzpatrick, 'Eamon de Valera at Trinity College', *Hermathena: A Trinity College Dublin Review*, 133 (1982), pp. 7–14.
66 'Cecil to speak at T.C.D.', *Irish Press*, 7 March 1934.
67 'President de Valera at Trinity College', *Irish Times*, 17 November 1934.
68 De Valera speech notes, UCDAD, P 150/2355,
69 'Mr de Valera's visit to T.C.D.', *Irish Press*, 3 July 1937.
70 'Trinity and Ireland', *Irish Times*, 3 July 1937.
71 Clair Wills, *That Neutral Island: A Cultural History of Ireland during the Second World War* (London: Faber, 2007), pp. 364–5; Leonard, 'The Twinge of Memory', p. 102.
72 'Malicious reports', *Irish Press*, 10 May 1945.
73 McDowell and Webb, *Trinity College Dublin*, pp. 464–5.
74 'A disgraceful incident', *Irish Press*, 8 May 1945.
75 Stanford to Alton, 8 May 1945, TCDDM, MUN/P/46/31/4.
76 Alton to Iveagh, 14 May 1945, TCDDM, MUN/P/46/31/17.

8. From Landlordism to Citizenship: Edward Richards-Orpen and the New State

1 I am indebted to Jeremy Hill for advice and comments on this chapter based on his knowledge of his grandfather and his activities. The research for this chapter has been made possible by funding from the Centre for the Study of Historic Irish Houses and Estates at Maynooth University.

2 Margaret Tomalin to Edward Orpen, mostly undated letters, 1913–14, Monksgrange archives [MGA]/VII(2b-e).
3 Edward Richards-Orpen [hereafter ERR-O], Autobiographical notes, 'The Somme in early 1917', MGA/VII/D(4a).
4 Adela Orpen to ERR-O, 15 February 1919, MGA/I/U(7).
5 Margaret Richards-Orpen [hereafter MR-O] to ERR-O, 23 February [1919], MGA/VII/A(4n).
6 Iris Orpen, Journal, 2 April 1923, MGA/VI/C(20).
7 For an account of the burning of houses in Ireland generally and of the motivations for these, see Terence Dooley, *The Decline of the Big House in Ireland: A Study of Irish Landed Families, 1860–1960* (Dublin: Wolfhound, 2001), pp. 171–207.
8 Dooley, *Decline of the Big House*, p. 189.
9 George Atkinson to ERR-O, 29 June 1928, MGA/VII/C(2f).
10 See Nicola Gordon Bowe, 'A Cotswold-inspired Venture towards Modernism in Ireland: Edward Richards Orpen (1884–1967) and the Grange Furniture Industry, 1927–1932', *The Decorative Arts Society 1850 to the Present Journal*, vol. 27, 2003, pp. 95–111.
11 Michael Doyle to ERR-O, 23 June 1923, MGA/VII/C(2c).
12 ERR-O to Adela Orpen, 30 June [1923], MGA/I/U(7d).
13 Charmian Hill, unpub. reminiscences of her childhood, MGA/VII/D(19), p. 5.
14 Margaret Tomalin to Edward Richards Orpen, n.d. [early 1914], MGA/VII/A(2b).
15 ERR-O to Adela Orpen, 30 June [1923], MGA/I/U(7d).
16 Ibid.
17 Marked-up Labour Party canvassing sheets for Chipping Campden for the 1924 General Election, MGA/VII/D(6a).
18 ERR-O, Autobiographical notes, 'The RIB period', MGA/VII/D(4b).
19 Ibid.
20 See, for example, Henry H. Hill (architect) to Manning Robertson, 15 April 1929, MGA/VII/C(2g).
21 See extensive correspondence and papers, 1925–7, in MGA/VII/C(2e-g) and H(20).
22 Donal O'Sullivan, *The Irish Free State and Its Senate: A Study in Contemporary Politics* (London: Faber & Faber, 1940), p. 299.
23 For a full account of the development and character of this organisation, see Raymond Ryan, 'The National Farmers' and Ratepayers' League', *Studia Hibernica*, no. 34, 2006–7, pp. 173–92; for a succinct statement of the realignment of opposition parties at this time, see John Coakley, 'The Significance of Names: The Evolution of Irish Party Names (1)', *Études Irlandaises*, no. 5, December 1980, p. 174.
24 *Irish Times*, 7 October 1932.
25 See papers for the local organisation at MGA/VII/I(1c-e).
26 ERR-O, Autobiographical notes, 'The Farmers & Ratepayers League', pp. 2–3, MGA/VII/I(1f).
27 See for example letter to branch secretaries, 21 August 1933, MGA/VII/A(9).
28 ERR-O, 'The Farmers & Ratepayers League', p. 3v.

29 ERR-O to MR-O, 8 October 1934 and n.d. [October-November? 1934], MGA/VII/A(9).
30 ERR-O to MR-O, 16 March 1935, MGA/VII/A(9).
31 Ibid.
32 ERR-O to MR-O, 7 March 1935, MGA/VII/A(9).
33 ERR-O to MR-O, 28 March 1935, MGA/VII/A(9).
34 ERR-O to [Patrick] Baxter (copy), 15 August 1933, MGA/VII/C(2m).
35 Ibid.
36 ERR-O to Eoin O'Duffy (draft), n.d [*c.* September 1933], MGA/VII/C(2m).
37 ERR-O to Eoin O'Duffy, 23 February 1934 (copy), MGA/VII/C(2n).
38 Liam Burke (General Secretary, Fine Gael) to ERR-O, 18 August 1934, MGA/VII/C(2n).
39 ERR-O to [Patrick] Baxter (draft), 7 September 1933, MGA/VII/C(2m).
40 ERR-O to James Dillon (copy), 18 July 1934. There are three drafts or copies of this letter, each varying from the other, but reference is here made to the one dated 18 July, which appears to be the final version, but which is incomplete. The other two are dated 6 and 8 July. MGA/VII/C(6a).
41 James Dillon to ERR-O, 8 September 1934. 'Confidential', MGA/VII/C(6a).
42 ERR-O to James Dillon (copy), 2 July 1938, MGA/VII/C(6a).
43 Liam Burke (General Secretary, Fine Gael) to ERR-O, 9 August 1944, with attachments, MGA/VII/C(2cc).
44 This statistic is compiled on the basis of the published articles which he retained within his papers, but given a very large gap between 1947 and 1956 it may be that there were even more, copies of which he did not retain, MGA/VII/H(6-8, 17a and 22) and VII/I(110).
45 Joseph Johnston, *Irish Agriculture in Transition* (Dublin: Hodges Figgis, and Oxford: Basil Blackwood, 1951), p. 166.
46 MR-O to [James Dillon] (draft), [*c.* 15 March 1944], MGA/VII/C(6a).
47 'Pat Murphy's Jottings', *Standard*, undated newspaper cutting, MGA/VII/I(11k).
48 Leonard Cox, 'Farming in a National Plan', *Standard*, 5 May 1944, p.6.
49 See, for example, letters to various people and other documents, 8 and19 April, 4 and 12 May, 6 June, 19 July 1933, MGA/VII/C(2m) and 31 July and 13 August 1934, MGA/VII/C(2n).
50 Department of Agriculture to ERR-O, 25 March 1942, MGA/VII/C(2w).
51 ERR-O, Autobiographical notes, 'The beginnings of agricultural research–Johnstown Castle', MGA/VII/D(4b).
52 Ibid.
53 Michael Neenan to Jeremy Hill, 21 November 1989, MGA/VII/D(3).
54 Undated document in ERR-O's hand setting out the conditions [June 1950], MGA.
55 See Michael Neenan, 'Agriculture in the New State', in P.L. Curran (ed.), *Towards a History of Agricultural Science in Ireland: Commemorating the Golden Jubilee of the Agricultural Science Association, 1942–1992* (Dublin: Agricultural Science Association, 1992), p. 114.
56 Neenan to Hill, 21 November 1989.
57 Michael Neenan, 'A Popular History of Irish Agriculture, 1879–1972', unpublished manuscript, pp. 151–2 and 165. I am indebted to Matt Wheeler of the Irish Agricultural Museum, Johnstown Castle, for access to this manuscript.

58 Neenan to Hill, 21 November 1989.
59 'Professor Gulliver Builds a Village', *Irish Press*, 19 August 1947.
60 See various news cuttings and letters in Esther Bishop's scrapbook, MGA/VIII/D(3).
61 *Irish Times*, 18 March 1949.
62 See especially MGA/VII/I(6).
63 Edward Richards-Orpen, *The Economic Farm Unit*, Reconstruction Pamphlet No. 6, published in connection with the National Town Planning Exhibition, Dublin, 25 April–5 May 1944.
64 MGA/VII/I(7a-d).
65 Johnston, *Irish Agriculture in Transition*, pp. 166ff.
66 Richards-Orpen, *The Economic Farm Unit*, p. 4.
67 Roy Johnston, *A Century of Endeavour: A Biographical and Autobiographical View of the 20th Century in Ireland*, 2nd ed. (Dublin: Lilliput Press, 2006), pp. 457 and 523.
68 Roy Johnston, 'The Richards Orpen plan', http://www.rjtechne.org/century130703/1940s/orpen.htm (accessed 2 May 2017).
69 Notice of meeting, 30 January 1931, MGA/VII/C(2j).
70 See MGA/VII/H(18a-e).

9. 'Old Dublin Merchant "Free of Ten and Four"': The Life and Death of Protestant Businesses in Independent Ireland

1 *Reply to the Catholic Association and Its Allies: 'The Leader' and 'The Irish Rosary'* (Dublin: Society for the Protection of Protestant Interests, 1903), pp. 6–8.
2 Tony Farmar, *Heitons—A Managed Transition: Heitons in the Irish Coal, Iron and Building Markets, 1818–1996* (Dublin: A. & A. Farmar, 1996), p. 34.
3 Mary E. Daly, *Sixties Ireland: Reshaping the Economy, State and Society, 1957–1973* (Cambridge: Cambridge University Press, 2016), p. 126.
4 F.S.L. Lyons, 'Reflections on a Bicentenary', in F.S.L. Lyons (ed.), *Bank of Ireland 1783–1983, Bicentenary Essays* (Dublin: Gill & Macmillan, 1983), pp. 207–8.
5 Louis Cullen, *Eason & Son: A History* (Dublin: Eason, 1989), p. 111.
6 Terence Brown, *The Irish Times: 150 Years of Influence* (London: Bloomsbury, 2015), p. 293; Kurt Bowen, *Protestants in a Catholic State: Ireland's Privileged Minority* (Dublin: Gill & Macmillan, 1983), p. 95.
7 Charles Flynn, 'Dundalk 1900–1960: An Oral History' (unpub. PhD thesis, Maynooth University, 2000), p. 129.
8 Cited in Tony Farmar, *The Versatile Profession: A History of Accountancy in Ireland since 1850* (Dublin: Chartered Accountants Ireland, 2013), p. 66.
9 Oliver MacDonagh, 'The Victorian Bank, 1824–1914', in F.S.L. Lyons (ed.), *Bank of Ireland 1783–1983, Bicentenary Essays* (Dublin: Gill & Macmillan, 1983), p. 44.
10 F.S.L. Lyons, 'Reflections on a Bicentenary', in Lyons, *Bank of Ireland 1783–1983*, pp. 207–8.
11 Tony Farmar, *Versatile Profession*, p. 65.
12 Anne Haverty, *Elegant Times: A Dublin Story* (Dublin: Sonas, 1995), p. 77.

13 Ronald Nesbitt, *At Arnott's of Dublin, 1843–1993* (Dublin: A. & A. Farmar, 1993), p. 38.
14 Tony Farmar, *Heitons*, p. 34.
15 James Quinn, 'Industry Evolution: A Comparative Study of Irish Wholesaling' (unpub. PhD thesis, DCU, 2002), p. 124.
16 For a history of the Findlater family, see Alex Findlater, *Findlaters: The Story of a Dublin Merchant Family, 1774–2001* (Dublin: A. & A. Farmar, 2001).
17 Cullen, *Eason & Son*, p. 390.
18 Mary E. Daly, *The First Department: A History of the Department of Agriculture* (Dublin: Institute of Public Administration, 2002), p. 112.
19 Daly, *The First Department*, p. 114.
20 CSO, *Life in 1916 Ireland* (Dublin: Central Statistics Office, 2016), p. 6; Paul Rouse, *Ireland's Own Soil: Government and Agriculture in Ireland, 1945 to 1965* (Dublin: Irish Farmers Journal, 2000), appendix 5, p. 260.
21 Terence Dooley, 'Estate Ownership and Management in Nineteenth- and Early Twentieth-Century Ireland', in Raymond Refaussé and Terence Dooley, *Sources for the History of Landed Estates in Ireland* (Dublin: Irish Academic Press, 2000), pp. 3–16.
22 Maurice Manning and Moore McDowell, *Electricity Supply in Ireland: The History of the ESB* (Dublin: Gill & Macmillan, 1984), p. 37.
23 Louis Cullen, *Princes and Pirates: The Dublin Chamber of Commerce, 1783–1983* (Dublin: Chamber of Commerce, 1983), p. 92.
24 John Coakley, 'Minor Parties in Irish Political Life, 1922–1989', *Economic and Social Review*, vol. 21, no. 3, 1990, pp. 269–97.
25 Mícheál Ó Fathartaigh, *Irish Agriculture Nationalised: The Dairy Disposal Company and the Making of the Modern Irish Dairy Industry* (Dublin: Institute of Public Administration, 2014), passim.
26 *Irish Times*, 28 June 1966.
27 Farmar, *Versatile Profession*, p. 70.
28 Cited in Cullen, *Eason & Son*, p. 385.
29 Mark Frankland, *Radio Man: The Remarkable Rise and Fall of C.O. Stanley* (London: Institution of Engineering and Technology, 2002), passim.
30 Restrictive Practices Commission, *Report of Studies into Industrial Concentration and Mergers in Ireland* (Dublin: Stationery Office, 1976), passim.
31 Lyons, 'Reflections on a Bicentenary', p. 209.
32 Farmar, *Versatile Profession*, p. 119.
33 Quinn, 'Industry Evolution', p. 137.
34 Patricia Kelleher, 'Familism in Irish Capitalism in the 1950s', *Economic and Social Review*, vol. 18, no. 2, 1987, pp. 75–94; Colm O'Gorman and Declan Curran, 'Strategic Transformations in Large Irish-owned Businesses', *Business History*, vol. 59, no. 4, 2017, pp. 497–524.
35 M. O'Brien, *The Irish Times: A History* (Dublin: Four Courts Press, 2008), pp. 146–7.
36 Homan Potterton, *Rathcormick: A Childhood Recalled* (Dublin: New Island Books, 2004), p. 59.
37 Terence Brown, *The Irish Times: 150 Years of Influence* (London: Bloomsbury, 2015), pp. 293, 305, 340.

10. 'The jersey is all that matters, not your church': Protestants and the GAA in the Rural Republic

1 L.W. White, 'Rackard, Nicholas ("Nicky")', *DIB*, vol. 8, pp. 367–8.
2 M. Cronin, M. Duncan and P. Rouse (eds), *The GAA: A People's History* (Cork: Collins Press, 2009), pp. 253–6.
3 Cronin, Duncan and Rouse (eds), *The GAA*, pp. 253–6.
4 Ibid., p. 142.
5 Telephone call between author and Pat Daly, Director of Games, Croke Park, 12 September 2013.
6 Name and address of interviewee with author.
7 J. Sugden and A. Bairner, *Sport, Sectarianism and Society in a Divided Ireland* (London: Leicester University Press, 1995), p. 23.
8 D. Hassan, 'The GAA in Ulster', in M. Cronin, W. Murphy and P. Rouse (eds), *The Gaelic Athletic Association 1884–2009* (Dublin: Irish Academic Press, 2009), pp. 77–92.
9 *Irish Times*, 10 August 2007.
10 Email communications between Donal McAnallen and the author.
11 *Gaelic Athletic Association Official Guide, Part I* (Dublin: Central Council of the Association, Croke Park, 2013).
12 P. Rouse, 'The Politics of Culture and Sport in Ireland: A History of the GAA Ban on Foreign Games, 1884–1971. Pt I 1884–1921', *International Journal of the History of Sport*, vol. x, no. 3, December 1993, pp. 333–60; Neal Garnham, 'Accounting for the Early Success of the Gaelic Athletic Association', *Irish Historical Studies*, vol. 34, no. 133, May 2004, pp. 65–78.
13 M. de Búrca, *The GAA: A History*, 2nd ed. (Dublin: Gill & Macmillan, 1999), p. 18.
14 W. Murphy, 'The GAA during the Irish Revolution, 1913–23', in Cronin, Murphy and Rouse (eds), *The Gaelic Athletic Association*, pp. 61–76.
15 Interview with sports historian and journalist Eoghan Corry, 13 July 2014.
16 P. Downey, 'Flaherty is Offaly's Galway Connection', *Irish Times*, 30 August 1985.
17 Interview with Jack Boothman, Blessington, County Wicklow, 3 February 2010.
18 C. O'Connor, 'Southern Protestantism: The Inter-relationship of Religious, Social and Gender Identity in the Diocese of Ferns 1945–65' (unpub. PhD thesis, University of Limerick, 2007).
19 Interview with Eoghan Corry, 28 May 2014.
20 Telephone interview with Colin Regan, 10 February 2010.
21 The Angelus is a bell for Catholic prayer. It is also broadcast twice-daily since 1950 on RTÉ radio and television.
22 Interview with Sheila Milne, Wexford, 27 August 2013.
23 Telephone interview with Eric Deacon, Wexford, 20 September 2013.
24 Email communication with John Nangle, Wexford, 26 February 2013.
25 Email communication with Senan Lillis, Wexford, 15 September 2013.

11. Protestant Republicans in the Revolution and After

1 Niall Whelehan, 'The Irish Revolution, 1912–23', in Alvin Jackson (ed.), *The Oxford Handbook of Modern Irish History* (Oxford: Oxford University Press, 2014), pp. 621–44, p. 635.

2 For an early discussion of these themes, see Martin Maguire, 'Harry Nicholls and Kathleen Emerson: Protestant Rebels', *Studia Hibernica*, no. 35, 2008–2009, pp. 147–66.
3 León Ó Broin, *Protestant Nationalists in Revolutionary Ireland: The Stopford Connection* (Dublin: Gill & Macmillan, 1985).
4 Valerie Jones, *Rebel Prods: The Forgotten Story of Protestant Radical Nationalists and the 1916 Rising* (Dublin: Ashfield Press, 2016).
5 R. Foster, *Vivid Faces: The Revolutionary Generation in Ireland, 1890–1923* (London: Allen Lane, 2014), pp. 70–2.
6 http://www.bureauofmilitaryhistory.ie/; http://www.militaryarchives.ie/collections/online-collections/military-service-pensions-collection.
7 Evi Gkotzaridis, 'Revisionist Historians and the Modern Irish State: The Conflict between the Advisory Committee and the Bureau of Military History', *Irish Historical Studies,* XXXV, no. 137, May 2006, pp. 99–116; Eve Morrison, 'Bureau of Military History Witness Statements as Sources for the Irish Revolution', at www. bureauofmilitaryhistory.ie; Eve Morrison, 'The Bureau of Military History and Female Republican Activism, 1913–23', in Maryann Gialanella Valiulis (ed.), *Gender and Power in Irish History* (Dublin: Irish Academic Press, 2009), pp. 59–83.
8 Senia Pašeta, *Irish Nationalist Women, 1900–1918* (Cambridge: Cambridge University Press, 2013).
9 Oonagh Walsh, *Anglican Women in Dublin Philanthropy, Politics and Education in the Early Twentieth Century* (Dublin: UCD Press, 2005), pp. 35–6.
10 Sydney Gifford Czira, *The Years Flew By: Recollections of Sydney Gifford Czira* (Dublin: Gifford & Craven, 1974), p. 46.
11 Joep Leerssen, *National Thought in Europe: A Cultural History* (Amsterdam: Amsterdam University Press, 2008), pp. 159–70.
12 Fearghal McGarry, *The Abbey Rebels of 1916: A Lost Revolution* (Dublin: Gill & Macmillan, 2015).
13 Fintan Lane, *The Origins of Modern Irish Socialism 1881–1896* (Cork: Cork University Press, 1997), pp. 158–219.
14 McGarry, *The Abbey Rebels of 1916*, pp. 109–15.
15 Jones, *Rebel Prods*, pp. 276–332.
16 Foster, *Vivid Faces*, pp. 70–2.
17 Foster, *Vivid Faces*, p. 137.
18 Captain Jack White, *Misfit: A Revolutionary Life* (London: Jonathan Cape, 1930; Dublin: Livewire Publications, 2005), p. 32.
19 'Miss Elizabeth Bloxham', Military Archives, BMH, ws 632 http://www.bureauofmilitaryhistory.ie/reels/bmh/BMH.WS0632.pdf (accessed 12 June 2017).
20 *Irish Times,* 11 October 1911.
21 For a further discussion of this, see Felix M. Larkin's essay in this volume.
22 Jones, *Rebel Prods*, pp. 77–111.
23 Hilary Pyle, *Cesca's Diary 1913–1916: Where Art and Nationalism Meet* (Dublin: Woodfield Press, 2005), pp. 197–216.
24 Foster, *Vivid Faces*, p. 36.
25 McGarry, *The Abbey Rebels of 1916,* p. 157.
26 Foster, *Vivid Faces*, pp. 281–5.

27 Jones, *Rebel Prods*, pp. 348–54.
28 William Murphy, 'Green, Alice Sophia Amelia Stopford', *DIB*, at http://dib.cambridge.org/viewReadPage.do?articleId=a3602 (accessed 12 June 2017).
29 Jones, *Rebel Prods*, p. 288.
30 Diarmaid Ferriter, 'Heron, Archibald ("Archie")', in *DIB*, at http://dib.cambridge.org/viewReadPage.do?articleId=a3963 (accessed 12 June 2017).
31 Michael Kennedy, 'Lester, Seán (John Ernest)', in *DIB*, at http://dib.cambridge.org/viewReadPage.do?articleId=a4809 (accessed 10 June 2017).
32 Valerie Jones, *A Gaelic Experiment: The Preparatory System 1922–61 and Coláiste Móibhí* (Dublin: Woodfield Press, 2006).
33 Martin Maguire, 'Harry Nicholls and Kathleen Emerson "Protestant Rebels"'; Martin Maguire, 'Henry (Harry) Nicholls (1889–1975) Assistant City Engineer and Republican Revolutionary', in John Gibney (ed.), *Dublin City Council and the 1916 Rising* (Dublin: Dublin City Council, 2016), pp. 106–19, 147–65; Jones, *Rebel Prods*, p. 201.
34 C.J. Woods, 'Owen McGee, Allan, Frederick James ("Fred")', in *DIB*, at http://dib.cambridge.org/viewReadPage.do?articleId=a0108 (accessed 10 June 2017).
35 *Dáil Debates*, vol. 15, no. 13, 12 and 13 May 1926. Recently, the GAA has part-funded the installation of the 'Sam Maguire Community Bells' in St Mary's Church of Ireland, Dunmanway.
36 Brian Hanley, 'The Irish Citizen Army after 1916', *Saothar*, vol. 28, 2003, pp. 37–47.
37 *Irish Labour Party and Trade Union Congress, Report of the Twenty-Fifth Annual Meeting, August 1919*, p. 80.
38 Michael Moroney, 'George Plant and the Rule of Law: The Devereux Affair 1940–1942', *Tipperary Historical Journal*, 1988, pp. 1–12.
39 Jones, *Rebel Prods*, pp. 42–9.
40 Holmes/Nicholls papers, typescript memoir, Military Archives, Cathal Brugha Barracks, Rathmines.
41 Robert Tobin, '"Tracing again the tiny snail track": Southern Protestant Memoir since 1950', *The Yearbook of English Studies*, vol. 35, no. 1, January 2005, pp. 171–85; Elizabeth Grubgeld, *Anglo-Irish Autobiographies: Class, Gender and the Forms of Narrative* (Syracuse, NY: Syracuse University Press, 2004).
42 Hubert Butler, 'Portrait of a Minority', in *Escape from the Anthill* (Mullingar: Lilliput Press, 1985), p. 116.
43 J.J. Lee, 'Pearse, Patrick Henry', in *DIB*, vol. 8, p. 24.
44 *Collected Works of Patrick H. Pearse: Political Writings and Speeches* (Dublin: Phoenix Publishing Company, 1916), p. 94.
45 Joost Augusteijn, *Patrick Pearse: The Making of a Revolutionary* (Basingstoke: Palgrave Macmillan, 2010), pp. 288–96.
46 *Collected Works of Patrick H. Pearse*, pp. 219–372.

12. 'We're Irish, but not that kind of Irish': British Imperial Identity in Transition in Ireland and India in the Early Twentieth Century

1 Dave Blair recorded by Niamh Dillon, 7 June 2012.
2 Interview with Olive Stevenson, born in Surrey in 1930, social worker; recorded by Niamh Dillon on 14 December 2004, © BL, C1155/01.

3 *Census of Ireland, 1926*, at http://www.cso.ie/en/census/censusvolumes1926to1991/historicalreports/census1926reports/ (accessed 17 September 2017).
4 David Cannadine, *Ornamentalism: How the British Saw their Empire* (London: Allen Lane, The Penguin Press, 2001), pp. 41–5.
5 L.P. Curtis Jr, *Apes and Angels: The Irishman in Victorian Caricature* (Washington DC: Smithsonian Institution Press, 1997).
6 Diarmaid Ferriter, *The Transformation of Ireland 1900–2000* (London: Profile Books, 2005), p. 110.
7 Jan Morris, *Farewell the Trumpets: An Imperial Retreat* (London: Faber & Faber, 1998), pp. 207–12.
8 John Biggs-Davison, *The Cross of St. Patrick: The Catholic Unionist Tradition in Ireland* (Bourne End: Kensal Press, 1984); Alison Blunt, *Domicile and Diaspora: Anglo Indian Women and the Spatial Politics of Home* (Malden, MA: Blackwell Publishing, 2005).
9 Linda Colley, *Act of Union, Acts of Disunion*, BBC Radio 4 broadcast, 24 January 2014.
10 Linda Colley, *Britons: Forging the Nation 1707–1837* (New Haven and London: Yale University Press, 2005), pp. 3–6.
11 Colley, *Britons*, p. 5.
12 Benedict Anderson, *Imagined Communities* (London: Verso, 1983), p. 15.
13 Ibid.
14 Reprinted by permission from *The Death of Luigi Trastulli and Other Stories: Form and Meaning in Oral History* by Alessandro Portelli, the State University of New York. All rights reserved.
15 These matters are further discussed in the Introduction and Brian Hughes' chapter in this volume.
16 Peter Hart, *The IRA at War 1916–23* (Oxford: Oxford University Press, 2003), p. 237.
17 R.B. McDowell, *Crisis and Decline: The Fate of the Southern Unionists* (Dublin: Lilliput Press, 1997), pp. 95, 135–6.
18 http://theirishrevolution.ie/cork-fatality-register-2/#.WcDG8CMrKhg (accessed 16 September 2017).
19 Lord Ashton, IGC papers, TNA, CO 762/15.
20 William Bateman, TNA, 762/50, 776.
21 Transfer of Power, 29 July 1947, BL, Mountbatten Papers, 267.
22 Interview with Wallace Burnet-Smith, born in Calcutta in 1922; recorded by Niamh Dillon on 1 February 2013, BL, C1508/4.
23 Lady Sylvia Corfield, 'Plain Tales from the Raj', BBC, BL, MSS EUR T. 17, p. 9.
24 Mo Moulton, *Ireland and the Irish in Interwar England* (Cambridge: Cambridge University Press, 2014), p. 206.
25 Sir Olaf Caroe, 'Plain Tales from the Raj', BBC, BL, MSS EUR T. 10.
26 Vere Birdwood, 'Plain Tales from the Raj', BBC, BL, MSS EUR T. 7.
27 'Debates in the Dail', *Weekly Irish Times*, 7 January 1922.
28 Terence Brown, *Ireland: A Social and Cultural History* (London: Harper Perennial, 2004), p. 119.
29 Andy Bielenberg, 'Exodus: The Emigration of Southern Irish Protestants during the Irish War of Independence and the Civil War', *Past and Present*, no. 218, February 2013, p. 231.

30 Judith M. Brown, 'India', in W. Roger Louis and Judith M. Brown (eds), *The Oxford History of the British Empire: Volume IV The Twentieth Century* (Oxford, New York: Oxford University Press, 1999), p. 423.
31 Transfer of Power Collection, Indian Independence Act, 1947, BL, L/P & J/10/124: ff 2–12.
32 Brown, *Ireland*, pp. 37–41.
33 Interview with Peter Walton, born in north Wales, 1939; recorded by Niamh Dillon on 13 November 2012, BL, C1508/5.
34 Interview with Ron Alcock, born in Dublin in 1938; recorded by Niamh Dillon on 5 July 2012, BL, C1508/2.
35 E.M. Collingham, *Imperial Bodies: The Physical Experience of the Raj* (Oxford: Polity Press, 2001), pp. 50–5.
36 Peter Walton, recorded on 27 November 2012, BL, C1508/5.
37 Interview with Robert Maude, born in Dublin in 1929; recorded by Niamh Dillon on 12 July 2012, BL, C1508/3.
38 Ron Alcock, recorded on 14 September 2012, BL, C1508/2.
39 Blunt, *Domicile and Diaspora,* p. 23.
40 Interview with Sue Sloan, born in Quetta, India, in 1934; recorded by Niamh Dillon on 16 April 2013 BL, C1580/8.
41 Interview with John Outram, born in Malaya in 1935, architect; recorded by Niamh Dillon, BL, C467/86.
42 Interview with Betty Gascoyne, born in Jubbulpor, India, in 1925; recorded by Niamh Dillon on 16 July 2012, BL C1508/10
43 Fourth report from the Select Committee on Colonization and Settlement (India); together with the proceedings of the Committee, minutes of evidence and appendix, p. iiii – 23 July 1858.
44 Elizabeth Bowen, *Bowen's Court & Seven Winters* (London: Vintage, 1999), p. 3.
45 Ibid., p. 367.
46 Ibid., pp. 384–5.
47 Peter Walton interviewed by Niamh Dillon on 13 November 2012, BL, C1508/5.
48 Roy Strong, *Visions of England* (London: The Bodley Head, 2011), pp. 145–90.
49 Paul Colley, 'From Londonderry to London: Identity and a Sense of Place for a Protestant Northern Irish Woman in the 1930s', in Donald M. MacRaild (ed.), *The Great Famine and Beyond: Irish Migration in Britain in the Nineteenth and Twentieth Centuries* (Dublin: Irish Academic Press, 2000), p. 191.
50 Mark Harrison, *Climate and Constitutions* (Oxford: Oxford University Press, 1999).
51 Colonel Rivett Carnac, 'Plain Tales from the Raj', BBC, BL, MSS EUR T. 4, p. 3/8.
52 Collingham, *Imperial Bodies*, p. 165.
53 Ibid., p. 171.
54 Lady Dring, 'Plain Tales from the Raj', BBC, BL, MSS EUR T. 28.
55 John Outram, BL, C467/86.
56 Interview with Verna Perry, born in Dartford, Kent, in 1939; recorded by Niamh Dillon on 4 February 2014, BL, C1508/13.

13. 'My mother wouldn't have been as hurt': Women and Inter-church Marriage in Wexford, 1945–65

1 D. Keogh, F. O' Shea and C. Quinlan (eds), *The Lost Decade: Ireland in the 1950s* (Dublin: Mercier Press, 2004).
2 Interview DT, 2 August 2003, one of twenty-one oral history interviews conducted by the author with married Church of Ireland women who lived in the diocese of Ferns, part of the research for C. O'Connor, 'Southern Protestantism: The Inter-relationship of Religious, Social and Gender Identity in the Diocese of Ferns 1945–65' (unpub. PhD thesis, University of Limerick, 2007). Names were anonymised at request of interviewees.
3 With the exception of four parishes, Carnew, Crosspatrick, Clonegal and Inch.
4 *Report of the Commission on Emigration and Other Population Problems* (Dublin: The Stationery Office, 1954), para. 99, p. 201.
5 F. Glenfield, 'The Protestant Population of South East Leinster, 1834–1981' (unpub. MLitt thesis, University of Dublin, 1991), p. 17.
6 D. Ferriter, *The Transformation of Ireland 1900–2000* (London: Profile Books, 2004), p. 498.
7 Interview JC, 14 July 2004.
8 Report of the Board of Education, *Journal of the General Synod* (1949), p. 194.
9 For example: 'Young man, clean job, would like to meet Christian domestic servant, 24 to 28, slimly built, good appearance. Box 48 at this office.' *CoIG*, 23 February 1945.
10 Advertisement in *Diocesan Magazine of Ossory, Ferns and Leighlin*, May 1962.
11 *CoIG*, 19 Februrary 1965.
12 Hilary Pratt, in C. Murphy and J. Adair (eds), *Untold Stories: Protestants in the Republic of Ireland 1922–2002* (Dublin: Liffey Press, 2002), p. 181.
13 *Diocesan Magazine*, February 1949, p. 11.
14 Primate's Address, *Report of the General Synod*, 1951.
15 Interview SM, 11 February 2004.
16 Interview JR, 28 August 2002.
17 Interview LJ, 4 February 2004.
18 Interview MA, 25 August 2003.
19 Interview JA, 26 August 2004.
20 Interview SW, 11 February 2004.
21 Interview HB, 16 September 2004.
22 Interview HB, 16 September 2004.
23 Interview HL, 5 August 2004.
24 Interview JA, 26 August 2004.
25 On one occasion an interview was abruptly terminated by the interviewee when the topic of mixed marriage was introduced: interview JR, 28 August 2002.
26 See C. O'Connor, 'Protestantism and Social Identity: The Diocese of Ferns 1945–65', in B. Browne (ed.), *The Wexford Man: Essays in Honour of Nicky Furlong* (Dublin: Geography Publications, 2007), pp. 147–59.
27 *Diocesan Magazine*, Newtownbarry notes, December 1948, p. 11.
28 *Diocesan Magazine*, Kilnamanagh notes, October 1960, p. 6.

29 See C. O'Connor, 'The Diocese of Ferns, 1945–65: A Female Perspective', in M. Busteed, F. Neal and J. Tonge (eds), *Irish Protestant Identities* (Manchester: Manchester University Press, 2008), pp. 113–25.
30 Interview LJ, 4 February 2004.
31 Interview SM, 11 February 2004.
32 J. Jenkins, *The Tate School Wexford 1867–1949* (Wexford: Impression Print, n.d), p. 7.
33 Interview YC, 27 August 2004.
34 Interview LP, 19 February 2004.
35 Interview MA, 25 August 2003.
36 Interview JA, 26 August 2004.
37 Interview LP, 19 February 2004.
38 Interview JC, 14 July 2004.
39 Interview HB, 16 September 2004.
40 Interview SM, 11 February 2004.
41 This is referenced in detail in Ida Milne's chapter in this volume.
42 Interview SM, 11 February 2004.
43 *Enniscorthy Echo*, 18 April 1953.
44 Glenfield, 'The Protestant Population', p. 264.
45 See C. O'Connor, 'Mixed Marriage, "a grave injury to our church": An Account of the 1957 Fethard-on-Sea Boycott', *The History of the Family: An International Quarterly*, vol. 13, no. 4, 2008, pp. 395–401.
46 For detailed accounts of the Fethard-on-Sea Boycott, see E. Broderick, *The Boycott at Fethard-on-Sea, 1957: A Study in Catholic–Protestant Relations in Modern Ireland* (Newcastle: Cambridge Scholars Publishing, 2011), and T. Fanning, *The Fethard-on-Sea Boycott* (Cork: Collins Press, 2010).
47 *The Wexford People*, 6 July 1957.
48 *Diocesan Magazine*, August 1957, p. 3.
49 *Diocesan Magazine*, November 1957, p. 3.
50 *Dáil Éireann Debates*, 4 July 1957, vol. 163, no. 6, col. 731.
51 Interview HL, 5 August 2004.
52 Canon E.F. Grant, 'The Fethard Boycott, 1957: Recollections and Reflections', undated typescript copy held at the RCBL, PC, pp. 3–14.
53 S. Poyntz, *Memory Emancipated* (Dublin: Poyntz, 2005), p. 41.
54 Interview EK, 28 February 2004.
55 Interview YC, 27 August 2004.

14. Carson's Abandoned Children: Southern Irish Protestants as Depicted in Irish Cartoons, 1920–60

1 My thinking and writings about cartoons have been greatly enriched by the work of other scholars in the field of cartoon studies, specifically L.P. Curtis Jr, James Curry, Ciarán Wallace, Tim Ellis, Roseanna Doughty, Pól Ó Duibhir and Barry Sheppard. I am most grateful to them and to Ian d'Alton, whose seminal work on southern Irish Protestants has helped shape this essay.
2 Quotation from 'If', song written by David Gates (1971).
3 F.M. Larkin, *Terror and Discord: The Shemus Cartoons in the* Freeman's Journal, *1920–1924* (Dublin: A. & A. Farmar, 2009), pp. 72–3. See also R.

Douglas, L. Harte and J. O'Hara, *Drawing Conclusions: A Cartoon History of Anglo-Irish Relations, 1798–1998* (Belfast: The Blackstaff Press, 1998), pp. 232–3.

4 E. Biagini, 'Edward Carson', in E. Biagini and D. Mulhall (eds), *The Shaping of Modern Ireland: A Centenary Assessment* (Dublin: Irish Academic Press, 2016), p. 107.

5 R.B. McDowell, 'Edward Carson', in C.C. O'Brien, *The Shaping of Modern Ireland* (London: Routledge & Kegan Paul, 1970), p. 97.

6 Quoted in Geoffrey Lewis, *Carson: The Man who Divided Ireland* (London: Hambledon Continuum, 2005), p. 231.

7 McDowell, 'Carson', p. 97.

8 See Lewis, *Carson*, pp. 214–15, 224, and Noel Dorr, *Sunningdale: The Search for Peace in Ireland* (Dublin: Royal Irish Academy, 2017), pp. 176–98.

9 McDowell, 'Carson', p. 87.

10 Published 28 May 1921; the election was held on 24 May.

11 P. Maume, 'Moran, D.P.', in *DIB*, vol. 6, pp. 666–70.

12 I am grateful to Ted Smyth for this most apposite phrase.

13 I. d'Alton, '"A Vestigial Population"? Perspectives on Southern Irish Protestants in the Twentieth Century,' *Éire-Ireland*, vol. 44, nos 3 and 4, Fall/Winter 2009, p. 14.

14 Ibid.

15 See M.C. Rast, 'The Ulster Unionists "on velvet": Home Rule and Partition in the Lloyd George Proposals, 1916', *American Journal of Irish Studies*, vol. 14, 2017, pp. 113–38 (pp. 125–31).

16 See, for example, Garry Trudeau's remarks delivered on 10 April 2015 at the Long Island University's George Polk Awards ceremony: https://www.theatlantic.com/international/archive/2015/04/the-abuse-of-satire/390312/ (accessed 7 September 2016). See also F.M. Larkin, 'Free Speech and Charlie Hebdo', *Studies*, vol. 105, no. 418, Summer 2016, pp. 192–8.

17 M. Beard, *Laughter in Ancient Rome: On Joking, Tickling and Cracking Up* (Berkeley: University of California Press, 2014), p. 33. The quoted phrase comes from Aristotle's *Rhetoric*.

18 V. Mercier, *The Irish Comic Tradition* (Oxford: The Clarendon Press, 1962), p. ix.

19 L.P. Curtis Jr, *Images of Erin in the Age of Parnell* (Dublin: National Library of Ireland, 2000), pp. 13–15, 19.

20 L.P. Curtis Jr, *The Depiction of Eviction in Ireland, 1845–1910* (Dublin: UCD Press, 2011), plate 8. See also another cartoon by O'Hea, 'The most noble' (ibid., plate 6), in which he caricatures the marquess of Clanricarde, one of the principal landlords targeted by the Plan of Campaign, as a black devil with horns.

21 *United Ireland*, 23 October 1886.

22 Curtis, *Depiction of Eviction*, pp. 159–60.

23 David Fitzpatrick has argued that the decline by about one-third in the southern Irish Protestant population between 1911 and 1926 was 'mainly self-inflicted', not due to 'excess migration', but rather to 'already low fertility and nuptiality, exacerbated by losses through mixed marriages and conversion': D. Fitzpatrick, *Descendancy: Irish Protestant Histories since 1795* (Cambridge: Cambridge University Press, 2014), p. 180.

24 See *The Revolution Papers, 1916–1923*, no. 48, 29 November 2016. Tony Varley's essay in this volume references the suspicion in which some ex-landlords were held by the IFU.
25 That quaint phrase is how Donal O'Sullivan, clerk of the Senate, describes them: D. O'Sullivan, *The Irish Free State and Its Senate* (London: Faber & Faber, 1940), p. 90.
26 Ibid., pp. 81–2, 90.
27 Larkin, *Terror and Discord*, pp. 15–16, 19, 76–7.
28 O'Sullivan, *The Irish Free State and Its Senate*, p. 82.
29 For an account of the *Freeman*'s last years, see F.M. Larkin, '"A great daily organ": The *Freeman's Journal*, 1763–1924', *History Ireland*, vol. 14, no. 3, May/June 2006, pp. 44–9 (pp. 48–9).
30 *Dáil Debates*, 26 June 1923, vol. 3, col. 2935. O'Shannon was speaking against a government proposal to prescribe a sentence of flogging for some offences. The *Freeman* had strongly opposed a similar measure introduced earlier in Northern Ireland—thus inspiring several mordant Shemus cartoons emphasising the cruelty of such punishment—but it had not spoken out against the government proposal.
31 *Dublin Opinion*, vol. 1, no. 9, November 1922.
32 C.E. Kelly, '*Dublin Opinion, 1922–1968*', *Irish Press*, 15 October 1970.
33 For an account of the history of *Dublin Opinion*, see F.M. Larkin, '"Humour is the safety valve of a nation": *Dublin Opinion, 1922–68*', in M. O'Brien and F.M. Larkin (eds), *Periodicals and Journalism in Twentieth-century Ireland* (Dublin: Four Courts Press, 2014), pp. 123–42.
34 Kelly, '*Dublin Opinion*'.
35 *Irish Press*, 29 January 1940.
36 *Dublin Opinion*, vol. 12, no. 144, February 1934. See also *Forty Years of Dublin Opinion* (Dublin: Dublin Opinion, n.d. [1962?]), pp. 144–5.
37 D'Alton, '"A Vestigial Population"?', pp. 17–18.
38 The earl of Dudley was lord lieutenant of Ireland from 1902 to 1905; he and his wife make cameo appearances in James Joyce's *Ulysses*: V. Igoe, *The Real People of Joyce's* Ulysses*: A Biographical Guide* (Dublin: UCD Press, 2016), pp. 91–3.
39 *Dublin Opinion*, vol. 9, no. 103, September 1930. See also M. O'Brien, *The Irish Times: A History* (Dublin: Four Courts Press, 2008), plate 5 and p. 67.
40 See Larkin, '"Humour is the safety valve of a nation"', p. 131. Another outlier among Irish Protestants, Erskine Childers, was the subject of a number of very bitter Shemus cartoons in the *Freeman's Journal* during 1922: Larkin, *Terror and Discord*, pp. 18–19, 38–9.
41 d'Alton, '"A Vestigial Population"?', pp. 14, 38. The 'vestigial population' quotation is from J. O'Neill, *Blood-dark Track: A Family History* (London: Granta Press, 2001), p. 326.
42 *Dublin Opinion*, vol. 14, no. 167 (January 1936). See also Larkin, '"Humour is the safety valve of a nation"', pp. 133–4.
43 See note 28 above.
44 F. Ó Riain, 'What Makes a Cartoonist?', *Irish Independent*, 5 June 1970.
45 For background information on Brewster, see two blogs by P. Ó Duibhir: http://photopol.com/gordon/ and https://blog.nli.ie/index.php/2013/03/25/death-in-a-sweetshop/ (accessed 9 June 2016).

46 Regarding the fate of the National Land Bank, see J. Meehan, *The Irish Economy since 1922* (Liverpool: Liverpool University Press, 1970), p. 240.
47 For background information on Brown, see B. Sheppard, 'Historical Political Cartoons', https://shephistory.wordpress.com/author/bshephistory/ (accessed 3 October 2017). Sheppard's collection of historical cartoons is an invaluable resource.
48 See note 25 above.
49 *Irish Press*, 12 December 1931.
50 Ibid., 15 February 1932.
51 Beard, *Laughter in Ancient Rome*, p. 15.
52 W. Lippmann, *Public Opinion* (New York: Harcourt, Brace, 1922), p. 144.

15. Patrick Campbell's Easy Times: Humour and Southern Irish Protestants

1 *Seanad Éireann Debates*. vol. 5, no. 7, col. 442, 11 June 1925.
2 All of the following present a much more complex portrait of southern Protestants than their titles indicate, but indicate the dominance of the received story: David Fitzpatrick, *Descendancy: Irish Protestant Histories Since 1795* (Cambridge: Cambridge University Press, 2014); Heather W. Crawford, *Outside the Glow: Protestants and Irishness in Independent Ireland* (Dublin: University College Dublin Press, 2010); Robin Bury, *Buried Lives: The Protestants of Southern Ireland* (Dublin: History Press, 2017); Colin Murphy and Lynne Adair (eds), *Untold Stories: Protestants in the Republic of Ireland, 1922–2002* (Dublin: Liffey Press, 2002); Michael McConville, *Ascendancy to Oblivion: The Story of the Anglo-Irish* (London: Quartet Books, 1986).
3 A nearly random search brings up Colin W. Reid, 'Citizens of Nowhere: Longing, Belonging and Exile among Irish Protestant Writers in Britain, *c.*1830–1970', *Irish Studies Review*, vol. 24, issue 3, 2016, pp. 255–74; Raphael Ingelbien, 'Gothic Genealogies: Dracula, Bowen's Court, and Anglo-Irish Psychology', *English Literary History,* vol. 70, no. 4, Winter 2003, pp. 1089–1105; Ellen Crowell, 'Ghosting the Llangolen Ladies: Female Intimacies, Ascendancy Exiles, and the Anglo-Irish Novel', *Éire-Ireland*, vol. 39, 3 and 4, Fall/Winter 2004, pp. 202–27; James F. Wurtz, 'Elizabeth Bowen, Modernism and the Spectre of Anglo-Ireland', *Estudios Irlandeses*, no. 5, 2010, pp. 119–28.
4 Ian d'Alton, '"A Vestigial Population"?: Perspectives on Southern Irish Protestants in the Twentieth Century', *Éire-Ireland*, vol. 44, 3 and 4, Fall/Winter 2009, p. 41.
5 Henri Bergson, 'Laughter', in Wylie Sypher (ed.), *Comedy* (Garden City, NY: Doubleday, 1956), p. 187.
6 See Standish O'Grady, *Toryism and the Tory Democracy* (London: Chapman & Hall Limited, 1886), p. 238, and Daniel Corkery, *Synge and Anglo-Irish Literature* (Cork: Mercier Press, 1996), p. 16.
7 D.H. Munro, *Argument of Laughter* (Melbourne: Melbourne University Press, 1951), p. 45.
8 Sigmund Freud, *Jokes and Their Relations to the Unconscious* (New York: W.W. Norton, 1960).

9 John Morreall, *Comic Relief: A Comprehensive Philosophy of Humour* (Chichester, West Sussex: Wiley-Blackwell, 2009), pp. 102–10.
10 Ibid., pp. 112–19.
11 Patrick Gordon Campbell, third Baron Glenavy (1913–1980).
12 Vivian Mercier, *The Irish Comic Tradition* (Oxford: Oxford University Press, 1962).
13 Frank Muir (ed.), *The Oxford Book of Humorous Prose* (Oxford: Oxford University Press, 1990), p. xxix.
14 Ibid., p. 819.
15 Beatrice Lady Glenavy, *Today We Will Only Gossip* (London: Constable and Company Ltd., 1964), p. 115.
16 Patrick Campbell, *My Life and Easy Times* (London: Pavilion, 1988), p. 39.
17 Murphy and Adair, p. 227.
18 *My Life and Easy Times*, p. 45.
19 *My Life and Easy Times*, p. 67.
20 Beatrice Lady Glenavy, *Today*, p. 142.
21 *My Life and Easy Times*, p. 117.
22 *My Life and Easy Times*, p. 146.
23 *Irish Times,* 26 September 1987.
24 *Irish Times,* 25 September 1944.
25 *Irish Times,* 14 February 1946.
26 *Irish Times,* 12 June 1946.
27 *Irish Times,* 1 May 1946.
28 *Irish Times,* 7 May 1946.
29 *Irish Times,* 11 December 1944.
30 *Irish Times,* 30 November 1945.
31 *Irish Times,* 13 November 1971.
32 'Armed incendiaries' burned the family house, Clonard, at the end of December 1922. See *Irish Times*, 19 December 1922.
33 Elizabeth Bowen, *Bowen's Court* (New York: The Ecco Press, 1979), p. 441.
34 Patrick Campbell, 'A Boy's Best Bodyguard', in *Come Here Till I Tell You* (London: Hutchinson & Co., 1960), p. 174.
35 Ibid., p. 175.
36 Ibid., p. 176.
37 Beatrice Lady Glenavy, *Today*, p. 115.
38 'A Boy's Best Bodyguard', p. 179.
39 Elizabeth Grubgeld, 'Castleleslie.com: Autobiography, Heritage Tourism, and Digital Design', in *New Hibernia Review/Iris Éireannach Nua*, Spring/Earrach 10.1, 2006, pp. 46–64.
40 *My Life and Easy Times*, p. 127.
41 Ibid., p. 16.
42 Ibid., p. 16.
43 Ibid., p. 8.
44 Ibid., p. 14.
45 Ibid., p. 14.
46 *Irish Times,* 10 June 1967.
47 *My Life and Easy Times*, p. 28.
48 Ibid.

Afterword: Ireland's Mysterious Minority—A French–Irish Comparison

1 Brian Inglis, *West Briton* (London: Faber & Faber, 1962); Michael Viney, *The Five Per Cent: A Survey of Protestants in the Republic* (Dublin: Irish Times, 1965); Jack White, *Minority Report: The Protestant Community in the Irish Republic* (Dublin: Gill & Macmillan, 1975); Kurt Bowen, *Protestants in a Catholic State: Ireland's Privileged Minority* (Dublin: Gill & Macmillan, 1983); Colin Murphy and Lynne Adair (eds), *Untold Stories: Protestants in the Republic of Ireland, 1922–2002* (Dublin: Liffey Press, 2002); Heather Crawford, *Outside the Glow: Protestants and Irishness in Independent Ireland* (Dublin: UCD Press, 2010); Brian Walker, *A History of the Two Irelands: From Partition to Peace* (London: Palgrave Macmillan, 2012); Robin Bury, *Buried Lives: The Protestants of Southern Ireland* (Dublin: History Press, 2016).

2 See for instance, Ian d'Alton, 'Journeying into a Wider World? The Development of the Histories of the Church of Ireland since 1950', in M. Empey, A. Ford and M. Moffitt (eds), *The Church of Ireland and its Past: History, Interpretation and Identity* (Dublin: Four Courts, 2017), pp. 220–36.

3 Dennis Kennedy, *The Widening Gulf: Northern Attitudes to the Independent Irish State, 1919–49* (Belfast: Blackstaff, 1988); Brian Walker *passim*.

4 Ireland, *Census 2016 Summary Results* (Dublin: CSO, 2016), Part 1 (Section 8).

5 Ireland *Census 2011—Religion, Ethnicity and Irish Travellers* (Table 5).

6 As in the Irish case, the focus is on the historic Protestant population. Estimating its size is also difficult. The French state does not keep religious statistics and estimates are based on surveys. The most recent IPSOS survey (2017) gives a figure of 3.1 per cent. See 'Sondage: les protestants français, 500 ans après la Réforme', *Réforme*, 11 Décembre, 2017. Cabanel gives a figure of 2 per cent for the historic Protestant population, in Patrick Cabanel, *Les Protestants et la République: De 1870 à nos Jours* (Paris: Editions Complexe, 2000), pp. 18–20.

7 Bury, *passim*.

8 Bury, *passim*.

9 See the essays in Murphy and Adair, *passim*, and Stephen Mennell et al., 'Protestants in a Catholic State—A Silent Minority in Ireland', in Tom Inglis (ed.), *Religion and Politics: East-West Contrasts from Contemporary Europe* (Dublin: University College Dublin Press, 2000), pp. 68–92.

10 Peter Hart, *The IRA at War, 1916–23* (Oxford: Oxford University Press, 2005), pp. 240, 246. In a 1996 publication dealing with the killings, Hart evoked the 'ethnic cleansing' of the twentieth century. He later (2003) distanced himself from the argument.

11 In Hart's words, 'In the end, however, the fact of the victims' religion is inescapable. These men were shot because they were Protestant', *The IRA at War*, p. 288.

12 For example, Eoghan Harris, 'The Continuity of the IRA and Bodies Buried in Bogs', *Sunday Independent*, 10 November 2013.

13 Gerard Murphy, *The Year of Disappearances: Political Killings in Cork 1920–22* (Dublin: Gill & Macmillan, 2010); RTÉ Press Centre, 'Hidden History: The Killings at Coolacrease', 23 October 2007, at https://presspack.rte.ie/2007/10/23/hidden-history-the-killings-at-coolacrease/ (accessed 15 October 2015).

14 See John M. Regan, 'The Bandon Valley Massacre as a Historical Problem', *History*, vol. 97, no. 325, 2012, pp. 70–98; Niall Meehan, 'Examining Peter Hart', *Field Day Review*, vol. 10 (2014), pp. 102–47; P. Heaney, P. Muldowney and P. O'Connor, *Coolacrease: The True Story of the Pearson Executions—An Incident in the Irish War of Independence* (Aubane: Aubane Historical Society, 2008).

15 John A. Murphy, 'Reform ignores the realities of history', *Sunday Independent*, 10 October 2004, and 'There was no Kristellnacht on the South Mall', *Irish Examiner*, 10 November 2010. The South Mall in the centre of Cork city contained the offices of wealthy Protestant professionals.

16 Demography is never wholly predictable. Irish reunification in the future might well see the movement of northern Protestants southwards in a reversal of the trend of the early part of the twentieth century.

17 The term is Ian d'Alton's. See Ian d'Alton, 'Religion as Identity', in J. Hill and M.A. Lyons (eds), *Representing Irish Religious Histories: Historiography, Ideology and Practice* (Cham [Switz]: Palgrave Macmillan, 2017), p. 205.

18 For a comparative overview of the two cases, see Joseph Ruane, 'Majority–minority Conflicts and their Resolution: Protestant Minorities in France and in Ireland', *Nationalism and Ethnic Politics*, vol. 12, nos 3–4, 2006, pp. 509–32.

19 Mack Holt, *The French Wars of Religion, 1562–1629* (Cambridge: Cambridge University Press, 1995).

20 Cabanel, *passim*, p. 18.

21 Ibid.

22 John McManners, *Church and Society in Eighteenth-Century France: Volume 2* (Oxford: Clarendon Press, 1999), chapters 44–5, offer an excellent overview.

23 See Patrick Cabanel, *La Tour de Constance et le Chambon-sur-Lignon: L'oubli et le Royaume* (Cahors: La Louve, 2007).

24 André Encrevé, 'French Protestants', in Rainer Liedtke and Stephan Wendehorst (eds), *The Emancipation of Catholics, Jews and Protestants: Minorities and the Nation State in Nineteenth-century Europe* (Manchester: Manchester University Press, 1999), pp. 56–82.

25 Mireille Gueissaz, 'Protestants et Laïques d'origine Protestante dans la Loi de 1905', *Matériaux pour l'histoire de notre temps*, vol. 78, no. 1, pp. 16–26.

26 P. Joutard, 'Le Musée du Désert: La Minorité Reformée', in P. Nora (ed.), *Les Lieux de Mémoire, vol. 2* (Paris: Gallimard, 1997), pp. 2653–77. For a comparison with Irish Protestants, see Joseph Ruane, 'Ethnicity, Religion and Peoplehood: Protestants in France and in Ireland', *Ethnopolitics*, vol. 9, no. 1, 2010, pp. 121–35.

27 J. Baubérot and V. Zuber, *Une Haine Oubliée: L'antiprotestantisme avant le 'Pacte Laïque' (1870–1905)* (Paris: Albin Michel, 2000); for the long history of the Catholic/French identity entanglement, see Joseph F. Byrnes, *Catholic and French Forever: Religious and National Identity in Modern France* (Pennsylvania: Penn State University Press, 2005).

28 Many of these observations are based on interviews in the department of the Gard, a religiously mixed region in the south of France with a history of conflict. See Joseph Ruane, 'After Conflict: Protestant Identity in the Gard today', in P. Bénédict, H. Daussy and P.-O. Léchot (eds), *L'identité*

Huguenote: Faire Mémoire et écrire l'Histoire XVIe–XXXIe siècle (Paris: Droz, 2014).

29 Jean Baubérot, *Le Protestantisme: Doit-il Mourir?* (Paris: Seuil, 1988); Jean-Paul Willaime, *La Précarité Protestante* (Genève: Labor et Fides, 1992).

30 For a recent addition, see Patrick Cabanel, *Le Protestantisme Français: La Belle Histoire, XVIe–XXIe* (Nimes: Editions Alcide, 2017).

31 'Discours d'Emmanuel Macron à l'occasion du 500ème Anniversaire de la Réforme Protestante. Hôtel de Ville de Paris, 22 September 2017', http://www.elysee.fr/videos/new-video-66/ (accessed 30 May 2018).

32 '2018: Vingt Protestants s'adressent à Emmanuel Macron', *Réforme*, 23 Janvier 2018.

33 For example, Heather Jones, 'Church of Ireland Great War Remembrance in the South of Ireland: Personal Reflections', in John Horne and Edward Madigan (eds), *Towards Commemoration: Ireland in War and Revolution 1912–1923* (Dublin: Royal Irish Academy), pp. 74–82.

34 The quarterly *Crane Bag* (1979–88), edited by Richard Kearney and Mark Patrick Hederman, set it in motion.

35 Jacqueline Hill, 'Popery and Protestantism, Civil and Religious Liberty: The Disputed Lessons of Irish History, 1690–1812', *Past and Present*, 118, 1988, pp. 96–129.

36 D. George Boyce, *Ireland 1828–1923: From Ascendancy to Democracy* (London: Wiley, 1992).

37 See Gerard Hogan, 'A Fresh Look at "Tilson's" Case', *Irish Jurist*, 33, 1998, pp. 311–32; David Jameson, 'The Religious Upbringing of Children in "Mixed Marriages": The Evolution of Irish Law', *New Hibernia Review*, 18, 2, 2014, 65–83; Ian d'Alton, 'Navigating the Minefield: How *The Irish Times* and the *Church of Ireland Gazette* Approached the Tilson Case and the Dogma of the Assumption in 1950', unpublished paper read at the Church of Ireland Historical Society, 7 November 2015.

38 This comes across clearly in the essays in Murphy and Adair, *passim*.

39 See Ian d'Alton, '"A Vestigial Population"? Perspectives on Southern Irish Protestants in the Twentieth Century', *Éire-Ireland*, 44, 3 & 4, 2009, pp. 9–42.

40 Anne Dolan, 'Politics, Economy and Society in the Irish Free State, 1922–1939', in T. Bartlett (ed.), *The Cambridge History of Ireland*, volume 4 (Cambridge: Cambridge University Press, 2018), pp. 323–48.

41 See J.H. Goldthorpe and C.T. Whelan (eds), *The Development of Industrial Society in Ireland* (Oxford: Oxford University Press, 1993); A.F. Heath, R. Breen and C.T. Whelan (eds), *Ireland North and South: Perspectives from Social Science* (Oxford: Oxford University Press, 1999).

42 Compare the tone of Terence Brown, *Ireland: A Social and Cultural History 1922–2002* (London: Harper Perennial 2004), with that of the writings of (say) Desmond Fennell, Fintan O'Toole or Tom Garvin.

43 The first phase of the process is well described in Bowen, *Protestants in a Catholic State*.

44 See the account in Michael Smurfit, *A Life Worth Living: The Autobiography* (Dublin: Oak Tree Press, 2014).

45 See note 30 above.

46 There are parallels in the identity preoccupations of French Protestants and Irish Catholics rooted in their common history of displacement and marginalisation. For a four-way comparison (French Protestant, French Catholic, Irish Protestant, Irish Catholic), see Joseph Ruane 'Comparing Protestant–Catholic Conflict in France and Ireland: The Significance of the Ethnic and Colonial Dimension', in John Wolffe (ed.), *Irish Religious Conflict in Comparative Perspective* (London: Palgrave Macmillan, 2014), pp. 146–66.

47 Irish Catholics once had a heroic narrative, but it struggles in the face of revisionist critique. There has been no corresponding critique of the French Protestant heroic narrative.

Index